W9-ANV-844

WITHDRAWN

Gramley Library
Salem Academy and College
Winston-Salem, N.C. 27108

Watching Rape

Watching Rape

Film and Television in Postfeminist Culture

Sarah Projansky

NEW YORK UNIVERSITY PRESS

New York and London

Gramley Library
Salem Academy and College
Winston-Salem, N.C. 27108

NEW YORK UNIVERSITY PRESS
New York and London

© 2001 by New York University
All rights reserved.

Library of Congress Cataloging-in-Publication Data
Projansky, Sarah, 1965–
Watching rape : film and television in postfeminist culture / Sarah
Projansky.
p.   cm.
Includes bibliographical references and index.
ISBN 0-8147-6689-7 (alk. paper) — ISBN 0-8147-6690-0 (pbk. : alk. paper)
1. Rape in motion pictures. 2. Women in motion pictures. 3. Women on
television.   I. Title.
PN1995.9R27 P76 2001
791.43'655—dc21   2001002283

New York University Press books are printed on acid-free paper,
and their binding materials are chosen for strength and durability.

Manufactured in the United States of America
10 9 8 7 6 5 4 3 2 1

Contents

Acknowledgments

Many people have contributed to the project, many more than I have the space to thank here.

Faculty at the University of Iowa helped prepare me to write this book. In particular, I want to thank Lauren Rabinovitz, Bruce Gronbeck, Rick Altman, Dudley Andrew, and Barbara Eckstein for their insights and encouragement.

At New York University Press, Eric Zinner, Cecilia Feilla, Emily Park, and Despina Papazoglou Gimbel have been both encouraging and rigorous in their responses to the manuscript. Here in Davis, California, Christina Acosta created the index. I have benefited from all their expertise.

The University of California, Davis, supported this research with several faculty research grants and a faculty development grant. Davis's Consortium for Women and Research sponsored a weekend retreat for assistant professors that significantly strengthened the manuscript. I appreciate these financial resources and this sabbatical time.

Many friends and colleagues have read and responded to my work, offering invaluable suggestions and always improving the project. In particular, I would like to thank John M. Sloop and Leah R. Vande Berg for taking the time to respond to various portions of the manuscript. Lisa M. Cuklanz, Sujata Moorti, and Patricia Priest have shared in particularly generous ways their own knowledge about rape and sexual violence. I am fortunate to have encountered such a committed group of feminist scholars. The members of the Bay Area Consortium for Research on the Moving Image offered useful advice on an early draft of chapter 1. In particular, I would like to thank Carol Clover, Margaret Morse, Louis Schwartz, Eric Smoodin, and Shelley Stamp.

The women and gender studies program at the University of California, Davis, has been extremely supportive of me and my scholarship. In particular, Judith Newton and Rosa Linda Fregoso have been unselfish mentors. I deeply appreciate the ways they have nurtured me both personally and professionally over the past five and one-half years. Rosa Linda Fregoso also read and responded to portions of the manuscript at key times. Wendy Ho has been particularly encouraging throughout the writing process.

Four friends and colleagues, in particular, made a huge difference toward the end of this project: Elizabeth Constable, Ella Maria Ray, Karen Shimakawa, and Sophie Volpp. Their cogent insights, raucous humor, and eclectic cooking skills were invaluable. I thank them for taking the time to read my entire manuscript and for providing a perspective on both life and scholarship on which I continue to draw. Thanks also to Ella Maria Ray for our intellectually challenging and emotionally satisfying talks during our many walks. My friend Elizabeth M. Barnett, as well, has been particularly supportive. I appreciate her investment in this project and take inspiration from her as a feminist scholar.

Over the years, many research assistants have helped me collect the materials I use in this book. Kathleen Brady, Andreana Clay, Hoa Giang, Kyra Pearson, Laura Schooling, and Karla Segura all made it possible for me to develop my research. Lena Carla Gutekunst and Joan Chan, in particular, contributed immeasurably. I could not have finished the project without their outstanding research skills and tireless efforts in the final stages. I would also like to thank my students, particularly those in my "Feminist Approaches to Inquiry" and "Cultural Representations of Gender" classes, who read drafts of chapters and took seriously my encouragement to respond with their usual critical acumen.

Throughout the process of researching and writing this book, my parents and siblings have been extraordinarily supportive and (mostly) patient. I deeply appreciate their interest in and commitment to this project and their care and concern for me and my scholarship. I would like to thank my brother Daniel Projansky, especially, for his thoughtful comments on the project.

My partner, Kent A. Ono, generously read and commented on every page of every draft of this book. His attention to detail, commitment to social change, and intellectual, physical, and emotional nurturing were (and are) absolutely invaluable to me.

Finally, I would like to thank my daughter, Yasmin Projansky Ono, for waiting an entire week after I finished the manuscript to make her appearance in the world. It is an absolute joy to have her in my life.

Introduction

Just this week, as I was writing this introduction, I walked across campus to clear my head, only to encounter numerous antirape messages. Printed in chalk on the sidewalk beneath my feet and on sidewalks all across heavily traveled sections of campus were antirape writings, no doubt put there by activist feminist students. These writings declared, "One out of four women will be sexually assaulted on a college campus." "Around the world at least one woman in every three has been beaten, coerced into sex, or otherwise abused in her lifetime. Most often the abuser is a member of her own family." "Rape is not sex." "He simply didn't stop when I asked him to. Sound familiar? Rape." "April is sexual assault awareness month. Be aware."

One week earlier, during a public lecture a colleague quoted a scholar of sports culture as saying that in the United States sports, war, and rape are inextricably linked phenomena. After his lecture, my colleague asked me as an expert on rape what I thought about this claim. I told him that comparing rape to other social experiences was, in fact, not an unusual thing to do: scholars and media pundits alike casually invoke rape metaphors, for example, to convey a sense of the "ultimate" degradation or horror or to illustrate the humiliation of nations (e.g., the "rape of Kuwait"). Simultaneously, they neglect the particular experiences of women (and some men) who actually experience rape in masculinized contexts such as sports culture and war.

Over the last ten years, while researching representations of rape in popular culture, I have had innumerable experiences like these, during which rape emerges as a topic, image, narrative, trope, or metaphor in unexpected moments seemingly unrelated to my process of research and writing. Admittedly, encountering activist antirape graffiti (even when written in an ephemeral medium such as chalk) is (unfortunately) not a common experience for most people. Nevertheless, frequent encounters with rape messages are not limited to scholars and/or antirape activists,

1

such as myself, who strive to be aware of representations of rape in social environments. Whether or not one is conscious of it, beyond the physical rapes taking place every two and a half minutes in the United States (United States Department of Justice 1993), representations of rape pervade contemporary popular media and thus our everyday lives. For example, during every visit to the checkout stand at major U.S. grocery stores, a shopper is apt to see at least one magazine or newspaper with a story about rape advertised on the cover; these might include "special" multipart stories, such as "A Year in Rape" (Bizjak 1995), or continuing stories about specific cases, such as the University of California, Davis, student accused of raping a number of women on campus over several years.[1] And, more often than not Hollywood films represent rape. Stories about rape are also commonplace in first-run and rerun television dramas, talk shows, soap operas, "reality" shows, news programs, and even sometimes situation comedies. Currently, at least in northern California, public service announcements decrying statutory rape appear on the sides of moving buses and on billboards, cautioning men that "sex with a minor is a crime."

In short, given the ubiquity of representations of rape, even someone who is a moderate consumer of mass media would have difficulty spending a week (possibly even an entire day) without coming across the subject.[2] The existence of rape is thus naturalized in U.S. life, perhaps seemingly so natural that many people are unaware of the frequency with which they encounter these representations. I would go so far as to argue that rape is one of contemporary U.S. popular culture's compulsory citations: from talk in public service announcements about statutory rape to talk on the news about the "date rape drug," depictions of rape are a pervasive part of this culture, embedded in all of its complex media forms, entrenched in the landscape of visual imagery.

By suggesting that these examples illustrate an "experience of rape," I do not mean to suggest that encountering discourses about rape is *equivalent* to experiencing the physical act of rape. This book is about representations of rape, not physical rapes. Nevertheless, as AIDS discourse is to AIDS and cancer discourse is to cancer (Sontag 1990), rape discourse is *part of* the fabric of what rape is in contemporary culture. Discourses of rape are both productive and determinative. They are not simply narratives marketed for consumption in an entertainment context or "talk" about real things. They are themselves functional, generative, formative, strategic, performative, and real. Like physical actions, rape discourses have the capacity to inform, indeed embody and make way for, future actions, even physical ones. They are not simply metaphors for how people behave; as Raymond Williams (1977) puts it, they are "structures of feeling" for how people act in social contexts. The pervasiveness of representations of rape naturalizes rape's place in our everyday world, not only as real physical events but also as part of our fantasies, fears, desires, and consumptive practices. Representations of rape form a complex of cultural discourses central to the very structure of stories people tell about themselves and others. This book is about representation and narrative in relation to rape in U.S. popular culture since the 1980s; it develops and offers a feminist critical perspective on these depictions and stories.

Some Historical Functions of Rape Narratives

This book focuses primarily on representations of rape in post-1980 fictional film and television. However, as a topic rape is virtually "timeless," functioning as a key aspect of storytelling throughout Western history. Importantly, despite this "timelessness," the structure of rape narratives varies historically, depending on cultural and national contexts. Rape is a particularly versatile narrative element that often addresses any number of other themes and social issues. In this section I offer a brief discussion of just a few examples of the social function of rape narratives in various historical contexts prior to the emergence of film as a medium. My goal here is to identify the long-standing discursive effectivity of rape narratives—an effectivity that continues into the present. Furthermore, I choose examples that address issues of gender, race, class, and nation in different, sometimes even conflictual, ways in order to emphasize just how malleable rape is as it helps to produce and maintain social relations and hierarchies.

For instance, Stephen P. Pistono (1988) focuses on the ways rape narratives have functioned in various legal contexts. He finds that in fifth-century B.C.E. Athens the penalty for *seduction* of a married woman was death or torture, whereas for *rape* of a married woman the penalty was only a monetary fine. Pistono argues that this counterintuitive difference between the penalties for seduction and those for rape depended on the assumption that a seducer—but not a rapist—would have regular access to a "man's" home and could even conceivably be the biological father of that man's children without his knowledge: hence, the harsher punishment for access to the man's "property"—his home, wife, and children. While this historical example places the "wronged man" at the center of the drama, in other legal contexts women held center stage. For example, Pistono reports that prior to 1285 in England women were responsible for bringing forth their own rape charges. In such cases, charging a man with rape often resulted in a forced marriage between the woman and the man who raped her. Alternatively, the woman would be prosecuted for making a false accusation, if her case remained unproven. While either of these outcomes was punitive for women, Pistono reports that couples began to use this legal definition of rape to force their parents to accept marriage based on romantic love rather than on familial arrangement. Presumably, a woman would (falsely) accuse the man she desired to marry of rape; he would not deny the charge; and then the parents would have to allow their marriage. Pistono writes that in 1285, however, the Statute of Westminster gave the king the right to press rape charges, taking from women what little control they once had over the rape scenario. In 1382 a new statute gave fathers, husbands, and next of kin the right to press charges for rape of the women in their families. Pistono argues that as the voice of the accuser shifted from women to the king and finally to the male-headed family, these changes in law resulted in rape becoming an issue of property—protecting the family's land and identity, defining women as the property of the men in their family, and maintaining class and gender relations.

Given the fact that marriage law originally conceived of women as men's property, Frances Ferguson (1987) points out that in Hebrew and Saxon law, a husband's rape of his wife was theoretically impossible, since she "belonged" to him. Shifting her attention from legal to literary narratives, Ferguson goes on to argue that in his mid-eighteenth-century novel *Clarissa* Samuel Richardson challenged the law's definition of rape. Whereas the law viewed rape as a matter of form—that is, of whether or not one was married—Richardson's novel developed a definition of rape as a matter of "psychological states" (99), including questions of desire and intent. Ferguson argues that *Clarissa* thus offered a radical shift in public discourse away from formal familial relationships to questions of individual experience. Ferguson shows how *Clarissa* as a narrative about rape responded to legal structures, helped produce a new literary form (the psychological novel), and redefined rape in terms of individual desire rather than of social structure.

The previous examples illustrate the versatility of rape—functioning both to define property and the family and to support new literary forms and psychological interiorization—but these are only a few of many complex ways rape has functioned historically. In the context of the colonization of the United States, Antonia I. Castañeda (1993) argues that in the eighteenth century U.S. colonists told *narratives* about Native American men raping white women to justify white male armed violence against Native Americans, while simultaneously using *physical* rape of Native American women as a tool of war against Native Americans and in the name of cultural and national development.

In the later context of the early nineteenth century, James R. Lewis (1992) argues that captivity narratives supported a Puritan worldview, furthered anti–Native American propaganda, and provided entertainment. In these narratives, Lewis argues, an allusion to rape or attempted rape was necessary in order to justify showing or describing nudity (which was generally prohibited) in nineteenth-century representations. Lewis argues, nevertheless, that nude women in "the state of bondage, which was supposed to legitimate nudity by separating it from sensuality, actually *increased* the image's power to titillate by adding intimations of sexual dominance and sadism" (70). Lewis argues that these narratives produced a link between violence and sex, often in the character of the hero who would save the white woman just in time, do violence to her Native American captors, and then marry the former captive, achieving the thwarted sexuality the represented captors implicitly desired. Here, rather than justifying and enacting colonial war, rape justified violent masculine sexual and racist spectatorial pleasure.

In relation to U.S. slavery, Anthony S. Parent Jr. and Susan Brown Wallace (1993) argue that rape, the threat of rape, and even the forced observation (by African Americans) of slave owners' rape of African American women functioned as forms of social control, particularly as it shaped the sexual identity of slave children.[3] While this research is based on oral history testimony from ex-slaves, both Peter W. Bardaglio (1994) and Diane Miller Sommerville (1995) examine abolitionists' (e.g., Sarah Grimké) use of narratives about the rape of African American women by white men to argue against slavery, regardless of the fact that antebellum courts did not define the rape of an African American woman as illegal. Several other scholars argue that, in contradistinction to the abolitionists, southern U.S. courts used legal cases involving African American men as accused rapists during the later decades of slavery as evidence that (male) African Americans were actually treated fairly under the law, regardless of their status as slaves. Despite the fact that laws were different depending on the race of both the rapist and the victim, these courts claimed that the fact that the accused African American men had the legal protection of a court of law in which they were presumed innocent until proven guilty illustrated that they were not discriminated against as slaves.[4]

During slavery rape narratives might either condemn or justify slavery; after slavery rape emerged again as a key narrative through which to understand race relations in the United States. Many scholars point out that while the myth of the African American rapist was used after the Civil War to justify lynching, that same myth did not operate during slavery when bondage, rather than lynching, maintained racial hierarchies.[5] Angela Y. Davis (1981a) argues that the "myth of the black rapist" not only was meant to justify lynching of African American men, but simultaneously served to cloak continued violations of African American women by white men. Davis criticizes this myth (as well as some 1970s white feminist scholars) for depending on and perpetuating images of the violent African American man as rapist, the virginal white woman as rape victim, the benevolent white man as savior, and the oversexed African American woman as harlot.[6] Davis argues that this model of rape has functioned historically to define African American women as unrapable and African American men as out of control, thus justifying continued discrimination against African Americans.[7] Robyn Wiegman (1993) further argues that newspapers would document the violence of lynching in graphic detail, "extend[ing] the function of lynching as a mode of surveillance by reiterating its performative qualities" (230) and producing a forum for the expression of social anger and horror regarding African American bodies.

Narratives about postslavery rape also were sometimes invoked to call for a return to slavery. For example, Sommerville argues that at the turn of the twentieth century some racist discourse romanticized slavery by arguing that African American men did not start to rape white women until *after* slavery, once they were ostensibly "free" to become a sexual threat to white women. Martha Hodes (1993) points out that this discourse operated in the courts as well, citing a case in which a judge claimed that rape of white women by African American men occurred more often during Reconstruction than during slavery, although he offered no substantiating evidence. In these various examples, racialized narratives about the absence of rape in the past naturalize racialized narratives about the (supposed) presence of rape in the contemporary moment.

Whether in the form of legal documents, literature, or folklore, these admittedly brief examples hint at the versatility and ubiquity of rape narratives, illustrating how they have, among other things, operated historically to define the masculine familial subject; to structure women's relationship to love, family, and the law; to define property; to transform the structure of the novel; to justify and perpetuate U.S. colonialism; to define the nation; to produce masculine spectatorial pleasure predicated on illicit (violent) sexuality and culturally sanctioned racism; to perpetuate and justify slavery; to resist slavery; and to perpetuate racism. Operating in literature, law, the courts, social activism, family and plantation life, newspapers, paintings, and war, rape narratives help organize, understand, and even arguably produce the social world; they help structure social understandings of complex phenomena such as gender, race, class, and nation. Additionally, they help inscribe a way of looking, the conditions of watching, and the attitudes and structures of feeling one might have about rape, women, and people of color. I turn now to an examination of how 1970s and 1980s feminist antirape rhetoric and activism drew on, contributed to, and responded to the social functions of rape.[8]

Feminism and the Rape Reform Movement

In the 1970s and 1980s, feminist activism against rape and for rape law reform radically redefined rape. A few key texts and events that received widespread attention and helped to make at least some feminist understandings of rape common knowledge during this time include the New York Radical Feminists' 1971 "Speak-out" on rape, which defined talking openly about rape as part of politicized consciousness raising and drew attention to rape as a widespread problem (Rosen 2000, 182); Joanne Little's highly publicized trial for killing her rapist, a guard at the jail in which she was incarcerated;[9] Susan Brownmiller's 1975 book *Against Our Will: Men, Women, and Rape* (a best-seller offered through several book clubs, including the Book-of-the-Month Club), which defined rape as a form of patriarchal control of women through, for example, marriage and war and redefined rape in a (then) radical way as violence, not sex; Diana E. H. Russell's 1982 book *Rape in Marriage*, which drew attention to the existence of and problem of rape in the context of marriage; and Robin Warshaw's 1988 *Ms.* magazine–sponsored report on acquaintance rape, titled *I Never Called It Rape*, which acknowledged women's experience of, but lack of vocabulary to describe and social support to protest, rape by men they knew and often trusted.

As Lisa M. Cuklanz (2000) argues, this large body of feminist sociological, psychological, and legal work on rape offered various explanations of the "causes and purposes of rape, . . . but they nonetheless expressed remarkable unity in their assertions both on how rape had traditionally been viewed and on how this traditional view should be rejected in favor of a feminist understanding" (9). In her summary Cuklanz notes a number of traditional assumptions to which this work refers: that women who report rape often lie; that rape only takes place between people who do not know each other; that women who dress or behave in particular ways are "responsible for their own attacks"; that all rapists are "abnormal, depraved, or marginal men"; that women who are raped are placed on trial and forced to prove their "moral purity" through discussions of their previous sexual activities; and that African American men are more likely to rape than are white men (10).

In response, feminist scholars and activists articulated "counterformulation[s]" (9) that argued (and usually used statistics as support) that false accusations are no more common for rape than for other violent crimes; that rape most often takes place between people who know each other, either acquaintances, "friends, dates, partners, or spouses"; that the idea of an individual being responsible for or causing someone else's violent attack on her/him is incomprehensible in any context other than traditional patriarchal conceptions of rape; that most men who rape appear "normal in other ways" and are not especially "depraved"; that the sexual history of a woman who has been raped is irrelevant to a particular accusation and that even if a woman has given her consent to a man in the past she has not given up her right to withhold consent at some point in the future; and that intraracial rape is by far the most common form of rape and that, further, white men are more likely to rape both white women and African American women than are African American men likely to rape white women (Cuklanz 2000, 10).[10]

Some of these counterformulations have become so commonplace, they have produced well-known phrases that literally change language. For example, the concepts of *acquaintance rape, date rape,* and *marital rape* refer to the fact that rape can take place between people who have a variety of types of prior relationships. *Rape shield laws* now protect women in court against defense lawyers who attempt to ask questions about their sexual history. Davis's (1981a) phrase *the myth of the Black rapist* articulates a double meaning of myth: it points out the falsity of white assumptions that African American men rape more often than white men and rape white women in particular, and it identifies a cultural narrative used to structure racial relations and maintain racist social and legal practices against African American men (who are more often brought to trial, convicted, and given maximum sentences for rape) and African American women (who are less likely to be believed when they report rape).[11] Additional legal changes that feminists have advocated for include the protection of *anonymity* for a woman who makes a charge of rape, both in the press and in the courtroom. Overall, much feminist antirape discourse defines rape trials as *second rapes* or *re-rapes* of women who feel that they—rather than the men who raped them—are on trial and who experience the lawyers' questions not only as assaultive but, particularly when those questions address their sexual past and the actual rape itself, as *sexually* assaultive.[12] Feminists also introduced the term *rape culture*[13] to describe a culture in which sexual violence is a normalized phenomenon, in which male-dominant environments (such as sports, war, and the military) encourage and sometimes depend on violence against women,[14] in which the male gaze and women as objects-to-be-looked-at[15] contribute to a culture that accepts rape, and in which rape is one experience along a continuum of sexual violence that women confront on a daily basis.[16] Antirape activists also often replace the term "rape victim" with "*rape survivor*" to emphasize women's agency in response to their victimization and to address the complexity of women's *post*-rape experiences.[17]

Rape crisis centers and rape crisis counseling are additional forms of feminist antirape work. These nonprofit organizations (among other things) provide anonymous telephone counseling for women who have been raped; help women understand common post-rape experiences, such as a constant feeling of being dirty and wanting to shower, uncomfortableness with sex or even physical touch, a sense of being responsible for the attack, or guilt over accusing a loved one; accompany women to the hospital to provide emotional support and material resources (such as a ride home or a pair of sweatpants and a sweatshirt to replace the clothes the police will keep as evidence); accompany women to court as a source of emotional support and to counsel women on courtroom strategies from a feminist perspective; testify as experts in court; consult with local police; work in tandem with the police to help encourage women to report rape and to take steps to preserve evidence (e.g., not showering after a rape, understanding the legal need for a hospital examination that involves a "rape kit"); and provide or support self-defense classes[18] that encourage women to claim their bodies as their own and to defend those bodies against assault.[19]

Many scholars and activists have challenged rape crisis centers that emphasize the strategies I list in the above paragraph because of their lack of awareness of class, race, and cultural differences at all levels—the act of rape, the experience of rape, post-rape experiences, interaction with the police and courts, and experience of counseling (Crenshaw 1991)—and because of their "hierarchical, service-providing structure" (Bhattacharjee 1997, 30) that focuses on "individualism" (33) and "belief in the legal system" (37) rather than on "collective action" (34). Some of these activists have been involved in or report on rape crisis and domestic violence centers that specifically address the needs of women of color and/or low-income women. These centers, primarily located in urban areas, provide multilingual services, work with the police and hospitals to acknowledge women's varying cultural experiences, address economic needs for travel and survival, and provide counseling that is geared toward specific issues within, for example, African American, Asian American, Latina, and South Asian immigrant populations. These centers also often struggle, however, to raise and maintain funding. This difficulty occurs in part because major funding agencies often do not recognize that a multilingual counselor, for example, might be more important than a legal advocate for an immigrant Latina who, in general, is less likely to report a rape to legal authorities than is an English-speaking nonimmigrant white woman and less likely to see her case make it to court even if she does choose to report it.[20]

As both a feminist activist against rape and a feminist media critic of representations of rape, I understand the feminist activism and theory I have just briefly detailed from two perspectives.[21] First, I see this activism as an intervention, as part of a continuing political movement that has produced important changes that have benefited—in significant ways—women and others who face rape.[22] While I remain critical of some of these formulations of rape (for example, those that implicitly hold the person who has experienced rape responsible for taking action against rape, those that use horror stories to frighten women, those that tout self-defense as the answer to all rape but only address stranger rape models, and those that neglect racially and culturally specific details that affect *all* aspects of how a person will experience rape), I am committed to feminist activism that addresses intersections of gender, race, and class in the process of redefining what rape is and of changing legal, court, community, and family practices. Second, I also see this feminist redefinition of rape as another example of rape's versatility, its availability as a social narrative through which to articulate anxieties, to debate, and to negotiate various other social issues, in this case feminism. In other words, I acknowledge an important history of feminist activism against rape, while I also pay attention to how representations of and narratives about rape in that context function to help define feminism, as well as the related issues of gender and race, in popular culture. Throughout this book, the former perspective functions implicitly, driving my choice of examples, my critical perspective, and the arguments I make; however, the latter perspective emerges much more explicitly as it shapes my critical approach to fictional representations of rape in film and television and, as I discuss in the next section, their relationship to postfeminism.

Why Rape and Postfeminism?

By the end of the 1970s and the beginning of the 1980s, some of the feminist concepts I discuss in the previous section had some success at infiltrating mainstream popular culture, although often in truncated and altered forms. These discourses marked a partial acceptance of some feminist arguments about rape: they acknowledged rape as a social problem and accepted the need for reform of rape law, court practices, and social and familial attitudes toward rape, but they also negotiated and "resisted" (Cuklanz 1996, 12) other aspects of feminist arguments.[23] This negotiated acceptance also coincided with cultural discourses that defined the 1980s (and later the 1990s) as a "postfeminist era," one in which, as I discuss in more detail in chapter 2, feminism had supposedly arrived, successfully made changes that gave women "free choice" and "equality" with men, and as a result was no longer needed as an activist movement. With so many representations of successful women in the mainstream media —collectively forming a seductive and alluring image of success—logically, one might want to assume that historical, activist feminism had achieved sufficient social change to belay the need for further activism. Paradoxically, as I discuss in more detail in chapter 3, the popular acceptance of some feminist antirape discourses *contributed to* a cultural representation of feminism as "already successful" and thus no longer

Gramley Library
Salem Academy and College
Winston-Salem, N.C. 27108

necessary: rape narratives helped support postfeminism, which in turn implied that feminist activism was no longer necessary.

Concomitantly, postfeminist discourses defined both feminism and rape in particular ways, affecting social understandings of both in the process. For example, the central figure of postfeminist discourses is a white, heterosexual, middle-class woman. Whether she is a professional or a homemaker, a mother or a (hetero)sexually active and expressive twentysomething single woman, postfeminist discourses define the feminism that made her choices possible as focused entirely on a deracialized (but implicitly white) desire for "sameness" with men, particularly in terms of economic success and (hetero)sexual freedom. When these postfeminist discourses intersect with rape narratives, they inevitably limit social understandings of rape by deracializing the experience (but defining it as something that happens almost exclusively to white women), defining it as an aspect of heterosexuality while nevertheless simultaneously recuperating heterosexuality through romantic subplots, and neglecting class differences in women's experiences of rape and rape law. In short, in this book I argue that these representations of rape and these postfeminist discourses, which emerged during approximately the same time period, are co-constitutive, depending on and supporting each other while simultaneously contributing to cultural definitions of feminism that are limited in relation to race, class, and sexuality.

It is important to pause briefly to acknowledge that, despite their pervasive intersections, discourses of rape and discourses of postfeminism also exist separately from one another, intersecting with other social issues. For example, contemporary representations of rape can be understood in the context of nationalist and militarist discourses, especially in relation to Rwanda, the Gulf War, Bosnia, and Kosovo, or as Susan Jeffords (1991) puts it, in the context of the "new world order."[24] Contemporary representations of rape also can be understood in the context of discourses of criminalization and heightened fear for the self in a postmodern world in which the rule of law and the clear difference between "right" and "wrong" supposedly are breaking down.[25] Criminalization of (dark) "others" coupled with heightened fear for the (white) "self" appear in television shows such as *Cops* and *America's Most Wanted,* in legislation that requires convicted sex offenders to register in their communities upon release from prison, and in the current northern California public service campaign (which I mention above) that depicts young men serving time in prison for statutory rape and warns the (implied male) spectator that "sex with a minor is a crime."

While I occasionally address discourses about (among other things) nationalism, militarism, and criminalization in my discussion of film and television rape narratives throughout this book, particularly as they intersect with postfeminism, the links between these discourses and rape go beyond postfeminism and certainly could be (in fact, should be) studied in their own right. Similarly, postfeminism does more than provide a discourse through which rape narratives are told. Recent media depictions of battered women who kill, abortion, "fetal rights," and women's leisure, for example, all draw at least in part on postfeminist discourses.[26] Furthermore, I would point out that a large portion of postfeminist discourse defines issues of family and work in ways that *exclude* the existence of rape and sexual assault in these contexts. Again, while I occasionally refer to these postfeminist issues (and others) in this book, each needs to be (and in some cases has been) studied in more detail elsewhere.

I focus on the relationship between discourses of postfeminism and representations of rape in particular, however, for several reasons. First, this book is about representations of rape because of their ubiquity and versatility, not only in recent popular culture contexts but also in innumerable historical cultural contexts. If rape narratives can function in so many different ways in so many different contexts, as I illustrate only briefly above, this book asks what roles they play in recent popular culture in particular. Second, I use postfeminist discourses as a lens through which to understand recent film and television rape narratives because through my research I discovered that postfeminism intersects, in at least some way, with the vast majority of mainstream films and television shows from the late twentieth century that include rape or the threat of rape. Here, my goal is to understand how rape in particular is positioned in relation to pervasive postfeminist discourses. Third, and most important, I focus on the intersections of representations of rape and discourses of postfeminism because each is a dominant means through which contemporary popular culture discursively defines feminism. As Lauren Rabinovitz (1999) puts it in relation to one particular medium, "television's representation of feminism is a central, crucial means by which feminism is framed for the public" (163). In contemporary society, popular culture redeems rape by transforming it into a consumable product that earns the sanction of (a particular type of) feminism. Thus, one way of thinking about the role of representations of rape in contemporary society is as a marketing strategy linked to the political economy, with media as a pedagogical instrument, providing a stream of imagery that creates a context for consumer desires linked to and sanctioned by postfeminist discourses' co-opted versions of feminism.

Feminist Analysis of (Postfeminist) Media Culture

This is not to say that I see postfeminist discourses, generally, or popular texts' incorporation of some feminist antirape rhetoric, more specifically, as useless or, worse, simply hurtful to feminism. Rather, my goal is to offer a feminist analysis of these discourses that articulates a perspective *different from* contemporary culture's definition of feminism while simultaneously acknowledging that the way postfeminist discourse defines feminism is now part of what feminism *is*. In other words, I am not saying that "my feminism is right and popular culture's feminism is wrong," but rather that "my feminist analysis offers a particular critical perspective on the strengths and weaknesses of popular feminism." A brief discussion of the early 1980s—in both popular culture and academic scholarship—as the particular historical moment when the social concept of postfeminism emerged will help illustrate some of the distinctions I draw here between postfeminism and my own critical approach.

Because postfeminist discourses work hegemonically to transform feminism in the service of heterosexual masculinity and a dispersed, depoliticized, and universalized white, middle-class feminine/feminist identity, they must sidestep feminist theory and activism that, by addressing the intersections of gender, race, sexuality, nation, and class, complicate and problematize a feminism (visible in popular culture) that focuses exclusively on (white) gender. Barbara Ryan (1992) illustrates and implicitly perpetuates this primary focus on gender when she argues that postfeminism began as a concept in 1982 because that was the year the (race- and class-nonspecific) Equal Rights Amendment was defeated (136, 164 n.6). In the very same year, Susan Bolotin (1982) illustrates postfeminism's single focus on (middle-class) gender when she coins the term in a *New York Times Magazine* article in the process of declaring the success of a middle-class equality feminism that ensures women's access to professional work. While these positions are contradictory from the perspective of feminism's failure

(Ryan: ERA) or success (Bolotin: professionalism), they also coalesce: both
positions depend on a definition of feminism that ignores any feminism
that addresses issues other than gender.

Ryan and Bolotin make persuasive arguments about the reasons for the
emergence of the concept of postfeminism in the early 1980s in relation to
the ERA and women's professionalism, both of which were feminist issues
relatively visible in popular culture. I would suggest additionally, however,
that postfeminism entered popular culture in the early 1980s because that
decade was a particularly fruitful time for feminist theory that addressed
gender *and* race. In a sense, then, I am suggesting that postfeminist discourses emerged as a "reaction formation" in defense of a version of feminism that had already achieved a certain amount of purchase in popular
culture and against work such as Davis's *Women, Race and Class* (1981b),
bell hooks's *Ain't I a Woman: Black Women and Feminism* (1981), and Cherríe Moraga and Gloria Anzaldúa's anthology *This Bridge Called My Back*
(1981/1983). While, as (for example) Davis makes clear in *Women, Race and
Class*, women of color already had a long history of feminist activism and
theorizing, the nearly simultaneous emergence of these three highly influential books, in particular, marks a shift in feminist publishing in the early
1980s.[27] Rosa Linda Fregoso (1999), in fact, calls *Women, Race and Class* a
"foundational text for what we now call 'multicultural feminism,' 'women of
colour feminisms,' 'Third World' feminisms, or racialized women as a 'political project'" (214).

Moraga and Anzaldúa and hooks report on the struggles they faced
getting their feminist work on women of color published and the ambivalent relationship they had to white feminism at the time. For instance, hooks (1989a) writes,

> When I finished *Ain't I a Woman* . . . I sent it off to a number of publishers
> who rejected the work. Discouraged, I put the manuscript away. Then
> "race" became an important topic in feminist circles. It was important be-
> cause white women had decided that they were ready to hear about race.
> When black women had been talking about race in our own way they did
> not deem it relevant. (153)

While hooks eventually negotiated a satisfactory relationship with the
white feminist press that published her book, Moraga and Anzaldúa had
to take Persephone Press to court when it ceased operation to force the
press to give the editors permission to publish their book elsewhere. In
1983 Kitchen Table: Women of Color Press published a second edition of

This Bridge Called My Back. These now well-known stories mark both the emergence of more published work by feminists of color and the troubled relationship between their work and white feminism in the early 1980s. In this context, I would argue that the simultaneous emergence of postfeminist discourses is both a response to the success/defeat of the kinds of feminisms with which Ryan and Bolotin are concerned and a way to redefine feminism in order to perpetuate heterosexual whiteness as universal, despite significant shifts taking place in how feminist scholars and activists, such as Davis, hooks, Moraga, and Anzaldúa were conceiving of feminism.[28]

In contrast to the version of feminism that postfeminist discourses define, the feminism I draw on and hopefully contribute to engages a complex conglomeration of social and ideological analyses and political activism that seeks to criticize and transform the social category of gender in relation to the social categories of race, class, and sexuality. Specifically, I draw on what Ella Shohat (1998) defines as a "yoking" of feminism with "polycentric multiculturalism." Polycentric "multicultural feminism" offers a perspective that is neither willing to give up the term "feminism" (and "the critique of masculinist ideologies and the desire to undo patriarchal power regimes" it implies) nor willing to let feminism stand alone, which would implicitly disconnect an analysis of gender from the representational, material, and historical ways it intersects with race, class, and nation (2). As Kimberlé Crenshaw (1991) argues, particularly (although not exclusively) in terms of sexual violence, "an analysis of what may be termed *'representational intersectionality'* would include both the ways in which these images are produced through a confluence of prevalent narratives of race and gender, as well as a recognition of how contemporary critiques of [just] racist [or just] sexist representation marginalize women of color" (1282–83, emphasis added). My point in drawing on Shohat and Crenshaw to define my critical approach is not to mandate one particular method of feminist praxis. Rather, I engage a multiperspectival approach that is shaped in part by the complexity of the subject under study—in this case film and television rape narratives. Using this perspective, I ask how postfeminist and rape discourses define, delimit, and use feminism, and to what ends. Additionally, I explore how the intersection of rape narratives with postfeminist discourses defines and delimits rape, and thus potential antirape activism.

Throughout this introduction, I have also been drawing on a poststructuralist theoretical assumption that public discourses have material effects and that representations are as important to understanding what rape and feminism "are" as are laws, theory, activism, and experience. In order to enact this theoretical framework in the book, I examine fictional representations of rape as they trace their way through films, some television shows, and sometimes other popular media. This approach, admittedly, produces only a partial picture of what rape "is" in late-twentieth-century popular culture. Given the pervasiveness of rape representations, however, no one book could hope to provide a "complete" picture. I choose to focus on fictional film and some television narratives in a U.S. popular culture context, while simultaneously attending to their interrelationships with other types of media, most simply because film is the least discussed aspect of media culture in relation to rape within the scholarly literature. Overall, while a significant amount of research has already been conducted on the subject of rape in literature, drama, poetry, sociology, psychology, law, and rape prevention and survival, those in film studies have not paid the same kind of serious attention to rape. Furthermore, collective work on rape consistently neglects analysis of visual culture. For example, *Rape and Society* (Searles and Berger 1995), an important anthology of feminist analyses of rape that claims to be a comprehensive overview, addresses law, literature, poetry, rape prevention, and ethnographic work with rapists and women who have been raped, but it does not consider the profound impact media representations of rape have on popular culture and on consumers of popular culture. *Watching Rape* thus begins to fill a gap in both feminist and media research on rape.[29]

My approach to film and its intersections with other media emphasizes transtextual media relations (Stam et al. 1992, 206–13). My goal is not to identify the specificity of rape within particular genres (e.g., melodrama, comedy, horror), show types (e.g., soap opera, cop show, advertisement, talk show), or media (e.g., film, television, print). Because representations of rape appear indiscriminately in nearly all genres, show types, and media, a genre- or media-specific approach would not allow me to address how rape and feminism *cross* popular and local cultural texts and how they can help us understand *systems* of media and representation.[30] From this transtextual critical perspective, I examine the ubiquitous nature of rape in the context of a "media culture" in which media are interconnected through marketing, transnational conglomerate ownership, and diverse localized consumption and production practices; and in which media provide a cumulative set of discourses that saturate the cultural landscape and compete for spectators' attentions (Kellner 1995).

There has been a recent move to analyze "[media] spectacles of social and cultural conflict" (Garber et al. 1993, x) or "media events," about which John Fiske (1996) asks, "Can we separate media events from non-media events, or are all events today, or at least the ones that matter, necessarily media events?" (1). Scholars have produced whole books on spectacular events such as, for example, the Tonya Harding/Nancy Kerrigan assault in the context of figure skating competition, the television show *Twin Peaks*, the Rodney King beating and Los Angeles uprising, the Anita Hill/Clarence Thomas sexual harassment/Supreme Court confirmation hearings, the U.S. war against Iraq, and the *Star Trek* franchise.[31] Such an approach to individual texts, subjects, and/or events is useful in understanding a series of complex social issues and discourses. My project in this book can best be described as one that sees media products, such as films, themselves as "events," and one that sees rape as a hypermediated "spectacle" in that context.

Depending in part on the scholarship of audience researchers of the past two decades, I take for granted that we use and respond to popular culture artifacts in complex and varied ways.[32] While I do not focus on audience responses to rape narratives, I use theoretical, critical, and analytical reflection to engage particular films in multiple ways.[33] Without assuming that all audiences will read the texts as I do, I suggest a variety of ways to understand individual examples and their relationships to other texts. As I analyze these examples, I emphasize the versatility of representation (e.g., villains are not always [or even often] men of color who wear dark clothes), and I seek out contradictions and pressure points that prevent me from resolving my readings too easily; rather, I attempt to play up media's intricacy.

In the process of engaging this complexity and the feminist critical perspective I define above, I make choices about the kinds of examples I examine and about my own representational practices. First, I define "rape narratives" broadly to include representations of rape, attempted rape, threats of rape, implied rape, and sometimes coercive sexuality. While it is crucial to make distinctions among all these types of representations of rape, it is most important to me in this book to acknowledge commonalities among various forms of sexual violence against women in general. I do not use the term "rape narratives" as a metaphor for other kinds of violations (such as "rape of . . ." discourses), but instead as a feminist tool to read rape back into texts that sometimes attempt to cover over their own use of rape, for example, to initiate narratives or to tell stories about characters other than the women who face rape (Higgins and Silver 1991). In short, by defining rape narratives broadly my goal is to make visible and explicit myriad invisible or implicit references to rape.

Second, throughout the book I discuss and confront a feminist paradox between a desire to *end* rape and a need to *represent* (and therefore perpetuate discursive) rape in order to challenge it. In chapters 1, 3, and 6 in particular, I discuss texts that perpetuate rape discursively, even "give" rape to the spectator, in the process of arguing against rape. While there is no absolute way out of this representational conundrum, in this book I choose not to describe any rape scenes in detail. While this choice runs the risk of contributing to a long-standing "absent presence" of rape in social narratives that sidestep addressing women's experience of rape, it nonetheless helps me create a distance between myself (and hopefully my readers) and the pervasiveness of depictions of rape in our everyday lives, a distance that allows for critical and activist insights.[34] Coupled with my insistence on defining rape narratives broadly, of holding texts responsible for the sexual violence they depict yet sometimes repress, hopefully my decision to exclude detailed analyses of rape scenes does not unduly perpetuate a textual neglect of women's experiences of rape.

The Structure of the Book and a Preview of Chapters

Based on my critical skepticism about the kinds of representations of rape and feminism possible in the context of postfeminist discourses, I divide this book into two parts. The first part—chapters 1, 2, and 3—offers an overview of postfeminist discourses and of rape narratives in fictional film and television, exploring the intersections between representations of rape and social issues of gender, race, class, sexuality, nation, and feminism. The second part—chapters 4, 5, and 6—includes three case studies that offer the potential to explore (and perhaps widen) the "limits" of the social concept of postfeminism. I use "limits" here in two senses: first, to point to the kinds of *restrictions* postfeminism places on social understandings of feminism and rape and, second, to point to the fact that postfeminism is *partial*: despite its pervasiveness in popular culture since the 1980s, it does not necessarily extend to all texts. The two parts of the book, together, characterize and challenge postfeminist rape narratives. In what follows, I describe each chapter in more detail.

Chapter 1 offers a historical overview of rape in film from 1903 to 1979, using a feminist critical perspective that focuses on issues of gender, class, race, nationality, and their intersections. Despite the fact that the Hollywood Production Code forbade representations of rape in film, rape did not disappear; the strategies for representing it simply changed such that it became more implicit. Thus the chapter looks at the ubiquity of representations of both implicit and explicit rape in the *pre*-postfeminist era and argues that rape is central to cinema itself. This overview of the ways rape helps define gender, class, race, and nation as social categories offers one feminist perspective on the history of rape in film. The chapter also, however, engages a second feminist perspective, one that explores the possibility of reading rape films in ways that impose a feminist understanding of women's experiences of rape on films that may, in many other ways, deflect attention away from women's experiences and understandings of rape. In other words, the second section of the chapter asks how to read feminism into rape narratives critically. Overall, the chapter introduces two key aspects of my feminist critical approach—looking at the intersections of gender, class, race, and nation and bringing one's own feminism to bear on the examples at hand—and it offers a historical background against which to understand the focus on rape narratives in a postfeminist context in the remainder of the book.

Chapter 2 sets rape aside momentarily in order to define the term "postfeminism" in detail and to illustrate the historical and cultural context in which popular culture representations of rape since the 1980s have appeared. Drawing on previous studies of postfeminism as well as on a thorough examination of popular discourses that have used the term "postfeminism" since the early 1980s, the chapter illustrates how postfeminist discourses paradoxically both incorporate feminism into and purge feminism from popular culture, engaging in a depoliticization of feminism through both hegemonic moves. I argue that, like rape narratives, postfeminist discourses are particularly versatile. For example, they incorporate both antifeminist new traditionalism and "choiceoisie" (which Elspeth Probyn [1993] defines as having the supposed freedom to choose among particularly limited choices) around issues of work and family; and they engage a backlash against feminism and violent assaults on women while simultaneously celebrating women's right to bodily pleasures such as (hetero)sexual desire and display and active physical engagement in sports. Additionally, I point out that while women are most often at the center of postfeminist discourses, men emerge as well, either as models to be emulated or as "feminists without women" (Modleski 1991) who are better informed about the history of feminism and better prepared to shape its history than are women. Despite these variations in postfeminist discourses, white, middle-class, and heterosexual concerns are central to *all* postfeminist discourses. In chapter 2, I analyze these particular foci, as well as the particularly narrow ways postfeminist discourses define feminism (e.g., as a two-way "choice" between work and family), in order to highlight the versatility, pervasiveness, and limitations of postfeminism.

Chapter 3 articulates the central argument of the book—since the early 1980s, rape and postfeminism have been co-constitutive in U.S. fictional film and television narratives—and asks what versions of feminism are produced discursively in that context. A survey of numerous films and television shows illustrates that these texts incorporate some aspects of feminist antirape logics. They do so, however, in ways that link those logics to postfeminist conceptions of white, middle-class, heterosexual women's independence and equality that depend on either a family identity or a supposedly degendered desire to engage in traditionally masculine endeavors. I also argue that graphic representations of rape, even in popular culture texts that define themselves as profeminist, can contribute to a postfeminist backlash against women and feminism if they heighten spectatorial anxiety. And I argue that, as in postfeminist discourse generally, men can again take center stage in narratives in which *they* experience rape, usurping women's role in feminism, recovering from a supposed "feminization" produced by feminism (and initially heightened by the experience of rape), or engaging in male bonding that supplants women and feminism altogether.

In many of these contexts, rape functions as the narrative event that brings out a latent feminism in the woman (or man) who experiences rape; thus the texts make rape necessary for the articulation of feminism. Furthermore, the narratives tend to develop in ways that hold women responsible for using the feminist aspects of (now reformed) rape law, and that provide men with more knowledge of rape law and feminist perspectives on rape than women have, thus positioning men as feminist educators of women. These texts do incorporate some feminist criticisms of rape and rape law—for example, that women's experiences and credibility are generally ignored but should not be and that acquaintances and friends rape more often than do strangers. In each of these examples, however, the texts transform a feminist argument into limiting postfeminist tropes that imply that feminist activism on these issues has been successful and therefore is no longer necessary.

Furthermore, overall postfeminist rape narratives demonstrate no racial specificity: women are racially undifferentiated, yet almost always white. As a result, these texts offer a whiteness that is "everything and nothing" (Dyer 1988, 45): it pervades the texts but nothing in the texts (explicitly) draws attention to it as meaningful. As a result, the feminism these postfeminist rape narratives offer is oblivious to race or racial analysis, depending instead on a universal conception of "woman" in relation to rape, but simultaneously representing her almost always through white characters who move through racially undifferentiated worlds.

My argument in chapter 3 is not that the acceptance of some feminist analysis of rape and rape law in popular culture *completely* undermines feminist logics. Instead, I argue that feminist logics and knowledges forged through resistance and activism are often incorporated in ways that primarily depoliticize feminism by suggesting that its success means activism is no longer necessary, by reducing it to a trope or stereotype that does little to shift a narrative's structure or trajectory, and by limiting it to an uncritical representation of whiteness as universal.

As chapter 3 argues, most popular culture rape narratives since the early 1980s support and depend on the social concept of postfeminism. Nevertheless, postfeminism has contradictions, and thus chapters 4, 5, and 6 examine narratives that highlight postfeminism's limitations. In these chapters I ask, What do texts do when they intersect with, but do not quite fit, postfeminist logics? What tensions do they produce? How do they help illuminate the limitations of postfeminism?

Chapter 4 focuses on a "media spectacle" that continues to resonate in popular culture: the film *Thelma and Louise* (1991) and its critical reception. I begin the second section of the book with *Thelma and Louise* most simply because it is the most discussed (in both popular culture and scholarly criticism) rape film to appear since 1980. Furthermore, in some ways it is an ideal illustration of a postfeminist text; yet, it also produces great public anxiety about women, feminism, and gendered violence (as evidenced by various popular press responses to the film) and *continues* to be a reference point for feminist criticism and various narratives that represent women as rejecting masculine society and embracing feminine community. Chapter 4 argues that the film has a feminist radical potential, particularly in relation to its representation of rape, but that the film's reception in popular culture discourses that interpret the film as conforming to a depoliticized postfeminist perspective tends to diminish that potential. I end the chapter by examining the ways various feminist film and media critics have used and embraced the film, and I ask what roles narratives of rape and discourses of postfeminism play in these scholarly feminist uses of the film—including my own.

In chapter 5 I address postfeminism's limitations by purposefully turning my critical attention to one group of women who are generally excluded from both postfeminist discourses and mainstream fictional rape narratives: Black women.[35] Here, I ask what happens to postfeminism, rape, and their intersections in the relatively few films and television shows about rape that do include Black women. Some narratives about African Americans and rape displace their stories to a former historical era and thus avoid critique of present-day racialized gender relations. Such films invent a history and displace African American women's experiences of rape into it, without seriously considering rape as a contemporary social problem for African American women. Displacements also occur in texts that take place in the present. While Black women are sometimes highly visible in such texts, they are rarely heard, as the stories are not specifically about them. For example, in narratives in which white men rape African American women, African American men are falsely accused of rape, and Black women are raped, Black *men's* more serious traumas diminish the importance of Black women's experiences. Some of these texts are not postfeminist. In other texts, however, representations of African American women do intersect with many standard aspects of postfeminist rape narratives. In these examples, African American women most often exist next-to-but-just-outside postfeminism: the narratives are often multiple-focus, for example telling one story about an African American woman's experience of rape outside the (postfeminist) law and another about white men's education of white women to use the (postfeminist) law to end what becomes a deracialized story about rape. I end the chapter by examining three films that offer more nuanced and explicitly antiracist depictions of rape: *Rosewood* (1996), *She's Gotta Have It* (1986), and *Daughters of the Dust* (1991). I argue, however, that while these films challenge postfeminism's hegemony more fully than do the other examples I discuss in this chapter, they nonetheless marginalize African American women, centering African American men instead.

If chapters 4 and 5 examine texts that challenge—however fleetingly—both postfeminism and its whiteness, the final chapter of the book takes up texts that, at least at the level of production and consumption, exist much more marginally in relation to mainstream postfeminist popular culture: feminist rape prevention and education films and videos that are marketed to feminist classrooms, rape crisis centers, and the like. I further challenge postfeminism in this chapter by including texts produced in the 1970s, when feminist discourses (but not yet postfeminist discourses) had emerged in popular culture. In this chapter I illustrate how films and videos from the 1970s and early 1980s move from making women aware of the prevalence of rape, to suggesting ways women can prevent rape, to educating women about self-defense techniques. After the mid-1980s, however, films and videos emphasized personal therapeutic recovery rather than addressing the need for social and legal changes in relation to rape. From the 1970s to the 1990s, films and videos also moved from depicting more rare stranger rapes to more prevalent acquaintance rapes, illustrating a shift in feminist logics about rape. Nevertheless, a contradiction emerges in these films and videos between a claim that rape is violence, not sex, and representations of nevertheless *eroticized* date circumstances in which rape is most likely to take place.

The earlier films and videos tend to be more focused on activism, empowerment, and social change than are the later films and videos. Some more recent films and videos do offer more variety, however, depicting rape in multiple ways, including discussing rape in terms of war, as an aspect of media culture generally, and through more avant-garde experimental techniques. Overall, however, I argue that while some antirape films and videos take up larger feminist perspectives such as these, more often than not these productions, through the narratives about rape they tell, augment women's vulnerability and social isolation as individuals. Moreover, like postfeminist rape narratives, the vast majority of antirape films and videos fail to explore racial themes in complex ways, ultimately placing spectators' empathy with white women and leaving women of color out of the picture. While I conclude by suggesting alternative possibilities for video- and filmmakers (and for those of us who teach film and video) that might more effectively respond to the social problem of rape, I remain relatively pessimistic, since the patterns I describe in this final chapter essentially parallel those of postfeminist discourses generally.

By developing a feminist cultural studies approach that moves among film, television, and video—and between mass-mediated and local activist texts—I hope to offer a nuanced intertextual and cross-media argument about the place of representations of rape and discourses of postfeminism in popular culture and in feminist cultural studies and activism. Additionally, by using the book's structure to examine the intersections of popular film and television and independent film and video depictions of rape both in the context of postfeminist culture and at critical disjunctures from postfeminism, I hope to illustrate the complex interrelationships among contemporary cultural understandings of feminism, activism, and the plethora of representations of rape in our daily lives. Finally, by drawing on an antiracist polycentric multicultural feminist critical perspective that is opposed to many of postfeminist discourses' definitions of feminism, I hope to illustrate how these interrelationships in the late twentieth century contribute to racial formations, nationalism, cultural understandings of and anxieties about sexuality, and gendered categories of social identity. Overall, I hope this book will offer a significant contribution to film and television studies, feminist and antiracist theory and criticism, a variety of feminist activist projects, and thereby to women's lives.

1

A Feminist History of Rape in U.S. Film, 1903–1979

This chapter is *a* history of the representation of rape in mainstream[1] U.S. film from 1903 through 1979, but it is not a *comprehensive* history of these representations during this time period.[2] To write such a history would be nearly to write the history of cinema itself. Scholars argue that rape is pervasive in narratives generally, and cinema is certainly no exception.[3] Quite probably not a year has gone by since the beginning of cinema when any number of films have not represented, implied, or alluded to rape, attempted rape, or other forms of sexual violence. I would argue, in fact, that rape is a key force throughout the history of U.S. cinema and that one cannot fully understand cinema itself without addressing rape and its representation.

While representations of rape are ubiquitous throughout the history of film, shifts in the frequency of particular modes of representation of rape have occurred. Up until the early 1930s, explicit references to rape and onscreen depictions of attempted rape were relatively common. By the mid-1930s, films with explicit rape themes appeared less often; however, allusions to rape and sexual violence continued. In the 1960s, explicit representations of rape once again became commonplace.

The development of self-regulation in Hollywood and the eventual formation (and then demise) of the Production Code offer one perspective from which to understand these shifts. Focusing on self-regulation in the 1910s, Janet Staiger (1995) argues that narrational techniques—such as a clear motivation for a character's immoral act or a moralistic ending in which the "bad" characters face punishment—regulated, but also justified, representations of sexuality. In relation to rape, films might represent a character who rapes or attempts to rape someone in a variety of ways: he could be saved through transformation, function to teach other characters or the audience a lesson, help to define a film as "serious" or "high art," or face the consequences of choosing to take a "bad" action. Additionally, narratives might depict rape as a punishing consequence of women's inappropriate actions. In this context, one might argue that self-regulatory practices actually *invited* (particular kinds of) representations of rape.

When the Production Code began to take effect in the late 1920s and early 1930s, it held that representations of rape and seduction "should never be more than suggested, and only when essential for the plot, and even then never shown by explicit method. They are never the proper subject for comedy" ("Documents" 1995, 62). Thus, rather than eliminating rape altogether, the code prescribed certain narrational strategies that, as Ruth Vasey (1995) argues, led to "elision, or effacement of sensitive subjects" (81) such as rape.[4] The Production Code's call for effacement was not a new mode for representing rape, however. The development and codification of this Production Code–sanctioned approach followed logically from preestablished modes of representation. As both Vasey and Richard Maltby (1995) point out, the code was based on existing practices of city censorship boards, and it corresponded with many of the methods of self-regulation developed in the 1910s, such as the narrative and moral imperatives for representing rape that I mention above. Furthermore, earlier censorship boards and film producers were themselves drawing on precinematic rape narrative forms. In fact, the Code's imperative that rape "should never be more than suggested, only when essential for the plot" mirrors the findings of the essays in *Rape and Representation*, an anthology that examines both ancient and contemporary rape narratives in oral culture, prose, literature, film, and elsewhere. Summarizing the collective findings of the anthology, the editors write,

> What remains is a conspicuous absence: a configuration where sexual violence against women is an origin of social relations and narratives in which the event itself is subsequently elided. . . . The simultaneous presence and disappearance of rape as constantly deferred origin of both plot and social relations is repeated so often as to suggest a *basic conceptual principle* in the articulation of both social and artistic representations. (Higgins and Silver 1991, 2–3, emphasis added)

The censorship boards and later the framers and interpreters of the Production Code, then, drew on well-established modes of representation when making their decisions about "appropriate" and "inappropriate" depictions of rape in the relatively new medium of film. The result was that by the second half of the 1930s and continuing into the 1940s representations of rape and sexual violence were predominantly an "absent presence" in cinema. Films alluded to rape obliquely but nonetheless *systematically depended on rape* to motivate narrative progression.

After federal antitrust actions against the film industry and the 1952 U.S. Supreme Court decision that films were to be considered under rules of free speech, the Production Code gave way to a new form of self-regulation: a ratings system, a descendant of which is used today. Concomitantly, the number of films depicting explicit rape or attempted rape increased. For example, Aljean Harmetz (1973) examines nearly twenty films from the late 1960s and early 1970s that include rape, calling rape "the new Hollywood game" (1).[5] While, as I illustrate in this chapter, rape was anything but new to Hollywood, Harmetz's article is an example of public discourse noting a shift in the representation of rape toward more explicit depictions during the late 1960s and early 1970s.[6] Harmetz's article also illustrates, however, that implicit representations of rape continued during this era. For example, Harmetz criticizes the writer/director Paul Mazursky for claiming that what Harmetz considers to be a rape scene from *Blume in Love* (1973) is not a rape scene: Mazursky claims, "on some level, [the character in *Blume in Love* (1973)] permit[s] it to happen" (quoted in Harmetz, 11). This scene, then, is an example of the continuation of implicit representations of rape.

In short, while the number of explicit representations of rape in cinema has varied historically, standard narrative conventions that contribute to rape's elusiveness, many of which were codified during the Production Code era, appeared regularly during the *entire* time period under study here, blurring firm distinctions one might want to draw between pre-/post-Code and Code films and maintaining a consistently high number of representations of rape in film overall. Given this elusive/ubiquitous history, I have the following two goals. First, I seek to *demonstrate just how pervasive rape is* in mainstream U.S. films up until the 1970s, regardless of shifts in self-regulation and modes of representation. In order to illustrate this with as many examples as possible, I draw on my own viewing of more than fifty films from 1903 to 1979 that represent rape in some way; on the subject indexes and plot descriptions in the American Film Institute (AFI) *Catalog of Motion Pictures Produced in the United States* for 1911–1920 (Hanson 1988), 1921–1930 (Munden 1971), 1931–1940 (Hanson 1993), 1941–1950 (Hanson and Dunkleberger 1999), and 1961–1970 (Krafsur 1976) and the AFI special topic catalog on ethnicity in U.S. cinema for 1911–1960 (Gevinson 1997); and on keyword searches of Web sites that include plot descriptions of films.[7] In order to include many films that subtly imply rape rather than explicitly represent it and thus are not indexed under rape (or related terms) in the AFI catalogs or on the Web sites, I also draw on other scholarly work that explores implicit representations of rape in film[8] and on other relevant films I have seen while researching this book.[9]

Throughout the chapter I rely on brief summaries and downplay some of the more canonical examples of films that include rape (such as *Birth of a Nation* [1915] and *Gone with the Wind* [1939]) in favor of texts that have received less critical attention in order to emphasize how *standard* these representations are *throughout* cinema, not just in the relatively unique films of cinema studies' canon. This approach to criticism helps illustrate rape films' ubiquity and begins to *challenge the elusiveness* of many of these representations, the second goal of this chapter. To further this goal, I also include some close textual analyses, particularly of films that elide the sexual violence on which their narratives depend. If rape is everywhere in film and yet often offscreen, alluded to, or not acknowledged as "really" rape, this chapter offers a critical analysis that insists on identifying all these types of representations and naming them as forms of rape within narrative.

Specifically, the particular history I tell in the first section of this chapter explores the multiple, ambivalent, and contradictory ways rape narratives have contributed to and depend on social categories of gender, class, race, and nation. The second section addresses the relationship between rape narratives and the representation of feminism. In this second section I ask specific questions about how representations of rape have helped to negotiate social understandings of feminism and women's activism historically and about how these representations intersect with the social categories of gender, class, race, and nation described in the first section.

Rape in Film: Gender, Class, Race, and Nation

In what follows, I separate my discussion of gender, class, race, and nation into separate subsections in order to pay due attention to each issue. By addressing each issue separately, I illustrate a distinct difference between a *mutability* of gender and class and a *reification* of race and nation in these films. In addition to considering gender, class, race, and nation singly, however, I also address the intersections of these issues, arguing, for example, that some rape narratives draw on a relationship between gender and class in ways that reaffirm a heterosexual family structure. And, for instance, I suggest that the mutability of gender is a key part of the process of maintaining national boundaries through depictions of rape. By addressing gender, class, race, nation, *and* their intersections, I hope to illustrate the complex and versatile roles rape plays in U.S. film. Throughout this section I also emphasize that there are no consistent stereotypes in rape narratives that appear in all or even most cases. For example, a man of color, a white man, a wealthy man, or a poor man might each just as easily be a savior as a villain. Similarly, a woman's desire for a "foreign" man might lead to rape, or it might lead to the assimilation of the foreign man into U.S. society. This point is particularly important because much previous research on one or several rape films depends on generalizations about *consistency* in representations of rape.[10] My examination of a large number of films from a wide time period illustrates that rape narratives are much more versatile and varied than this research has suggested. My overall goal, then, is to describe both consistencies and inconsistencies, emphasizing the *pervasiveness of the appearance* of representations of rape while highlighting the *versatility of the forms* they take.

Women, Vulnerability, Independence, and the Family

Women are often vulnerable in rape films, but the relationship between rape and women's vulnerability is complex. Specifically, two seemingly antithetical types of narratives are common: those that depict women's vulnerability as leading to rape and those that depict the rape of an independent woman as making her vulnerable. Paradoxically, the first set of texts suggests that women should be more self-sufficient and independent in order to avoid rape, while the second set of texts suggests that independent behavior and sometimes independent sexuality can lead to rape. In both cases, however, most narratives resolve the paradox between vulnerability and independence by providing a conclusion that successfully incorporates the woman into a stable heterosexual family setting.

In the films that depict women as innocent, naive, and vulnerable, and as facing rape as a result, the women may lack control over their own lives or bodies; hence, they lack agency and therefore logically must be rescued from rape. Some 1910s films depict men's use of drugs, alcohol, or hypnotism or women's amnesia or fainting to indicate women's hypervulnerability.[11] Other films from the same period represent young orphaned women as particularly vulnerable because they are parentless.[12] In some, rescue by a male guardian culminates in romance.[13] Other films heighten the orphaned woman's vulnerability by depicting her seemingly "kindly" guardian, often a single man, as a rapist.[14]

In the 1948 film *Johnny Belinda*, Belinda is particularly vulnerable because she is both deaf and mute. When Belinda begins to become more integrated into the community her vulnerable naïveté leads to a rape that makes her even more vulnerable. The rape also naturalizes her return to passivity through her eventual incorporation into marriage as the institution most likely to protect her from future rapes. Some scholars have claimed that this is the "first" post–World War II film to address rape *directly*, and rape *is* central to the narrative's development, but *Johnny Belinda* nevertheless relegates the rape and Belinda's experience of that rape to the margins of the text.[15]

The first section of the film depicts Dr. Robert Richardson's attempts to teach Belinda American Sign Language. Belinda, however, already communicates well through smiles, gestures, and body language, and she even keeps track of the customers at her family's flour mill by using a written symbol system she and her father have developed for this purpose. After Lucky McCormick, one of Belinda's customers, rapes her, however, Belinda stops communicating, which isolates her even more than her pre–American Sign Language life did. As a result, after the rape Robert communicates and translates for her, initiating the narrative repression of the rape that Belinda's silence facilitates. For example, when Belinda's father finds out that Belinda is pregnant and demands that she tell him who did this to her, Robert erroneously says, "Even if she could talk she couldn't tell you. . . . [It's] blotted out of her mind." Here, Robert "forgets" that Belinda can communicate and that, because Lucky is one of her customers, she even has a specific linguistic symbol to represent him.

Belinda's vulnerability increases further when Lucky and his new wife, Stella, convince the town that Belinda, impregnated as a result of the rape, is an unfit mother and that Lucky and Stella should therefore adopt Belinda's child. However, Belinda fights physically to prevent Lucky from taking her child, which leads to his accidental death and her subsequent trial for murder. At the trial, Belinda is unable to communicate because the lawyers face away from her, making it impossible for her to read their lips. Ultimately, Belinda is acquitted only when *Stella* speaks up, admitting that Belinda killed Lucky in self-defense. After the trial, Belinda begins to sign something to Robert, who is now her fiancé, but he stops her and says, "You don't have to say anything." By the end of the film Belinda has become even more silent, vulnerable, and dependent on others than she was at the beginning of the film, (supposedly) having lost her language skills, her ability to think, and even her right to talk.[16] Overall, the flow of the narrative suggests that, given her vulnerable state—which led to rape, which led to the birth of a child, which led to an accidental murder, which led to a trial—the film's culmination in heterosexual romance is even more necessary for her protection and happiness.

In such films with drugged, hypnotized, orphaned, and silenced women, innocence makes women vulnerable to rape; other films transform previously independent women into vulnerable women by subjecting them to rape or sexual violence. Some films emphasize this causality by depicting women's strength or independence as an explanation for why they face rape. Thus, the films use rape to discipline independent women into vulnerability. In films from the very first years of the 1900s, being active or visible in public—for example, the street,[17] a train,[18] or even just near a country stream[19]—is enough to put women in danger of peeping Toms, attempts at seduction, or rape. Later films drop the general theme of women in public spaces per se; however, 1910s films commonly include threats to women who express their independence by working for a wage. In *The Ruse* (1915), for example, a man identified by a title as a "crooked mine operator" repeatedly tries to touch his stenographer, Miss Dawson. She pulls away, but he eventually kidnaps her. Crosscutting between a scene of the kidnapper with Miss Dawson and a scene of Miss Dawson's mother with Miss Dawson's soon-to-be-fiancé, Bat, builds suspense and emphasizes the opposition between the dangers of Miss Dawson's independent work life and the security of her protected home life. While Miss Dawson bangs on her boss's shoulders and continually resists him, he does, eventually, manage to kiss her. The film ends after Bat rescues Miss Dawson and proposes marriage, which she accepts with her mother's blessing.[20]

In other films, women's independent expressions of sexuality, in particular, eventuate in rape, which in turn threatens the family. A common 1910s narrative includes a woman agreeing to elope with a man, only to face his rape or attempted rape of her before the marriage takes place.[21] A similar narrative involves a false marriage ceremony, after which the woman is raped or almost raped.[22] Here, a woman's independence of thought and her interest in leaving her family without her parents' permission ultimately endanger her. A related narrative includes women who are romantic dreamers and who get into trouble as a result. Some romantic dreamers are unmarried,[23] but most are married and thus threaten the family when they consider or engage in adultery. (*The Cheat* (1915) is perhaps the most famous example of this kind of narrative.) *The Talk of the Town* (1918) makes clear the threat women's extramarital flirting poses to marriage when the husband, after the fact, actually *pays* the man who attempts to rape his wife for "curing" his wife of her desire to flirt.[24]

These examples from the 1910s and early 1920s suggest that a woman's active sexuality, in particular, results in rape or attempted rape, which in turn threatens her place in the family. In the 1930s, women's sexual expression leads to sexual violence in a variety of films. For example, in many films women attempt various modes of self-defense, but are ultimately trapped by melodramatic circumstances in contexts where they face repeated sexual violence—at least until the very last moments of the film when marriage, as it is for Belinda, is often their only way out.[25]

I would argue that 1930s and 1940s screwball comedies, as a genre, offer another example of a group of films that include sexual violence as a central narrative element. These films depend not only on sexual tension, but also quite often on violent sexual battle (in the context of the sexual tension) that is ultimately resolved through heteronormative coupling at the narrative's conclusion.[26] For example, sexual violence appears as comedy in this genre when a man uses his knowledge that a marriage ceremony is false—knowledge the woman does not share (but spectators *do* share)—to pretend to want to consummate that marriage against the woman's will[27] and when an attempted rape, brought on by a woman's insistence on independent movement in social space, brings her together with the hero when he rescues her.[28]

I choose to examine one representative screwball comedy in some detail here because, as comedies, screwballs perhaps seem to be the least likely genre to depict sexual violence, and thus an analysis of a film from this genre emphasizes how pervasive implicit sexual violence is in film. Two scenes in particular from *We're Not Dressing* (1934) depict sexual violence. In the first scene, Doris Worthington, a wealthy yacht owner, fights with Stephen Jones, a sailor working on her yacht, to whom she is attracted and who is attracted to her. Stephen has been remiss in his duties, and Doris confronts him. She says, "You annoy me so, I could slap your face." He encourages her to do so, and she does; a reaction shot shows his surprise, and then he leans forward and kisses her. Here, while they are both acting violently, he links the violence to sex by kissing her in response to her violence and by kissing her without her permission (she slaps him with his permission, after all).

They are soon stranded on a desert island, where Doris becomes dependent on Stephen's working-class, manly savvy for her survival, and where sexual and physical vulnerability replace her independence and class privilege. As his power over her grows, so does his sexual violence. For example, when he frustrates her again and she threatens to throw a rock at him, he says, "Remember what happened when you just slapped me," explicitly threatening a more violent sexual assault. Later, when Stephen discovers that Doris has hidden the fact that there are other people on the island who could help them, he drags her off and ties her up. In response, Doris jokes, "I suppose a fate worse than death awaits me," referencing rape. His response implies that she is right, adding the jibe that he assumes she has been raped before. He says, "How would you know? You've never been dead, have you?" Next Doris pulls away in fright and tells him he "wouldn't dare." He responds with a speech that references the class tensions of screwball comedy: "Why wouldn't I? Tomorrow you'll be back in your own sheltered world, spoiled and petted and sheltered and out of my reach. In all my life I'll probably never see you again. But tonight you're mine." As in many screwball comedies, while Doris and Stephen ultimately engage in consensual coupling at the end of the film, they arrive there only after Doris faces repeated sexual violence as a result of her sexual desire and her independence (enabled by her class privilege).[29]

While I choose to pause over sexual violence in a screwball comedy of the 1930s in order to emphasize that rape can be central in even unlikely places such as comedies, which the Production Code explicitly states should "never" include rape, the number of films that associate women's independence and sexuality with sexual violence is overwhelming. Perhaps the scene from *Gone with the Wind* in which Rhett carries Scarlett up the stairs to her bedroom—despite her explicit physical and verbal protestations—is the most famous rape that a female character's independence and expressive sexuality within the narrative transforms into not-(really)-a-rape after the fact. Examples of women's expression of sexuality leading to rape from 1940s and 1950s films include women who contemplate leaving their marriages only then to face rape, which eventually leads them back to their marriage;[30] women who suffer from some kind of psychological affliction defined as feminine by the film—such as kleptomania,[31] repressed sexuality,[32] excessive sexual behavior (such as sometimes not wearing panties),[33] or delusion[34]—which in turn puts them in danger of rape; and entire narratives structured so that women have no choice but to capitulate to love/marriage, thus blurring the line between coercion and consent.[35] Additionally, being a former prostitute[36] or even just using femininity as a disguise (e.g., by faking a faint)[37] might eventuate in a woman facing rape or coercive sexuality.

Numerous 1960s and early 1970s rape films depict women's sexuality as even more explicitly excessive, suspect, or unhealthy. In *Straw Dogs* (1971), for example, Amy repeatedly flirts with a group of men working on her and her husband's property, one of whom is a former lover. Eventually, the former lover and another man rape her. While she initially struggles during the rapes, at the end she seems to give in, at least to the first rape. Whether or not she actually consents to any aspect of the rapes, the film implies that her expression of sexuality contributes to the rapes and then to the subsequent drawn-out violent confrontation between the working men and Amy and her husband, David. Thus a woman's expression of sexuality, followed by a violent rape, unleashes even more excessive and sustained violence in the text.[38]

In these films, women's vulnerability is complex and sometimes contradictory. Women may lack control over their own lives and thus need to be rescued, as in *Johnny Belinda*; or they may act independently, moving about alone in public space, working for a wage, or defending themselves, but still face sexual violence, as in *The Ruse*. Expressing their sexuality may be followed by rape that threatens their family structure, as in *Straw Dogs*; or expressing sexuality might lead to sexual violence that helps bring a couple together, as in *We're Not Dressing*. What is consistent here is that no matter how independent and self-sufficient a woman is in these films, rape heightens her vulnerability. Her gender identity may be mutable, oscillating between vulnerability and independence, but, more often than not, the narrative ultimately represents the family as a refuge and heterosexual romance as her salvation.

Economic and Social Class Ambivalence

In addition to addressing women's vulnerability and independence, their sexuality, and their relationship to family, some rape films explore themes of class. For example, in some films women become even more vulnerable as a result of economic losses, such as being orphaned or having to work for a wage. In these contexts, class disadvantage helps absolve women of responsibility for rapes or attempted rapes. In other films, trouble follows women's access to wealth. In a screwball comedy such as *We're Not Dressing*, for example, Doris's wealth renders her oppressive toward her employee, Stephen. This behavior then provides a motivation for his anger toward her, which he expresses through sexual violence. Similarly, in *Straw Dogs*, Amy taunts her former lover, a working man, both by displaying her status as mistress of her house and by using high-priced fashion to express her sexuality. Eventually he rapes her, moving the film forward to a violent confrontation between the land-owning couple, Amy and David, and the working-class men in whose community Amy and David are out of place.[39]

Overall, films representing a relationship between rape and social and economic class express an underlying ambivalence about a classed society. Both the films about working women and the screwball comedies about wealthy women discussed above, for example, include both anxiety about and desire for movement across class divisions. In these films, the sexualized violence can express the anxiety (if a woman crosses a class division she may face rape), or it can make the movement possible (once she faces rape, she may find love in a new class context).[40] As I discuss below, comparing films about villainous wealthy men to films about villainous working-class men illustrates ambivalence about class, as does comparing films that champion social reform of work conditions to films that are explicitly antisocialist. Furthermore, paradoxically, in some films women's desire for wealth may result in a potential rape, but the films nevertheless detail a sumptuously wealthy mise-en-scène as a source of spectatorial pleasure.[41] Ambivalence about class emerges again in films about distinct social groups, whether or not those distinctions are based in economics; for example, artists may be either villains or saviors, and youths may be both wildly violent and potentially reformable.

The villainous wealthy or aristocratic rapist is a stock character in 1910s and 1920s films.[42] The villainous (or at least misguided) wealthy or aristocratic woman also appears either as a mother or sister who insists on a "class-appropriate" marriage[43] or as a young woman who misuses or inappropriately desires wealth.[44] Any of these behaviors can lead to situations that eventually include rape or attempted rape. In *The Auction of Virtue* (1917), for example, a wealthy man is villainous *and* a woman is overly concerned with acquiring wealth. While she desires money only in order to help a friend, her desire nevertheless leads to a situation in which a wealthy man has an opportunity to rape her. The narrative culminates in an attempted rape and rescue, which naturalizes her return to poverty and to romantic love within that class context.

In contrast, other narratives unabashedly celebrate society or aristocratic life, depicting working-class, poor, or uneducated men as rapists.[45] Although it does not depict a wealthy world in opposition to a working-class world, *Broken Blossoms* (1919) does use a metaphorical rape and (unsuccessful) rescue narrative to depict the villainy of the working class. In this film Lucy, abused by her working-class father, Burrows, runs away. She is taken in by a Chinese man, Cheng, who is attracted to her and begins to approach her sexually without her consent (or, arguably, knowledge), but ultimately stops himself. Burrows then kidnaps Lucy and beats her to death with what Julia Lesage (1981) defines as a "whip-phallus" (53). Consequently, Cheng kills Burrows, reclaims Lucy's body, and finally kills himself. Lesage and Gina Marchetti (1993) both offer persuasive readings of Burrows's sexualized and violent treatment of Lucy[46] and of Cheng's approach to Lucy[47] as depictions of metaphorical rape. Marchetti further argues that although Cheng becomes the avenger when he shoots Burrows, because he is not white he must also die, returning to an emasculated, masochistic role of an Asian man in Hollywood. This difference from standard narratives (of attempted rape leading to rescue, leading to love, leading to heterosexual romantic/family coupling) highlights the racialized nature of the film. Here, the issue of rape emerges in the context of class in such a way that the film depicts both working-class and Asian men as rapists, even though the Asian man simultaneously functions as a(n ineffectual) savior.

Films that draw a relationship between rape and a need for labor reform were also common in the 1910s. Most films that bemoan work conditions primarily do so in order to tell a story about attempted rape—caused by the work conditions—rescue, and a fantasy of reform. Thus, the films acknowledge exploitive labor conditions, but the endings imply that "good men" (and occasionally "good women") are already making all the changes that are needed.[48] Other films, however, are explicitly antisocialist. For example, in *Bolshevism on Trial* (1919), which Kevin Brownlow (1990) suggests "was an attack on socialism, intended to make it seem ludicrous in theory and impossible in practice" (443), Barbara and Norman work together to establish a "Bolshevist" utopian island community where everyone is equal. The leader, however, is villainous: he is married, but advocates free love, which includes an attempt to rape Barbara, whom Norman rescues. The film ends with the U.S. flag being raised and the (capitalist and masculinist) U.S. Marines restoring order to the island. Here sexuality, sex, and attempted rape signify socialism, and advocating "free love" leads to rape.

While a large number of films link rape and *economic* class conflict in the 1910s, by the 1920s this particular pairing drops out almost altogether.[49] The theme of *social* class continues to appear, however. In 1910s and 1920s films, for example, entertainment professions, such as artist, actor, dancer, or singer, function as a social class associated with rape and the threat of rape. These professions are not economically class specific: these films depict artists, whether wealthy or poor, as on the fringe of mainstream society. In this context, artists can be said to function as a social class. Like films dealing specifically with economic class, films that depict rape in these various contexts collectively portray ambivalent class politics. While they primarily depict these settings as dangerous for women, a savior also sometimes emerges from this world.[50] In *Infidelity* (1917), for example, Elaine is an art student who is taken with another art student who is "Hindu," Ali. The film exoticizes Ali when he uses hypnosis to force Elaine to be alone with him and then attempts to rape her. Her sweetheart, a white man in the art class, rescues her. This film does depict the art world as dangerous for women, and does depict an artist as villainous, but simultaneously depicts a (white) artist as savior. Furthermore, the villain's racialized use of hypnotism, which renders the woman blameless for the attempted rape, makes this film less wary of women's participation in the art world and more critical of immigration and racial difference.

The association of rape with particular social classes continues in the 1930s, 1940s, and 1950s, although with less frequency. In this time frame, rape might occur in the context of the circus,[51] the dance world,[52] a nightclub,[53] or among sailors at sea.[54] In *The Pitfall* (1948), a model, Mona Stevens, faces a relentless pursuit by MacDonald, a man who does occasional private detective work for the hero, with whom Mona is having an affair. In one scene, MacDonald comes to the department store where Mona works and insists that she model for him, thus illustrating his threat to her. In a medium close-up that reveals her discomfort and then a close-up of him watching, he forces her to turn around for him, telling her to lower her shawl to reveal her bare shoulders. While not an explicit rape per se, this scene does include class-based and explicitly coercive sexuality. The 1950 film *The House by the River* does include an explicit attempted rape. This film depicts a villainous author who not only attempts to rape his maid, Emily, but accidentally kills her when she resists him. Here, simply working for an artist/author endangers Emily.

In 1950s and 1960s films "juveniles" function as yet another kind of social class with a connection to rape. These films weigh two alternatives to controlling youth violence: nurturing psychology or aggressive social control. The young men and women almost always are incontrovertibly "bad," however, and thus by the end of the films aggressive social control appears to be the only solution, suggesting less ambivalence about (marginalized "youths" as a social) class than the other films I discuss in this section. *The Purple Gang* (1960), which takes place in Detroit during Prohibition, explicitly depicts a therapeutic approach as dangerous. In this film, a social worker wants to rehabilitate juvenile delinquents while the police disagree with her, believing prison to be the answer. Eventually, the teenagers rape and murder the social worker, violently proving her wrong.[55]

Like films that use rape to work through social understandings of women's relationship to independence and vulnerability, films that link rape to issues of economic and social class articulate anxiety about these social categories. In this context, rape functions as a narrative tool first to raise anxiety and then either (1) to provide a means of returning characters to a gendered and classed status quo in which gender and class differences, particularly differences associated with social power, are obscured and the heterosexual family is valorized; or, especially in the later films, (2) to articulate an apocalyptic perspective on shifts in these social categories that suggests the worst will happen if one (whether character or spectator) does not remain in one's designated gender and class position.

Solidifying Race

Rape films that address gender and class imply at least a potential mutability and permeability of these social characteristics—as the social definition of women shifts in relation to, for example, mobility in social space, waged work, the family, and expression of sexuality; and as class categories are transgressed and complicated when wealthy men and poor men, artists and other entertainers can be either villainous or virtuous. Conversely, rape films that foreground race tend, overall, to solidify racial categories, perhaps "incorporating" a racialized minority into dominant society,[56] but nevertheless also suggesting the impossibility of shifting what race *is*.[57] For example, the villainous artist in *Infidelity*, discussed above, illustrates this overdetermined racial solidification: he is an artist, he incapacitates his victim, *and* his method of subduing the woman—hypnotism rather than drugs, for example—is coded as foreign and therefore particularly dangerous. And, in *Broken Blossoms* the strength of Cheng's racial identity is sufficient to "bend" the standard rape/rescue/romance narrative. This melodrama has a particularly tragic ending: both Lucy and Cheng die rather than develop the romantic familial relationship that follows a typical rescue from rape in innumerable other films.[58] Despite this stability of racial *categories*, however, often the particular racial *identity* of the depicted rapists and, to some extent, the women who are raped shift from film to film. In the discussion that follows, I illustrate the reification of race in films that depict men of color as rapists of white women, that depict men of color as saviors, and that depict white men as rapists of women of color. Additionally, I point out that even in explicitly antiracist films, rape's place in the narrative generally helps to solidify racial categories.[59]

One might expect that I would begin this section by discussing films that depict men of color as rapists of white women. While scholars have most often discussed this racist characterization in relation to African American men,[60] it functions in relation to other racialized groups as well.[61] For example, in *Her Debt of Honor* (1916) a Native American man attempts to rape a white woman who is saved by her white sweetheart. In *The Border Raiders* (1918), a presumably Chinese or Chinese American man, Mock Sing, attempts to rape a white woman. She is rescued by her white sweetheart. In *Cora* (1915), a character named José (presumably Mexican American, but certainly racialized) attempts to rape a white woman. She defends herself against him, accidentally causing his death in the process.[62] *Birth of a Nation* (1915), which represents an African American man as (attempted) rapist of a white girl/woman, is probably the most written about film that fits into this category.[63]

The western, in particular, is a genre in which men of color, usually Native American men, regularly appear as villainous rapists. For example, in westerns a woman's bonnet caught on a broken wagon, a silver bracelet on a Native American man's wrist,[64] a darkened room whose contents (presumably a dead and raped woman) are visible only to the hero,[65] a darkened pass between two rocks, again visible only to the hero,[66] an extreme close-up of a woman's frightened face coupled with the sound of approaching Indians,[67] or a white man about to kill a woman he deeply cares about to save her from a "fate worse than death" each symbolizes rape or potential rape within a complex semiotic system of inference.[68] In these examples (symbolic) rape serves as a justification for white men's (more literalized) massacre of Native Americans. In *The Searchers* (1956), in particular, rape serves as the precipitating event for the entire narrative progression as well as the potential threat that keeps the search for the white child kidnapped by Native Americans—and the narrative— going.[69] Westerns depicting Native American rapists continue into the 1960s and early 1970s.[70] This trope is so common that in some 1970s self-referential comedic westerns, rape becomes a joke. In *Little Big Man* (1970), for example, Native Americans who rescue a young woman frighten her because she assumes they will rape her. The antiracist (but sexist and homophobic) joke turns on the Native American men's sexual disinterest in her, including their initial assumption that she is a boy.[71]

In contrast to films such as *Birth of a Nation* and *The Searchers* that depend on the stereotype of the racialized man as a rapist, some films depict Native American men, in particular, as saviors who sacrifice themselves (usually including their lives) to save white women. Here, heroism rather than villainy defines the man of color's fixed racialized identity.[72] *The Rainbow Trail* (1932), in which a Native American man rescues a white woman from rape, is somewhat more complicated, however, because this rescue is not purely self-sacrificial. Rather, the Native American man rescues the white woman in *exchange* for a white man rescuing a Native American woman. Furthermore, in both cases men rescue the women from attempted rape by a white man. This film includes both a "noble" Native American man *and* a villainous white man who attempts to rape a Native American woman. By placing these characters in relation to each other, the film adds a racialized motivation for the Native American man's "nobility" beyond a more simplified "positive" stereotype.

Most often, however, men of color as cross-race saviors and white men as cross-race rapists do not appear in the same film. Furthermore, when the white man as cross-race rapist does appear, the narrative often veers away from the subject of rape. For example, *The Grip of Jealousy* (1916) displaces the story of a white man raping an African American woman to the pre-film time frame of slavery, seemingly unable to imagine this interracial rape in the present.[73] *The Goddess of Lost Lake* (1918) explicitly suggests that a Native American woman's racial identity places her in danger of rape by white men. In this film Mary, a woman who is mixed race Native American and white, returns from the East with a college degree. She decides, however, to "pretend" to be a "full" Native American. Presumably as a result of her performance of what they understand to be a provocative racialized identity, two white men who visit her white father find her attractive. One attempts to rape her, while the other saves her from the rapist. In this film and others like it,[74] a white hero rescues the woman of color threatened with a cross-racial rape brought on by her racialized identity and then ends up marrying her, thus drawing her into white culture.[75] By representing a mixed race character, *The Goddess of Lost Lake* has the *potential* to represent race as mutable, but the narrative structure—in which rape emerges only in response to (a pretend) "full" Native American identity and in which marriage to a white man emphasizes the character's whiteness—reifies distinctions between racial categories.

While the representation of Native American men as rapists of white women is pervasive in westerns, often leading to violent colonial incursions, it is also important to note that white men as cross-race rapists appear in this genre as well. In *Wagon Master* (1950), for example, a white man—Reese, an outlaw—rapes a Navajo woman, an act that marks him as villainous. While the rape takes place offscreen, represented visually only by a Navajo woman crying, yelling, and pointing toward Reese after the rape, the Mormons and the two wagon masters traveling with them tie Reese to a wagon wheel, shirtless, and whip him—onscreen. Thus, punishment for rape is a matter to be settled between white men; the Navajo people, while threatening, ultimately simply watch from a victimized position. Other westerns, such as *Canyon Passage* (1946), *The Hellbenders* (1967), and *Firecreek* (1968), however, do include a violent "Indian uprising" in response to a white man's rape or attempted rape of a Native American woman; here, rape provides narrative motivation for a violent confrontation between the two opposed racialized groups.[76] Overall, films that depict white men's rape of women of color also draw attention away from these interracial rapes by displacing the rape as a problem of a former historical period, by folding the women into white culture through marriage, or by following an individual rape with a large-scale, bilateral racialized conflict.

Despite the overwhelming number of films that link rape and race in racist ways, there are also a number of films that depict rape as part of an effort to articulate an antiracist stance. For example, rape is a theme in some of Oscar Micheaux's early films, made and released in the context of independent African American film production and culture during the late 1910s and 1920s and engaging contemporary cultural narratives about rape and African Americans in order to critique white racism. Micheaux's *Within Our Gates* (1919) includes a flashback in which Sylvia's (adoptive) father is unfairly blamed for his white employer and landlord's murder. In response, a lynch mob hangs and burns Sylvia's mother and father in a scene crosscut with Sylvia experiencing an attempted rape by the landlord's brother, Armand, who is white. When Armand rips Sylvia's dress and sees a scar, however, he realizes that Sylvia is his own daughter and stops attempting to rape her. When the flashback ends, Sylvia is reunited with the man with whom she has fallen in love, a doctor.

The film's *separation* of the rape and the lynching articulates the contemporary antiracist argument that lynchings of African Americans were taking place for reasons other than rape of white women (such as keeping a saloon or having smallpox), but that lynch mobs nevertheless used stories about rape or attempted rape of white women to justify those lynchings (Wells-Barnett 1909, 99). Parallel editing produces a temporal *association* of lynching with rape, however, which ironically mimics the contemporary culture's link of acts of racist mob violence with stories about racialized rape. Furthermore, the film's reversal of race in the standard rape story used to justify lynching, so that in the film a white man attempts to rape an African American woman, not only undermines cultural narratives about rape that "justified" lynching but also alludes to the long history of white men's rape of African American women. The fact that Sylvia is Armand's *unrecognized daughter* emphasizes the frequency with which white men historically created sexual access to African American women's bodies and to the daughters those women sometimes bore as a result of rape. Jane Gaines (1993) argues, "The scene is thus symbolically charged as a reenactment of the White patriarch's ravishment of Black womanhood, reminding viewers of all of the clandestine forced sexual acts that produced the mulatto population of the American South" (56–57).[77]

A few films from the 1930s also use rape to critique racism. In *Eskimo* (1934), when a white captain rapes Mala's wife, Aba, causing her death, Mala kills the captain and then is forced into hiding. Eventually the sympathetic Mala makes friends with Canadian Mounties who are searching for him. When they discover his identity, they let him go. On the one hand, this film depicts the "white man" as dangerous because he rapes and murders. On the other hand, the Canadian Mounties function as a sympathetic representation of the white man's law and thus as an alternative white masculinity. For the indigenous characters, white men's entry into their community is dangerous, but the white man's law is necessary.[78]

Several films from the 1950s and early 1960s, such as *The Sun Shines Bright* (1953) and *To Kill a Mockingbird* (1962), support antiracism by depicting an African American man falsely accused of rape but defended in court by a liberal white man. While these films confront racism, they also take place in a former era, making the false accusation and racist legal system appear to be a thing of the past. As a result, the films implicitly suggest that the legal system contemporary to the era in which the film is produced need not be similarly examined for racism. In these films, rape "justifies" attention to race relations, but when the accusation turns out to be false, the film displaces concern about rape. Furthermore, by drawing on a false accusation model that holds the white woman who (falsely) accuses the African American man at least partially responsible for the racism in the courts, these films further deflect a critique of the racist legal system they seem to set out to address.[79]

All these antiracist films overwhelmingly focus on how rape, attempted rape, and false accusations of rape affect men of color. Occasionally, however, films depict rape in order to address the intersection of racism and sexism for women. For example, in *Lady Sings the Blues* (1972) the rape of Billie Holiday as a child initiates the narrative. While she works in a brothel, she seems blissfully unaware of where she is, listening to music and generally ignoring her surroundings. The camera, however, emphasizes the setting, lingering over her surroundings and on an African American man who leers at her. This split between the knowing spectator and the innocent Billie continues as she walks home. While she skips along, the camera fragments her body, at times showing just her legs or just her face. In one shot of her legs the camera picks up the man from the brothel as he first watches her pass and then gets up and follows her. The next scene shows Billie's coming to consciousness when he intrudes on her while she listens to music and offers to pay her "two dollars" for sex. She attempts to escape by pretending to be interested and inviting him to sit down and take off his hat, but when she tries to run, he grabs her. While the film does not code the rape itself as racialized in any specific way, it does focus on the racism Billie Holiday faces later in life in getting a job, in getting her music on the radio, in facing the Klan, and in facing prosecution for drug possession. Thus, in the film rape initiates her into an adult world in which she must face not only her own sexuality but also racism.[80]

While each of these films relies on and reasserts the stability of racial identities, they do so in a variety of sometimes contradictory ways. Many films depict men of color as inherently rapists; others depict Native American men as (again) inherently self-sacrificial saviors. Films may depict a white man's rape of a woman of color, paradoxically, as justification for a later massacre of people of color; or they may depict a white man's rape or attempted rape of a woman of color, again paradoxically, as a precursor to the woman of color's assimilation into white culture through marriage. In each case, however, the racial category of various characters remains static. Even antiracist films tend to reify racial categories, as in the 1950s films that depict African American men as inherently innocent, and as in *Lady Sings the Blues* in which (following rape) Billie Holiday confronts her own inescapable identity as an adult African American woman in a racist world. Overall, then, unlike rape films with ambivalence about gender and/or class, rape films that address race stabilize racial categories, even when they sometimes also challenge racism.

Maintaining the Nation

A number of the films I discuss in the previous section use rape not only to reify racial identity but also to link race to questions of nation and nationality. For example, *Birth of a Nation* suggests that an African American man's attempted rape of a white girl/woman produces the white Klan, which (vaguely) saves the infant nation (from reconstruction). Some westerns define Native American rapists as, historically, a cause of white colonization. A link between rape and race thus precipitates what appears to have been an unavoidable contemporary neocolonialist national structure (whether the film represents that link as justified or not). Films from the 1950s that depict African American men as falsely accused of rape—at some time in the past—acknowledge historical racism and sometimes even acknowledge historical racism in the United States in particular; but, they also celebrate the power and justness of abstract Law available in U.S. courts by relegating the problem to the past and by holding (lying) white women primarily responsible. If the woman had not falsely accused the man, some of the films imply, the law, even "back then," might not have led to injustice. Even the socially critical *Within Our Gates* relies on a pastoral version of an antiracist struggle that views rape and lynching as part of the United States' (near) past, ending on an optimistic note when intertitles represent the suddenly patriotic doctor saying, "Be proud of our country, Sylvia. We should never forget what our people did in Cuba under Roosevelt's command. . . . And later in France, from Bruges to Chateau-Thierry, from Saint-Mihiel to the Alps! . . . In spite of your misfortunes, you will always be a patriot—and a tender wife. I love you!"

As this brief discussion of the link between race and nation implies, rape films that address issues of nation, nationalism, and nationality struggle to construct national cohesion, even (or especially) in the face of pressures on the shape of the nation. For example, films might use rape to mark the dangers of immigration for the nation or to encourage assimilation into the nation. Films about war often use rape to distinguish enemies from friends (a fixed binary that helps justify wars between nations) or to attest to the horrors of war, particularly when those horrors infiltrate the United States through the figure of the returning veteran.[81] Even colonial films, located in various "desert locale[s]" (Shohat and Stam 1994, 169), can maintain racialized U.S. borders when rape delineates "us" versus "them" or defines a white woman's appropriate (or at least safe) place as "here" rather than "there."

Films that link immigration to rape include 1910s white slavery films that depict sexual coercion as a dangerous outcome of immigration and portray women as passive victims.[82] While early-twentieth-century white slavery narratives in the popular press initially focused on the supposed dangers posed by ethnic immigrant men to ethnic immigrant women, in 1909 the Immigration Commission Report shifted attention to the supposed vulnerability of native-born women, rather than immigrant women (Grieveson 1997, 158).[83] Lee Grieveson's (1997) analysis of the documentary versus fictional elements of *Traffic in Souls* (1913) points to this kind of slippage, as the film shifts from representing the danger of forced prostitution for recently arrived immigrant women, represented by documentary footage shot on the streets of New York, to dangers for *any* woman (i.e., the native-born woman around whom the primary fictional abduction narrative functions). This shift in the film's form (from documentary footage to narrative centrality) corresponds with a shift from cultural anxiety about abduction of immigrants to cultural anxiety about abduction of native-born U.S. women.[84] Thus, collectively, the white slavery narratives blamed ethnic and racialized men for the victimization of white native-born women and "the quality and integrity of 'the race'" that they represented (Grieveson, 158).

Later films also link rape to immigration. *Daughter of Shanghai* (1938), for example, represents Chinese immigration. When Lan Ying's father is killed for refusing to smuggle immigrants into San Francisco, she decides to help break the smuggling ring, posing as a man aboard a smuggling ship. The immigrants, however, discover that she is a woman and promptly attempt to rape her; she is rescued by Kim, a detective and her sweetheart. Rape helps define immigrants and immigration as problems in this film, but in *Blue* (1968) a Mexican man who prevents a rape is an idealized—although doomed—U.S. immigrant. Azul leaves his Mexican adoptive father and brother's gang after he kills one of his brothers to prevent him from raping Joanne, a Texan. This action initiates a narrative in which Azul goes to Texas, changes (i.e., translates) his name to Blue, and falls in love with Joanne. Blue is literally caught between Mexico and the United States in the final shoot-out when he dies in the Rio Grande. Joanne then swims out into the river to recover Blue's body, bringing him back to the United States as a martyr for the protection of both white womanhood and the U.S. nation.

While the films I have just discussed are about or allude to dangerous outsiders coming into the United States, other films that involve rape depict a colonial setting in which U.S. nationality and/or white identity are defined—in part through rape—in relation to racialized foreign others. Some films, much like some westerns set in the United States, depict a villainous white man who rapes an indigenous woman, thus precipitating a violent attack by the indigenous people against the white colonists/travelers. Here, a single white man is villainous, but the indigenous people as a whole are violent by nature, as exemplified by their undifferentiated and excessive attack on the entire group in response to one individual's actions. In response, the white colonists have no choice but to protect themselves in order to return to the safety of their nation.[85]

Other films depict racialized men as villains and white women traveling in their country as victims. *Auction of Souls* (1919), for example, depicts both Turks and Kurds as villainous rapists. Furthermore, the exhibition system for the film used the narrative to justify U.S. imperialism *beyond* the text. Not only did the film tell a story about real people, Edith Graham and Aurora Mardiganian, but it opened at ten dollars a seat, with the proceeds going to the Armenian War Relief Association.[86]

Several rape films from the late 1910s draw on the representation of the foreign man as violent but also include a colonialist white woman who is attracted to that violent man. These films intersect with those that define rape as a danger faced by women who actively express their sexuality in a U.S. context, but here women's sexual desire is particularly dangerous because it is both cross-racial and cross-national, thus threatening the loss of white U.S. (or British) citizenship. In *Barbary Sheep* (1917), for example, a married British woman in Arabia indulges her romanticism by engaging in a flirtation with an Arabian chief. When he attempts to rape her, however, her inattentive husband, who has been off hunting Barbary sheep, arrives just in time to rescue her. This film's focus on the difficulties in, and then the reconciliation of, this white couple's marriage makes particularly clear the way the colonialist setting and the threat of rape in that setting are metaphors for danger outside traditional heterosexual whiteness. Other films, such as *The Arab* (1915), contain an explicitly villainous Arab character, but also provide another racialized man as savior. *Flame of the Desert* (1919) plays with this structure, but ultimately reveals the Egyptian savior, Essad, actually to be an English nobleman disguised as a sheik in order to quell a rebellion in Egypt. An Egyptian rebel remains the primary villain of the film.

These films prefigure the "sheik genre" of the 1920s by representing the white woman as attracted to an "Arab sheik," but the earlier films generally portray the villainy of the racialized man with much less ambiguity than do the later films.[87] In *The Sheik* (1921), *The Thief of Bagdad* (1924), and *Son of the Sheik* (1926), three of the most economically successful and historically famous colonialist films containing rape narratives, the Arab man (played in each case by a non-Arab white man, although Rudolph Valentino was coded as ethnic Italian) initially plans, attempts, or completes the rape of a woman, but later is transformed by love and/or the power of the woman's morality or beauty.[88] By the end of the film, he is drawn into "civilized" white culture (i.e., love not rape) and away from the "barbaric" Arab culture (i.e., rape not love). Looking at *The Thief of Bagdad* in the context of Douglas Fairbanks's relation to "boyishness" as star, Gaylyn Studlar (1996) argues that this film transforms "the boyish criminal, the juvenile delinquent, whose strong, manly instincts have . . . led him into crime" (including, I would add, planned rape) into a moral man. "He has a spiritual conversion sparked by [the princess's] utter chasteness" (82).[89] After the conversion, he then saves "his" princess from rape by another, more villainous, dark man, the Mongol prince. Valentino, on the other hand, who was already coded as ethnic, began *The Sheik* and *Son of the Sheik* not as a boyish criminal, but as one of "many variations on [a] stereotype of sexualized and greedy masculinity, [who] at his most dangerous . . . was darkly foreign" (Studlar, 151). Nevertheless, in *The Sheik* he does not rape his captive; instead, as Joel Shrock (1997) argues, "the moral power of his female prey transforms his primitive manhood into a masculinity more civilized and respectable" (73). And, like Fairbanks in *The Thief of Bagdad*, Valentino later saves "his" captive from another, more villainous Arab man. In *Son of the Sheik*, however,

Valentino *does* rape his captive; thus, while he ultimately also still "saves" her from a villainous dark man at the end of the film, when they do declare their love, in effect he saves her from his former self. By the end of each of these films, the characters reject Arab culture in favor of white Western culture.

While these desert locale narratives were common in the 1920s, they appear in later films as well.[90] Making the jungle's danger to "whiteness" explicit, *Forbidden Adventure* (1938) includes a "white goddess." Before the film begins, a planter kidnaps her and her mother and repeatedly rapes her mother. When they escape, a "Borneo tribe" takes them in. While the Borneo people are not the cause of the "white goddess's" exile from "civilization," the film makes it clear that their kindness is not sufficient for her happiness. The film ends with her mother's death in an accidental fire, freeing the white goddess to return to civilization with a white "explorer" with whom she has, of course, fallen in love.[91] In the more recent *Genghis Khan* (1965), the kidnapping, raping, and branding of a princess illustrate the extreme villainy of a Merkit Mongol leader.[92]

While not all the films I discuss here portray the victim or potential victim as a white woman, the majority do. Ella Shohat and Robert Stam (1994) argue that film narratives that depict rape as taking place in a desert setting away from a Western European context elide "the history of subordination of Third World women by First World men" (157). Furthermore, when a woman of color is the victim, she often functions as what James Snead (1994) calls a "prop" in the plot—important to the flow of the narrative but not central to the narrative itself—as in the westerns and colonialist films in which a white man's rape of an indigenous woman precipitates a conflict between two groups of racialized men as a narrative climax. Other films use the rape of a woman of color or ethnically coded woman as a narrative device to tell a story about a *man's* bravery—often in relation to his desire to protect or redefine the nation. In *The Yaqui* (1916), for example, the Native Mexican Yaqui Indians are enslaved by a plantation owner who attempts to rape Modesta, the wife of the Yaqui leader, Tambor. Modesta kills herself, and then Tambor kills the plantation owner, going on to lead a successful revolt.[93] Overall, films that take place in a colonialist setting use rape, whether of a traveling/ colonialist white woman or of an indigenous woman of color, to mark the danger of the exotic, to highlight the unchangeable nature of race, and, as Shohat and Stam argue, to displace questions of sexualized violence from a U.S. context.

War films similarly depict rape in foreign or historical settings. Some World War I films, for example, use rape as a means of reforming an enemy soldier, usually a German. In these films, the soldier either plans, attempts, or actually enacts the rape of a woman (usually a woman with whom he is falling in love), but then has remorse. Sometimes, he subsequently rescues her from another attacker and then reforms himself in relation to the woman, often even going so far as to revise his position on the war.[94] Sometimes, the reformed rapists are German *American* but have returned to Europe to fight for Germany during the war. In these cases, even when the United States is not directly involved with the war, immigrants or children of immigrants who choose to give up their national identity as "American" illustrate the error in their choice by becoming enemy rapists. Even more complexly, that traitor may be redeemed if he subsequently saves the woman and then chooses to return to the United States, reclaiming his identity as "American" through heroism and patriotism.[95] By 1918 and 1919, however, World War I films tend to depict unilaterally villainous enemy rapists, whether or not the rape is central to the narrative.[96]

World War I films tend to be about foreign villainy and the potential for men's redemption through assimilation into the United States, in part by saving women. Like the sheik films, they also depict women's transformative powers. The tension in these films often is not between men, but between women and men. Conversely, later war films tell stories about men's relationship to each other and to their own patriotism. For example, in *China* (1943), a World War II film, Japanese soldiers rape and kill a Chinese woman, thus illustrating that the Japanese soldiers are evil.[97] In terms of narrative development, the rape then transforms a formerly apathetic U.S. "war profiteer" into a patriotic ally who helps the Chinese fight the Japanese.[98] Similarly, in *Edge of Darkness* (1943), when a German soldier rapes a Norwegian village woman, the underground resistance in town, which has been relatively passive, finally takes action against the Nazis.[99] *The Nun and the Sergeant* (1962), set during the Korean War, involves a group of unsuccessful soldiers on an extremely dangerous mission. It also focuses on rape's effects on men. While the sergeant who leads the soldiers is skilled, the men resist following him until he takes in and protects a nun and a group of schoolgirls. The men begin to respect him, but one remains villainous, attempting to rape one of the girls. The rest of the men, then, reform themselves as soldiers by banding together with the sergeant against the rapist.[100] Other war films from the early

1970s depict returning Vietnam veterans driven to rape in the present context of the United States by their horrific prior experience of war in Vietnam.[101]

Overall, whether films depict immigrants as rapists or saviors, define foreign men as villainous or transformable, represent soldiers who rape or attempt to rape as enemies of women or as enemies of men, these films construct a specifically U.S. identity and do so by linking that national identity to a whiteness distanced from rape. Even when films celebrate a desire for immigration, as does *Blue,* or when white women travel and even sometimes find love in various "desert locales," as they do in *The Sheik* and *Forbidden Adventure,* rape in these films helps to delineate national borders and national identities, holding up the United States, whiteness, or very often both as protected contexts where women do not face rape. Even when white slavery films or returning Vietnam veteran films show rape in the United States, rape often implies a "problem" with an individual's incorporation or reincorporation into U.S. society. If that problem is resolved, then the nation is healed and rape will no longer be a threat. In sum, in all these examples rape represents a threat to national cohesion; thus, the absence of rape at the narrative's conclusion—often replaced by romantic heterosexual love—reaffirms national coherence.

Feminism in the Texts

Many of the films I have discussed so far at least implicitly link rape to feminism. For example, in the early part of the twentieth century, while suffrage may have dominated popular feminism, other feminist issues also emerge in rape films.[102] These include an antilynching campaign; challenges of work conditions, generally, but especially for women and children; the role of women in public spaces, including spaces of entertainment; and women's relationship to sexuality and the family.[103] Thus, the rape films that engaged these issues at least implicitly spoke to and about what feminism was. Similarly, in the 1960s and 1970s, when feminism once again became widely visible in popular culture, questions about women's sexual independence, their right to defend themselves, and their place in the civil rights movement intersected both with feminist activism and with the many films that represented rape.[104] In this section, I trace some of the ways rape films have engaged with feminism. I do not argue that the films "reflect" the historical moment. In fact, I would suggest that the way these films collectively define feminism is far from an "accurate" portrayal of the complexity of feminist activisms during these respective periods. Rather, I am interested in the ways rape in these films participates in the *discursive production* of what feminism is and can be.

I explore this discursive production of feminism first by looking at films that depict feminism explicitly, particularly in two eras in which feminism was often discussed publicly: the 1910s and the 1960s and 1970s. I then shift my approach and ask how my own particular feminist critical perspective on narrative and representation might reveal "feminist moments" in rape films, whether or not those films appeared when feminism was in the public eye. Here, I am interested in how critical practice can itself participate in the discursive production of feminism by reading films as offering a feminist response to the social and discursive existence of rape. Finally, I combine these two critical approaches when I turn to a particular issue that has been central to feminist discussions of rape since the 1970s: self-defense and revenge. In the process, I use a late-twentieth-century feminist perspective to read self-defense and revenge in a variety of earlier films, and I examine 1970s films that explicitly take up the issues of self-defense and revenge. Overall, by examining a variety of ways rape films intersect with feminism, I hope to provide a background against which to understand the more recent films I discuss in the remainder of the book.

Depicting Feminism

Early films that include women who face rape after engaging in feminist activities—such as moving about in public space, immigrating to the United States, migrating from country to city, working for a wage, participating in reform activities, or attempting to leave a monogamous heterosexual family/marriage—implicitly acknowledge these activities and goals as a possibility for women but also represent them as dangerous and atypical for women. *The Cheat* (1915), for example, addresses a woman's active cross-race sexual desire, her attempts to manage money, her (excessive) participation in a new consumer culture, and her independent freedom of movement.[105] The film represents *all* these issues as potential threats to family life *because* they can lead to a situation in which rape (and in this racialized text in which an Asian/Asian American man obsessively marks everything he owns, literal branding) is a possibility. Similarly, the colonialist films of the late 1910s and 1920s about white women's sexual desire for men of color, particularly "sheiks," acknowledge a specific form of (white) women's sexual desire while simultaneously depending on categories of race and nation to represent that sexuality as dangerous for women. Nevertheless, when the films transform the violent men of color into romantic lovers and even sometimes into *white* romantic lovers, they simultaneously fold the women's sexuality back into a monogamous heterosexual—even familial—context, and thus accept that sexuality. Similarly, in screwball comedies when women are sexually expressive, the threat of sexual violence in response helps fold the characters back into relatively stable class and family positions by the end of the films.[106]

Other early films address women's activism more directly. For example, in *The Woman under Oath* (1919) Grace becomes the first woman to serve on a jury in New York.[107] The trial is a murder case in which Jim, the accused, admits that he had planned to kill a man who had raped his sweetheart, but that the man was dead when he arrived. The jury deadlocks, eleven for and one (Grace) against conviction, until Grace finally admits to her fellow jury members that *she* killed the man because he had refused to marry her sister after seducing her. Although Grace is, in fact, a murderer, that murder takes place in a context of avenging a woman who is raped, and thus the film not only implies that women ostensibly would bring a unique perspective to the jury process, but it does so by suggesting that women have the right to defend their family against sexual assault.[108]

Other films may acknowledge sexism and champion a feminist response to it, but rather than locating the sexism in the U.S. legal system, as does *The Woman under Oath*, they distance the United States from sexism, representing it as endemic to other nations instead. These films link the common displacement-of-rape-to-elsewhere I describe above to feminism, thus depending on feminism to help define the United States as an enlightened feminist nation and a foreign nation as sexist and sexually assaultive. For example, in *The New Moon* (1919) Theo, a dictator of an unnamed Bolshevist country, passes a decree that all women (between seventeen and thirty-two years of age) must register as state property; he does this because he wants to "possess" the Princess Marie. Marie then disguises herself as a male shopkeeper and begins organizing women to refuse to cooperate. Theo continues to pursue Marie, however, and attempts to rape her. The film ends when Marie ultimately abandons her feminist activism in the face of the overwhelming brutality of the

"Bolshevists" and escapes across the border with the man who rescued her from rape (although unspecified in the film, perhaps to the more enlightened United States).[109]

Bolshevism on Trial (1919) also rejects socialism, but, in contrast to *The New Moon*, it draws a *link* between feminism and socialism by connecting the concept of "free love" (which could be associated with women's activism) to "Bolshevism."[110] When "free love" then leads to rape, "feminist Bolshevism" is to blame. From this perspective, the film simultaneously embraces feminism by bemoaning the sexism of others and takes an antifeminist stance by defining "free love" as necessarily sexist. Other films from the time period also explicitly undermine feminist ideals. In *Human Collateral* (1920), for example, Patricia recognizes that she is being treated as "human collateral" when her father borrows money from her fiancé, Roderick. As a result, she rejects both of them, encouraging the attentions of another man, Richard. Richard, however, attempts to rape her. Roderick saves her just in time, and she then realizes he truly loves her. She ignores her previous feminist insight that she is "collateral"—whether or not Roderick loves her—and accepts him as her future husband.[111]

Rape films from the 1960s and 1970s also emerge in an era when feminist activism was particularly visible. Rape, however, was much more prominent as a feminist issue itself by the 1970s.[112] As a result, when these films represent rape, by definition, they at least implicitly also represent feminism. Some films do confront feminist arguments about rape more directly, however. For example, *The Mad Bomber* (1972) implies that pornography, which was an important feminist issue at the time, causes rape.[113] Alternatively, *The Seven Minutes* (1971) explicitly argues against the assumption that pornography encourages rape, implicitly responding to some feminist activism, as well as other contemporary films, such as *The Mad Bomber*. Dealing with another feminist (re)definition of rape as something that happens to women of any age and body type, not just young attractive women, *The Boston Strangler* (1968) dramatizes the sexual assault and murders of thirteen women in the early 1960s.[114] The film emphasizes that the victims were all elderly women and thus works against stereotypes of rape victims as young, sexually attractive women. And, as I discuss later in this section, many 1960s and 1970s rape films deal with feminist issues of self-defense and revenge as a response to rape.

Overall, the films I discuss in this section engage feminism directly, either by supporting or by challenging it. In the 1910s and 1920s, the films often used rape to address other feminist issues, such as a woman's right to express sexuality actively, her right to serve on a jury, or her role as commodity undergirding the institution of marriage. The structure of some films' narratives connects rape to these issues in ways that support feminism; other films imply that the practice of feminism could produce situations in which women face rape—i.e., feminism causes rape. Nevertheless, as Marchetti argues in relation to *The Cheat*, even films that seem to work against feminism still raise the issues and thus contribute to a cultural interest in women's independent sexuality, for example, as much as they suggest that that independence is dangerous for women. Some 1960s and 1970s films go further still by addressing feminist arguments about rape itself; however, the particular versions of feminism they draw into the text, such as the possibility that pornography "causes" or is linked to rape, are problematic because they simplify and in many ways misrepresent the complexity of feminist activisms against rape.[115]

Reading Feminism

Given that many of these films are ambivalent about feminism, at best, I turn now to a critical practice that seeks to read feminism in and through rape films. Here I want to think more about the possibilities that particular aspects of some films—such as Patricia's insistence in *Human Collateral* that women *are* collateral in marriage (regardless of her subsequent actions)—provide for reading a feminist depiction of rape in a film. Can moments like these produce alternative stories about rape?

Some films from the 1910s and 1920s, for example, take a typical rape narrative structure and turn it around for feminist purposes. In *Brand's Daughter* (1917), Alethea *pretends* she is willing to elope with Norvinsk in order to trap him into revealing that he is trying to rob her father's bank. She nevertheless ends up alone with him as a result. Subsequently she still faces his attempted rape of her, and she still is rescued by her sweetheart. In *Lover's Island* (1925), Clemmy's father decides that he will force the man who raped Clemmy to marry her. Rather than submitting to this patriarchal structure, Clemmy simply announces (falsely) that it was her sweetheart, Avery, who raped her, thus taking control over her own marriage away from her father. Here rape becomes a vehicle for feminist independence, even if her independence from her father leads Clemmy right back into a heterosexual family structure with Avery. While these films end in heterosexual coupling, as do almost all rape films from that same era, along the way they alter standard narrative structures, revealing those structures as conventions and—at least temporarily—considering other narrative possibilities for rape.[116]

Narratives that increase women's vulnerability by subjecting them to repeated acts of sexual violence can be read similarly. Despite the oppressive traps in which these women are caught, as some feminist scholars have argued in relation to melodrama as a genre, one can read the texts as defining women's circumstances as oppressive through the subjective and sustained representation of that oppression. Thus the films express a feminist perspective on, in this case, the roles rape plays in gendered oppression.[117] For example, *Sadie Thompson* (1928) links a religious interest in reforming prostitution and in colonizing the "south seas" to a patriarchal oppression of women.[118] Into a typical distanced exotic setting come a missionary, Alfred Davidson, and a former prostitute, Sadie Thompson.[119] Tensions increase as Alfred begins to persecute Sadie relentlessly, attempting to force her to repent, to reform, and then to return to San Francisco. While Sadie falls in love with a marine, Sergeant Tim O'Hara, Alfred refuses to let her go on to become Tim's wife, instead insisting on his own right to control her life. As Alfred's reformative pursuit of Sadie heightens, she begins to realize that she has no escape, and thus she approaches him, presumably to try to reason with him. The scene is shot from her emotional point of view, including long drawn out extreme close-ups of his fingers drumming the table, his foot tapping the floor, and his face, with his head in his hands, staring at her unwaveringly. Eventually, when Sadie's attempts to reason with him and to appeal to the governor fail, Alfred's desire to control her, depicted as torturous through her point of view, wins out. Sadie finally agrees to atone, acting, as Tim says, as if she's "doped."

Her newfound faith does not satisfy Alfred's desire for control, however. After an extended crosscutting scene between Alfred sitting on the porch, unable to sleep, and Sadie in her own room, unable to sleep, Alfred rapes her.[120] Having revealed the sexually violent desire for control at the base of his antiprostitution reform, he then commits suicide. Ironically, Alfred's suicide produces a "happy ending," because his death frees Sadie from the oppressively gendered context in which the entire film traps her. The film's conclusion is thus extremely ambivalent about its critique of gendered oppression. While the film has revealed Sadie's oppression, and while Alfred's rape of her ironically frees her from his ability to persuade her that she needs to repent (the morning after the rape she announces that "all men are pigs"), she also forgives Alfred when she hears that he has committed suicide and then agrees to give up her independence by going to Sydney with Tim when he announces that he still wants to marry her. Furthermore, by focusing on Alfred's pursuit of Sadie rather than on his colonialist role as a missionary, the film leaves colonialism unchallenged, depending, in fact, on the status of "exotic locales" as a displaced site at which rape is likely to take place.

Aspects of *Duel in the Sun* (1946) also can be read as feminist in relation to the film's depiction of sexual violence as pervasive in Native American women's lives. The film defines Native American women's race itself, however, as the source of the problem. The film opens in an unnamed town in which a Native American woman knowingly dances provocatively in a saloon, while her mixed race daughter, Pearl, naively dances provocatively in the street. Men approach both women in these contexts, although Pearl pulls away. Pearl then watches as her white father murders her unfaithful mother. This scene suggests that Native American women's sexuality is innately excessive, passed on from one generation to the next (regardless of a father's racial identity), and implies that it is and will be the ruin of both those women and the white men who become involved with them.

The bulk of the narrative reinforces this idea in the context of Pearl's subsequent life with her father's former lover, a wealthy white woman named Laurabell, and her family. At Laurabell's ranch, Pearl meets Laurabell's two sons, Jesse and Lewt, both of whom fall in love/lust with her. While Pearl is interested in Jesse (the "good" brother), Lewt (the "bad" brother) pursues her, forces his way into her bedroom, and eventually rapes her. After the rape, Jesse rejects Pearl, assuming she consented. Caught as she is in the melodramatic structures of a racialized and gendered fate she cannot escape, Pearl begins a relationship with Lewt. He continues his abuse of her, however, by refusing to marry her and also refusing to let her marry anyone else. The film ends with Lewt and Pearl's death as a result of a shoot-out between them.

By describing the film this way, especially in relation to *Sadie Thompson* in which the act of rape *ends* the man's control over the woman, I hope to illustrate that *Duel in the Sun*'s narrative takes a decidedly unfeminist path from rape to love to death. Nevertheless, there are also moments when the film pauses to define not only Lewt but Pearl's entire life as sexually assaultive. For example, when Lewt (falsely) implies to Laurabell that he and Pearl are engaged in a sexual relationship, Laurabell wakes Pearl in the middle of the night and forces her to come in her nightclothes to talk with a reverend, who, while telling Pearl that she is sinful, stares at her lustfully and touches her face. In this brief moment, the text reveals its own sexual violence toward Pearl by offering an understanding of Pearl's experience of sexuality as men's assault on her, facilitated in this case by a white woman. This perspective directly contradicts—if only for a moment—the film's overwhelming general implication that Pearl's identity as a hypersexual Native American woman means that, just like her mother, she cannot help but die tragically.

Similarly, when the film emphasizes Pearl's (rather than Lewt's) perspective during his pursuit of her, it again makes possible a reading of both Lewt and the film's own narrative trajectory as assaultive.[121] For example, the first time Lewt enters Pearl's bedroom uninvited his spurs jingle and his shadow is huge. He kisses her, but she hits his face and says she hates him. When she spits at the door after he leaves, the film further emphasizes her point of view of his villainy. When Lewt does eventually rape Pearl, not only do his spurs jingle but lightning flashes as she resists him. Lewt again kisses Pearl while she tries to pull away from him, but just before the scene ends she seems to kiss him back, beginning the troubling narrative trajectory from rape to love to tragic death as a result of their shoot-out.

Responding to Rape

As satisfying, assuaging, productive, or affirming as it may be to read feminist moments into films like *Sadie Thompson* and *Duel in the Sun*, in the end, as in the majority of the films addressing rape and feminism, while they may offer a woman's *experience* of rape, even a feminist *perspective* on rape, they do not engage a particularly feminist *response* to rape. I turn now to films that do, particularly those that represent various kinds of self-defense and revenge.

One form of self-defense is to engage in self-protective behavior after a rape. For example, both *Johnny Belinda* and *Straw Dogs* seem to pause after the rapes, elaborating on the women's experience of post-rape trauma before moving on to the business of increased vulnerability and class and national warfare, respectively. In *Johnny Belinda,* when Belinda jumps at Robert's touch on her shoulder rather than responding to his attempts at communication, she seems to be dealing with her own experience of nonconsensual touch rather than operating as victim-to-be-rescued-by-Robert. Similarly, in *Straw Dogs,* before the film moves forward from the rape to the working men's violent attack on Amy and David's house, it pauses long enough to portray Amy's fear and trauma through very brief subjective flashbacks of the rapes when Amy ends up in the same space with the rapists at a public event.[122]

Some films depict women's acts of physical self-defense during an attempted rape not as leading to increased vulnerability, as in some of the films I discuss above, but rather as successfully *reducing* women's vulnerability. For example, a few early silent films celebrate new communication technologies as a means of self-defense by depicting a woman using them to discover the leader of a white slavery ring and thus to rescue her sister (*Traffic in Souls*) or to communicate with the Allies during World War I and thus avoid enemy rapists, simultaneously protecting both herself and the nation (*The Little American* [1917] and *To Hell with the Kaiser* [1918]). *Wild Party* (1929) also includes successful self-defense, although it is only successful in a particular context. Rejected by other women at her college for not following the dress code for a party (she dresses too provocatively), Stella and her friends decide to leave, ending up at a roadhouse. There, several men try to assault all the women, and as Judith Mayne (1994) argues, "what was playful in the previous scene [the clothes] here becomes dangerous" (135). The central character sacrifices herself, performing femininity not to protect herself but to protect her friends, pretending to be interested in the men and saying she will stay if the others can go. As she is about to face rape, her male professor, who is quickly becoming her sweetheart, arrives and rescues her. As Mayne points out, however, at the next dance organized by the college Stella again performs femininity by pretending to be interested in a man in order to distract him from his assault on her friend, Helen. In this context, her performance is successful: neither she nor Helen needs further rescuing.[123] More recently, *Saturday Night Fever* (1977) portrays one woman's use of self-defense as successfully stopping a rape.[124]

Related to these potentially empowering (although ambivalently so) depictions of self-defense are films that portray women's acts of revenge. For example, in *Shanghai Express* (1932) Hui Fei kills Cheng in revenge for his rape of her. This act is important not only for her but also for the narrative, because it frees her and her white traveling companions from Cheng's captivity. In this film, a white woman, Lily, is traveling by train to Shanghai. She strikes up a friendship with a Chinese woman, Fei, in part because they are both rejected by other travelers on the train for being too sexually expressive (the film implies that Fei is a prostitute and that Lily is a "kept" woman). Cheng first attempts to rape Lily, but when Lily's former lover rescues her, Cheng sends for Fei. As the women pass on the stairs, they exchange a look after which Lily struggles aggressively against her guards, although she is unable to break away to protect Fei. When Cheng rapes Fei he precipitates her revenge, which leads to the prisoner's freedom and ultimately to Lily's reconciliation with her former lover. Thus, on the level of the narrative, Fei's revenge works in the service both of confirming a racist depiction of Cheng's intense villainy, so intense he "deserves" to die, and of precipitating the standard romantic heterosexual coupling for the white stars. Nevertheless, the brief moments in which Fei and Lily exchange a glance and in which Fei takes her revenge acknowledge the intensity of the violence of rape, problematize the rape of a woman of color (in part) as a form of protection of a white woman, and offer an image of women resistant to that racialized sexual violence.

Rape-revenge narratives are particularly common in the 1970s. In a historical context in which feminism defines self-defense and revenge as aspects of antirape activism, it is no longer necessary to read feminism into isolated moments of resistance to a man's touch (*Johnny Belinda*) or an exchange of looks as two women pass on the stairs, acknowledging their shared but racially differentiated roles in an inevitable rape scenario (*Shanghai Express*), for example. Rather, 1970s rape-revenge films offer an entire genre with the potential to articulate a feminist response to rape.

In these films, sometimes the revenge is taken by a man who loses his wife or daughter to a rape/murder, and sometimes the revenge is taken by women who have faced rape themselves. The films in the first category depend on rape to motivate and justify a particularly violent version of masculinity, relegating women to minor "props" in the narrative.[125] The films in the second category, however, can be understood as feminist narratives in which women face rape, recognize that the law will neither protect nor avenge them, and then take the law into their own hands. Carol J. Clover (1992) argues that rape-revenge films "share a set of premises [including] ... that we live in a 'rape culture' in which *all* males—husbands, boyfriends, lawyers, politicians—are directly or indirectly complicit and that men are thus not just individually but corporately liable" (138–39). More specifically, she argues, for example, that *I Spit on Your Grave* (1977) analyzes how the "dynamics of males in groups" can lead to rape (144) and that both *Rape Squad* (a.k.a. *Act of Vengeance*) (1974) and *Lipstick* (1976) criticize the failure of "the law and the legal system" to respond to rape (145). Revenge, then, becomes women's only viable response to rape.[126]

Foxy Brown (1974) is a particularly interesting example because it puts a woman at the center of both a blaxploitation film and a rape-revenge narrative. While Foxy Brown's primary goal is revenge for her boyfriend's and brother's murders, rape is also one of the acts of violence and racism with which she has to contend. Immediately after the rape, she attacks the men who are holding her captive, one of whom raped her, and escapes. Continuing her vengeance, she ultimately has the main villain, a white drug dealer and high-class pimp, castrated. This act forces him to live on with a lifetime reminder of his racist and sexist acts.[127]

In the end, the films I describe in this section offer feminist depictions of rape, but they do so in ambivalent ways. Collectively, they contribute to a discursive production of feminism that keeps it fragmented, links it to racist, colonialist, and xenophobic ideologies, supplants it with heterosexual romance, and limits a woman's response to rape to violent vengeance. Nevertheless, I consider it useful to pause over the moments during which the films provide an opportunity for reading the representation of rape in ways that have the potential to empower characters and/or spectators rather than, for example, to increase their experience of vulnerability.[128] The trick is to pay attention to how the films then seek to recuperate or undermine that empowerment without giving up the potential resistant reading a feminist perspective can bring to the film. In other words, I choose to dwell on Patricia's critique of women's role in marriage as "human collateral," on Sadie's resistance to Alfred's reformative pursuit, on Pearl's hatred of Lewt, on Belinda's rejection of Robert's touch, on Fei's murder of Cheng, and on Foxy Brown's escape, while nevertheless remembering that my feminist readings and the characters' self-protective actions do not decrease the existence of discursive rape.

Conclusion

Rape narratives are so common in cinema (and elsewhere) that they seem always to be available to address other social issues. In this chapter, I draw attention to a variety of ways rape has functioned throughout the history of film, and I suggest there is not simply one way that rape intersects with gender, class, race, nation, or feminism. Thus, while I argue that films often link rape to women's vulnerability, the place of rape in the narrative may be a result *or* cause of vulnerability. And, while the expression of sexuality may lead to rape, rape in turn may lead to a romantic rescue that accepts the woman's sexuality within a heterosexual family context. The ambivalence about social and economic class in many of these films emerges through rape narratives that can just as easily condemn the wealthy as the poor, the "insider" as the "outsider"; can just as easily reassert a class status quo in which unique individuals cross boundaries as articulate an apocalyptic vision of "outsiders" (e.g., youths) as wholly different and unreformable. Similarly, the reification of racial categories in many of these films depends on rape narratives that work equally well to further racism (e.g., *Birth of a Nation*) as to (at least attempt to) work against racism (e.g., *Within Our Gates, To Kill a Mockingbird*); to depend on stereotypes of men of color as villainous or as self-sacrificial; and to define women of color as inconsequential "props" or to incorporate them into a mainstream white society purged of all marks of cultural identity. Rape narratives' versatility also means they can work either to incorporate immigrants into or to exclude racialized others from the nation, to attest to the horrors of war (for the United States) or to argue for the necessity of war (to protect the United States). Finally, the complexity of rape narratives allows them to evoke feminist issues and perspectives, to make possible critical readings that can find feminist responses to and critiques of rape in the text, while simultaneously undermining those critiques with narratives that end in marriage or death, for example.

The complexity and contradictions in the ways rape interacts with gender, class, race, and nation in these films illustrate the importance of a feminist intersectional analysis that goes beyond a sole analysis of gender by addressing specificities as well as linkages among social positions. In this case, an intersectional analysis of these films illustrates the ways rape narratives function to suggest a mutability for gender and class—to imply that women's relationship to vulnerability and independence can change and that class boundaries are permeable—while also maintaining clear boundaries around social identities of race and nationality. An intersectional approach forces additional looks at the films in order to see how, for example, the depiction of women's independence and its relationship to rape can work narratively in the service of maintaining classed and national boundaries, or how depictions of African American men as innocent of rape can work in the service of blaming women for lying or of celebrating the present (of the film's production and reception) as a historical moment in which the nation has supposedly exorcised racism.

To put it simply, this chapter argues that film criticism needs to go beyond pointing out that rape films punish women and vilify economic, social, racial, and national others.[129] While some do include these types of representations, many do not. Furthermore, as I have shown, even those that do are often ambivalent about their own depictions. Instead, if anything is common to all the texts I address in this chapter it is the way rape functions to work through tensions and anxieties surrounding gendered, classed, raced, and national border crossings. In other words, I am suggesting that what is particularly troubling about rape films is not that they are sometimes sexist, capitalist, racist, nationalist, and colonialist (although, of course, many are), but that violence against women is so central to the films, so key to character transformations and narrative development and resolution, so *versatile*, that it not only seems to be necessary to the film itself, but it concomitantly naturalizes the policing and negotiating of gendered, classed, racialized, and national boundaries these films engage.

I would suggest that one of the reasons rape in film is so versatile, beyond its overall ubiquity, is its existence in so many different narrative forms that endure across time. For example, I have illustrated rape's central role in screwball comedies and westerns, as genres. On the one hand, it is important to pay attention to the specificity of the roles rape plays in each genre. Thus, for example, in screwball comedies sexual violence can help articulate tensions about women's independence and class divisions, themes central to the genre, while in westerns racialized rape often plays a more central narrative role by motivating an escalating conflict between two groups and helping to naturalize the narrative conclusion in an "unavoidable" violent colonial confrontation. On the other hand, the fact that sexual violence is central to *both* genres suggests that, despite particular genres' specificities, it is important to understand the role rape plays in supporting genre itself as a narrative form in cinema.

Rape does not only support genre. Other common rape narrative forms include the rape/rescue/romance trajectory; pervasiveness on an implicit—but nonetheless narratively significant—level of the text; the threat to and/or protection of the heterosexual family; the exportation of rape into other racialized, exotic, or historical locales; rape's precipitation and sometimes justification of a more violent, more social, more narratively significant conflict; the use of rape of women to focus on relationships among men; and the woman of color as prop. Through these and other common narrative forms, rape functions both as the narrative motor for individual films and as a cultural reference that connects any number of films together—forming genres, shaping expectations, and naturalizing the cultural pervasiveness of sexual violence against women.

In the process of identifying rape's pervasiveness, I have included examples of films in which rape is obvious, such as *Johnny Belinda* and *Sadie Thompson,* and of films where it is less obvious, such as *The Ruse, We're Not Dressing, Broken Blossoms, The Pitfall,* and *The Cheat.* On the one hand, the employer's kiss of Miss Dawson in *The Ruse,* Stephen's threat of a "fate worse than death" for Doris in *We're Not Dressing,* Cheng's thwarted sexual approach to an unconscious Lucy and Burrows's sexualized violent murder of Lucy in *Broken Blossoms,* MacDonald's insistence that Mona bare her shoulders in *The Pitfall,* and the Asian/Asian American man's branding of Edith in *The Cheat* are *not* rapes. On the other hand, they *are* all examples of sexualized violence that draw on many of the same narrative and representational conventions as do more literal rape films. Thus, the pervasiveness of rape in film naturalizes the existence of all these other forms of sexual violence. By reading these other kinds of sexual violence as *part of* the matrix of rape in film, I am insisting on understanding how they contribute to and depend on the elusive/ubiquitous place of rape in U.S. cinema. Examining both obvious and not-so-obvious representations of rape emphasizes and challenges the pervasiveness of rape in film—two of my central goals in this chapter.

Overall, by identifying these narrative structures I hope, at base, to have illustrated the centrality of rape to cinema itself. While not all films include rape, an overwhelming number not only include but *depend on* rape and sexual violence to generate narrative action. As a result, various critical models that film studies has brought to bear on cinema (i.e., Production Code history, genre theory, feminist theory/criticism of romance and the preservation of the heterosexual family, and antiracism work on the history of racialization in cinema) also implicitly depend on rape. Why has an analysis of rape, except for a few important works, been overwhelmingly absent from film studies in general and feminist film studies in particular?[130] What aspects of our theory and history in film studies might we want to rethink and rewrite, given how elusive yet ubiquitous cinematic rape is? While I would not want to suggest that all studies of film be done through the lens of rape, I do want to pause over these questions, to acknowledge—at least for a moment—how central rape is to film, and therefore to film studies.

In this context, rape films also sometimes provide cultural definitions of feminism. In the early twentieth century, despite the fact that rape was not necessarily a visible feminist issue, rape narratives that already raised issues about women's relationship to independence, vulnerability, and family could easily provide a context in which to explore specific feminist issues such as women's right to serve on juries, free love, and the oppressiveness of marriage. In the late 1960s and 1970s, when rape was a central feminist issue, rape films sometimes more directly engaged feminist perspectives on rape, such as the relationship between rape and pornography or the validity of self-defense and revenge in response to rape. No one version of feminism emerges from these films, however. Like the complex and varied representation of gender, class, race, and nation, the films' depictions of feminism are ambivalent and contradictory, certainly across films but also sometimes even within individual films. Reading feminism into the texts through critical methods that focus on brief moments in the texts, temporary shifts in standard narrative forms, or the acknowledgment of women's experience of oppression through the excessive representation of that oppression is similarly ambivalent in that this critical method depends on finding feminism in the text *despite* the text.

Overall, then, by focusing in this chapter on ambivalence and contradiction as well as on consistency and repetition, I hope to emphasize the complexity of the discursive production of rape and of feminism and to illustrate how criticism can point to—and thereby expand—the partiality of popular culture's ability to define both rape and feminism.

2

The Postfeminist Context
Popular Redefinitions of Feminism, 1980–Present

Most simply, given a dictionary definition of "post" as "after," popular texts that use the term "postfeminism" imply that the contemporary moment is "past" feminism. These texts promise that postfeminism has moved us beyond feminism; yet, in the process they also produce the particular versions of feminism that are supposedly defunct. Thus the concept of postfeminism *perpetuates* feminism in the very process of insisting that it is now *over*. But what kind of feminism is perpetuated? As Judith Stacey (1987) puts it, postfeminism is "the simultaneous incorporation, revision, and depoliticalization of many of the central goals of second-wave feminism" (quoted in Dow 1996b, 87). According to Stacey, postfeminism absorbs and transforms aspects of feminism in ways that, at minimum, dissociate feminist concepts from political and social activism. Suzanna Danuta Walters (1991) argues that this "revision . . . of second-wave feminism" not only depoliticizes feminism but can go so far as to kill it off. She writes, "[Postfeminist] discourse . . . has declared the [feminist] movement (predictably if illogically) dead, victorious, and ultimately failed" (106). In Walters's discussion, postfeminism defines feminism as dead and gone either because it has been successful and is therefore no longer necessary ("victorious") or because it was unsuccessful and therefore proves itself to be unnecessary ("failed"). According to postfeminist discourses, what specific victories has feminism won? And what aspects of it have failed?

In this chapter I focus on the emergence of the concept of postfeminism in popular culture since the early 1980s. I have two goals here: first, to identify and analyze the definitions of postfeminism circulating in popular culture for the last twenty years or so; and second, to detail and critically examine the particular versions of feminism those postfeminist discourses offer. Thus, I ask both "What are the themes and concerns of postfeminism?" and "What kind of feminisms do those postfeminist themes and concerns discursively produce?" While I do not address depictions of rape directly in this chapter, the answers to these questions are particularly important to understanding the rape narratives I discuss in the remainder of the book, all of which are influenced by and contribute to postfeminist discourses in some way.

In what follows, I discuss five interrelated categories of postfeminist discourses that emerge in the popular press. I focus first on what I call *linear postfeminism*: the representation of a historical trajectory from prefeminism through to feminism and then on to the end point of postfeminism. The construction of linear historical relations between feminism and postfeminism ensures the impossibility of feminism and postfeminism coexisting. Since postfeminism always supplants feminism, feminism logically no longer exists. The second category of postfeminist discourses I discuss is *backlash postfeminism*. Rather than simply declaring feminism over, these discourses aggressively lash back at feminism. For example, what might be called "antifeminist feminist postfeminism" introduces a "new" type of feminism as a corrective for a previous problematic "victim" feminism. Alternatively, "new traditionalist postfeminism" appeals to a nostalgia for a prefeminist past as an ideal that feminism has supposedly destroyed. Overall, both linear and backlash postfeminism represent feminism in a particularly negative light.

In contrast, *equality and choice postfeminism*, the third category of postfeminist discourse I identify, consists of narratives about feminism's "success" in achieving gender "equity" and having given women "choice," particularly with regard to labor and family. While this type of postfeminist discourse represents feminism in a relatively positive light, it nonetheless suggests that women now have greater access to choice and hence can avoid having to fight further for equality; therefore, women presumably no longer need feminism. The fourth category of postfeminist discourse I discuss is a more recent development, emerging first in the 1990s rather than the 1980s. This version of postfeminism defines feminism as antisex and then offers itself as a current, more positive, alternative *(hetero)sex-positive postfeminism*; this version nevertheless also incorporates aspects of feminism that promise women's independence. Thus, it both rejects an antisex feminism and embraces a feminism focused on individuality and independence. In most postfeminist discourse, men are in the background as objects of desire, role models, or villains. A fifth category of postfeminist discourse, however, focuses directly on men. Here, since feminism has been successful and women are now equal, *men can be feminists too*. Again, while these postfeminist discourses offer a relatively positive version of feminism by embracing it for both women *and* men, not surprisingly men turn out to be *better* feminists than are women.

These five categories offer some structure for understanding the complexity of postfeminist discourses in the popular media. They illustrate the adaptability and pervasiveness of the assumption in popular culture that feminism existed, was wholeheartedly absorbed by the mainstream, and therefore is no longer needed. Because postfeminism is and can be so many different things, it is a powerful, pervasive, and versatile cultural concept. However, as I will argue, postfeminism is also limited by its overwhelming focus on white, heterosexual, middle-class women (and sometimes men). Its complexity and adaptability, as well as its essentialist and universalizing logic about "women" and "gender equality," tend to cover over postfeminism's race, sexuality, and class specificity. Thus postfeminist discourses not only shape what feminism is and how women are positioned in relation to work, family, and sexuality, but they do so in ways that deny the relevance of race, sexuality, and class to considerations of gender—and therefore to feminism.

A Linear History for Feminism, Ending in Death

Time magazine's June 29, 1998, cover nicely illustrates the kind of linear history much postfeminist discourse assumes.[1] The cover features the disembodied heads of four women, three actual women and one fictional woman: Susan B. Anthony, Betty Friedan, Gloria Steinem, and Ally McBeal. The name of each woman appears above her head, in case, perhaps, the reader does not recognize these famous feminists or "misinterprets" the head of television character Ally McBeal as the head of Calista Flockhart, the actor who portrays Ally. Ally's is the only picture in color; the other women are in black and white. This opposition between color (for the fictional present) and noncolor (for the actual past) suggests that Ally's feminism has supplanted the three earlier "out-of-date" versions. But her feminism is tenuous. Below Ally's chin, *Time* poses the question "Is Feminism Dead?" The question, printed in red, is particularly authoritative since the color matches the magazine cover's title and border.

This cover depicts a linear history of feminism that is white, middle-class, and heterosexual, ending in "death" with the figure of Ally McBeal. In terms of race, by beginning the history of feminism with Susan B. Anthony, who is probably best known as a suffragist, *Time* disconnects "first-wave" feminism from its earlier roots in the mid-1800s abolition movement and thus elides analysis of race and gender as co-constitutive aspects of feminist activism historically.[2] Anthony herself was involved with the abolition movement (Ryan 1992, 14), although by the 1870s she was using racist rhetoric to argue for women's suffrage.[3] Furthermore, *Time*'s depiction of Anthony, who worked most extensively for suffrage, neglects many other aspects of feminist thought that coincided with the push for suffrage, including, among other issues, working women's rights, birth control, and sexual freedom.[4] Whether or not a *Time* reader is aware of these details in Anthony's history or the history of feminist thought and activism, generally, is beside the point; by depicting Anthony rather than, say, Angelina Grimké, Sojourner Truth, or Frederick Douglass as the "first" feminist, the magazine cover ensures an explicitly white-focused and implicitly racist depiction of the "beginning" of U.S. feminism.[5]

Jumping ahead nearly a hundred years, *Time* represents Betty Friedan as the next stage of feminism. While the cover thus connects disparate historical moments in feminism, these moments nonetheless share a focus on whiteness and middle-class life. Friedan's (1963) best-selling book, *The Feminine Mystique*, focuses primarily on white middle-class women (a default, given the absence of a discussion of racial and class specificity in her book) and thus conceptualizes a version of feminism that neglects women of color and working-class white women. Friedan is followed by Gloria Steinem, known for her active, independent, heterosexual feminism. As a young, traditionally attractive, openly heterosexual white woman in the 1970s, Steinem became (and continues to be) an acceptable feminist figure in the popular press (Dow 1996b, 29–30).[6] Again, *Time* might have pictured Angela Davis, Ti-Grace Atkinson, or Rita Mae Brown to symbolize late 1960s and early 1970s feminism but chose instead the middle-class, white, and heterosexual Friedan and Steinem. Perhaps most troubling, though, is *Time*'s choice of Ally McBeal to represent contemporary feminism. Rather than depicting one of many feminists who are currently active and visible in the popular press, such as bell hooks, Alice Walker, or even Ellen DeGeneres (as herself, rather than a fictional television character), *Time* ensures at least the potential for an affirmative answer to its question—"Is Feminism Dead?"—by depicting an imaginary (i.e., *nonliving*) television character who represents heterosexuality, obsession with body image, and aggressive get-ahead professionalism.

My point is not that picturing these other feminists (or any other feminists) would somehow be more accurate, or that *Time*'s version of feminism does not actually qualify as feminism. Rather, my point is that this depiction, in fact, *is* (at least one representative example of) what feminism *is* in the popular press; it is an example of how the media play a powerful role in defining feminism. This is the version of feminism—which *Time* and many other popular media sources repeatedly discuss in stories about feminism, the death of feminism, and postfeminism—that has emerged since the early 1980s. This version of postfeminism defines feminism as having followed along a linear historical trajectory focused, as I discuss in more detail below, almost exclusively on "equality" for white, heterosexual, middle-class women. It suggests that feminism has now ended (died) because, as the existence of Ally McBeal illustrates, women have achieved full access to independence and high-paying jobs and now have the right to choose whether or not to engage in heterosexualized bodily display in those contexts.

Antifeminism, New Traditionalism, and the Assaultive Backlash

This *Time* magazine cover also includes an implicitly aggressive assault on the feminism about which it simultaneously purports to be concerned. The question "Is Feminism Dead?" is not new; the popular press has asked this question repeatedly since the early 1980s, thus ensuring both "yes" and "no" answers to the question.[7] On the one hand, if the question has to be asked repeatedly every few years (if not every year), often on the cover of a widely distributed national magazine such as *Time*, feminism is clearly not dead. It lives on, if only to instigate this question. On the other hand, however, the repetition of the question, especially when paired with layouts like the *Time* cover I describe here, also leaves open the potential for a "yes, it's dead" answer. From this perspective, the question itself is a backlash against feminism. As Amelia Jones (1992) puts it, while a text that includes this question "appears to 'ask' innocently if there is 'a future for feminism,' it effectively precludes any consideration of this future by using the term 'postfeminism,' inexorably linking feminism to the highly charged image of 'being strident and lesbian,' a state of 'being' that is implicitly undesirable" (11).[8] While the

Time cover defines feminism through Anthony/Friedan/Steinem rather than "'being strident and lesbian,'" as in the example Jones analyzes, *Time* nevertheless implies that feminism has no future, in this case because it has already passed into the "historical" black and white imagery of Anthony/Friedan/Steinem.

Another assault on feminism within postfeminist discourses comes from antifeminist (self-defined) feminists, such as Shahrazad Ali (*The Blackman's Guide to Understanding the Blackwoman* 1989),[9] Sylvia Ann Hewlett (*A Lesser Life* 1986, 1987), Wendy Kaminer (*A Fearful Freedom* 1990), Daphne Patai and Noretta Koertge (*Professing Feminism* 1994), Katie Roiphe (*The Morning After* 1993, 1994), Christina Hoff Sommers (*Who Stole Feminism?* 1994),[10] and Naomi Wolf (*Fire with Fire* 1993, 1994), many of whom receive substantial press coverage.[11] While these authors often define themselves as feminist, their perspectives are simultaneously antifeminist because they call for the "death" of (another version of) feminism in the process of articulating their own feminism. Specifically, while claiming to stand for women's "equity" with men, antifeminist feminist postfeminists reject a "victim" feminism that they assert has great cultural ethos, particularly on college and university campuses. As Patrice McDermott (1995) points out, these books and the popular press's celebration of them focus on, attack, and, in fact, *define* one version of feminism (victim feminism); in the process, they neglect and thus negate many other versions of feminism. As a result, they are able to hold "exaggerated feminist propaganda . . . responsible for the oppression of women in contemporary society" (671). Bell hooks (1994) points to the "frightening dismissal and belittling of feminist politics that is at the core of" Naomi Wolf's *Fire with Fire,* in particular (97). In other words, these antifeminist postfeminist feminists blame the oppression of women on a version of feminism that they imagine to exist. As a result, it must be eliminated and replaced with "better" feminism.

These two assaults on feminism—asking whether feminism is dead and blaming an imaginary feminism for women's oppression—are part of a larger postfeminist cultural backlash against women and feminism. Susan Faludi (1991) details this assault in her best-selling book *Backlash,* which focuses on demeaning depictions of feminism and women. In part, Faludi examines explicitly antifeminist and antiwoman rhetoric in the media, politics, and popular press that virulently opposes feminism and sometimes women as a whole. Collectively, these discourses do not even bother to "ask" whether feminism is dead (which might at least imply a concern about its future) or to replace a problematic feminism with a more useful one. Instead, they explicitly attack feminism.

One example of this backlash is the idea of "new traditionalism." Jones (1992, 1994) illustrates the emergence of new traditionalism in the popular press's use of rhetorical appeals to nostalgia and the pastoral. These discourses construct a postfeminist woman as someone who rejects feminist ideology altogether and hearkens back to a time when traditional values were (supposedly) popular. Jones (1992) uses the example of a series of early 1990s ads that appeared in a variety of magazines, including *Woman's Day* and *Good Housekeeping*. These ads feature "new traditionalist" women, such as Barbara Bush, as the postfeminist replacement for the "professionally powerful . . . feminist subject," such as Murphy Brown. The depiction of feminism (which Jones argues is already a "limited" version of feminism) as threatening to the family in these particular new traditionalist postfeminist representations "legitimates and in fact necessitates its obliteration" (11).

Jones (1991) argues that feminism is under fire not only in new traditionalist discourse but also in what she calls neo-noir films. In these films, "bad news" women—of *Fatal Attraction* (1987) and *Presumed Innocent* (1990), for example—receive "punishment and/or annihilation by the patriarchal system [they] so overtly [transgress]" (297). Both new traditionalism and the neo-noirs see feminism as victimizing women and threatening the family. Having defined feminism as all-powerful, these backlash postfeminist discourses then set out to "promote" its "death" (Jones 1992, 10).

Equality and the Choice between Work and Family

While Faludi and Jones discuss postfeminist texts that set out to destroy the sexually and professionally independent feminist New Woman, not all postfeminist discourses reject this New Woman. Some texts declare feminism to be a positive success within the postfeminist moment, representing today's women as "equal" to men. These examples still suggest that feminism is no longer necessary, but, unlike the backlash depictions, they celebrate what they define as feminism's historical usefulness for women. For example, a 1985 *TV Guide* "Cheers 'n' Jeers" column claims that in 1985 female characters approached "numerical parity with males." Of the 143 new characters that season, 46.85 percent were women. Furthermore, the article claims that 76 percent of adult women on mid-1980s television shows had jobs outside the home.

While similar in certain respects, Nancy Gibbs's 1992 review of Faludi's *Backlash* in *Time* is somewhat more complex than this *TV Guide* example in its representation of "equality." Gibbs acknowledges that a backlash against feminism exists, but then opposes Faludi's critique of Hope Steadman ("the submissive wife" on *thirtysomething*) and Glenn Close as Alex Forrest ("the crazed career woman" in *Fatal Attraction* [51]), which she considers justified, with "feminist" images of the television characters Roseanne and Murphy Brown. While the first two pages of the article label several pictures "backlash stereotypes" in large, bold type (50–51), the second two pages label several pictures "feminist images" in large, bold type (52–53). The two layouts are identical, as are the number of "backlash" and "feminist" images. By representing Murphy Brown and Hope Steadman as opposites, the positions of the photographs and their captions suggest a stalemate between Faludi's critique and Gibbs's "interesting parlor game" (53) of thinking up counter-images. Because the "feminist images" *follow* the "backlash stereotypes," however, the "feminist images" indirectly counter Faludi's critique of the backlash against feminism. While Gibbs does not consider the contemporary moment unambiguously ideal for women, the reduction of the debate about feminism to a dichotomy between positive and negative "images" does use the mere existence of Roseanne and Murphy Brown to highlight a positive, utopian "feminist" interpretation of the "postfeminist age" (50).

These two examples of equality postfeminism, like almost all postfeminist discourse, make no distinctions among the various social and cultural positions and experiences of women; instead, they celebrate depictions of white, middle-class, heterosexual women's success as markers of all women's supposed success. Even when articles about postfeminism do occasionally discuss or include photos of women of color or white working-class women, the articles do not address how these women might have specific racialized or classed experiences that could impact their place in postfeminism. Herman Gray (1995) calls similar representations of African Americans "assimilationist." Focusing on television, he writes, "I consider shows assimilationist to the extent that the worlds they construct are distinguished by the complete elimination or, at best, marginalization of social and cultural difference in the interest of shared universal similarity" (85). When postfeminist discourses simply include African

Americans and/or other people of color, they depend on an assimilationist mode of representation so that "the privileged subject position is necessarily that of the white middle-class. That is to say, whiteness is the privileged yet unnamed place from which to see and make sense of the world" (Gray, 86). For example, in *USA Weekend* Patricia Edmonds (1998) both quotes from and pictures an African American woman (all other women pictured are not only white, but blonde; and two of them appear with their two blonde children), but makes no mention of how African American women and white women might experience discrimination differently in the workplace.[12] As a result, her article implies that all women are the same.

Of course, it would be equally problematic if these texts addressed race in stereotypical ways, such as defining all African American mothers as inadequate single mothers, for example.[13] My point here is that, in general, postfeminist representations depend on an assimilationist mode of representation to erase race as a legitimate social category for analysis. As a result, "woman" is meant to stand for all women but does so through the lens of whiteness. Relatedly, in terms of class, while Gibbs draws on an image of Roseanne, "the working-class hero" of *Roseanne* (52), she uses it as just another example of a generic woman who appears as a "feminist image" equivalent to Murphy Brown, "the savvy professional" (53). Thus the class differences between the two fictional television characters disappear. Similarly, the new traditionalist and neo–femme fatales of backlash postfeminism *depend on* their stable middle-class status for their identities as nonprofessional homemakers and vicious career women, respectively.

Given this implicit middle-class focus of postfeminist discourses, it is no surprise that many articles define women's success in politics in particular as evidence of an equality feminism's success. For example, Ellen Hume (1986) argues that when women enter politics as a matter of course and do so without referring to gender as a campaign issue, then postfeminism has arrived. In a *Wall Street Journal* article she demonstrates this by discussing two women from the two major parties who are running against each other for the Nebraska governorship, hence assuring Nebraska a female governor. She claims that neither woman is involved in feminist networks and each avoids women's rights issues in her campaign platform (although they both believe that feminism made their campaigns possible), but she also claims that "feminists are clearly delighted" that a woman will be governor. This version of postfeminism depends on essentialist definitions of women and of feminism, suggesting that as long as women are succeeding in typically male arenas, regardless of their political affiliations, feminism has worked, feminists are happy, and thus there is no longer a need for feminist activism. Deirdre English (1992) makes a similar move in her *Mother Jones* article "Through the Glass Ceiling." English, in fact, suggests that the successful campaigns of women politicians, such as Barbara Boxer, Carol Moseley Braun, Diane Feinstein, and Ann Richards, signal the advent of a post-postfeminist moment. Of the "culture war" between the Democrats' "Year of the Woman" and the Republicans' "Family Values," she writes, "At least the smug postfeminist mood of the last decade is over" (49). While English does not define what she means by postfeminism, she paints an optimistic picture of today's women, who are "on the verge of finally breaking through" the "glass ceiling" (49). That women (whether in the 1986 or the 1992 version of postfeminism) are perpetually "on the verge" but never quite "there" inadvertently reveals the underside of this optimism.

Bonnie J. Dow's (1996b) analysis of Murphy Brown as the postfeminist who "has made it" in the 1980s as opposed to Mary Richards of *The Mary Tyler Moore Show*, who was "emerging" (136) as a feminist in the 1970s, illustrates that there are representations that manage to escape this "almost equal" and "on the verge" version of postfeminism in the above examples. As Dow shows in her analysis of *Murphy Brown*, however, to achieve full equality the postfeminist woman must give up all connections to feminism, other than the "right" to function in the professional world—the right to be like a man. As Dow sees it, Murphy Brown is a "male persona in a female body" (140).[14] Despite the fact that the show was often heralded as "feminist" (e.g., Gibbs), Dow's close analysis of several episodes illustrates how the narrative often displaces potentially feminist ideas and issues. For example, in an episode based on the Anita Hill/Clarence Thomas hearings, "the issues of gender, race, and sexual harassment . . . are completely ignored" (157). Instead, the episode focuses on what Murphy calls the senators' "grandstanding and shameless self-promotion" in a story line in which the "Senate Ethics Committee" (157) questions her. Furthermore, Dow argues, Murphy's professional success comes at the cost of her personal happiness, which renders her a comic scapegoat. "Unmarried, childless, and without a satisfying romantic relationship, Murphy's character embodies what media constructions of postfeminism posit as the negative consequences of female independence" (144).[15] Thus, while for many popular press critics (as Dow acknowledges) *Murphy Brown* represents the success of feminism, Dow shows that that success is empty both of feminist specificities and of femininity.

Some popular press critics, like Dow, are suspicious of the emergence of the masculine New Woman (such as Murphy Brown), arguing that, although women's equality is important, it is unfortunate that women have to become just like men to be professionally successful. Generally, unlike Dow (who addresses complex activist feminism), these critics represent the masculinized New Woman as a problem because her feminist desire for equality with men means she must repress her maternal feminine side —her desire to have children or even just to nurture in any context—in order to succeed. Thus, these examples set up a tension between work and (heteronormative) family, which is supposedly produced by feminism's demand for women's equality. Erica Jong (1986) draws on (antifeminist feminist postfeminist) Hewlett to make this kind of argument in *Vanity Fair*, defining second-wave feminism as having been focused on equal rights and thus leading to "career paths [for women] identical to men" (118). For Jong, this is a problem because it denies women's "biological need" (119) to have children. While she does not go so far as to claim that women "need" to have children, Geneva Overholser (1986), writing in the *New York Times*, also worries over professionalism's interruption of maternalism when she criticizes what she sees as two related versions of postfeminism: the idea that working women are cheating their families and the idea that women are beginning to work part-time because they are realizing that work is not so great after all. While Overholser accepts the premise that "no women, even superwomen" can do all the work both at the office and at home, she rejects what she defines as postfeminism's assumption that women need to make even more changes. As Arlie Hochschild (1983) does in *Mother Jones*, Overholser suggests that men need to change at home to match women's changes at work and thus to eliminate (or at least reduce) the profound tension between work and family in women's lives. Both Overholser and Hochschild paradoxically move in a simultaneously progressive and conservative direction by making a feminist argument for the social transformation of gendered family roles, while nevertheless depending on a heteronormative middle-class conception of the male/female two-parent middle-class nuclear family in which one or both parents would have the economic resources to be able to work less in order to spend more time providing child care.

Mary Anne Dolan (1988) addresses the issue of nurturing in the workplace, rather than in the family. In a *New York Times Magazine* article she explains that despite her efforts as "the first woman in America to rise through the ranks to the editorship of a major metropolitan newspaper" (21) to hire as many women in high-level positions as possible, her feminist "experiment" failed (22). The women, she says, simply acted like men, chasing power and "goodies" and mistreating their employees in the process. In her *Washington Post* review of *Working Girl* (1988), Ellen Goodman (1989) defines postfeminism similarly, arguing that as postfeminists, rather than change patriarchy, women simply become like men. She writes, "Finally, what makes this a truly postfeminist flick is that not even the heroine really expects that women can change the system anymore. Tess just wants a chance to get in it." Like Dolan, Goodman seems to prefer representations and contexts in which women *are* able to bring a (feminine) "difference" into the workplace.

Other articles are similarly pessimistic about New Women postfeminists, not because they reject femininity but because these "New Women," especially young New Women (whether or not they act like men and/or neglect their families), take feminism for granted. Susan Bolotin introduces this idea in her October 17, 1982, *New York Times Magazine* article, "Voices from the Post-Feminist Generation," which Walters (1991) suggests was probably the first use of "the term 'postfeminism' . . . in *public discourse*" (105).[16] After interviewing a number of professional women who had recently graduated from college, Bolotin calls their attitudes toward feminism "post-feminist" because they accept what she defines as the basic principles of feminism but reject the label of "feminist" and criticize those who do label themselves feminist for being "bitter" and "unhappy" and for lacking "warmth" (31). Barbara Ehrenreich (1987) also suggests that "especially on the elite campuses [some young women have] the assured conviction that, whatever indignities women may have suffered in the remote past (for example, 1970), the way is now clear for any woman of spirit to rise straight to the top of whatever fascinating, lucrative profession she chooses" (168). Pointing out the class specificity of this particular version of feminism, Ehrenreich nevertheless does accept that feminism was a success in a middle-class context and that—as a result of its success in that context—it has now foundered.[17] Thus, while her *Ms.* article is relatively unique because it addresses class issues, Ehrenreich also reinscribes the focus on professionalism in much postfeminist discourse. By December 1989, writing in *Time*, Claudia Wallis coins a term for the type of young women Bolotin and Ehrenreich discuss: she calls them the "no, but . . ." generation; "no," they are not feminists, "but" they expect to be treated "equally" in their professional lives. As she puts it, "In many ways, feminism is a victim of its own resounding achievements. Its triumphs—in getting women into the work place, in elevating their status in society and in shattering the 'feminine mystique' . . .—have rendered it obsolete, at least in its original form and rhetoric" (82).[18]

It is important to point out that the no, but . . . woman is a media construction, a figure that contributes to the cultural "posting" of feminism. This figure is perpetually young and dismissive of the women who preceded her, emerging in 1982 as a recent college graduate (Bolotin), re-emerging in 1987 as a college student (Ehrenreich), and returning again in 1989 for Wallis's use.[19] The no, but . . . woman has faith that feminism has paved the way for her and other women and as a result is no longer useful. Because this particular postfeminist woman is young, she is on the verge of entering professional life and has not yet had to confront a tension between work and family. Nevertheless, most writers reintroduce the issue of family, confronting the no, but . . . woman with what the authors portray as an inevitable conflict. Wallis, for example, claims that working mothers (who are the implied future for the no, but . . . woman) feel cheated because they are discovering that they cannot manage "it all." Like Hochschild and Overholser, Wallis ends with a call for more men to participate in child care by quoting Gloria Steinem: "If men start taking care of children, the job will become more valuable" (89).

Overall, these articles initially set up a tension between work and family, defining these two aspects of women's lives as "it all." They then suggest, first, that women want "it all" but, second, that women cannot successfully have "it all" because they turn into men as a result of their professionalism and therefore are not able to remain nurturing in the workplace or at home. While some of the authors suggest that more involvement by men with child care will help, others revert to what Elspeth Probyn (1990, 1993) calls "choiceoisie." Separating the feminist concept of "choice" from the particular issue of abortion and linking it to a more nationalist concept of "equality," postfeminist representations use choice to set up an equivalency between work and family as either/or options.[20] Thus a woman can "choose" to work (New Woman), or she can "choose" to have a family (new traditionalist), or she can "choose" to try to do both (failed feminist).

The topics of choiceoisie and the tension between work and family that I describe throughout this section reveal the class biases of postfeminism: only middle-class mothers who have some nonwork means of support (i.e., a working husband/partner) could, theoretically, make such a "choice" between work and family. Furthermore, because the women pictured, quoted, and discussed are overwhelmingly white and inattentive to issues of race in any context, these examples illustrate the dominance of whiteness in postfeminist discourse. These examples reveal how postfeminist discourses define and depend on a version of feminism that focuses on individual rights rather than, for example, a structural analysis that might suggest that unequal pay at work, the intersection of racism and sexism, and cultural assumptions about femininity make the concept of "free choice" an oxymoron.[21] From this perspective, there is little difference between these pessimistic and optimistic representations of women's relationship to postfeminism. Whether celebrating feminism for enabling women politicians who are on the verge of breaking through the glass ceiling or bemoaning feminism for encouraging the masculine and self-centered behavior of professional women, collectively these examples define feminism as no longer necessary because it already has successfully secured access to equality and choice for middle-class white professional and/or family women.

Choosing (Hetero)Sexuality

In the 1990s, popular media began to represent choiceoisie as a *three-way* tension among work, family, and dating/sexuality; now postfeminism includes women's "choice" to engage in heterosexually attractive bodily behavior. Elyce Rae Helford (2000) argues that even female action heroes who "shed traditional feminine traits, such as passivity, gentleness, and emotionality" (294) and have "thin, fit bodies and prowess with a weapon are saved from being alienatingly strong by the camera's emphasis on their bodies" (295). Furthermore, Helford argues that postfeminists who "choose" sexuality "find their individual 'activism' primarily in battle against what they must first establish to be a legacy of feminist antisexuality" (296). This celebration of (hetero)sexuality is in tension with representations of women who, having supposedly achieved professional success, now realize that "having it all" often means giving up a boyfriend/husband and a family (e.g., Suplee 1987). Thus, along with challenging an assumed "sex-negative" feminist legacy, these discourses construct sexual interaction with men as a core desire for women. In other words, these discourses suggest, if feminism means not sacrificing personal desires and aspirations, why should women have to give up (hetero)sexuality in order to have a professional career?

Ally McBeal is a good example of this angst over the lack of a husband/ family combined with excessive displays of active sexuality (Heywood 1998). Furthermore, her hyperthin body, in opposition to the contemporary wave of self-defense feminists (McCaughey 1997) and muscle-bound action heroes like those Helford discusses (e.g., the television character Xena and WNBA and Olympic athlete stars), functions as part of choice-oisie. In other words, the existence of highly sculpted muscle-bound women naturalizes Ally's hyperthin body as a viable alternative (choice) rather than as a cultural imperative. As Robert Goldman, Deborah Heath, and Sharon L. Smith (1991) put it, "Meanings of choice and individual freedom become wed to images of sexuality in which women apparently choose to be seen as sexual objects because it suits their liberated interests" (338). In the 1990s, women simply "choose" either sculpted muscles or hyperthin bodies.

This celebration of women's play with the heterosexual male gaze—their invitation of the gaze and their own fascination with and attention to the object of that gaze (their own bodies)—not only intensifies heterosexuality within the postfeminism depicted in the popular press, but it also ensures a place for femininity in postfeminism. Advertising, in particular, contributes to this version of postfeminism, celebrating women's "equality" and their access to "choice" (feminism), while marketing commodities that call for and support constant body maintenance (femininity). Goldman, Heath, and Smith call this "self-fetishization" and argue that "commercial attempts to choreograph a non-contradictory unification of feminism and femininity have given rise to an aesthetically depoliticized [commodity] feminism" (334). Whether advertisements encourage women to buy products, such as comfortable jeans, as "the agent of progressive social transformation" (347) or to buy products, such as makeup, because women have the freedom to "choose" to engage in femininity, the ads link feminism and femininity so that they become "interchangeable alternatives" (348) and feminism becomes a style, easily acquired and unproblematically worn.

While these examples are concerned with *women's* pleasure in relation to commodity feminism and pro-sex postfeminism, other postfeminist discourses celebrate the "return" of (hetero)sexuality for the pleasure it provides to *men*: a to-be-looked-at postfeminism. For Michael Angeli (1993), writing in *Esquire*, Teri Hatcher/Lois Lane (of the television series *Lois and Clark: The New Adventures of Superman*) embodies this sensuous, feminine, to-be-looked-at postfeminist woman. Teri/Lois is "equal" to Superman (Angeli describes her as "faster than a speeding bullet," "more powerful than a locomotive," and "able to leap tall buildings in a single bound"), yet still a sensuous and vulnerable woman. More specifically, it is Teri Hatcher's *stereotypical femininity* as the "postfeminist Lois Lane" (98) that makes her "equal" to Superman. For example, Angeli argues that Hatcher is "more powerful than a locomotive" because she has failed. He quotes her as saying, "I've been knocked flat on my face, sure. But it just makes me stronger" (98). Similarly, he argues that she is "able to leap tall buildings in a single bound" because she is a vulnerable and compulsive consumer. He quotes her again as saying, "The only way to get anything wonderful out of life . . . is to risk big and jump off the cliff. It makes you incredibly vulnerable, but you know that on the other side, that's where all the *goodies* are" (98, emphasis added). Finally, Teri/Lois is a "woman of steel" because she "could tempt even the Man of Steel to abuse his X-ray vision" (98). Angeli's version of postfeminism equates gender equality with failure, compulsive consumption, and (most important in the context of *Esquire* magazine) exhibitionist feminine beauty. More recently, David Handelman (1996) titles his *Vogue* review of two of John Dahl's films (*Unforgettable* [1996] and *The Last Seduction* [1994]) "Postfeminist Mystique." His article seems to suggest that this "mystique" is a "dangerous, mysterious element" of women that men find "quite appealing" (295). Similarly, in Peter Plagens's (1996) *Newsweek* review of three women painters he celebrates their postfeminism, defining it as "some of the best—the craftiest, funniest and, in a dark way, sexiest—art around" (82).

Other male columnists seem more irritated with women's postfeminist play with feminine heterosexuality than attracted to it. For example, in James Wolcott's (1996) *New Yorker* review of Maureen Dowd's journalism he repeatedly discusses his irritation with her for "becom[ing] increasingly kittenish in her columns. She rubs up against the reader's leg. Her work lacks any sense of social dimension: everything is about her, her, her" (57). Furthermore, he repeatedly calls her a "chick," claiming that the term has made a comeback as a way to describe "a postfeminist in a party dress, a bachelorette too smart to be a bimbo, too refined to be a babe, too boojy to be a bohemian" (54).[22] Throwing around insulting terms because (he says) they have now made a comeback, Wolcott aptly defines a postfeminist chick as fashionably feminine (party dress) and professionally successful (smart, refined, and bourgeois).

Other postfeminist discourse discusses "do-me feminists" whose active sexuality is as much for themselves as for the male gaze, whether appreciative (like Angeli's) or irritated (like Wolcott's).[23] Mary Ann Doane's (1982) theorization of the masquerade is relevant here. Drawing on Joan Riviere's psychoanalytic work, Doane attempts to theorize women's film spectatorship through characters that heighten femininity so much that they draw attention to its social constructedness. Thus, the excessive femininity becomes a "mask," making it possible for a woman (character or spectator) to perform femininity while simultaneously functioning independently and successfully in masculine arenas.[24] This theoretical model explains both the excessiveness of do-me postfeminism's femininity (e.g., the impossibly short television skirts of *Melrose Place*'s Amanda and *Ally McBeal*'s Ally) and the ironic combination of this bodily display with aggressive and successful professionalism. Doane's original theorization of the masquerade was, in part, an attempt to get beyond the impasse of masochism and male-identification for a woman spectator in 1970s psychoanalytic film theory. Analogously, the masquerade works in postfeminism as a way out of the impasse of new traditionalism in the home (masochism) and nonnurturing masculine behavior at work (male-identification).

As with most versions of postfeminism, critics find this do-me masquerade postfeminism both disturbing and pleasurable. In the *New Republic*, Ruth Shalit (1998) criticizes it in the televisual representation of Ally (*Ally McBeal*), Dharma (*Dharma and Greg*), and Ronnie (*Veronica's Closet*) because it emphasizes self-absorption and consumerism. "To them, a job is a lifestyle accoutrement, a crisp stratagem to make themselves more attractive" (29). Furthermore, their sexuality is paired with professional failure and vulnerability, all of which "are supposed to be part of [their] charm" (30). While Shalit acknowledges that Ally "has been embraced as a canonical statement of postfeminist exhilaration" (30), this version of postfeminism only works, she argues, because it attracts men. Similarly, Ginia Bellafante (1998) suggests in *Time* that feminism is indeed dead because it succeeded for a select group of middle-class women and then "devolved into the silly. And it has powerful support for this: a popular culture insistent on offering images of grown single women as frazzled, self-absorbed girls" (58). While she acknowledges the role of cultural representations in the production of this version of postfeminism (the critical approach I take here), she nonetheless also blames feminism for moving toward sexuality: "You'll have better luck becoming a darling of feminist circles if you chronicle your adventures in cybersex than if you churn out a tome on the glass ceiling" (57). Paradoxically, she then praises antifeminist feminist postfeminist Camille Paglia for "catapult[ing] feminism beyond an ideology of victimhood" (58) but nevertheless critiques "lesser minds" for using Paglia's work as "an excuse for media-hungry would be feminists to share their adventures in the mall or in bed" (59).

In contrast to these irritated responses to postfeminist self-directed sexuality, Plum Sykes (1998), writing in *Vogue*, is not at all disturbed by her desire to link work with sexuality. In a discussion of her pursuit of the perfect postfeminist bra (a pursuit made possible by her class privileges), she suggests that both the frilly feminine styles and no-nonsense practical styles that she can find off the rack at her local department store do not go with her "trouser suit[ed] . . . fashionably postfeminist New Me" (142). Eventually, she writes that she had to have a bra personally made for her. The designer came up with a reversible bra: "The Prince of Wales check flips over to reveal blood-red satin" (144). Similarly but more graphically, the "Postfeminist Playground" Web site celebrates the fact that *Playboy* online chose it as a "pick of the day" on July 2, 1998.[25] As an announcement sent to their e-mail list says, the site celebrates books such as *The Great Taste of Straight People*, "written by Lily James of the Postfeminist Playground. . . . 19 short stories about sex, math, vivisection and real estate will vibrate your mind, your muscle, and your wicked sense of humor. WARNING: This book may offend diehard feminists." On the Web, a potentially more sexually explicit forum than the mainstream press, the heterosexual and antifeminist focus of masquerade postfeminism is more explicit, in part through its ironic humor.

Overall, then, whether a postfeminist woman engages in active, even excessive, bodily display of (hetero)sexuality—what I have termed masquerade postfeminism—in pursuit of a man, to irritate others, to get ahead at work, or to please herself, these representations assume the centrality of heterosexuality in women's lives in opposition to what postfeminist discourses portray as an antisex feminism. While these examples "add" sexuality to the postfeminist mix, they also link that sexuality, if only tenuously, to either work, family, or both. In other words, in the 1990s, consumerism, bodily display, and active sexuality are the routes provided by postfeminist discourses out of the (alleged) feminist-produced impasse of having to choose between family and work, routes that lead women right back to the individualism of "equality" or the compulsory heterosexuality of "new traditionalism."

Postfeminist Men

Most of these versions of postfeminism focus on women, whether they are raving feminists who need to be eliminated, new traditionalists who "choose" home, successful professionals who depend on but no longer need feminism or who act like men, unfulfilled successful professionals, or sexily feminine heterosexuals. Nevertheless, men do appear in the background of some of this discourse, as negative, nonnurturing role models that women too readily adopt; as heterosexual gazers, delighted with postfeminism's turn toward hypersexualized women in the 1990s; or as objects of desire, just beyond the reach of the professional woman who thought she could have it all but has since found that all she has is her job.

Occasionally, though, men emerge at the center of postfeminist discourses. A number of articles shift the focus from women's to men's oppression, arguing, like the antifeminist feminist postfeminists, that "the women's revolution has succeeded to an amazing degree" (Mansfield 1998, 14). This success, they argue, has led to the "Post-Feminist Male (PFM)—and he is a lugubrious specimen indeed: trend-whipped, wary, variously deranged" (Suplee, B1). Men's mistake, Curt Suplee (1987) suggests in the *Washington Post*, is to become passive (read: feminine), thus, he argues, allowing women to define masculinity. According to Suplee, it is women/feminists (like most postfeminist discourse, he collapses the terms) who have produced the "Mr. Right" who "turn[ed] out so wrong" (B1).

While Suplee constructs a bleak picture of the postfeminist man produced by feminism, other articles focus on what they call the "nascent men's movement" (Allis 1990, 80) as a potential savior. While the feminist movement is still at fault for producing the postfeminist wimp through "two contradictory messages—'Open up and share your feelings' alternating with 'Shut up, you disgusting beast!'" (Epps 1987), the emergent men's movement redefines the postfeminist man as an agent on a path to self-discovery. Sam Allis (1990) writes in *Time*, "In the wake of the feminist movement, some men are beginning to pipe up. They are airing their frustration with the limited roles they face today, compared with the multiple options that women seem to have won" (80). Allis suggests that feminism has been so successful in reversing patriarchal power and authority that women now oppress men; therefore, men need a social movement. Harvey Mansfield (1998) is optimistic about this new masculinity, arguing in the *Times Literary Supplement* that now that feminism has succeeded, "manliness," which he defines as a complex form of courage, can be "humaniz[ed]" and turned into a "virtue." He is even willing to let women express this new version of masculinity themselves, just as they have succeeded in participating in (men's) professional life:

> The price of humanizing manliness, of raising it from quality to virtue, is allowing women to participate in it. It will not be equal participation, because, as Aristotle said, men find it easier to be courageous—and likewise, women find it easier to be moderate. . . . For the most part, men will always have more manliness than women have, and it is up to both sexes, having faced that fact, to fashion this quality into a virtue. (16)

Like the postfeminist discourse that assumes nurturing is an essential female quality/virtue, but one in which men can learn to engage, Mansfield assumes that courage is an essential male quality/virtue, but one to which women now have access. In both cases it is the success of feminism, and thus the existence of postfeminism, that makes this revaluing of traditional descriptions of "sex differences" possible. Overall, in the postfeminist discourse that focuses on men, feminism (and by default women in general) produces miserable and unappealing men; as a result, men must (re)take center stage and return to their traditional roles as "manly" saviors in order to fix what women/feminists unwittingly have made inoperable.

While the above examples focus on returning masculinity to men, another version of postfeminism represents men who take over women's roles as feminine subjects, feminists, or both. For example, Wolcott's critique of Maureen Dowd as a "chick" sets him up as a better feminist than she, because he understands that he needs to be "serious" and he pays attention to the history of feminism in the 1960s and 1970s. Tania Modleski (1991) has termed this version of postfeminism "feminism without women." In her book of that title, she details how in popular culture men replace women as mothers (including even sometimes disguising themselves as pregnant women [77]) and how women celebrate this new nurturing masculinity. For example, she argues that in *Three Men and a Baby* (1987) "father's rights, male appropriation of femininity, and male homoeroticism fuse perfectly in a film that nearly squeezes woman out of the picture altogether, just as the mother is squeezed to one side of the frame in the last shot of the film" (82). The film "constitutes a flagrant encroachment of the (ever multiplying) fathers onto the mother's traditional domain" (86).[26] Similarly, in her analysis of *China Beach*, Leah R. Vande Berg (1993) claims the television series portrays "male Vietnam warrior veterans as the only characters equally capable of performing traditionally female roles and values (nurturing children) as well as traditionally masculine roles (fighting wars)" (359). In both of these examples, while men may take on markers of femininity, even discourses of (particular versions of) feminism, they nevertheless do so without giving up their centrality within the narrative. Thus, men embrace feminism, but only as long as women are absent from it.

Conclusion

As a discursively produced concept that incorporates, coopts, and reworks feminism, postfeminism is extremely versatile, containing appeals to multiple and contradictory audiences. Given its many configurations, some of which almost seem to be opposites of each other (e.g., the new traditionalist versus the woman who plays with sexuality on the "postfeminist playground"), postfeminism refers to many aspects of contemporary women's lives. There is linear dead-feminism postfeminism; assaultive backlash postfeminism, which includes antifeminist feminist postfeminism, new traditionalist postfeminism, and bad news women postfeminism; equality postfeminism, which includes New Women postfeminism, women on the verge postfeminism, masculine women postfeminism, no, but . . . postfeminism, and choiceoisie postfeminism; pro-sex postfeminism, which includes commodity feminism postfeminism, to-be-looked-at postfeminism, do-me postfeminism, and masquerade postfeminism; and men's postfeminism, which includes wimpy men postfeminism, masculine men postfeminism, and feminism without women postfeminism. In these contexts, feminism is understood variously as a former event, obsessed with victimization, all-powerful, threatening to the family, successful in having achieved individualistic equality and choice for women, in pursuit of masculine identities for women, rejecting of women's nurturing roles, antisex, and antimen.

Importantly, most versions of postfeminism can function as either a condemnation or a celebration of women and feminism. For example, equality postfeminism can lead to bitter, nonnurturing masculine women or to women either on the verge of or having achieved professional success. Similarly, postfeminist definitions of feminism can celebrate the achievement of equality at work or condemn an all-powerful victim feminism. This collective ambivalence in the popular press about postfeminism and the feminism it replaces leads to perpetual discussions about the central issues of postfeminism—work, family, sexuality—and naturalizes the proliferation of multiple forms of postfeminism, each of which is concerned with the effects of feminism on contemporary culture and life. In short, the collective ambivalence ensures that postfeminism is wide-ranging, versatile, and influential.

Despite the multiplicity of postfeminism and its definitions of feminism, it also has many consistencies—especially the assumption that feminism is no longer necessary and the promotion of white, middle-class, heterosexual women and men as culturally central. Postfeminism's multiplicity, however, makes it more difficult to see such consistencies. In other words, if some postfeminist discourses celebrate what feminism has wrought while others bemoan changes produced by feminism, it is harder to see that *all* these discourses imply that feminist activism is no longer needed. And if, for example, as is the case in the majority of postfeminist discourses, questions about sexual identity never even emerge, heterosexuality is naturalized for contemporary women, whether they prefer to practice that heterosexuality in the confines of a middle-class home or the confines of an independent single-girl life. Similarly, if the feminism that postfeminist discourses depict is not attentive to class difference, then a possible tension between working women who work because they have to and working women who work because they are beneficiaries of the "right" to work for which 1960s and 1970s feminists supposedly fought dissipates. And because women of color *do* appear in some postfeminist discourse as assimilated "equal" beneficiaries of the same "rights" that feminism supposedly provided to white women, the specific intersection of gender and race oppressions that women of color may face in the United States is ignored.

In short, postfeminism is the depiction of the present as the end point of a linear feminism that promotes "equal rights," "choice," and individualism for white, middle-class, heterosexual women. Having achieved (or even almost achieved) this version of equality, in which women can choose "to have it (work, family, [hetero]sexual expression) all" or choose not to have it all, the contemporary era follows a feminist era and inherits the benefits, failures, and pitfalls of that feminism, whether or not particular writers interpret the postfeminist era as having profited or suffered from the feminism that preceded it.

In this chapter, I have emphasized the ways much of this discourse defines the era since the early 1980s as postfeminist, as a historical moment that follows a presumably prior feminist moment. Much of the scholarship on postfeminism in popular culture draws on a similar model, arguing that postfeminist discourse emerged in a particular historical moment as a response to feminism. For example, Modleski subtitles her book "Culture and Criticism in a 'Postfeminist' *Age*" (emphasis added) and Dow (1996b) details the shift from what she defines as depictions of feminism in 1970s television sitcoms, such as *The Mary Tyler Moore Show* and *One Day at a Time*, to depictions of postfeminism in 1980s and 1990s television shows, such as *Murphy Brown* and *Dr. Quinn, Medicine Woman*.[27] And certainly, it is important to my own argument throughout this book to point to the historical context of the late twentieth century as an era during which sustained feminist activism is less often visible in the popular media than are postfeminist women.

Nevertheless, throughout this chapter, by emphasizing popular culture discourses and representations, I have suggested that it is also useful to approach postfeminism as a cultural *discourse*—an attitude, a reaction formation, an always available hegemonic response to feminism—not entirely linked to any particular historical moment. From this perspective, it is no surprise that postfeminism emerged as a concept in the 1920s United States as well, immediately after women got the vote.[28]

Thinking critically about postfeminism in this way, first, helps resist a linear historical trajectory that defines postfeminism as the natural updated progeny of (a no-longer-needed) feminism along an evolutionary continuum. Rejecting the historical linear representation of the relationship between feminism and postfeminism helps reveal the ways feminism continues to exist not only as a discursively defined thorn in the side of postfeminist popular culture but also as a complex and varied social movement; an epistemological and philosophical standpoint; a critical and analytic methodology; a race-, sex-, and class-based pedagogy and scholarship; and a powerful strategic rhetoric (among other things). Furthermore, critically resisting postfeminism's linear narrative, in which feminism has supposedly already been successful, makes it possible to see ways women are not necessarily on a long march toward equality but instead, for example, continue to be unemployed or underemployed and to make less than men for doing the same job, continue to struggle for access to legal abortion, and continue to face sexual and racial assault and sexual and racial harassment in their work and home lives.[29] Thinking of postfeminism discursively helps illustrate how postfeminism is a *cultural response to feminism*, one that seeks to rework—to *steal* rather than to supersede—feminism.

Second, paying attention to postfeminism as a cultural discursive strategy, rather than as an "actual" historical event, also helps emphasize how easily the discourse moves between "real" women and fictional women (like the *Time* cover's move from Steinem to McBeal) without considering any differences between them. This collapse of "women" with "women in popular culture" helps carry the weight of the discourse's suggestion that postfeminist attitudes have become pervasive and that gender traits are innate, since they appear both in polls (whose methodologies are never divulged) and on fictional television. As a result, no attention to actual women's complex relationships to work, family, sexuality, and feminism in the contemporary moment is necessary. Using a critical and theoretical analysis of postfeminist discourse in response to its claim of universality helps to emphasize that the fictional Ally McBeal and the living no, but . . . women Bolotin and Wallis interview are *both* cultural constructions that do the work of defining both feminism and postfeminism in at least some of the many ways they function in late-twentieth-century culture. This critical perspective, which I endeavor to take here, helps dismantle postfeminism's ubiquity by insisting on a disjuncture (which postfeminist discourse seeks to deny) between representations of postfeminism and the complexity of women's actual lives.

In short, my goal is to understand postfeminism both as a self-defined particular historical moment and as a versatile cultural discourse, one that negotiates, defines, and ultimately limits what feminism is within popular culture. Nevertheless, I also consider it important to acknowledge the space some postfeminist discourses make for feminism within popular culture. This is a space in which many rape narratives emerge. As I discuss in the next chapter, discourses of postfeminism, feminism, and rape intersect in this space, simultaneously transforming and reinforcing each other.

3

Film and Television Narratives at the Intersection of Rape and Postfeminism

Rape is in the news constantly, and, as Helen Benedict (1992) and Marian Meyers (1997) both argue, contemporary news coverage of rape is problematic from a feminist perspective. For example, they argue that news media represent violence against women as "a matter of isolated pathology or deviance" (Meyers, 117); privilege whiteness and "stereotypes" African Americans (Meyers), blame "rape on the assailants' color and class, rather than their gender" (in the Central Park jogger case) (Benedict, 248); and reproduce a "virgin/vamp" dichotomy.[1] Benedict argues in fact that, while the press did include coverage of feminist perspectives (such as the idea of "sexual violence as a phenomenon" and an emphasis on the importance of "rape crisis counseling" [248]) during the earlier 1983–84 New Bedford "Big Dan's" case, by the late 1980s when the Central Park jogger case occurred, the press did not discuss *any* feminist activism against rape.[2] Sujata Moorti (1995) makes a similar claim about televisual news from April 1989 to March 1992. She argues that, "in general, news discourses re-produce dominant rape myths and the act of rape remains an 'unspeakable' event" (7). Taking these studies together, one could argue that by the 1990s rape coverage in the news drew on a linear historical postfeminism, not bothering with a feminist perspective at all, now that feminism was supposedly "over."

Unlike the above three authors, Lisa M. Cuklanz (1996) looks at representations of rape across multiple media. While Benedict and Meyers both explicitly examine journalists' discourse, even offering suggestions for how to improve news coverage, Cuklanz offers a rhetorical analysis of news coverage of famous rape trials, as well as subsequent print, television, and film fictionalizations of those cases. Cuklanz focuses specifically on the representation of feminist antirape activism and law reform in these contexts. She argues that "certain highly publicized trials can be seen both as a means through which feminist meanings are curtailed and delimited and as a vehicle through which these reinterpreted feminist ideas are broadcast to the general culture" (6). Pointing out that news coverage is generally more conservative than fictionalized forms, such as made-for-television movies and the film *The Accused* (1988), she nevertheless argues that both have begun to acknowledge antirape activists as experts and to focus on women's points of view, for example. As Cuklanz argues, this is not a direct representation of feminist definitions of rape, but it is a shift in how rape is understood in popular culture, a shift that responds to and incorporates some feminist antirape activism. While Cuklanz does not call this shift in representation "postfeminist," the limited incorporation and transformation of feminist ideas about rape into the popularly available views in mainstream media that she describes correspond with the definition of postfeminism I lay out in chapter 2.

Despite my brief reading of Benedict, Meyers, Moorti, and Cuklanz through the lens of postfeminism, it may well be the case that their collective focus on *actual rape cases* in the news (and, for Cuklanz, Moorti, and Benedict, only nationally known cases) illustrates that representations of real rape cases do not directly contribute to postfeminism and feminism in popular culture. In fact, Cuklanz shows that *fictionalized* versions of the famous rape trials she studies are more likely to incorporate representations of feminism than are news versions. Stepping back from the focus on actual rape cases as I do in this chapter, in fact, reveals a plethora of representations of rape drawing on and contributing to postfeminism and postfeminism's feminism in popular culture.

For example, just the titles of a number of popular press articles on rape in general (rather than actual cases) reveal attention to feminism and/or postfeminism: "A New Way of Looking at Violence against Women" (Heinzerling 1990), "The Tyranny of Modern-Day Feminism" (Amiel 1994), "Postfeminist Images Begin to Blur" (Goodman 1991), "Are You a Bad Girl?" (Wolf 1991b), "We're All 'Bad Girls' Now" (Wolf 1991a), and "Rape: The Conservative Backlash" (Johnson 1992). As these titles suggest, and as the complexity of postfeminist discourses would lead one to suspect, these articles move in a number of different directions, from taking an antifeminist position that feminism has a "new and terrible power" in Canada that controls the courts and thus leads to trials based on "charges of sexual assault that are patently false" (Amiel) to taking a profeminist position that violence against women motivated by hate, such as the Montreal massacre in which the gunman left a suicide note "declar[ing] that women had ruined his life," should be classified as hate crimes under new hate crime legislation in the United States (Heinzerling). These two examples illustrate competing representations of feminism as either negative or positive, but *both* depend on claims of unequivocal clarity ("patently false" charges and a clearly hate-filled suicide note, respectively) to make their case.

More often, however, popular culture texts that discuss rape in the context of feminism claim there is a "murkiness" surrounding rape, and they blame that murkiness (at least in part) on feminism. For example, while Ellen Goodman (1991) and Naomi Wolf (1991a, 1991b) both take feminist perspectives in their articles, each depicts contemporary U.S. culture as confused about rape, in part as a result of feminism. Drawing on two conflicting versions of feminism—one that encourages women to be free to express their sexuality and another that warns women to protect themselves from sexual violence—Goodman writes that as a result of social changes surrounding sexuality, "cultural cues are no longer universal and the likelihood that two people who meet will share the same assumptions isn't as high as it once was." Furthermore, she suggests that supposedly new definitions of sexual assault and consent, again implicitly available because of feminist activism, "lead to enormous confusion around the words that infiltrate [women's] single lives with less terror than the word rape: words like sexuality, sexiness and the nature of 'consensual sex.' It is as if a huge gray spot has covered these topics too, making it hard to see clearly." The gray spot to which Goodman alludes temporarily masked the identity of Patricia Bowman during the television broadcast of William Kennedy Smith's rape trial and thus provided the kind of protection that some feminist rape law reform demands.[3] In this context, however, Goodman uses the gray spot as a metaphor for what feminist activism against rape has done to all (hetero)sexuality: made it hard to see clearly. While Goodman, unlike Barbara Amiel (1994), holds men (not women) responsible for sexual assault throughout her article, she nonetheless implicitly suggests that the way feminism has been incorporated into women's lives (she reports on several interviews with "young women" in the article) has led to the blurry "postfeminist images" of both rape and sexuality. Wolf (1991b) moves in a similar direction when she draws on a pro-sex postfeminist position to illustrate that both news coverage and court treatment of rape victims define the sexual practices of "all of us, America's daughters" (275) as "bad."[4] She writes, with ironic humor, "*I have talked to boys ... I too have bantered ... on more* than one occasion as an undergraduate, *I too had too much to drink.* The more I think about it, the more depressed I get. Not only am I a bad girl, but nearly every girl I know is just as bad" (212). While Wolf articulates the feminist position that "consenting to sex with one or more men in the past does not indicate consent for all future time to anyone who demands it" (274), she also suggests that the confusion around sexuality and rape is caused by the contradiction between a pro-sex feminism and news coverage and court practices that depend on women's asexuality to ensure credibility. Thus, (her version of) feminism, which introduces women's active sexuality into the mix, is at least partially responsible for that confusion.

For antifeminist feminist postfeminist Katie Roiphe (1993, 1994), the confusion around rape is produced *entirely* by that all-powerful postfeminist-defined feminism that supposedly controls college campuses and makes women's lives miserable. Drawing heavily on Neil Gilbert in her book *The Morning After,* Roiphe argues that the "rape epidemic" is an exaggeration, produced simply by a change in perspective, "a way of interpreting" (53) that feminists use to "sequester feminism in the teary province of trauma and crisis" (56).[5] Furthermore, like Wolf, she aims to reclaim sexuality for women, holding feminists' "interpretation" of rape responsible for a "denial of female sexual agency that threatens to propel us backwards" (84). Wolf and Roiphe do distance themselves from each other. In *The Morning After* Roiphe critiques Wolf's discussion of rape culture in *The Beauty Myth* (56), and in *Fire with Fire* Wolf critiques Roiphe's rejection of rape as a real problem (Dow 1996b, 211). Nevertheless, both Wolf and Roiphe argue against a "victim feminism" and for a pro-sex feminism. Roiphe makes this typical postfeminist argument by *rejecting* women's claims of rape, and Wolf makes this same argument by *criticizing* rape culture and legal practices. Despite their differences, however, both Wolf and Roiphe say that rape is confusing and that feminism (at least in part) produces that confusion. As bell hooks (1994) points out, "many passages in Wolf's work [*Fire with Fire*] could easily have been excerpts from *The Morning After*" (93).

With this brief discussion of the representation of rape in the popular press, I hope to begin to illustrate the way these representations intersect with postfeminism, particularly antifeminist feminist postfeminism, backlash postfeminism, and pro-sex postfeminism. In the process, particular versions of feminism emerge in relation to rape. For antifeminist postfeminists such as Roiphe and Amiel, feminism sees women as victims; paradoxically, feminism is also powerful enough to confuse people about what rape is. For profeminist postfeminists such as Goodman and Wolf, feminism demands women's "equal" access to sexual expression and behavior, as well as their right to "choose" to say no, no matter how many times they may have said yes in the past. From both perspectives, however, it is the changes feminism has wrought that lead to confusion around rape and sexuality.

Postfeminist Rape Narratives

Both the larger field of postfeminist discourse I discuss in chapter 2 and the more specific intersection of rape and postfeminism in the popular press, which tends to hold feminism partially responsible for a confusion around rape, serve as contexts in which to understand the post-1980 films and television shows to which I now turn. I ask, How do these texts use, respond to, or challenge postfeminist discourses? In this context, how do they use, respond to, or challenge feminist antirape discourses? And what happens to rape and feminism as a result?

In the first section of the chapter, I examine links between specific aspects of postfeminism and various rape narratives. I offer four specific arguments: (1) the existence of a postfeminist backlash against feminism heightens a representational paradox in which all representations of rape contribute to a cultural assault on women, regardless of a text's more general ideological position; (2) many rape narratives contribute to a postfeminist definition of women's independence as limited to their relationships to family and/or to an abstract equality with men; (3) when men face rape in a postfeminist context, they emerge from the experience as idealized postfeminists who can embrace both masculinity and femininity and as a result become even better feminists than are women; and (4) the general white, middle-class, heterosexual focus of postfeminism is reinforced through post-1980 rape narratives. Overall, I argue that, like most postfeminist discourses, these rape narratives generally absorb and alter what feminism is, suggesting, in the process, that feminism is no longer necessary.

In the second section of the chapter, I focus more directly on the particular versions of feminism emerging in these texts. Here, I argue that some aspects of feminism have been absorbed into popular culture so fully that they have become truisms that help redefine rape in particularly narrow ways. Furthermore, I argue that rape narratives depend on a postfeminist assumption that feminism has been successful. Paradoxically, such narratives hold women responsible for using the (now improved) law to end rape and view men, who know more about the new laws, as better feminists than women. Overall, this chapter argues that many post-1980 rape narratives in film and television draw on and contribute to a cultural concept of postfeminism in a multitude of ways that collectively suggest there is no need for continued feminist activism, even against rape.

To support this argument, I analyze examples from film and television that are evocative or representative of the plethora of available media texts. While notes often point toward additional examples, and while I sometimes focus on relatively unusual examples to highlight their difference from more common forms of representation, inevitably other films and television shows will come to mind for readers. This is, in fact, my hope: that readers can expand the analysis I offer here through additional examples they bring to the experience of reading this book. Rape narratives are pervasive and their relationship to postfeminism is complex and far-reaching. In this chapter, as in chapter 1, I could not hope to touch on all the possible examples (given their ubiquity), and no one example matters *in particular*; instead, it is the cumulative stories and representations as well as the sum total of repetitive themes with which I am concerned.

Rape as Backlash: A Representational Paradox

Perhaps the most obvious way that contemporary representations of rape in film and on television can contribute to postfeminism is through a backlash against both feminism and women. The sheer number of representations of rape that have appeared on screen since the 1970s offer a sustained definition of women as sexually victimized and a sustained cultural assault on women.[6] In particular, graphic representations of rape, at least for the moment in the text during which the rape appears, can be understood to express hatred for and violence against women and thus can potentially increase anxiety and discomfort for many spectators. Any number of films and even some television shows include these gratuitous representations, not closely connected to the larger narrative.[7]

Paradoxically, even texts that explicitly articulate an antirape perspective can also inadvertently contribute to these backlash representations. For example, perhaps the most well-known self-defined antirape mainstream film, *The Accused,* includes a graphic rape scene (through a witness's flashback) at the end of the film.[8] The culmination of courtroom testimony, this scene emphasizes the horror of rape and illustrates the idea that even if a woman dresses and dances provocatively in a public bar, she is not responsible if a gang rape follows. But, the graphic representation is also explicit in its visual and aural depiction of sexual violence toward women, thus increasing the amount of violence against women that exists in popular culture representations. Thus, in this film the graphic rape scene functions, paradoxically, both to challenge rape myths from a feminist perspective and to contribute to the existence of violence against women in media culture.[9]

This paradox of discursively *increasing* (and potentially eliciting pleasure in) the very thing a text is working against is not unique to the representation of rape. The same argument can be made about representations of graphic war scenes in antiwar films,[10] or of explicit racism in antiracist films, for example.[11] Nor is it unique to a postfeminist era. As I discuss in chapter 1, a similar paradox emerges in 1920s and 1930s films, such as *Shanghai Express* (1932), increasing the pathos surrounding women's experience of gendered oppression, in part through the representation of rape. I raise the issue here, specifically, to illustrate how this paradox of representation is *heightened* by the fact that an antifeminist backlash is part of postfeminist culture. In other words, if postfeminist discourses were *only* positive about feminism, even as they shaped feminism itself, it would at least be more difficult to read graphic rape scenes as an assault on women themselves. But this is not the case; as I argue in chapter 2, postfeminist discourses include both celebration of and disdain for women and feminism. Thus postfeminism encourages a similar double reading of *any* representation of rape: both as an assault on women and as an expression of the horrors of that assault. My point here is that even an explicitly "progressive" film, such as *The Accused,* through its explicit rape scene, can participate in antifeminist aspects of postfeminist discourses: a violent backlash against both women and feminism.[12] Wherever a text falls on a continuum from misogynous and antifeminist to feminist and antirape, the simple fact that it includes a representation of rape contributes to the existence of rape on a representational level. I am not arguing here that representations of rape are *equivalent* to the experience of rape, but rather that all representations of rape necessarily contribute to the discursive existence of rape and that graphic representations do so in particularly powerful ways.

Independent Women and Their Families

Despite the potential backlash against women and feminism in any representation of rape, most 1980s and 1990s rape narratives intersect with aspects of postfeminism that seek to absorb and transform (rather than violently expel) feminism. As I discuss in chapter 1, rape narratives historically often linked rape to women's independence, depicting a two-way causality in which rape illustrated that women needed to be more independent and less vulnerable, or in which independent behavior led to rape. Not surprisingly—given that women's relationship to independence is a central concern of postfeminism—these narrative structures continue throughout the 1980s and 1990s. In the context of a postfeminist tension between independence and family, these narratives often use rape to help bring these two aspects of women's lives together, linking women's independent behavior to rape in the service of protecting the family. In these texts, experiencing rape helps women "have it all" (independence *and* family).

For example, thrillers or horror films that incorporate rape or the threat of rape specifically in order to produce spectatorial anxiety often resolve that anxiety through an independent woman character who triumphs in the end. Furthermore, these texts define this postfeminist New Woman's independence through her capacity to overcome victimization in order to protect herself and her family. In the film *Trial by Jury* (1994), Rusty, a mafia leader on trial for murder, threatens Valerie, a self-employed, divorced white single mother on the jury. Even Valerie's father recognizes her independence; in describing how his own experience of jury duty differs from hers, he says he "wasn't a single girl trying to survive in that jungle [the city]." Despite these explicit depictions of Valerie as independent, when Rusty threatens to kill her son if she refuses to find Rusty innocent, she is reduced to tears and falls into the arms of the man who carries Rusty's message. At the trial, she stares blankly ahead, twisting her hair and looking incapable of making an argument (let alone a decision) for either guilt or innocence. Given this behavior, which Rusty watches closely in point-of-view shots during a trial scene, he realizes that a verbal *threat* is not enough to ensure her cooperation; it has simply incapacitated her. So, he goes to her apartment and rapes her, making good his verbal threats through a physical assault. This rape transforms Valerie from a frightened and confused woman into one who is powerful and in control, a role naturalized by the initial portrayal of her character as independent.

After the rape, Valerie takes over the narrative in an effort to save her son and prevent further assaults on herself. No longer twirling her hair in the jury box and waiting to see what Rusty will do, she persuades three other members of the jury that Rusty's constitutional rights have been violated, leading to the hung jury that Rusty demanded of her as prevention against further assaults. Furthermore, she begins to stand up to the jury fore*man* in a way that emphasizes her independence as a woman, telling him, for example, that her name is not "*Mrs.* Alston." Thus, the film explicitly links her newfound post-rape persona to feminism. Then, when the prosecution team begins to investigate her in order to prove jury tampering and Rusty sends several people to try to kill her, she escapes. Rather than collapsing in tears as she does when first threatened, she continually bangs on the hood of the car trunk in which they have locked her in order to draw a passerby's attention. When that does not work, she fashions a weapon out of what looks like a nail file and uses it to wound all three of the people who have captured her (when they eventually open the trunk). Although she does not get away on her own (Tommy, the man who initially threatened her son and who seems to have fallen in love with her, arrives and shoots at her attackers), she is the only person to leave the scene alive (Tommy dies soon after the shoot-out).

Having moved from being an independent yet naive New Woman to an incapacitated potential victim to an actual victim to a post-rape independent woman who can do whatever it takes to protect herself and her family, Valerie now goes further and enters a rape-revenge narrative. Knowing she has no way out, Valerie goes to Rusty, offering herself to him sexually. Here, she easily changes from an independent single mother postfeminist to an independent strategically sexy masquerade postfeminist, drawing on her sexuality to manipulate Rusty. When he attempts to kill her anyway, she is prepared with her "bad news" postfeminist persona: she stabs him in the back and then kicks him viciously as he lies on the ground dying. While this scene accesses the feminist inflections of the rape-revenge films I discuss in chapter 1, Valerie nevertheless enacts revenge not to challenge men's perpetual assaults or because rape law is ineffectual for her, for example, but in order to protect herself and her son, in order to protect her *family*. Thus, in *Trial by Jury* the more feminist aspects of earlier rape-revenge films are replaced by postfeminist concerns.[13]

This example illustrates how films at the intersection of rape and postfeminism can fulfill conventions of the thriller or horror genre that build and then relieve anxiety, as is the case in some of the pre-1980 films I discuss in chapter 1. The post-1980 depiction of rape transforming a woman into an active, independent agent—allowing a woman to take control, not play the victim, and hence become postfeminist—is not confined to a particular genre, however. For example, the film *Rob Roy* (1995), like *Trial by Jury*, represents a transformation—enabled by a rape—of an independent-minded but still relatively meek woman into a powerful figure at the center of the narrative. A historical drama that takes place in early-eighteenth-century Scotland, *Rob Roy* represents a class battle between Robert Roy McGregor and the marquis of Montrose, from whom he borrows money. Archibald (Archie) Cunningham, a man from court who serves the marquis conspires with Killearn (another man at court) to steal Robert's loan money before he receives it. When the marquis tries to put Robert in prison for not paying back the loan he never received, Robert escapes and Archie pursues him. When Archie is unable to find Robert, he goes to Robert's home, kills his livestock, rapes his wife, Mary, and burns the house.

Prior to the rape, like Valerie in *Trial by Jury*, Mary is a latent independent woman. For example, she advises Robert not to borrow money, and she warns him that leaving her alone in the house is dangerous. In each case she speaks her mind, but in each case when Robert disagrees with her she capitulates. The film, however, takes her perspective over Robert's. Not only does the narrative prove her right when borrowing money places Robert in danger and when Archie's rape of her illustrates that she is not safe at home alone, it also places all these events in an explicit context of a misogynist environment, of which Mary is aware and Robert is oblivious. For example, although Robert tells Mary she will be perfectly safe alone at home because the quarrel is between men, repeated "atmosphere" scenes of explicitly sexist dialogue and behavior contradict Robert by making it clear that in general the men in the film disrespect women. Thus, the film provides two views of feminism: Mary is a latent feminist because she knows sexism when she sees it, while Robert is a postfeminist man, so sure everyone shares his belief in women's autonomy and equality that he is unable to see sexism when it is right in front of him.

The rape, however, transforms Mary from being simply outspoken-but-cooperative to being decisive and in control of herself, her family, and the narrative. Now, Mary's decisions, rather than Robert's, determine the narrative development. For example, Mary decides it is better to keep the rape to herself than to watch her husband die while trying to avenge her honor. Implicitly depending on a feminist assumption that rape is about power, not sex, Mary understands Archie's rape of her as an attempt to exert power over her husband. In response, by keeping the rape a secret from Robert, she refuses to allow Archie's actions to influence Robert. Instead, she sees the rape as about herself and her relationship to her family, and the narrative develops accordingly. Thus, Mary simultaneously illustrates both a postfeminist focus on family and a postfeminist definition of woman as self-confident, capable, and self-determined. And Robert, who is oblivious to the fact that other men do not share his nonsexist respect for women, is unaware that Mary has been raped, despite several clues, such as the fact that she is now uncomfortable with his touch. Thus, Robert's postfeminism-induced obliviousness facilitates Mary's postfeminist concern for her family and her control of the narrative.

Without telling Robert, Mary manages to negotiate a final sword fight between Robert and Archie, which will free Robert of his debt if he wins (which, of course, he does). Mary thus controls the circumstances of the confrontation between Robert and Archie. That Robert simultaneously escapes his debt and avenges Mary's honor by killing the man who raped her is perhaps more important to Robert than to Mary because she has *already* avenged her *own* rape by confronting Killearn, the man who watched Archie rape her. In this scene, Killearn moves toward her threateningly, and Mary begins to look vulnerable, but then an extreme close-up reveals her pulling out a knife, which she uses to stab him, making good on her threat to kill him if he does not confess.[14] Like Valerie in *Trial by Jury*, however, Mary takes her revenge not for rape per se, but in order to protect her family: the confession she wants is about Killearn's role in stealing Robert's money, not his role in her rape.

In these films and others like them, rape or the threat of rape is the lever that transforms the woman into a powerful and independent agent who can protect herself.[15] As I suggest by discussing films in two very different generic contexts, a thriller and a historical drama, this figure of the woman who achieves independence as a result of rape is versatile, made possible by a postfeminist assumption that all women have access to feminism and are in fact (at minimum) latent feminists who simply need a motivating event to catapult them into action. In other words, these examples represent rape as a painful but ultimately *positive* event, one that enables the emergence of a woman's latent independent identity. Furthermore, this independent woman responds to rape by becoming stronger, not weaker, so that she can protect her *family*. In short, in these examples rape is the generative element of a postfeminist liberation narrative.

While *Trial by Jury* and *Rob Roy* represent rape as an instigator of women's (latent) independence, other films represent rape as a potential *result* of women's already fully developed independent behavior. In these examples a woman begins the narrative as self-determined, resists an early romantic union, faces potential rape as a result of her determination to remain independent, and then recognizes her own latent desire for romance at the end of the film, a narrative trajectory that Mimi White (1989) explicitly calls postfeminist.[16] For example, in the film *Raiders of the Lost Ark* (1981) Marion Ravenwood refuses to do what Indiana Jones says, instead choosing to make her own decisions. As a result, she is captured by the enemy and faces potential rape, only to be rescued by Indiana. In the Disney film *Beauty and the Beast* (1991), Gaston has noticed and is attracted to Belle's independent, scholarly ways, and he tries to rape/possess her as a result. In the film *The Ballad of Little Jo* (1993), a western, when a man discovers that Jo is really a woman who has been masquerading as a man in order to live independently, he attempts to rape her.[17] Whether one reads these films as making a feminist statement about men's violent response to independent women (as I read *The Ballad of Little Jo*) or as warning women against living independently (as I read *Raiders of the Lost Ark*), in either case rape makes such a reading possible and, furthermore, functions as a response to a particular kind of equality feminism that is central to much postfeminist discourse.

By addressing race and sexuality, the made-for-television movie *Women of Brewster Place* (1989) slightly complicates this independence-rape-romance narrative trajectory. The movie includes the story of Lorraine, an African American woman living with her female lover, who is raped by men who yell homophobic comments at her during the rape. This movie explicitly depicts the rape as an assault not only on Lorraine's independence as a woman but also on her identity as a lesbian; it does not resolve the rape (to which her explicit independence leads) through heterosexual romance. Furthermore, it depicts the rape as one traumatic event among many faced by the "women of Brewster Place," all of which are produced by the intersections of gender, race, class, and sexuality. Thus, in contrast to postfeminist depictions generally, *Women of Brewster Place* reveals the dominance of heterosexuality and whiteness in postfeminist narratives, even as it also depends on a standard postfeminist representation of a woman as threatened by rape because of her independence.

Women Who Act like Men

Some texts depict independent women as interested in masculine careers. Rape emerges in these films as a mark of women's essentialized bodily gender difference that must be overcome before they can succeed in this masculine world. In a sense, these examples combine the two types of independent women rape films I discuss above: a woman *both* faces rape because of her desire to access her equal right to a masculine career *and* is fully transformed into an independent masculine subject (a version of a postfeminist feminist), ironically, as a result of rape. Examples of rape-in-the-military films illustrate the variety of ways the post-rape masculine postfeminist woman subject can emerge.

Susan Jeffords (1988) discusses *Opposing Force* (1986), a film that represents a military captain's use of rape as part of a training exercise for Casey, the only woman at his mock POW training camp. Jeffords points out that the film "teeters on the edge of" (106) an ambivalence about military rape. On the one hand, public worries about women in the military address the "danger" of rape by enemy forces. On the other hand, the military is likely to define a woman's rape or sexual assault by one or more of her U.S. military colleagues as incidental to her choice to serve in the predominantly male military. *Opposing Force* represents a captain who both believes the former (believes that women will face rape if captured by enemies) and enacts the latter (rapes her in order to prove his point).

Jeffords points out that, in the process of negotiating this ambivalence, the film "succeed[s] in rewriting the definition of enemy from 'the enemy is he who rapes,' to 'he who rapes is the enemy'" (111). As a result, both masculinity and rape become "performative": a man is the enemy only when he is in the process of performing rape; and masculinity is in flux and can even be taken up by women. Performative masculinity emerges not only through Captain Becker's transformation from leader into rapist, but also through Logan, another trainee, who takes on marks of femininity as the New Man who is a "friend" to women who are raped. In fact, it is Logan, not Casey, who expresses outrage and emotion after the rape. "By taking Casey's voice here, Logan permits Casey to become more soldierly, more 'masculine'" (114). Thus, the rape allows the text to acknowledge that women in the U.S. military may face rape by their "friends," but the film simultaneously distances the rape from "normal" men in the military by providing a second man to express a feminized response to rape. In turn, the evacuation of these two men from masculinity proper (one because he is a crazed villain and the other because he is feminized) leaves that masculinity available to the woman, who is thus able to succeed in her masculine pursuit of a career in the military. In short, *Opposing Force* addresses women's entry into the military by representing the experience of rape and the availability of New Men as friends as the means for women to achieve the masculine identity they desire/need in order to succeed in this predominantly male arena.

Military narratives such as *Opposing Force* also help maintain the centrality of whiteness to postfeminism.[18] While traditional "enemy as rapist" narratives generally depend on the racialization of the enemy as a threat to the purity of whiteness, when this narrative is displaced by the friend-turned-enemy rapist as a result of women's entry into the military, this new rapist, a figure of U.S. military authority and citizenship, is figured as white, as is the woman who gains access to equality with men through rape.[19] Nevertheless, the specter of the racialized enemy rapist remains a backdrop in these films, a potential for which Casey is now supposedly prepared, no matter how "demented and gone over the edge" (Jeffords 1988, 109) was the U.S. white man who used rape to prepare her. Thus, these narratives maintain an attention to whiteness without giving up the possibility of a racialized enemy rapist in some other context.

In a post-Tailhook context, the film *The General's Daughter* (1999) takes rape and sexual harassment within U.S. military units even more for granted than does *Opposing Force*, dropping the ambivalent tension between enemy rapists and friend-turned-enemy rapist.[20] Instead, it accesses the feminist antirape argument that male-dominated institutions, such as the military, sports, and fraternities, create environments in which rape is not only possible but often encouraged.[21] *The General's Daughter*, however, also transforms this aspect of feminist antirape logic. The film represents a gang rape of Elizabeth, a military trainee, carried out by a group of male in-training soldiers (rather than by a superior, as in *Opposing Force*), thus suggesting that perhaps something about their community led them to rape. The soldier who finally admits that the rape took place, however, explicitly says that Elizabeth's *presence* provoked the rape. In the end, the problem is not the military, but the presence of women in the military. This, in fact, is one of the arguments the military has used historically to exclude women (and African Americans and lesbians and gays).[22] Thus, the feminist argument that male exclusivity encourages rape becomes a *new postfeminist logic* that women's pursuit of independence and equality leads to rape. Paradoxically (at least for Casey in *Opposing Force*), that independence and equality is simultaneously only possible through the experience of rape.

Male Rape

If rape can masculinize women, it can also feminize men. In a postfeminist context, however, this feminization is not a straightforward emasculation, disempowerment, or displacement from the central role of narrative hero.[23] On the contrary, rape can place men squarely in the center of a narrative, in control of both masculinity and femininity. Some male rape narratives represent men who are raped as now being able to "understand women's experience," and thus they become postfeminist feminists without women. Other narratives about male rape solve an assumed postfeminist crisis of masculinity (such as the "trend-whipped PFM" over which some postfeminist discourses worry [e.g., Suplee 1987]), first by using rape to take that crisis to an extreme and then by suggesting that even this excessively feminizing experience only strengthens the stability of masculine identity. Still other male rape narratives emphasize men's ability to bond with each other in a world devoid of women.

The made-for-television movie *The Rape of Richard Beck* (1985) illustrates a transformation of an antifeminist man into a postfeminist feminist without women perfectly. While Richard begins the film as an insensitive police detective, dismissive of women's claims of rape and contemptuous of Ms. McKey, the "hotline volunteer" from the "community" with whom his department forces him to work, after he is raped he slowly comes to terms first with the traumatizing experience of rape and then with the sexism and callousness of the law to which McKey has been trying to draw his attention. In the final scene, Richard takes over McKey's role as a feminist antirape activist and seemingly single-handedly transforms the police department by initiating and leading a sensitivity training session for students at the police academy. The film promises a new postfeminist world in which the police have a sensitivity to the women (and the few men) who experience rape. McKey's feminist activism is thus no longer necessary by the end of the film.

Richard's masculinity is never in question in *The Rape of Richard Beck*; his problem is simply coming to terms with feminist understandings of rape through the experience of rape.[24] In this example the man's experience of rape transforms and strengthens his masculinity by forcing him to incorporate both a feminizing experience and a feminist perspective on that experience into his preexisting masculinity. Alternatively, Tom Wingo's rape in the film *The Prince of Tides* (1991) profoundly threatens his masculinity. Specifically, Tom simultaneously experiences rape and passively views the rapes of his sister and mother. Point-of-view shots during Tom's flashback of the rapes emphasize his inability to stop the horror and represent him as a passive and ineffectual feminine spectator both metaphorically and literally.

The problem for the adult Tom is that, having become a postfeminist man through violent and feminizing means, he is ill-equipped to handle his postfeminist responsibilities. Like the popular press's "trend-whipped PFM," Tom's encounter with the feminine makes him undesirable and undesirous. When the film opens, Tom is impotent with his (very successful professional) wife and constantly defines his problems in terms of his inability to fulfill a masculine role, especially given his wife's professional success. The film concludes, however, by suggesting that Tom never actually was emasculated; instead, he was only temporarily unable to come to terms with the intersection of femininity and masculinity within his own subjectivity. For example, Tom, an out-of-work football coach, successfully trains a young man, Bernard, who, because he plays the violin rather than sports, needs masculinization. By teaching Bernard masculinity, Tom confirms his own masculinity. And, by empathizing with Bernard's plight, Tom accesses his feminine side. At the end of the film, through therapy, Tom has come to terms with the rapes. He is then able to return to his wife and daughters, reentering and embracing a family that includes a professional woman who is unwilling to give up her career. Tom is an ideal postfeminist man because—having faced his experience with rape—he can reenter a postfeminist family as a masculine/feminine man with ease and comfort. Rape makes his postfeminism possible.

Other male rape films move in yet another postfeminist direction, eliminating women altogether and replacing the postfeminist man's acceptance of antirape feminist principles (Richard) or his return to the postfeminist family (Tom) with male friendship and bonding. For example, in the film *Pulp Fiction* (1994), rather than taking the opportunity to let the men raping Marsellus kill him, Butch chooses to rescue Marsellus, even though Marsellus has been trying to kill Butch. This bonding experience, one in which both men agree never to tell anyone what happened, saves both men's lives. They agree to end their feud to the death, as long as Butch leaves town—his goal anyway. While rape is not the only factor in producing a lifelong friendship between Andy Dufresne and Ellis Boyd

"Red" Redding in the prison film *Shawshank Redemption* (1994), Andy's ability to survive rape and then to use his education and intelligence to garner the guards' protection from further rape earn him Red's respect and friendship. In both films, then, rape is the catalyst for male bonding and justifies the narrative's preoccupation with men and men's issues.

Furthermore, as Jeffords (1994) argues is common in late 1980s and early 1990s films, in the process of bonding, white men often save themselves by paternalistically saving people of color. Both *Pulp Fiction* and *Shawshank Redemption* provide not only male bonding but also interracial bonding, post-rape. In *Pulp Fiction,* a white man (Butch) rescues an African American man (Marsellus) during his rape. Here, while the white man had been threatened previously by the more socially powerful African American man, the rape and rescue reverse their power. And, while a white man (Andy) experiences rape in *Shawshank Redemption,* the cross-race friendship that rape precipitates ultimately allows him to "save" an African American man (Red): while Red perceives himself as unable to survive outside prison, Andy's friendship gives him another option. In both films, then, rape not only allows an emotional connection between men that suggests a postfeminist comfort with a New Man persona, but it also represents that persona as color-blind.

Feminism in the Texts

Thus far, I have discussed several ways feminist antirape rhetoric and logic emerge in and are transformed by these texts in postfeminist ways. I have offered a brief rhetorical analysis of how discussions of rape and postfeminism in the popular press, whether engaging in a backlash against or absorption of feminism, imply that feminist redefinitions of rape and sexuality have led to a troubling confusion around rape and sexuality. I have pointed out that the graphic representation of rape in the name of a feminist insistence that rape is a violent assault, not a result of a woman's provocative sexuality, can concomitantly function as a backlash against women and feminism by potentially increasing spectatorial anxiety and expressing cultural violence toward women. I have argued that narratives that are driven by a rape that brings out the latent independent feminist in a woman imply that rape can produce positive results and that all women are already committed to independent action, they just need rape to "free" them to take that action. I have discussed particular examples that suggest that behaving in independent ways, such as "choosing" equality, leads to rape or at least the threat of rape, whether or not the text seems to use that causality to fold women back into heterosexual romance or to critique that causality. I have identified examples that suggest that male cultures, such as the military, foster rape but simultaneously imply that it is not until a woman chooses to enter that culture that a rape takes place. Finally, I have discussed texts that insist that men pay attention to rape by recentering men as the victims of rape and by providing them with an idealized postfeminist masculinity as a result.

Each of these types of representation includes a tension between an *acknowledgment* of feminist antirape arguments (e.g., a woman cannot provoke rape; women have a right to independence; rape is violence, not sex; exclusive male cultures can foster rape; and men need to take rape seriously) and a *transformation* of those arguments into postfeminist logics that often at least implicitly hold women and/or feminism responsible for producing the situations in which the rapes take place. Collectively, the examples in the previous section illustrate how rape narratives can facilitate the representation of feminism without giving up postfeminist perspectives on either feminism or rape. I turn now to a more sustained analysis of the particular versions of feminism that appear in this context.

Women's Perspectives

In *Rape on Trial,* Cuklanz argues that the representation of a woman's point of view in fiction (as opposed to in news reports on highly publicized rape trials) has the most potential for representing a coherent feminism in popular culture. For example, in relation to the made-for-television movie *Rape and Marriage: The Rideout Case* (1980), Cuklanz argues that all the changes in the facts of the case that the movie made helped to develop the wife, Greta's, point of view. "By developing this perspective and focusing on Greta's experiences, the film adds legitimacy to her claim of rape" (93). For Cuklanz, giving validity to a woman's perspective on rape means accepting a feminist insistence on the credibility of women who report rape.

Most post-1980 rape films include at least brief representations of a woman's point of view and of her experience of the trauma of rape and its aftermath. These scenes lend these characters credibility and emphasize that something traumatic really did happen to them, whether or not anyone else believes them.[25] For example, in *Rob Roy* not one but two scenes show Mary pulling away from Rob's touch after Archie rapes her; she is no longer able to enjoy the erotic sexuality the film emphasizes between her and her husband prior to the rape. The made-for-television movie *Settle the Score* (1989) begins with what will later be revealed as a flashback/dream in which Kate, a police officer, relives a rape that took place twenty years earlier. Diffuse light, shadows, soft focus, handheld and shaky camera movements, odd camera angles, and the fragmented bodies of both Kate and the rapist express Kate's emotional state in both the past and the present. In *The Accused,* Sarah repeatedly insists that she be able to tell her story in court, and, although she does not get a flashback, she does get an opportunity to take the stand and state her version of what happened. Even an episode of *Beverly Hills 90210* (November 17, 1993) that includes a flashback representing the point of view of Steve, a regular character who understood a sexual encounter to be consensual, *also* includes a flashback representing the point of view of Laura, a visiting character who understood their encounter as rape. Despite the fact that the multiple-episode narrative develops in such a way that Laura later *re*interprets the encounter as "not rape," the flashback of her initial point of view has already offered a woman's perspective on an "ambiguous" sexual encounter as potentially rape. While Laura may change her interpretation of the encounter, a spectator may not necessarily follow suit. This she said/he said model contributes to a redefinition of rape that legitimates charges of "acquaintance rape," a concept that emerged from feminist antirape activism and that Cuklanz (2000) argues is dominant in television rape narratives by the late 1980s.[26]

Representing a rape scene from a woman's point of view, as do *Settle the Score* and *Beverly Hills 90210,* may be the most explicit way to incorporate a woman's perspective on rape. Any number of other kinds of representations can communicate a woman's perspective, however, whether they move the narrative forward (e.g., *The Accused*) or simply exist as moments of narrative excess, defining the character but not structuring the narrative (e.g., *Rob Roy*). Perhaps the most common way of representing a woman's perspective is a scene in which the woman takes a shower after being raped, succinctly representing the feminist argument that women who experience rape often feel perpetually dirty after the rape. In *Trial by Jury,* immediately before the rape, a shot from Rusty's point of view pans up Valerie's body from her feet to her face, as she says, guessing he is about to rape her, "You're in control. You don't have to prove it." He responds, "This will make it official." The rape that occurs next takes place offscreen, but the film includes a standard crying-in-the-shower shot to cue the viewer that rape did, in fact, take place. In a camera movement reminiscent of the one that moves up Valerie's body before the rape, the camera tracks from the dress she had been wearing lying on the floor, up to the bathroom sink, and over to the shower, which is running. A cut reveals Valerie sitting on the floor of the shower crying. This shot offers Valerie's emotional point of view to counter Rusty's controlling visual point of view in the previous scene.

In *Trial by Jury* as well as *Leaving Las Vegas* (1995) (a film that also has a post-rape shower scene), the women are uninterested in reporting the rape—in *Trial by Jury* because Valerie would have to admit that Rusty was tampering with the jury through her, in *Leaving Las Vegas* because Sera interprets the rape as a moment in which "something went wrong" with one of her "dates" as a prostitute. She does not call it a rape, and, like Valerie in *Trial by Jury*, she is not in a legal position to report the rape safely. While Mary did not have access to a shower or twentieth-century evidence collection practices in 1700s Scotland in *Rob Roy*, she also gets a ritual washing scene, cleaning herself in a lake after the rape. Given that, for various reasons, these women are unable to enter a contemporary legal system to prove that rape took place, the post-rape washing scene becomes a trope, a very brief moment outside the narrative flow that stands in for "women's experiences of rape."[27]

The representations of women's perspectives on rape in these examples often also access contemporary therapeutic discourses. For example, the psychic realm of Kate's dream and the specific details of women's physical responses to rape (discomfort with touch, a desire to bathe) both gesture toward therapeutic understandings of women's responses to rape. White (1992) argues that "confessional and therapeutic discourse centrally figure as narrative and narrational strategies in television in the United States" (8). In the more specific context of rape narratives here, those therapeutic discourses also contribute to a postfeminist emphasis on the individual and her experience. Dana L. Cloud (1998) argues that "therapeutic rhetorics are situated at moments of social or political movement or crisis, delegitimating political outrage and collective activity in favor of more private endeavors" (xvi). Postfeminist discourses' emphasis on individual choice and on incorporating independence within heteronormative middle-class family contexts illustrates therapeutic rhetorics that seek to move "past" feminism's "political outrage and collective activity."

The Law

Other films and television shows include the flip side of this feminist dilemma, suggesting that, while a woman may desire the comfort of a shower after a rape, if she bathes she will be washing away "evidence," a point that rape law reform discourse explicitly makes and that films and television shows that depict a "rape kit scene" at a hospital also emphasize. These scenes generally depict the post-rape examination as a difficult but necessary event and often include explicit details to educate the audience, such as doctors explaining what they are about to do and rape crisis counselors arriving with a sweatshirt and sweatpants to replace the clothes the woman (and audience) learns she cannot keep because they are now evidence. These scenes sometimes even include the doctor questioning the woman about whether or not she showered, thus "teaching" the audience the right way to behave after a rape in order to ensure prosecution.[28]

Women's relationship to rape law, in fact, is central to many of these films and television shows. As Cuklanz (1996) argues about *The Accused*, many of these texts portray "as heroic the common woman struggling against the legal system and cultural bias" (102). For example, even when the D.A., Katheryn, plea bargains with the rapists in *The Accused*, Sarah does not give up; she insists that Katheryn find another way to tell Sarah's story. The solution to this narrative problem requires a significant change in the facts. As Cuklanz points out, in the "Big Dan" case on which the film was based, the rapists were convicted while the men who watched were acquitted; in the film, the rapists are dismissed early through a plea bargain, while the remainder of the film focuses on Katheryn's creative use of the law to prosecute the men who watched and facilitated the gang rape. Together, Sarah and Katheryn confront the law, and in the end they win. Thus, this film both shows women struggling against the legal system and provides a solution to that struggle in the legal system, since it is the existing legal system itself that makes it possible for Katheryn to prosecute the men who watched the rapes. In this example the legal system has the potential to work, it is only a matter of how one uses it.

Some texts, however, do not let the law off the hook so easily. In an early episode of *L.A. Law* (March 26, 1987), for example, Michael Kuzak (a regular character) takes the case of Lori Abrams, a woman suing an acquaintance rapist in civil court for damages. Lori wins the case, but is rewarded with a settlement of only one dollar. Michael explains to her that the jury is defining her experience as rape, but she must accept some blame—perhaps she did not say "no" clearly enough. Lori, however, resists this interpretation and consequently fires Michael. This particular narrative strand ends when a walk-on character, Fran Wilson, comes to Michael's office to tell him that she too was raped by the same man who raped Lori, convincing Michael (and presumably the audience) that the jury's decision was wrong and that Lori should not have had to take *any* responsibility for the rape.

Despite the law's error, however, Lori takes full responsibility for trying to *use it,* even to the point of firing Michael when he no longer cooperates with her. And, the episode emphasizes her own desire to take this responsibility. For example, when Michael tells Lori that the man she is accusing has offered to settle out of court, he encourages Lori to take the offer rather than assuring her that they can win. Here, Michael shifts the burden of responsibility and decision to Lori. Lori, convinced that acquaintance rape *is* a crime, immediately accepts the responsibility and says she is determined to go to court. Despite Michael's warnings that it will be difficult for her on the stand, alluding to his knowledge of feminist critiques of rape trials as "second rapes," she insists in saying, "Michael, he *raped* me," and walks away with determination. A long shot through the glass wall of the room in which they are talking shows both Lori crossing in front of the camera and Michael, behind her, watching her go. She is in control; she is taking responsibility for going to court and Michael is left to watch—a representative of the legal system and a sympathetic man, but no longer determining narrative events.

Whether or not these examples represent law or the practice of it as in need of change, as Cuklanz (1996) points out in relation to *The Accused,* these kinds of texts ultimately hold women responsible for convicting rapists (105). Thus, while a feminist critique of rape law emerges in these texts, the postfeminist representation of that critique holds women solely responsible for making social change possible through their individual actions in relation to the law. Furthermore, many texts suggest not only that the law has changed but that women need to adjust their behavior to accommodate the new law. While Sarah and Lori aggressively take responsibility for using the law, many other examples include women who—through their ignorance of the law—make conviction impossible. For example, as I discuss above, in some texts women take showers and wash away the evidence; other women mistakenly introduce information about their personal sex life, thereby negating rape shield laws and making it legally possible for defense attorneys to ask about their prior sexual experiences (e.g., *L.A. Law* [January 4, 11, and 18, 1990]). The problem now is a need not for feminist rape law reform but instead for women's appropriate use of the laws feminism has already provided.

Men: Friends or Rapists?

Very often, it is *men* who teach women their errors regarding the law, "respond[ing] with a unified spirit that actively promotes female-centered definitions of rape" (Moorti, 258). In these examples, men emerge as "better" feminists than women, taking over the voice of feminism in the text, and thus depicting feminism without women.[29] In *The Accused*, for example, a man who witnesses the rape, Ken, is the one who reports it. And, once Sarah and Katheryn have found a way to work together to bring to trial the men who watched and encouraged the rape, they focus on persuading Ken to come forward. As critics of the film have pointed out, while Sarah tells her story at the trial, the film does not provide a flashback to a visual representation of the rape until *Ken* takes the stand and tells *his* version of the story.[30] In *L.A. Law*, Michael, although occasionally less informed than his clients (e.g., Lori), most often teaches rape law to all the women around him, clients and fellow lawyers alike (e.g., January 7, 1988, and April 14, 1988). Another central character, Victor Sifuentes, plays a similar role in two additional story lines (November 12, 1987; January 4, 11, and 18, 1990). In the film *Back to the Future* (1985), Marty time travels back to the 1950s, bringing his 1980s postfeminist sensibilities with him. When he interrupts an attempted rape of the woman who will become his mother, he takes a 1980s "zero tolerance" stance toward rape, which, the film implies, is anachronistic in the 1950s. And, it is Marty's unwillingness to tolerate rape that sets the historical change in motion: he teaches the man who will become his father to behave in an aggressive and protective way, rather than in the wimpy and frightened way he is inclined to behave. As a result, Marty's mother transfers her affection from Marty to the more appropriate object: her future husband. The made-for-television movie *Johnny Belinda* (1982) makes it easy for the man to be more feminist than the woman who is raped because she is both deaf and mute, unable to explain what happened to her until a kindhearted, more educated man comes along and helps her.[31] The film *Casualties of War* (1989), like *The Accused*, offers a representation of the heroic man, Private Ericksson, in a particularly problematic way, depicting the kidnapping and repeated gang rape of a Vietnamese woman by U.S. soldiers during the Vietnam War. While *Casualties of War* represents the rapes as horrific and defines the rapists as villainous, the film primarily focuses on Ericksson while he watches the repeated rapes without stopping them and hesitates before coming forward to tell the truth of what happened. As in *The Accused,* the kindhearted man who just "happens" to witness the rape is the hero (played in *Casualties of War* by the well-known film and television star Michael J. Fox) who articulates the truth about rape. As an antiwar film, *Casualties of War* represents the rape as a vehicle for understanding men, much like the war films of the 1940s, 1950s, and 1960s I discuss in chapter 1. The raped Vietnamese woman (played by a less well-known actor, Thuy Thu Le), who semiotically stands in for "her country," is not the central figure of the narrative, and thus her depiction facilitates a shift to the perspective of the kindhearted (white U.S.) man's response to a horrific experience—both hers and *his.*

This sympathetic, legally informed man is the "friend" Jeffords (1988) describes in *Opposing Force.* He is the man whose identity as an idealistic, nonsexist, appreciative-of-women postfeminist ensures him his inevitable place at the center of the narrative, or at least as moral voice of the narrative. Paradoxically, however, he closely resembles the typical rapist in these texts. *Casualties of War* illustrates this starkly: the only difference between Ericksson and Sergeant Meserve is that the former does not rape and the latter does. Similarly, *Settle the Score*'s narrative structure and mise-en-scène draw on generic mystery conventions to suggest that Josh, the man who is trying to help Kate discover who the rapist is, may be the rapist himself. Thus, these examples illustrate Jeffords's argument that narratives like these discard the depiction of the enemy as (always) a rapist, reversing it so that one only knows one's enemy when he rapes.

This shift, in fact, draws on yet another element of antirape rhetoric, the argument that "regular guys" with whom one is acquainted not only *can* rape, but *are more likely* to rape than are strangers. This argument often merges with another feminist antirape argument I discuss above: that exclusive male environments, such as the military, fraternities, and sports, encourage rape. The figure of the white fraternity brother or sports star rapist is so common, in fact, I would say he is the normative rapist in contemporary popular culture. Not only do particular films and television shows depict rape as part of a sport[32] or fraternity[33] culture, but even when rape takes place in other contexts, minor elements in the mise-en-scène become motifs evoking these cultures. For example, sports team jackets or brief references to a rapist's membership in a fraternity depend on the sports star/fraternity brother image to reference—but not to confront—a feminist critique of rape in these contexts.[34]

While I want to pause over the fact that these representations *do* articulate an important feminist point about rape, I also want to stress that—through repetition—they simultaneously solidify the fraternity brother/ sports star rapist as a new stereotype. As a hypervillainous figure, he then begins to become "strange," once again to become the enemy. As a result, the feminist argument that "regular guys" can rape dissipates under the weight of the new stereotype that reduces "regular guys" to fraternity/sports star rapists. Furthermore, many of these examples depict *gang* rapes as *excessive* acts, which undermines the feminist argument that even the most respected *individual* man can rape in all sorts of *everyday* settings.[35] In other words, by collapsing two very different feminist arguments—any man can rape and male exclusivity can lead to rape—through the repeated theme of gang rapes enacted by seemingly "respectable" men, these examples can be understood to suggest that, while all-male contexts can produce inappropriate behavior toward women, in most other contexts when men and women exist together, by implication, rape is less common.

Whiteness

Importantly, the friend-turned-enemy rapist is almost always white.[36] Thus the texts represent the feminist argument that even the "popular boys," "our friends," and "average guys," can be rapists to mean average *white* guys. Implicitly, then, the women who face rape by these men are also almost always white.[37] A particularly telling example of the white imperative for the typical postfeminist rapist appears in an *L.A. Law* episode located at an intersection of the real-life rape trials of William Kennedy Smith and Mike Tyson. This episode first aired on March 26, 1992, only three months after the Smith trial ended in acquittal and the *same day* that Tyson was incarcerated after his February 10 conviction.[38] It tells the story of Robert Henry Richards, a baseball star, who, like Smith, is white and has an all-American three-part name but who, like Tyson, is an athlete. In the episode, Robert is acquitted, as was Smith, although the structure of the episode makes it clear that Robert *is* guilty, as was Tyson. Thus, while the episode is *more* similar to the Smith case, it nonetheless also draws on the context of athletics and guilt from the Tyson case. Furthermore, the lead-in to the evening newscast that followed the episode on my local NBC affiliate the day it originally aired featured images of and a voiceover narration describing Tyson being "fingerprinted, patted down, and handcuffed" on his way to prison.[39] Thus, despite the text's repression of Tyson in favor of a narrative about a white man who is acquitted of rape, the newscast's depiction of Tyson inadvertently draws attention to the fictional text's emphasis on whiteness.

On the one hand, the figure of the clean-cut white acquaintance rapist avoids a stereotyped image of an African American man as stranger rapist, thus on the surface avoiding racism. On the other hand, by simply *eliminating* the stranger rapist and the African American rapist, like the military films that replace the enemy rapist with the friend-turned-enemy rapist, these examples preserve the *possibility* of the reemergence of that racialized figure.[40] His absence in the majority of fictional examples, however, ensures a postfeminist definition of feminism as focused on whiteness.

Higher Learning (1995) is an unusual film because it represents feminism as limited to whiteness in order to *critique* that limitation.[41] In this multiple-focus narrative that takes place on a college campus and that addresses racial tensions and racism, rape is part of the story of Kris, a white first-year student, and influences her relationship with her roommate, Monet, an African American first-year student. At a fraternity party at which she is drinking, Kris flirts with and then goes to the bedroom of a white student she finds attractive, Billy. They begin to have sex, but she tries to stop him when she realizes he is not wearing a condom. He does not stop in response to her repeated "nos," but she does eventually escape from his room. Subsequently, the film critiques some feminist antirape activism by portraying the campus "blue light system" with irony in relation to this depiction of rape. Earlier in the film, Kris walks home alone, only to be confronted by a white woman for doing such a "dangerous" thing. Kris further expresses her naïveté by saying, "Look at all these pretty blue lights." Her new friend then explains to her that the lights point the way toward a phone at the end of each block, so that if she is attacked she can call for help. After the rape, as Kris runs home from the fraternity house in tears, she runs past the line of blue lights without seeing them, getting smaller and smaller in the frame. The shot ends with a pan over to a close-up of a brightly lit phone, clearly of little help to Kris who has been raped by an acquaintance in his home, rather than by a stranger who might grab her in the dark on campus. Thus, the film implicitly critiques some feminist antirape activism for overemphasizing stranger rape and, in the context of a film about race and racism, for drawing on stereotypes of dangerous "dark" men who emerge in the "dark." Like almost all contemporary films and television shows about rape, *Higher Learning* represents a white, "well-respected" (in this case, fraternity) man as the rapist. But, unlike most other narratives, it does not simply ignore men of color; instead, it implicitly points to at least potential racism in some approaches to rape prevention, such as the blue light system. Nevertheless, because the narrative represents rape as a white problem, African American *women's* potential experience of rape drops out of this film.

Watching Rape

If the typical rapist is a young clean-cut white man, quite often a sports star, fraternity brother, or soldier, the most *vile* villain in many of these texts is not the rapist but the man who *watches* the rape. In *The Accused*, it is the men who watch and encourage the rape who are convicted, not the rapists. In *Rob Roy*, Mary takes out her revenge, not on Archie (the rapist), but on Killearn, who watches the rape and even declines to take "his turn" when Archie offers it to him. In the western film *Bad Girls* (1994), it is Lilly's anger at and fear of Ned, the man who wanted to watch her being raped and who threatened to rape her next—*not* the man who actually raped her—that leads to a shoot-out in which she and her three companions nearly die. Furthermore, the confrontation scene between the four women and the outlaws who have stolen their money and captured one of their lovers continually emphasizes an exchange of looks between Lilly and Ned. Close-ups show them looking at each other: Lilly looking away from the main outlaw who offers the greatest threat, despite her friends' insistence that she concentrate on their task, and Ned making lewd gestures at Lilly. Finally, Lilly cannot stand it any longer: she turns and fires at Ned, beginning the shoot-out that will lead to all of the outlaws' deaths.

I would like to be able to argue that the indictment of those who watch rape offers a powerful feminist critique of a "rape culture" that encourages rape in part by giving men permission, even encouraging men, to watch women sexually and that acknowledges the male gaze as sexually assaultive.[42] And I would like to argue that the revenge some women take out on the men who watch rape is a response to the cultural pervasiveness of the male gaze as a form of sexual assault. I would especially like to be able to argue that *even a few* of these texts draw an association between the character who watches and the *spectator*, thus perhaps questioning the roles of the representation of rape and the consumption of those representations in contributing to a culture in which sexual assault is commonplace.

Typical aspects of the texts, however, make it very difficult to maintain this perspective. First, the focus on the men who watch detracts attention from the rape itself. This shift is particularly clear in *Bad Girls* when Lilly is distracted from a direct confrontation with *the man who raped her* by the taunts of the man who wanted to watch. Thus the texts do not maintain a critique of the acts of rape and of watching rape, simultaneously. Second, texts sometimes insert another potential point of identification between the spectator and the evil-man-who-watches, undermining a potential parallel between men who watch rapes and spectators who watch films about rape. For example, because *The Accused* actually represents one of the men who watches the rape, Ken, as a "friend" rather than "enemy" because he eventually speaks out about the rape that he saw, it offers a good example of how these texts can provide the spectator with a comfortable position from which to watch rape. Because the film delays the representation of the rape scene itself until the end and denies a visual representation of Sarah's verbal description when she is on the stand, it creates a spectatorial desire for Ken's testimony and for the representation of rape that parallels Sarah and Katheryn's desire for Ken's testimony. In a sense, the spectator of the film is invited to respond as Ken does, to *acknowledge* the story. Watching the film then potentially replaces other forms of activism one could take against rape. By assuming that the legal system will work to women's advantage if they can just discover the best way to use it, and by suggesting that watching a rape and then telling the story of that rape is sufficient to take action against rape, ultimately, the film implies that there is nothing left for spectators to do, as long as they are willing to "see" that what they are witnessing *is* rape. Similarly, *Casualties of War* and *The Prince of Tides* both represent men who watch rape as heroes because they (eventually) speak out against rape. And, in *The General's Daughter* Elizabeth goes so far as to restage her rape in order to force her father, a military general who helped cover up the rape (ostensibly to protect women's right to serve in the military), to "see" that she was raped. The film seems to share her perspective that her father's refusal to see that she was raped is particularly villainous when it ends with printed words on screen informing the audience that General Campbell—not the rapists—was court-martialed. In these examples, a man's ability and desire to *see* the rape, then, become feminist acts in a postfeminist world in which feminist activism has already achieved rape law reform and equality for women and thus is no longer necessary.

I am not arguing here that watching a film about rape is identical to watching a rape; nor am I arguing that watching and encouraging a rape are beyond critique and that rape itself should be the only "real" crime. Rather, I am arguing that many of these texts have the potential to offer nuanced critiques of both rape and the representation of rape that could encourage continued feminist activism against rape and for rape law (and legal practice) reform, but the texts undermine that potential by providing more comfortable positions for viewing rape.

Conclusion

Certainly, not all fictional films and television shows since 1980 that represent rape intersect with postfeminism and/or depict feminism in even a single one of the ways I describe in this chapter. While I would argue that the centrality and visibility of antirape activism to feminism during this period (as in the 1970s texts I discuss in chapter 1) mean that any post-1980 representation of rape intersects with feminism in some way, for some texts that is the extent of the intersection. For example, in some texts rape simply represents the villainy of a character.[43] And, in some texts *false* accusations of rape further other leftist arguments against, for example, class discrimination[44] or race discrimination.[45] In other examples, rape helps represent the men who rescue women from rape as heroes.[46] My point in this chapter is not to explore all the ways rape is represented during this period, but to point to the complexity and pervasiveness of the intersections between rape narratives and postfeminist discourses and to highlight how those intersections rework feminist antirape logic in popular culture.

Those intersections include a sense of a latent feminism that is available in all women's subconscious, only needing the experience of or threat of rape to bring it forward. Similarly, rape can be the event that helps a woman fully access equality in a masculine arena, such as the military. Ironically, in these examples one of the things feminism fights against—rape—is required to facilitate feminist goals. Alternatively, in some examples feminism can contribute to rape (e.g., advocating for women in the military can lead to situations in which women face rape), or can at least contribute to confusion around rape (e.g., she said/he said acquaintance rape situations and women's equal access to sexual expression can contribute to "murkiness"), or can produce reformed laws that women now must understand and use in order to take responsibility for bringing rapists to justice. These examples represent rape as becoming more difficult for women *because of feminism*. Simultaneously, sympathetic men are available to teach women the law, express women's emotions for them, accept women as "equals," or even just do the right thing by "watching" a rape. Thus, men can replace women as the center of concern and knowledge in relation to rape. Additionally, these texts often depend on distilled iconic scenes—such as post-rape shower scenes and medical rape kit scenes—to "teach" both characters and spectators particular feminist "facts" about rape. These images help a text access feminism but then quickly move on to other postfeminist concerns. Implicitly, since the texts depict these feminist ideas as standard, continued feminist activism is not at issue in these particular narratives. Furthermore, these rape narratives depend on and contribute to the white, middle-class, heterosexual focus of postfeminist discourse and the feminism it represents, defining the typical rapist *and* typical woman who is raped in these terms. Nevertheless, because the narratives avoid addressing the issue of race altogether, the specters of the racialized enemy rapist and the U.S. rapist of color who do continue to appear elsewhere in popular culture (e.g., news reports) remain as a subtextual threat in (other) rape narratives. Overall, while all rape narratives and all postfeminist discourses are not *identical*, they are mutually constitutive. In these texts, rape—in the name of feminism—produces postfeminism. Simultaneously, postfeminist definitions of feminism in the texts limit cultural understandings of rape.

Despite this relatively pessimistic reading of the feminist usefulness of postfeminist rape narratives, I do want to pause over some shifts in post-1980 representations of rape that I consider important, from a feminist perspective. Many of these texts acknowledge that U.S. soldiers rape, recognize that rape takes place between acquaintances, insist that a woman's dress and behavior cannot cause rape, address women's physical and emotional post-rape experiences, and critique the trial experience and men's gaze as forms of sexualized assault. These ideas are important aspects of long-standing feminist antirape work and thus their appearance in popular culture marks a distinct way that this activism can be considered to be at least partially successful. Nevertheless, long-standing narrative structures persist as well. For example, as I argue in chapter 1, since as early as 1903 many films have maintained a relationship between rape and women's independence, often providing narratives that end with heteronormative family resolutions. Similarly, at least since the 1940s, war films have often used representations of women's rapes to tell stories about men. Furthermore, rape has historically appeared not only in any number of genres but also as a crucial aspect of various generic narrative forms. At least in these ways, postfeminist rape narratives are not necessarily so different from all those that have gone before. In short, I would argue that despite some useful incorporation of aspects of feminist antirape arguments, both long-standing narrative forms and new postfeminist logics depoliticize feminism and feminist antirape activism in innumerable post-1980 films and television shows that represent rape.

While much feminist criticism of postfeminist culture expresses at least an implicit desire for alternative depictions of feminism in the media, that is not my goal here. The postfeminist version of feminism the media offer is market-driven, using feminism because it has become—because they have helped it become—a valuable commodity that does not undermine the gender system that helps to maintain the media. To desire a widespread structural critique of a system by the system itself is to desire the unlikely, to say the least. My goal here is not to imagine how the media could represent the world differently, but to draw on a poststructuralist critical perspective to illustrate how feminism is limited through postfeminist rape narratives and how this process functions, overall, to exclude people of color and constrain women's options.

That said, the remainder of this book takes up case studies of rape narratives that challenge the limitations of postfeminism I describe in this and the previous chapter. While I argue here that fictional rape narratives in popular film and television draw on and contribute to a postfeminist culture and thus discursively delimit both feminism and rape, the remaining chapters ask how particular high-profile fictional rape narratives or specific types of media texts do—and do not—resist postfeminism.

4

Feminism and the Popular
Readings of Rape and Postfeminism
in Thelma and Louise

Near the end of *Thelma and Louise* (1991), Thelma asks Louise if she is thinking about making a deal with Hal, the sympathetic, paternalistic cop who helps to track them for murdering Harlan, the man who rapes Thelma early in the film. While on the phone with Louise, Hal uses his inside knowledge about "what happened to [her] in Texas" (presumably rape) to try to persuade her that he understands her unlawful response to sexual assault (killing the rapist), while also trying to keep her on the phone long enough for fellow officers to trace the call. While Louise is at a loss for words, Thelma, who is standing next to Louise, cannot hear Hal's attempts at friendly persuasion; worried about being caught, Thelma hangs up the phone. Hal's spell over her now broken, Louise promises Thelma she will not make a deal and turn herself in, saying, "We don't wanna end up on the damn *Geraldo Show!*"

If "Geraldo" stands in for "talk shows" in general, which stand in for publicity, heated debates, scrutiny of feminine pleasures, and ultimately community sanction, then Louise is right about what will happen to her and Thelma if they reenter society. While Thelma and Louise avoid a mass-mediated fate by choosing death within the diegesis, the popular press reviews of and commentaries on the film place *Thelma and Louise* (the film) and Thelma and Louise (the characters) on a figurative talk show, debating issues such as feminism, feminine identity, violence, and women's pleasure in literally hundreds of reviews and articles that continue to appear even in the late 1990s, years after the film's release.[1] Furthermore, the scholarly press has responded to and participated in this media spectacle, publishing (so far) two forums in scholarly magazines,[2] three articles in the July 1991 issue of *Sight and Sound*,[3] and dozens of essays and book chapters about *Thelma and Louise*, most of which at least in part confront the issue of feminism in relation to the film.[4] In addition to articles specifically about the film, and thus fairly easily found through typical research methods, any number of scholarly essays and books, many more (I assume) than those I happen upon while reading on other topics, use *Thelma and Louise* as a representative example of a feminist (or occasionally nonfeminist) popular film.[5]

I choose *Thelma and Louise* for a single-film case study, then, because it is probably the most highly mediated fictional rape narrative to have appeared in U.S. popular culture since the early 1980s, establishing it as the single most talked about post-1980 rape film.[6] Furthermore, much of this discussion has focused on the film's relationship to feminism and postfeminism: the popular press primarily discusses postfeminist definitions of feminism in relation to the film, while the scholarly press asks how feminist the film's feminism really is. Given its hypermediation, *Thelma and Louise* offers an excellent opportunity to examine the relationships among postfeminism, feminism, and rape. Looking at the film from a double perspective, I ask two questions. First, how do the film and the scholarly response to it at least implicitly reveal ways feminism resists postfeminism? And conversely, does the postfeminist discursive context of the popular press's response to the film potentially limit any reading of feminism in the film, particularly a feminist perspective on rape?

While answering these questions, I examine (and, admittedly, add to) the discursive mediation of *Thelma and Louise,* paying particular attention to the representation of rape and the film's relationship to feminism and postfeminism in the process. While some feminist criticism of the film does discuss rape briefly, to the best of my knowledge, no sustained analysis of the representation of rape in the film has yet appeared in print.[7] Thus, in the first of three sections of this chapter, I consider *Thelma and Louise* as a rape film, related to the other rape films and television shows I discuss throughout this book. Taking my cue from many of the feminist scholars who find something of value in the film, I explore how the film's narrative about rape and sexual violence can be read to challenge sexualized violence. From this perspective, I argue that *Thelma and Louise* represents a critical and resistant relationship to rape by drawing attention to links between rape and men's control over language and the gaze.

Additionally, I argue that the film offers at least four potential responses to sexual assault, each linked to women's self-preservation in a context of gendered and sexualized oppression: run from it, ignore it, defend oneself from it and get revenge for it, and learn from and about it.

These multiple responses invite a complex understanding of sexual assault that leads to an ambiguous and ambivalent conclusion to the narrative: Thelma and Louise's climactic flight into/over the Grand Canyon is both utopic, because it evokes women's freedom and pleasure, and dystopic, because it suggests that the assaultive male-dominated social order is so powerful the only way to escape it is to die. Through my analysis of sexual violence in the film, I also argue that the film's relationship to postfeminism is ambivalent: it both draws on and revises certain aspects of postfeminist rape narratives, such as those I describe in chapter 3. Overall, I argue that the film's ambivalence about both rape and postfeminism allows *Thelma and Louise,* on its own, to articulate a resistant relationship to both sexual violence and typical postfeminist representations of rape, women, and feminism.

In the second section of this chapter, however, I argue that coverage in the popular press resolves the film's ambivalence over and implicit resistance to postfeminism by glossing over sexual assault and offering circumscribed answers to questions about feminism and feminine pleasure. The press asks whether or not the film is feminist (answer: mostly yes), what kind of feminism it offers (answer: mostly nonconfrontational and playful postfeminist feminism), and, later, how women in general can take pleasure in *Thelma and Louise* (answer: primarily as a means of cultural consumption). Thus, I argue that the popular press "posts" what could be considered feminism in the film.

The first two sections of the chapter, then, set up a tension between (1) a critical reading of the film as offering a feminist critique of sexual assault and a sexually assaultive culture and (2) a transtextual reading that places the film in relation to the constraints of its reception. I do not mean the tension between these two types of critical analysis to be a debate over where the meaning of the film "really" lies. Rather, I foreground this tension to emphasize *both* the feminist possibilities in a particular film *and* the ways the popular press implicitly works to contain those possibilities. From my critical perspective, the meaning in the film's representation of rape and feminism oscillates among definitions of the film as an individual text, definitions of the film as a media event, and the relationship between these two definitions.

In the third and final section of the chapter, I turn to other scholarly analyses of the film that argue for and illustrate a variety of feminist pleasures availed by the film. This scholarship offers feminist pleasures of science fiction (Barr 1991, 1993) and butch-femme coming out stories

(Griggers 1993), for example, both of which are distinctly absent from the popular press coverage. Here, I examine scholarly work on *Thelma and Louise* (including my own in the first section of this chapter) in order to identify what kinds of pleasures are being claimed in the name of feminism and whether and how those pleasures illuminate and escape the limits of postfeminist rape narratives that also exist in and through the film and its popular press reception. Overall, I argue that while the feminist critical pleasures associated with the film are multiple, like the popular press, the scholarly press tends to sidestep the role of rape in the film. As a result, these pleasures depend on—but do not address—rape: a paradoxical, even troubling, position for feminist criticism to take, particularly given that the popular press makes the same move, also in the name of a (postfeminist) feminism.

My goal throughout the chapter is to advance a critical practice that centers an analysis of the representation of rape in order to challenge various ways rape may be naturalized, ignored, or depended on—often in the name of feminism. *Thelma and Louise*—as text, media event, and site of feminist theory/criticism—both helps and hinders this process.

Thelma and Louise

> You watch your mouth, buddy.
> —Louise to the dead rapist, after shooting him

In *Thelma and Louise* the rape/death scene in a parking lot outside a bar (while not the first scene of the film), like so many other rape scenes, instigates the forward motion of the narrative. Until this moment, Thelma and Louise move in fits and starts, delayed by tasks at home, Louise's work, and Thelma's husband, only just barely getting out of town, buried as they are under the weight of Thelma's excessive luggage.[8] Even when they are on the road heading toward their weekend getaway in the woods, Thelma immediately persuades Louise to stop for something to eat.[9] That stop precipitates the rape and the death that set the narrative in linear motion, justify the road trip to Mexico, and change Thelma and Louise's future forever. In this section, I examine how the film represents this rape, Louise's memory of another rape in Texas, and a series of additional encounters with a sexually assaultive truck driver. In the process, I focus on how the film links men's use of language, the gaze, and rape; offers multiple and complex responses to rape; and negotiates its relationship to various aspects of postfeminist rape narratives. In each case, I argue that the film at least potentially offers a feminist perspective on and critique of rape that go beyond postfeminist definitions of feminism.

Critique of Language/Gaze/Rape

Particularly in the prelude-to-rape and rape scenes, the film offers a potentially powerful critique of women's everyday experiences of rape and sexual harassment, one that links sexual assault to masculine control over both language and the gaze. From the moment Harlan approaches Thelma and Louise in the roadside bar, calling them "Kewpie dolls" and complimenting them in polite language, Louise responds to his words and gaze as assaultive. Three close-ups capture each character's different perspective on the situation. While Thelma enjoys Harlan's attention, batting her eyelashes and smiling broadly, a close-up of Louise reveals her attacking Harlan's instrument of assault—his gaze—by blowing cigarette smoke in his face. A third close-up shows Harlan batting his own eyelashes in frustrated response and purposefully turning his gaze from Louise to Thelma. These three close-ups construct a complex power dynamic of sexual harassment and eventually rape. Louise understands and articulates the links among gentlemanly language, appreciative looks, and sexual threats, and consequently rejects Harlan; Harlan realizes Louise is resistant but is not dissuaded from using his tools of pursuit on Thelma; and Thelma, who does not yet understand Harlan to be a sexual threat, responds innocently by pursuing a sense of freedom from her controlling husband.

Theoretically, at the point at which these three linked close-ups appear, the film suggests that either Thelma's or Louise's interpretation of Harlan can be correct. The film quickly weights this opposition in Louise's favor, however, offering her perspective on both the bar environment and Harlan as foreshadowing Harlan's eventual rape of Thelma. While the narrative development has yet to prove her right, Louise senses the potential for rape from the moment she enters the bar. "I haven't seen a place like this since I left Texas," she says, as they cross the crowded bar toward their table. This is her first mention of Texas, the perpetually (just) offscreen site of her previous "unspeakable" experience, an experience that the film's enthymematic structure repeatedly alludes to as rape. Neither Thelma nor the spectator knows enough yet to understand the brief reference to rape that Louise makes here (subconsciously or not).[10] Nevertheless, by repeatedly illustrating that Louise's interpretation of Harlan as villainous is correct, the structure of the scene supports her omniscient knowledge that the narrative will inevitably move toward sexual assault.

For example, once Harlan and Thelma are on the dance floor, the handheld camera follows them closely, always remaining nearer to Thelma and showing Harlan's face as he purposefully spins her (in and out of the frame) in order to contribute to her drunkenness. The camera jerks as it follows Thelma, emphasizing the deliberateness of Harlan's actions and supporting Louise's perception that Harlan is a threat. Thus, this prelude-to-rape scene makes clear who is to blame for the upcoming rape. While Thelma's positive responses to Harlan may imply she is naive, his purposeful manipulation and Louise's intuitive understanding of his actions naturalize the feminist claim Louise and Thelma both articulate later in the film: the woman is never to blame for rape.

Having used alcohol and dancing to make Thelma dizzy and sick to her stomach, Harlan maneuvers her outside to the parking lot, ostensibly for fresh air but actually to rape her. This scene represents Harlan's body as a threat that his use of language and the gaze only thinly veil. Having used his gentlemanly and appreciative voice to promise Thelma he will not hurt her ("you're so beautiful"), having said he "only wants to kiss her," he resorts to physical force when she does not respond positively to his verbal manipulation as she did in the bar. After slapping her face once, he says, "Now, I said I wouldn't hurt you," making it ironically clear that he will physically do the opposite of what he verbally says. Only when Louise arrives and threatens to shoot him does Harlan stop raping Thelma.

In both the prelude-to-rape and the rape scenes, the film's framing of Louise's perspective of Harlan as purposefully manipulative connects men's use of sexualized language and the gaze to rape. By emphasizing Louise's perspective that Harlan's attempts at getting Thelma to consent are in fact coercive, the film offers what can be read as a feminist critique of rape by understanding it to be both linked to men's flirtations and an inevitable part of women's everyday experiences. When Louise shoots Harlan, not to defend herself physically or to stop his physical assault of Thelma but to stop his *verbal* assaults, her action conveys the language-gaze-rape links directly. After Harlan slides to the ground, eyes wide open in death, Louise leans over him and says, "You watch your mouth, buddy." Elayne Rapping (1991) argues, "that Louise shoots after the danger of rape is gone muddies the political waters hopelessly" (31); however, I consider that fact to provide much of the political power of the film from a feminist perspective that does not isolate one act of physical sexual assault from various forms of sexualized assault—including verbal assaults—that pervade women's lives.

By representing Harlan's actions as extensions of everyday forms of sexual harassment that include visual and verbal assault (even when they are appreciative or gentlemanly), privileging Louise's perspective on Harlan, and providing Louise with the means to stop the assault, the film both acknowledges the pervasiveness of rape (similar to some of the films I discuss in chapter 1) and provides an image of a woman who fights back powerfully against both verbal and physical assaults—hence, against rape culture. The film continues to offer this perspective on sexual assault and to depict the women fighting back when, for example, later in the film Thelma and Louise encounter a truck driver who has images of naked women on his mud flaps, makes obscene gestures and comments, and assumes (when they finally stop the car in response to his verbal and visual assaults) that they are actually interested in him sexually. While he does not physically rape them, as Harlan does Thelma, he nevertheless represents men's sexualized language and gaze as an assaultive part of women's everyday lives. As I discuss in more detail in the next section, as with Harlan, Thelma and Louise eventually are able to defend themselves against the trucker.

Responding to Language/Gaze/Rape

The film's powerful acknowledgment of the pervasiveness of sexual assault—as past unspeakable horror (Texas), present unavoidable event (Harlan), and future inevitable threat (truck driver)—leads to a variety of responses from Thelma and Louise. While some responses appear more often in the film than do others, all these responses circulate throughout the film, without replacing each other. Thus, the film acknowledges at least some complexity in women's potential responses to rape and resists simplistically privileging one particular response over all the others. None of the responses offered in the film ultimately is effective in preventing further rapes, however. Instead, they function as a series of options (rather than solutions) for dealing with a continuously assaultive world.

Running from rape is one way to understand Louise's response to what happened to her in Texas. Not only did she leave Texas some time prior to the beginning of the film, but she refuses to go back, presumably because the entire state represents rape to her. Even when she and Thelma are "running for [their] lives," as Thelma puts it, Louise refuses to travel through Texas on their way to Mexico. She is perpetually on the run from rape/Texas, despite the fact that she reencounters rape elsewhere. Through this response, Louise acknowledges rape (at least to herself) and then refuses to return to the location of that rape.

Simply *ignoring sexual assault,* refusing even to acknowledge that it has happened or is happening, is another option. For example, the second time Thelma and Louise begin to pass the truck driver Louise tells Thelma to "ignore him," knowing that as soon as they are in his line of vision he will assault them again. He does, but they just drive by, looking straight ahead. Nevertheless, they encounter him again later in the film and thus face his assaults yet a third time. Louise's refusal to talk about what happened to her in Texas is another way she ignores rape. Whenever Thelma or Hal mentions Texas, in fact, Louise either tells Thelma not to talk about it or becomes virtually catatonic. For example, when Thelma says that she thinks Louise was raped in Texas, Louise immediately stops the car. The camera cuts to outside the windshield, shifting from intimate shot/countershot close-ups to a crowded and anxious pan from Louise toward Thelma as Louise says, "Drop it. I'm not going to talk about that." When she begins driving again, she looks straight ahead, expressionless. Later she gets the same blank look on her face when Hal says, "I know what's making you run. I know what happened to you in Texas." If running from rape (for Louise, running from Texas) represents a determined action, ignoring rape (for Louise, refusing to talk about her past) represents inaction.

While Louise is perpetually both running from and ignoring the Texas rape, in the present Thelma and Louise also use versions of *self-defense and revenge* to respond to sexual assault.[11] For example, when Louise interrupts Harlan's rape of Thelma, Louise practices a form of self-defense, or more accurately, friend-defense. She holds a gun to Harlan's neck, and she tells him in no uncertain terms to "let her go." She articulates for him her knowledge about rape. She instructs him about women's communication by defining crying as a signal that he should let a woman go ("In the future, when a woman's crying like that, she's not having any fun"). Harlan, however, like the other men in the film, is not the learning type. He responds to Louise's "lesson" with more verbal assaults ("suck my cock," "I should have gone ahead and fucked her"). Louise has already had enough of these assaults in the bar and in her past, experiencing verbal taunts as directly linked to physical assaults. Louise neither walks away as Thelma suggests, ignoring his final assault, nor leaves/runs from the scene, having successfully interrupted the rape with friend-defense, because neither really stops Harlan or the men Louise sees reflected in him. So she kills him.

Relatedly, when they encounter the truck driver for a third time, they again take revenge. They take control of the situation through their own use of language, telling him they are interested in "get[ting] serious" and directly discussing his gaze by asking him to remove his sunglasses so they can see his eyes. While they are getting serious about stopping his harassment, he assumes they are getting serious about having sex. As with Harlan, despite the lesson they attempt to give him, he refuses to apologize, refuses to stop using his voice to assault. So Thelma and Louise use their guns to destroy his truck in one of the most spectacular "action" scenes of the film.

When Louise tells him that they will "make [him] sorry" if he does not apologize, she implies a connection to having made Harlan sorry for not apologizing; but instead of killing the trucker, instead of destroying his *power* to rape and harass, they destroy the *symbol* of his power to rape and harass; they blow up his truck.[12] The energetic music; the women's use of their car to circle the trucker as he gets down on his knees and calls them "bitches from hell," shot from an extremely high angle that captures the burning tanker; and Thelma's exuberant physical ability to lean out of the car to grab the trucker's hat off the ground all emphasize pleasure in the wild ride and the act of revenge. While a spectator may take pleasure when Louise shoots Harlan, this scene much more specifically *invites* a pleasurable spectatorial experience of their actions, coded, for instance, by the upbeat music and the main characters' laughter. Thus, the film not only offers self-defense/revenge as a viable response to sexual assault, but defines such actions as potentially pleasurable.

While avenging sexual assault is prevalent in the film, Thelma and Louise also *learn about and criticize rape and rape law*—a fourth kind of response. In particular, Thelma learns that the law will not believe them, that they will be blamed for the rape, and that going to the police is useless. In short, when the film begins Thelma is ignorant of this perspective on rape, which Louise has to explain to her, and when the film ends they both understand not only that the law is ineffectual but that Thelma was not at fault for the rape.

Nevertheless, Thelma and Louise do not move through this learning process in a linear fashion. The film includes a complex representation of the difficult process of understanding and criticizing rape. Immediately after the rape/death, Thelma and Louise discuss what to do. Thelma argues that they should go to the police and tell them what happened. Louise, however, articulates her knowledge about rape, teaching Thelma that the police will blame her for the rape, or worse, will not believe she was raped at all. "Just about 100 goddamn people saw you dancing cheek to cheek!" she says, emphasizing the disjuncture between the legal interpretation of "dancing" and "flirting" and her knowledgeable interpretation of Harlan's manipulative actions that the handheld, sick-to-its-stomach camerawork demonstrates. While Louise and the camera saw Harlan coercing Thelma, Louise assumes that the law will see Thelma consenting. Thelma learns quickly, however; when they stop for coffee immediately after the rape to figure out what to do, Thelma criticizes Louise for now implying that Thelma *is* at fault.

> *Louise:* If you weren't concerned with having so much fun, we wouldn't be here right now.
> *Thelma:* So this is all my fault, is it?[13]

Immediately after setting up an opposition between Louise's knowledge and Thelma's naïveté, the film reverses their positions. Now Louise takes the same naive position she was criticizing in the previous scene by blaming Thelma for the rape; and Thelma reminds her that a woman who is raped is not responsible for that rape. Louise does not function as an ideal toward which Thelma moves; instead each character influences the other in the process and illustrating that there is no one right way to respond.

As the film progresses, Thelma's naïveté resurfaces so that she and Louise must continually participate in the learning/teaching process. Their conversations about both Texas and Harlan structure this process. While Louise never actually tells Thelma she was raped in Texas, several scenes build on each other and lead Thelma to voice this interpretation. When Louise refuses to take the shortest route from Oklahoma to Mexico—through Texas—Thelma asks, "What happened to you in Texas?" While Thelma does not yet "know" that Louise was raped there, she begins to imagine this possibility. She understands that some horrible unspeakable thing happened. In a later scene, when Thelma again suggests going to the police, Louise reminds her that even if the police would have believed Thelma was raped if she had gone to them immediately, by this point all the physical evidence (blood and bruises) is gone. Thelma, sensing there is a source for Louise's knowledge and drawing attention to the structured absence of Louise's rape, asks, "How do you know all this stuff?" The last time Thelma confronts Louise about Texas, she finally shifts from questions to statements and actually tells Louise she was raped in Texas. While Louise continues to refuse to talk about it, Thelma responds with the knowledge she has gained from her own rape, soothing Louise with "It's O.K. It's O.K." and touching her tenderly.

Despite Thelma's overarching progression toward knowledge received from Louise, each character also sometimes contradicts her role in the learning/teaching process. For example, even after experiencing Harlan's assaultive combination of language/gaze/rape and even after Louise has explained how rape laws function, Thelma naively assumes the truck driver will be polite when he waves them by the first time they encounter him on the road. As they pass, the camera shows them from underneath the truck, tracking their car until it picks up the truck's mud flaps with silhouettes of naked women on them. While Louise says, "How typical," automatically articulating her knowledge about the links between her other experiences of sexual assault and the trucker's gaze at and display of naked women, Thelma forgets what she has already learned and is temporarily persuaded by the "gentlemanly" actions of the trucker, who moves over to let them pass. As their car gets closer to his cab, however, a shot from the women's point of view shows him making obscene gestures. Thelma is surprised, saying, "That's disgusting," while Louise, who presumably anticipated what was coming, gives him the finger and drives away.

In another example, Thelma and Louise reverse their positions on rape: late in the film, *Louise* takes responsibility for everything that has happened to them, saying, "I don't know why I didn't go to the police right away." *Thelma* then teaches Louise what Louise taught her earlier: "Nobody would have believed us." Shifting positions yet again, after the final chase scene begins, *Thelma* takes responsibility and *Louise* says, "If there's one thing you should know by now, it wasn't your fault." In short, while overall Louise functions as a more knowledgeable teacher and Thelma moves from being naive to being informed, both characters also continually shift positions. Thus the film not only offers a critique of rape law as a potential response to rape, but it does so *repeatedly* as a result of the characters' frequent conversations during which they tell each other not to accept blame. Furthermore, the film offers that response as one among many possible responses.

The end of the film combines all these potential responses—except ignorance—in Thelma and Louise's complex and contradictory choice of suicide over either murder or imprisonment by the law. While Louise loads her gun and prepares to fight back in self-defense, Thelma has another idea: she continues to learn from and develop a critical response to sexualized assault. Instead of submitting to the assault that the slow-motion extreme close-ups and the amplified sounds of the FBI and police loading and cocking their guns symbolically promise, Thelma suggests they drive away (run away), off the edge of the Grand Canyon. Thelma and Louise refuse to let the representatives of the law carry out the death threat that their looks through the crosshairs of their guns promise, choosing their own form of death instead. The freeze-frame that suspends Thelma and Louise above the Grand Canyon, moments before their inevitable death, represents a women's relationship and homosocial/homoerotic gaze, frozen in space and time, rather than the assaultive male gaze that pervades the film. Shot from the side, as though the camera/spectator is also in the air, the image excludes both the men and the men's perspective, freeing the spectator from the material and social order, as well. Furthermore, a close-up of a photograph flying out of the back seat shows Thelma and Louise together when they were relatively carefree at the beginning of their journey. This image anticipates the final credit sequence of clips from their happy moments on the road that focus on women looking at and being with women rather than on the punishing male gaze. In these final moments of the film, Thelma and Louise practice a variety of responses to sexual assault when they *run* from what they *understand* to be the law's assault, in an act of *revenge and self-defense* that denies the police the satisfaction of their deaths and Hal the satisfaction of saving them for the legal system.

Given the circularity of the narrative, as it moves continually from one assault to another, it is inevitable that the film ends in a way that does not allow Thelma and Louise to eliminate assault altogether. The film articulates a critique of men's language/gaze/rape through Louise's knowledge, Thelma's growing knowledge, and the camera's privileging of their perspective, while simultaneously defining this knowledge and perspective as ultimately ineffectual. Not only is rape a necessary precursor for Thelma and Louise to have this knowledge, but having the knowledge does no good; verbal, visual, physical, and legal assaults continue. The only option remaining at the end of the film is ambivalent: both a utopic freedom from masculine assault and a suggestion—through their deaths —that sexual assault is inevitable and women are helpless to do anything substantive to change it. At the end of the film, Thelma and Louise escape one final assault, but they do not end assault. They simply leap into a freeze-frame, hands clasped, music blaring, caught on the precarious brink between death and life, between feminist resistance to assault and a feminist critique of the inevitability of assault.

Is *Thelma and Louise* a Postfeminist Rape Film?

I primarily read this ambivalent representation of sexual assault as escaping the bounds of a postfeminist definition of feminism by offering a complex and multiple analysis of and response to sexual assault and a learning process that does not involve a more fully informed postfeminist man to bring the women to consciousness about rape. Nevertheless, the film corresponds with a number of the postfeminist rape narratives I discuss in the previous chapter. For example, the moment Thelma takes action independently of her husband, exploring her own pleasures and desires, the moment she claims a right to the independence postfeminism promises her, she faces rape. Conversely, Louise's previous rape has made her self-sufficient, wise, and independent, and Thelma moves toward a similar position through the course of the film after her rape and as a result of Louise's instruction about rape. Thus, as in many of the examples I discuss in chapter 3, rape both leads to (can be understood as a necessity to achieve) and is a result of (can be understood as a punishment for) a general postfeminist independence.

Furthermore, both Harlan, as a rapist, and Thelma and Louise, as women who face rape, correspond with many aspects of the typical rapist and the typical women who face rape in film that I discuss in chapter 3. Harlan is white, attractive, and acquainted with Louise.[14] He is not an enemy rapist, but a friend-turned-enemy rapist. While Christine Holmlund (1993) points out that, out of a series of recent "deadly doll" films in which women kill, *Thelma and Louise* is the only one to address "attempted date rape" (128), the fact that it represents acquaintance rape in particular is typical of many mainstream post-1980 film and television rape narratives.[15] Additionally, Harlan is unambiguously villainous, an individual whom the woman who serves Thelma and Louise in the bar identifies as particularly assaultive. While the film is relatively unusual because it does not define him as the *only* sexually assaultive man in the narrative, he and these other men are often read as an exaggerated "string of stereotypical male bimbos" (Rapping, 31), what Marsha Kinder (1991–92) calls "a veritable postmodernist parade of treacherous male characters from well-known movies and popular male action genres" (30). As stereotypes, these male characters can function as comical jokes that undermine the film's representation of *everyday* codes of masculinity as legitimating rape. Notably, Thelma and Louise are also typical of white and attractive women who face rape in innumerable postfeminist narratives.

The racial specificity of the story becomes particularly clear in one gratuitous scene, completely unrelated to the narrative, in which an African American man with dreadlocks, who is incongruously smoking what appears to be pot while riding a bike, happens upon the police officer Thelma and Louise have trapped in the trunk of his own car.[16] Surprised by the sound of banging, he looks around and finally sees the police car. When a voice from inside the trunk explains that he is a police officer, the man takes a huge puff of his joint and blows the smoke through the air hole Thelma has so thoughtfully shot into the trunk of the car so that the imprisoned cop can breathe. This is the only scene in which an explicitly nonwhite character appears as anything other than a fleeting background figure. He does not, however, speak; he is a spectacle of gratuitous humor rather than part of the movement of the narrative, marking the narrative as explicitly about whiteness.[17] The biker marks racial difference triply: he is not part of the narrative and does not speak (like white people in the film), he is not sexually assaultive (like white men in the film), and he offers comic relief (unlike Thelma and Louise, whose humor moves the narrative forward).[18]

Despite these ways the film does illustrate aspects of typical postfeminist rape narratives in terms of women's independence, acquaintance rape, and whiteness, there are also a number of ways the film is ambivalent about the common rape narratives that appear in other post-1980 films and television shows. For example, the film *does* consistently represent the women's point of view on sexual assault, making it clear that they do not desire the assaults they experience, but it *does not* rely on previously codified images (e.g., a post-rape shower) to represent their perspective quickly and then move on. Instead, the film returns again and again not only to their conversations about, perspectives on, and responses to the Texas rape and Harlan's rape, but also to a series of other assaults. Similarly, the rape event *does* give Thelma and Louise power over the narrative, setting it in motion around the decisions they make from the moment Louise kills Harlan, but that power over the narrative *does not* lead to the kinds of individualized triumphs over individualized crazed men and heteronormative family reunions that the raped women of *Trial by Jury* (1994) and *Rob Roy* (1995), for example, experience at the end of their films. Furthermore, while the film *does* criticize rape law repeatedly, it *does not* then hold the women responsible for either changing that law or finding a way to use law against itself, as does *The Accused* (1988), for example. Instead, the women's continuous inability to escape either sexual assault or the law reiterates criticism without offering an easy solution to the problem of rape in general.

Furthermore, while I argue above that the film links rape to the male gaze, thus accessing what I define in the previous chapter as a common element of postfeminist rape narratives—the critique of the male gaze—this film shows a link between the gaze and rape rather than either supplanting rape with the gaze or celebrating men who gaze and then speak out against what they have seen. In other words, while many other rape narratives from the same time period represent men who watch rape as either worse than rapists or as saviors for women who have been raped, this film suggests that gazing sexually at women is just one of many culturally sanctioned behaviors, including rape.

While from one perspective *Thelma and Louise* takes rape much more seriously than do other films and television shows that displace it with an excessively villainous watcher, from another perspective the film also downplays its own critique by at times representing the act of watching as humorous. The scene in which Thelma robs a convenience store after her one-night stand, J.D., first teaches her how to be a "gentlemanly" robber[19] and then enacts his lesson by stealing all her money after charming her into the best sex she has ever had, offers a good example.[20] The film represents the robbery from Hal, Darryl, and other officers' points of view while they watch a black-and-white security video image. Thelma begins to tell Louise the story ("Well I just said . . ."), but a cut interrupts her narration. Instead of depicting Thelma's experience or even Louise's experience of hearing the story, the film represents the robbery from the perspective of the law by cutting back and forth between the surveillance camera's image and the men's incredulous faces. One of the FBI agents, in fact, eats while he watches, suggesting a humorous correspondence between his watching Thelma's crime in progress and his watching, perhaps, a television drama in his living room at home. In the prelude-to-rape and the rape scenes the film aligns the spectator with Louise and her understanding of Harlan's gaze as sexualized assault, but in this scene the film aligns the spectator with the men. While the *disjuncture* between the spectator's ability and the men's inability to understand Thelma's actions contributes to the scene's humor, the surveillance camera also distances the spectator from Thelma's perspective and laughs at the men watching more than it emphasizes a link between their act of watching and the assaults that appear in the rest of the film. In short, *Thelma and Louise* both exceeds and deflects (through humor) postfeminist rape narratives' villainization of men who watch.

The representation of the "New Man" through Hal is perhaps the most ambivalent representation in the film in terms of postfeminism. On the one hand, Hal is a perfect example of a sympathetic and knowledgeable (about rape and women's experiences) postfeminist man. For example, when he breaks into Louise's apartment, he pauses to look at a picture of her as a little girl. In this scene, the film emphasizes his sympathetic attitude toward her with an extremely subjective brief sound of the birthday party Hal imagines as he says "Happy birthday, lady" to the picture. And when he brings J.D. in for questioning, he arranges to be alone with him, after which he yells at him for taking the only chance "those two girls . . . had" (their money). By phone, he asks Louise whether she wants to tell him what happened; tells her he feels he knows her; says "I believe you" when she implies he does not; and, finally, tells her that he understands her, that he knows that what happened in Texas is making her run now. Even in the last scene he is still trying to help them: he yells at Max, the man who is running the investigation, "How many times are these girls gonna get fucked over!?" in an attempt to prevent the shoot-out he thinks is coming but which Thelma and Louise evade.

Despite all these (and many other) representations of his sympathetic understanding of Thelma and Louise—depictions that mark him as a typical postfeminist man who knows more about rape and women's response to it than everyone else in a narrative—unlike typical postfeminist men, Hal is completely ineffectual. Not only do Thelma and Louise distrust his reassurances that he will help them if they turn themselves in, but the end of the film emphasizes just how ineffectual he is. A telephoto lens shows him running after them, but slow-motion and the lens distortion exaggerate the distance between him and the women, emphasizing the fact that he has never even been close to being able to catch or "help" Thelma and Louise. Furthermore, Hal exists in the context of a film that shows repeatedly that men's gentlemanly behavior masks their intent to rape (Harlan) or steal (J.D.): in short, to assault women. To be gentlemanly in this film is to be marked as untrustworthy and potentially dangerous, as much as is being explicitly nasty, like Darryl and the truck driver. Thus, the film undermines even Hal's attempt to "help" the women, whom he repeatedly calls "girls."

In short, I am suggesting that, as a rape narrative, *Thelma and Louise* is both postfeminist and not postfeminist, and that this ambivalent relationship to postfeminism contributes to a reading of the film as offering a critical feminist perspective on rape that cannot be entirely subsumed by postfeminism. *Thelma and Louise* accesses many of the standard elements of postfeminist rape narratives, but can also be read to undermine them, challenge them, or convert them into humor.

These readings suggest that the film offers a more complex and critical look at rape and sexualized assault than do the majority of (if not all) postfeminist rape narratives discussed in the previous chapter. Paradoxically, however, the film also takes postfeminism one step further, drawing on a postfeminist play with pleasure in scenes such as the convenience store robbery, killing the trucker's truck, and the utopic women-bonding death scene. This playful strain of postfeminism potentially undermines the critique of sexual assault that runs throughout the film and simultaneously invites the postfeminist definitions of the film's feminism that appear in the popular press, definitions that, as I argue in the next section, repress rape's place in the narrative.

Living in the Freeze-Frame of Postfeminism

I never had a second thought about the ending. It just seemed appropriate that they carry on the journey. It's a metaphorical continuation. The film's not about rape. It's about choices and freedom. The only solution is to take your choice which is to take your life.
—Ridley Scott, director of *Thelma and Louise,* quoted in Amy Taubin, "Ridley Scott's Road Work"

Of course they're feminists, but not because they have pistols tucked into their jeans. This is a movie about two women whose clasped hands are their most powerful weapon.
—Laura Shapiro, "Women Who Kill Too Much"

Our weekend would be *Thelma and Louise* without killing someone in the parking lot.   —Lynn Snowden, "Thelma and Louise, Part II"

The final freeze-frame of the film arrests Thelma and Louise in an other-time/other-space of a utopic separatism that they choose instead of the dystopic world of perpetual assault that they cannot escape. This freeze-frame allows Thelma and Louise to avoid the narrative and material logic of death. Oscillating between tragedy and utopic fantasy, both precipitated by rape, Thelma and Louise live on after the narrative ends, behind the final credits, in clips and freeze-frames depicting pleasurable aspects of their road trip. In the context of the film itself, this contradictory utopic/dystopic ending, which simultaneously enacts life and death, concludes where the film began, with a critique of male-dominated culture (marriage, work, heterosexuality, law) as sexually assaultive of women. As I discuss in this section, however, Thelma and Louise also continue to live on *outside the film* as cultural icons in such places as popular press articles that debate whether or not the film is feminist and whether or not its feminism is valuable; the June 24, 1991, cover of *Time*; editorial pages in the *New York Times*;[21] the 1991 Academy Awards ceremony; popular cartoons;[22] and subsequent women-road-trip films that refer back to *Thelma and Louise*[23] (among many other places). The critical tension in the impossibility of their immortal death thus dissipates as their immortality overpowers their diegetic death.

Not surprisingly, the extensive critical response to this film in the popular press does not address the film's lesbian possibilities[24] or the film's sustained critique of men's language/gaze/rape. Instead, Thelma and Louise's discursive immortality, supported by the immortal death in the film's final freeze-frame, constructs specifically nonconfrontational postfeminist subjectivities that all women are invited to emulate.[25] As Jane Arthurs (1995) argues, most of the reviews in the popular press represent the film's feminism as "funny, sexy, exciting, entertaining" (91). Avoiding a discussion of rape altogether, the popular press transforms *Thelma and Louise*, Thelma, and Louise into representatives of the postfeminism about which I have argued this film is ambivalent.[26] Becoming only a trace presence in the popular press, rape functions as a vague justification for Thelma and Louise's, then Geena Davis and Susan Sarandon's, and ultimately all women's playful response to gendered and sexualized assault.[27] This version of depoliticized and nonconfrontational postfeminist feminism—which I discuss below in relation to Thelma and Louise, then Geena Davis and Susan Sarandon, and finally represented spectators/readers—is unaware of (and certainly not critical of) rape.

Thelma and Louise

By early June 1991, only two weeks after *Thelma and Louise*'s theatrical release, nearly every review of the film begins with a summary of a debate over the value of the film's "feminism." While the reviewers represent the debate in which they themselves are engaging as "balanced" between celebrations and criticisms of the film, in fact, almost all reviewers praise the film. Each review generally uses the terms "man bashing" and "toxic feminism," quoting from two specific reviews (Novak 1991 and Leo 1991, respectively), to illustrate the criticism of the film. In the process, each review tends to misrepresent these two reviews as only a *fraction* of the negative criticism about the film, when in fact John Leo (1991) and Ralph Novak (1991) pretty much represent *all* the negative criticism.[28] The reviews then proceed to argue against that negative evaluation. Most reviews defend the film as life-affirming and fun, but in doing so they tend to deflect the critique of rape culture offered by the film. As a whole, then, the "debate" over *Thelma and Louise* is primarily a straw argument created by the reviewers and against which they then justify viewing *Thelma and Louise* as a harmless representation of feminism, a mere postfeminist pleasure. Collectively, the reviews represent Thelma and Louise as 1990s postfeminists, rather than as potentially radical outlaws in a perpetually sexually assaultive culture.

Reviews most often cite Leo's discussion of the film in *U.S. News and World Report* when mentioning "man-hating" interpretations of the film. Entitled "Toxic Feminism on the Big Screen," his article argues that the film is "fascist" because, like (his interpretation of) Andrea Dworkin's version of feminism, it represents men as completely evil:

> All males in this movie exist only to betray, ignore, sideswipe, penetrate or arrest our heroines. Anyone who has ever gotten to the end of a Dworkin essay knows how this movie will turn out: There is no hope for women. . . . Though the situation for women is hopeless, a form of pre-suicidal spiritual liberation is possible, and the key to this is violence. . . . With this repeated paean to transformative violence, found in none of the male-buddy movies, we have left Dworkin and entered a Mussolini speech. Here we have an explicit fascist theme, wedded to the bleakest form of feminism.

Leo objects to the pervasive "stereotypical" representations of men in the film, arguing that "violence" against the "phallic symbols" (trucks, "would-be rapists") is "fascist." Claiming that the film goes too far in reversing gender behavior, he suggests that the violence in this women's "buddy film" is problematic. For Leo, this simple reversal of women and men's roles defines the film as feminist—a bad thing. Novak, writing for *People*, implicitly agrees with Leo's critique of the film. Echoing the "negativity" in the women's "violence" against men, he writes, "Any movie that went as far out of its way to trash women as this female chauvinist sow of a film does to trash men would be universally, and justifiably, condemned."

While the positive reviews of the film obviously take issue with Leo and Novak, they do not challenge the terms of the debate. They accept the film as feminist, simply celebrating it as woman-affirming feminism rather than challenging it as man-hating feminism. Most strikingly, without exception, they collude with Leo and Novak in defining what happens between Harlan and Thelma as a "near rape" (e.g., Carlson 1991), "attempted rape" (e.g., Klawans 1991, 863; Rafferty 1991, 86), or "would be rap[e]" (e.g., Alleva 1991, 515). Without fail, the reviews accept Harlan's interpretation of the event as an uncompleted rape, an interpretation that leads him to say, "I should have gone ahead and fucked her," rather than Thelma's interpretation of the event as a rape, an interpretation that leads her to say, "He was raping me." In the process, each review covers over and neutralizes the threat that the representation of rape represents both to the pleasure the reviewer takes in the film and to a clearly defined dichotomous debate over feminism in the popular press. Having disregarded the actual violence against women in the film, the reviews quickly move on to an analysis of the women's friendship and their resistance to masculine assault as evidence of the film's pleasurable feminism. The reviews implicitly define feminism as a positive outcome of rape. They transform that rape, however, into an inconsequential almost-rape, focusing on the idea of a "female community" and "resistance" instead.

An article entitled "Women Who Kill Too Much" in *Newsweek* (Shapiro 1991), for example, avoids discussing rape by highlighting the women's connection to each other versus their "violence" against or "resistance" to men:

> What seems to disquiet this movie's critics is the portrayal of two women who, contrary to every law of God and popular culture, have something on their minds besides men. Yet they can't be dismissed as man-haters. . . . The simple but subversive truth is that neither woman needs a man to complete her. . . . Of course they're feminists, but not because they have pistols tucked into their jeans. This is a movie about two women whose clasped hands are their most powerful weapon.

Rather than praise the resistance in the image of "pistols tucked into their jeans" or address why they need guns to protect themselves, this article

explicitly claims that Thelma and Louise are not "man-haters" and focuses on the connection between them, arguing that women's solidarity
(their "clasped hands") is their most powerful weapon. The reading of the
film as a woman-bonding pleasure ride avoids the fact that their clasped
hands and (although this review does not mention it) their kiss represent
a death pact—necessary because of the unending sexualized assaults
Thelma and Louise face—just before they drive off the edge of the Grand
Canyon (Johnson 1993).

Geena Davis and Susan Sarandon

In the popular press, whether the authors consider the film's feminism
"good" or "bad," there is no discussion of rape. Instead, the women's connection to each other (as opposed to the male world through which they
move) comes to the fore as an ideal (or occasionally horrific) form of
"feminist" behavior. Star discourse about Susan Sarandon and Geena
Davis builds on this emphasis on "women's bonding," further transforming Thelma and Louise into celebrated postfeminists as the actors come
to embody this particular ideal. As Linda Frost (1998) puts it, "While
these periodicals obviously featured Davis and Sarandon to cash in on
the *Thelma and Louise* hype, their writers also carefully disarm the political possibilities of the characters" (157–58). The film's focus on a culture
in which women experience the violent effects of an unequally gendered
power structure (such as rape) becomes less and less important as
Thelma and Louise become more and more entrenched as immortal
icons of postfeminist pleasure.

At the 1991 Academy Awards ceremony, for example, while presenting
the award for best editing, Susan Sarandon and Geena Davis discuss the
possibility that Thelma and Louise actually live through their flight into
the Grand Canyon. Sarandon, drawing on her more realistic Louise character, laughs at Davis for suggesting that the film's ending is ambiguous
enough for Thelma and Louise actually to survive. Davis, however, draws
on her more hopeful and imaginative Thelma character and suggests that
they could have "grabbed onto something" or "made it to the other side."
When Davis points out that if Thelma and Louise do not survive there
will be no sequel, Sarandon, still drawing on the practical Louise character who lost her life savings, changes her mind and suggests that they
could have "bounced." In the face of the physical reality of death, the
film's and Davis's optimism persuades Sarandon. Despite Sarandon's

initial skepticism, this Academy Award reparteé plays on the fact that, sequel or no sequel, Thelma and Louise are still very much alive as part of Sarandon's and Davis's star personas.

The most telling example of the connection between the characters and the stars in terms of their relationships to men in particular appears, ironically, in the "Chatter" section of the same issue of *People* in which Novak's negative review appears:

> *Geena Davis* admits that costar *Susan Sarandon*, 44, became a role model for her during the making of their new film, *Thelma and Louise*. "She'll be embarrassed if I say this, but Susan is my hero," says Davis, 34. "She's very strong and outspoken and presents herself the way she is. The goal I had was to be stronger, more myself and more secure in how I feel. To claim my power and take responsibility for my life." Does that mean Susan influenced Davis's decision last year to divorce actor *Jeff Goldblum*? "No. Nothing like that," says Davis. "The sort of personal journey I'm talking about isn't freeing myself from men or in any way antimale." (Castro 1991)

This passage draws a direct connection between Davis and Sarandon's relationship and Thelma and Louise's relationship. The gossip suggests that Sarandon is strong and outspoken; whereas, Davis needs to be "stronger" and to "take responsibility" for her life. The relationship, however, is no longer about a shared experience of sexual assault but instead is about vague feminine power explicitly unconcerned with gendered power. That this quotation includes Davis's acknowledgment of a potential reading of the film (and of her decision to divorce Goldblum) as antimale reveals how purposefully the discourse works to move away from the "debate" over the film's feminism to a fun-filled celebration of the film. As though speaking to Novak's condemnation of the film published 103 pages earlier, the gossip diffuses the film's potential critique of men. Although Novak condemns the film, Davis asserts that the relationship she has with Sarandon, like Thelma's relationship with Louise, is based on women bonding rather than on women hating men. Additionally, this article displaces the lesbian potential in the relationship between Thelma and Louise, evoked in the film by Louise's explicit arguments against Thelma's marriage and Louise and Thelma's physical closeness: Davis assures the interviewer that Sarandon had nothing to do with her decision to leave Jeff Goldblum. Thus, Davis and Sarandon's relationship is an adjunct to, rather than a replacement for, heterosexuality; it is homosocial, not homosexual. In these reviews, Thelma/Davis and Louise/Sarandon have a fun, playful relationship, no longer precipitated by rape, sustained by self-defense and revenge, or motivated by lesbian desire.

With its May 1991 cover story on Geena Davis, *Harper's Bazaar* initially creates a similar parallel between the actor and the character, defining them both as independent women. The article curbs the feminism that independence might offer, however, when it asserts that Davis does not actually *want* independence from either men or femininity. The contents page blurb describing the cover photo of Davis reads, "Academy award–winning actress Geena Davis is driven by change. This spring, she blossoms in a bold, new direction: co-starring in the female buddy film *Thelma and Louise* and forming her own production company. (More on both, see page 140.) This take-charge attitude is reflected in her straightforward choice of makeup" (2). Using terms that allude to the film, such as "driven" and "new direction," this description draws a parallel between Davis and Thelma, aligning Thelma's journey with Davis's new production company and drawing on Thelma's growing knowledge and independence in the film to construct Davis as "blossoming" and "bold." Like the bit of gossip in *People,* however, the blurb quickly asserts that the parallel between Davis and Thelma does not extend to anything other than an independent, "take-charge" femininity (such as robbing convenience stores or choosing death over masculine police authority). The actual article published in this issue, entitled "Straight Shooter" (Rhodes 1991), makes the same two moves:

> Davis formed Genial Productions to develop projects in which she can star. Geena, just like Thelma, is trying to take control of her own destiny. "... I'd like to do more action stuff—maybe even play a cop. I think I have a *knack* for it. It does make me angry that more of those kinds of opportunities aren't out there for women. I'm trying to turn it around in whatever way I can. A lot of actresses are starting their own production companies now, and I guess that's the way to go. If they're not gonna do it for you, do it yourself." (175, emphasis added)

Quite explicitly, the article says Davis is "just like Thelma." The quotation from Davis, in fact, mirrors one of Thelma's lines from the film in which she says she has a "knack" for being an outlaw. But Davis's statement mutes the resistance and the refusal of the law that can be read in Thelma's statement, as her "knack" changes from being an "outlaw" to playing "action roles"; Thelma's resistance to the law becomes Davis's ability to enact the law. In short, *Harper's Bazaar* shifts the resistance both Davis and Thelma pose (to Hollywood, to men in general, to heteronormativity, to the institution of marriage) into a nonthreatening instance of homosocial woman-identified, non-antimale independence.[29]

The Rest of Us Women

As the furor died down in the press and the film's advertising moved from "the year's most sensational and controversial film" to "lay off Thelma and Louise" and finally to "everyone loves Thelma and Louise," the question of whether the film represents "good" or "bad" feminism began to disappear.[30] Later articles about *Thelma and Louise* have no need for this straw argument; they take the film's "feminism" for granted, continue to read Thelma and Louise as independent women who can survive in a "man's world" without challenging men, and then go one step further by using Thelma and Louise as stand-ins for all women, or rather, for specifically class-privileged postfeminist women who have access to both personal and economic independence. Perhaps Lynn Snowden (1992) illustrates this type of representation best in her *Working Woman* article, "Thelma and Louise, Part II." While describing her recent "spa weekend" with a close friend, she writes, "Our weekend would be *Thelma and Louise* without killing someone in the parking lot" (99). Or, I might add, without getting raped or losing one's entire life savings. Not only do Thelma and Louise live on in their freeze-frame of independence, not only do Davis and Sarandon embody their characters' friendship and independence as non-antimale, but Thelma and Louise become icons for all women to emulate. Their independence becomes a discursively constructed postfeminist subject position that hails the woman spectator/reader: to be a woman is to be like Thelma and Louise is to be playfully and nonconfrontationally empowered by spending time and lots of money with one's women friends—but only for a weekend.

Popular discussions that focus more directly on the film's audience generally assume that men feel threatened and women feel empowered by the film. Many articles quote Davis as saying, "If you're feeling threatened, you're identifying with the wrong character" (e.g., Rohter 1991, C24). While Davis's statement implies that men in the audience might identify with, as Charla Krupp (1991) puts it, "the rapist—or the trucker," most articles that discuss the audience simply focus on women, repeatedly constructing images of "real" women who playfully enact (who "are") Thelma and Louise:

> Among women moviegoers, *Thelma and Louise* has tapped a passion that hasn't had a decent outlet since the 70s, when the women's movement was in flower. Last week four women who had seen the film were walking down a Chicago street when a truck driver shouted an obscenity at them. Instantly, all four seized imaginary pistols and aimed them at his head. "*Thelma and Louise* hit Chicago!" yelled one. (Shapiro)

This *Newsweek* article explicitly defines *Thelma and Louise* as offering a feminism through which women can express their resistance to, or at least frustration with, men's sexual harassment without facing the threat of death or retribution, no matter what the narrative and/or legal logic might suggest. Focusing on the film's trucker rather than the rapist, the article emphasizes Thelma and Louise's playful response and, furthermore, replaces their actual pistols with imaginary ones.[31]

In a *New York Times* editorial, Mary Cantwell (1991) offers a similar position for her readers but further curbs the resistance and, like Snowden, depends on class privilege to do so. Cantwell begins by recounting a story about eight recent college graduates who rented a cottage on Cape Cod: "All they wanted to do was lie on the beach, swim if it was warm enough and eat as many lobsters as possible. What they did not want to do was spend any time with the young men . . . who'd rented the house next door." The men, however, "couldn't imagine eight young women choosing to forego the pleasure of their company" and continued harassing the women, finally throwing a brick through a window. As Louise would expect and Thelma learns to expect, when the police arrived they told the women they were inviting the attention by renting the cottage "by themselves." Cantwell tells this story, and then, rather than criticizing the men or the police or discussing the women's response to this treatment, she suggests that these eight women would "enjoy the new movie *Thelma and Louise.*" Cantwell simply juxtaposes this story of sexual assault and police sexism with a quick plot summary of the film, implying that the eight women's experience is similar to Thelma and Louise's experience. By depending on juxtaposition to make her argument, Cantwell drops Thelma and Louise's specific rape experience and the real women's greater economic advantages (cottage on Cape Cod, eating lobsters).

Furthermore, her focus on the women's pursuit of pleasure before the assault (beach, swim, lobsters) and then her suggestion that, after the assault, these women would "enjoy" *Thelma and Louise* emphasize a process of consumption as a means to middle-class women's independence. Cantwell is not just arguing that "the pressures that propel" Thelma and Louise are very "real"; she is also arguing that these women, or any "young women" for that matter, will enjoy the film, will enjoy watching the representation of rape, will enjoy the process of learning the links between language, the gaze, and rape, will enjoy vicariously and playfully destroying *symbols* of men's sexual and social power, and then will enjoy watching women's playful and pleasurable death.

Like the examples from chapter 3 that implicitly invite spectators to fight rape simply by watching narratives about rape, Cantwell's article suggests that watching, consuming, and enjoying a film like *Thelma and Louise* can take the place of activism against sexual harassment or assault and police sexism. While sexual assault *instigates* independent postfeminism, this postfeminism is a freeze-frame of perpetually playful fun that traps Thelma and Louise on the brink of death and "real" women in the pleasurable act of consuming without being antimale. In short, in the popular press's response to *Thelma and Louise*, film viewing becomes the vehicle to women's freedom, while addressing a feminist critique of rape (which I have suggested the film at least gestures toward) appears outmoded and unnecessary.

Feminist Critical Pleasures

> In the end Thelma and Louise defy gravity, gaining mastery of themselves, becoming triumphant in death. The ending is courageous, profound, sublime.
> —Patricia Mellencamp, *A Fine Romance: Five Ages of Film Feminism*

Thelma and Louise opens up the possibility for critical and resistant responses to rape that draw on a feminist-informed understanding of connections among language, the gaze, and rape in both an explicit and everyday sense. Yet, simultaneously, the film includes and its reception emphasizes a playful and pleasurable response to sexual assault (a joyride) that sees feminism as ineffectual or beside the point, rape as inevitable and relatively unimportant, and the damaging effects of assault and resisting assault (like death) as avoidable. In short, I have argued so far that while the film's representation of rape is ambivalent in relation to typical postfeminist rape narratives, working both with and against them, the popular press's response almost exclusively focuses on and extends the ways the film accesses and supports postfeminism's ineffectual versions of feminism.

Recently, when I alluded to this argument about *Thelma and Louise* in a public presentation on the larger project of this book, a feminist scholar who has written on *Thelma and Louise* challenged me, saying (I paraphrase from memory), "How can you call *Thelma and Louise* postfeminist? I *like Thelma and Louise.*" In this last section, I want to address the irritation, anxiety, and possibly even anger that I read in (admittedly, perhaps "into") her comment.[32]

This critic's separation of feminist critical pleasure from postfeminist culture is a common, but I would argue problematic, one. Bonnie J. Dow (1996b), for example, argues that *Designing Women* is less postfeminist than is *Murphy Brown*, because the former represents women bonding while the latter represents an aggressive masculinized woman. But, as I have suggested in my analysis of the popular press response to *Thelma and Louise*, it is precisely the focus on women bonding in the press that diffuses much of the criticism of sexual assault in the film. This representation of "women together" as—*by definition*—feminism, in which I would argue *Designing Women* participates, is a key component of postfeminism's displacement of feminist activism, an aspect of postfeminism that Dow herself identifies.[33] Frankly, I take pleasure in watching *Thelma and Louise* (as does the feminist scholar to whom I refer above), and I will admit that (unlike Dow) I prefer *Murphy Brown* to *Designing Women*, but that does not stop me from identifying ways *all three* contribute to and depend on postfeminism. My point here is that women's pleasures, even feminist pleasures, can be gleaned from postfeminist culture. This is a resistant relationship to postfeminist culture that feminist criticism, I would argue, needs to articulate in order to break postfeminism's stranglehold on popular definitions of what feminism is.[34] In relation to a rape narrative such as *Thelma and Louise*, however, it is *also* imperative, I would argue, that feminist criticism address the role representations of rape play in both postfeminism and feminist critical resistance. I return to this point in the conclusion of the chapter. First, however, I examine some of the ways feminist scholars have taken and offered pleasure in *Thelma and Louise* through their writing, asking how these pleasures relate to the readings of rape in the film and postfeminism in the popular press that I offer above.

Marleen Barr (1991, 1993) and Sharon Willis (1993), in particular, articulate persuasive arguments about the importance of *Thelma and Louise*'s
pleasurable fantasy.[35] For Barr, Thelma and Louise are idealized heroes, driving their car/spaceship away from patriarchy until they leap impossibly *up*
into the Grand Canyon and enter an "alternative text" of feminist science
fiction. She writes, "Thelma and Louise plunge into a magical place of non-
human signification; they enter an alternative text. By doing so, they themselves become fantastic, magical, surrealist. Their car does not adhere to the
laws of gravity; instead of immediately falling, it flies. Thelma and Louise
are no longer brought down by patriarchal law" (1991, 85). Along with
Davis and Sarandon, who think Thelma and Louise may have grabbed onto
something or bounced, Barr specifically rejects the question of "reality"
some critics in the popular press raise. She admits that the male characters
"*truly* exemplify the sorts of men women routinely confront" (1991, 82, emphasis added) but adds that the film is a fantasy, anyway. More specifically,
she defines the film as a "power fantasy" that allows women to escape the
everyday reality the men in the film represent.

Willis (1993) further discusses the relationship of the film's fantasy to
a feminist reading. Refusing to reduce her interpretation to the "reality"
of Thelma and Louise's deaths at the end of the film, she looks at the fantasy of "partiality and disruption" (124) played out along the way. Willis
focuses on the pleasure of "travel, speed, force, and aggression" (125)
that the woman spectator's uncharacteristically non–cross-gender identification provides. While Willis does not unilaterally celebrate this pleasure, recognizing its grounding in consumer capitalism, she does argue,
primarily, for a focus on pleasure in what she calls the "fantasmatic identification" that Thelma and Louise's ride toward the Grand Canyon offers
to women spectators, in particular.

Many other scholars participate in the kind of fantasmatic identification Willis sees the film offering: Cathy Griggers (1993) reads Thelma
and Louise as lesbians who come out during the course of the film;[36] Ann
Putnam (1993) celebrates Thelma and Louise as women who share ownership of the gaze with men; and Cara J. MariAnna (1993) uses Thelma
and Louise as guides who draw the spectator through Native American
mythology and Mary Daly's radical feminism toward a new, nonpatriar-
chal state.[37] Patricia Mellencamp (1995), in her chapter titled "What Cin-
derella and Snow White Forgot to Tell Thelma and Louise," rewrites the
film as a fairy tale that addresses questions such as "What does 'happily'
mean for women? What does 'ever after' cost women?" (8).[38] And, in her

study of self-defense culture, Martha McCaughey (1997) argues that even though *Thelma and Louise* is "not a film about women's self-defense and contained no scene of justifiable violence, images of women's violence, whatever their cinematic context, might help women experience and deploy their bodies along the lines of differently fantasized self-definitions [and] . . . can produce a new body-consciousness complementary to women's self-defense training" (100). Although McCaughey offers a very literalized reading of the film's relationship to "self-defense" and "justifiable violence," she nevertheless claims the power of the film as fantasy to transform women's bodies in a feminist way.[39] Finally, Patricia S. Mann (1994, 1996a, 1996b) claims that *Thelma and Louise* is postfeminist, not feminist, but not in the way I define postfeminism in this book. Mann is one of a very few scholars who embrace postfeminist theory as a theoretically viable political project, as a theoretical move that incorporates postmodernism, addresses the ways the "issues raised by feminists twenty-five years ago have become mainstream concerns" (1996b, 24), and moves toward a "micro-politics."[40] For Mann, postfeminism is a contemporary, updated version of feminism. Thus, when she calls Thelma and Louise postfeminists, she makes a move similar to that of scholars who claim them as feminists. She writes, "Thelma and Louise are postfeminist heroines in their resourceful and courageous response to the unexpected turn their lives have taken. Accepting a gendered struggle on the terms by which it arose, they have seized the micro-political moment and made the most of it, as one must do on frontiers" (1996a, 236).

Other scholars take up *Thelma and Louise* in the process of theorizing specific issues in film studies, particularly genre.[41] In the process, many of them return to the question of the feminist value of the film. For example, Carol J. Clover (1992) argues, on the one hand, that *Thelma and Louise* is a perfect example of a rape-revenge film crossing over from low-budget video distribution to big-budget mainstream distribution.

> In its focus on rape, its construction of males as corporately liable, its overt mistrust of the legal system to prosecute rape, and its interest in self-help (= direct revenge) and sisterhood, *Thelma and Louise* is at dead center of a tradition [of rape-revenge films] that emerged and throve in the lowest sectors of filmmaking for years before it trickled into major studio respectability. (234)

On the one hand, generically *Thelma and Louise* does fit the category of rape-revenge films and does draw on the women's movement to put women in the center of the narrative and to give them the "property" of men: cars, guns, tee-shirts, and jeans. On the other hand, from the perspective of Clover's work on spectatorship in conjunction with genre, she argues that *Thelma and Louise* is a "very, very, safe" (235) film because Hal, as a "point of insertion for the male viewer" (234), belays the need for cross-gender identification for men in the audience. Susan Morrison (1992) is less ambivalent about the film. She explicitly begins her essay on *Thelma and Louise* as an example of the "woman's film" genre by opposing her reading of the film as "potentially progressive" to both popular critics and a fellow feminist who argue that "the film merely substitutes female 'buddies' for male ones in an otherwise conventional and regressive road movie" (48). In response, by shifting the film's generic category, she finds the conclusion an "ironic and conscious" comment on the inevitability in the woman's film of punishment for "women who choose . . . to live outside the socially framed parameters of middle class morality" (52). Also focusing on genre, in this case action cinema, Yvonne Tasker (1993) points out that *Thelma and Louise* is typical of the genre, by "figuring . . . possession of the gun as a symbol of power for women" (26) and representing "a rites-of-passage narrative" (137). But, she argues that the film also undermines and transforms the action genre through its representation of gender, for example by representing "the uniformed cop" not as a representative of the law with which a hero has "at best, a strained relationship" but as a "[caricature] of masculine identity" (62) and by using rape as the mark of "traditional vulnerability of the hero" in action films (151, see also 161). Furthermore, like Morrison, Tasker explicitly sets her own reading up against other (unnamed) critics who would reject the film, in this case for depending on a "masculine" genre. She writes, "Ironically a designation of 'inappropriate' images derived from a feminist critical tradition, coincides here with a more conventional sense of feminine decorum, a sense of knowing one's place within a gendered hierarchy. As much as anything, this critical trajectory reveals the operation within feminist criticism of a class-based, high-cultural, attitude towards the popular cinema" (136). For Tasker, it is important to claim *Thelma and Louise* not only as an action film but also as a potentially valuable action film from a feminist perspective so that she can illustrate how women in action films can transform both that film genre and feminist film criticism.

Pairing Tasker and Morrison, who have related interpretations of *Thelma and Louise* as generically transformative, points to an irony: *Thelma and Louise* can be "reclaimed" for feminism whether defined in the context of the "masculine" action film or in the context of the "feminine" woman's film. Furthermore, as in the popular press, Tasker's and Morrison's use of the oft-repeated feminist critic's need to "reclaim" the film is, in fact, a straw argument. Of the dozens of published scholarly pieces on the film, many of which I discuss here, the large majority argue that the film *does* provide feminist pleasures.[42] In short, *Thelma and Louise* is an extremely versatile film for feminist film critics, transforming both the most masculine and most feminine genres, accessing pleasurable fantasies of escape from patriarchal law, providing women with non–cross-gender identification, telling lesbian coming-out narratives, claiming the gaze for women, engaging in mythic cycles of beginnings, rewriting fairy tales, reshaping women's body-consciousness and deployment, illustrating micro-political action, infusing mainstream Hollywood with the concerns of the lowest sectors of filmmaking, and (to add my own argument to the list) identifying and challenging the pervasiveness of sexual assault in women's everyday lives. For feminist film scholars, while the popular press may "post" the feminism in the film, *Thelma and Louise* is still available for alternative feminist uses.

Conclusion

What then is *Thelma and Louise*'s relationship to postfeminist rape narratives? Does it test or does it reinscribe the limits of postfeminism? It is easiest to answer these questions in relation to the discursive reception of the film. The popular reviews and articles sometimes notice that the film depicts a "would-be" rape, but they go no further. Although rape precipitates the narrative and the women's bonding, the popular discussion focuses on the narrative effects of rape while dissociating those effects from sexual assault as the film's narrative fulcrum. This move in the popular discourses allows them easily to draw on and contribute to postfeminist celebrations of women's independence, distinct from any attention to what women may want to be independent *of*. In this context, because the popular press addresses, questions, and then overwhelmingly embraces what it defines as (a particular kind of) feminism in the film, *Thelma and Louise* functions as an ideal example of a postfeminist film.

Nevertheless, as many scholarly critics have shown, the film offers much more to feminism than the popular press takes up. Thus, one thing the collective scholarship on *Thelma and Louise* reveals is that no matter how large a mass media spectacle a film becomes, no matter how fierce the debates (even if they are straw arguments), the text itself is potentially more complex and radical than the hundreds of articles about it can ever show. In this case, even though the popular press closes down potential feminisms in the film, characterizing it as either a direct reversal (in search of equality) or a nonconfrontational bonding experience of non-antimale consumption, the scholarly press opens up the potential feminism in the film, importing spaceships, lesbians, and fairy tale characters into the diegetic world in order to envision that world differently.

As much as I do take pleasure in imagining Louise's car as a spaceship, Thelma and Louise as engaging in lesbian desire, and the film to be a rewritten feminist fairy tale, these scholarly critical interventions are nevertheless a little too close to the responses in the popular press for my comfort—at least in terms of the representation of rape. Like the mainstream press's pleasures, these feminist critical pleasures depend on rape as a legitimating reason, a narrative cause, but do not address what it means for feminism to depend on the representation of rape in order to access these particular pleasures. Thus, for example, even as I read Thelma and Louise through the lens of lesbian desire and against the grain of the pervasive heterosexuality in the text, I worry that it takes a man's rape of a woman to unleash that desire in the text.[43] In short, I am not arguing against taking any number of feminist pleasures in the text, but I am arguing for understanding how those pleasures depend on representations of rape and thus may contribute to the naturalization of rape in our representational world. When feminist pleasures elide rape, they contribute to the culturally structured absent presence of rape that precludes a critical confrontation with rape in postfeminist discourses and perpetuates a long-standing narrative dependence on rape. If feminist scholarship does not address this process, it may inadvertently collude with the many ways post-1980 rape films and television shows use rape in the service of constructing and maintaining particular versions of feminism.[44]

That leaves me with analyses of *Thelma and Louise* that directly address the sexual violence in the film: in particular, McCaughey's, Clover's, and my own.[45] Collectively, these analyses suggest that while the film depicts rape in a way that is potentially transformative from a feminist perspective, that transformation is limited. For McCaughey, while the images of violent women can help women transform their bodies, especially "if [they] already feel vulnerable to men precisely because they do not see images of women prevailing over men, and in fact routinely see the opposite" (100), the film nevertheless avoids a direct representation of women's violence as legitimate self-defense. While McCaughey herself articulates the power of fantasy here, she also implies a need for what I would call "practical" representations as well. Working more directly in the context of film studies than is McCaughey, Clover and I each place *Thelma and Louise* in relation to a set of rape narratives. For Clover, in the context of a tradition of rape-revenge films, *Thelma and Louise* is not only not unique in its representation of women's revenge for rape, it is relatively tame in its confrontation of the spectator with the act of revenge. For me, in the analysis in the first section of this chapter, *Thelma and Louise*'s representation of rape as pervasive and rape law as ineffectual may take it further than most contemporary postfeminist rape narratives that individualize rape and then show women as empowered when they overcome that individual rape. Nevertheless, I see the film as supporting many other aspects of postfeminist representations of rape, in particular the centrality of whiteness and an obsession with rape as inevitably linked to women's independence.

Overall, then, I argue that *Thelma and Louise* illuminates, tests, *and* reinscribes the limits of postfeminism to varying degrees in at least three contexts: the film itself, the popular reception, and the scholarly response. My particular approach to feminist criticism here has been neither to claim the film as feminist nor to reject it as non- or antifeminist. Rather, my goals have been to look at the multiple ways the film—as both text and media event—interacts with feminism and to examine the roles rape plays in those various interactions. By offering a sustained analysis of rape and its relationship to feminism in this film-as-media-event, I hope to have simultaneously highlighted the ways *Thelma and Louise* challenges postfeminism and cautioned against a feminist critical celebration of the film that does not take into account the role rape plays in enabling that celebration.

5

Persistently Displaced

Black Women in Rape Narratives

> The institutionalized rape of black women has never been as power-
> ful a symbol of black oppression as the spectacle of lynching.
> —Hazel Carby, quoted in Darlene Clark Hine, "Rape and
> the Inner Lives of Black Women"

> Rape law reform measures that do not in some way engage and
> challenge the narratives that are read onto Black women's bodies are
> unlikely to affect the way cultural beliefs oppress Black women in
> rape trials.   —Kimberlé Crenshaw, "Mapping the Margins"

> Relying on the *visibility* of African American women to generate the
> *invisibility* of exclusionary practices or racial segregation, this new
> politics produces remarkably consistent Black female disadvantage
> while claiming to do the opposite.
> —Patricia Hill Collins, "The More Things Change,
> the More They Stay the Same"

This chapter looks at a series of post-1980 films and television shows that represent a relationship between Black women and rape.[1] My choice of this critical focus speaks back to postfeminism, challenging its pervasive whiteness and thus further exploring its boundaries and limitations. I choose to focus on representations of Black women in particular here for two reasons. First, to address all women of color would be too general, as each racialized group has a specific relationship to feminism, postfeminism, and the history of rape in the United States and in U.S. media. In order to offer a sufficiently nuanced and detailed discussion that takes into account variability as well as issues of class, sexuality, and nationality in relation to gender and race (at least in the case of the topic of rape), I consider it necessary to focus on one particular racialized group. Second, I choose to focus on representations of Black women in particular because in contemporary U.S. film and television rape narratives they are the second most common racialized group of women to appear, after white women.[2] This is in part because the U.S. media often construct race as a black/white binary (e.g., Friedman 1995; Perea 1997) and in part because of the central role rape has played in the history of African Americans (including slavery) and in antiracist activism, particularly in terms of false accusations of African American men as rapists (e.g., Crenshaw 1991). My point in focusing on Black women in this chapter is not to begin a "catalog" that could be continued with separate chapters on Latinas, Chicanas, Asian Americans, Native Americans, Arab Americans, Jews, and other racialized groups. Rather, my goal here, as it is in the previous and subsequent chapters, is to turn a critical eye on a topic that helps break apart the hegemony of postfeminism, while simultaneously addressing the complexity and specificity of representations of rape in late-twentieth-century popular culture, in this case in terms of race.

In this introduction, I describe three contexts in which films and television shows that represent a relationship between Black women and rape can be understood. First, these narratives can be understood in relation to the intersection of racial and gender oppression in the sexual violence African American women have experienced historically in the United States, particularly during slavery and in the context of domestic work, and in relation to African American women's antirape activism. Second, these films and television shows can be understood in relation to a broad field of contemporary representations of Blackness in which African American women often have, as Michele Wallace (1990) puts it, "high *visibility*" combined with an "almost total lack of *voice*" (5). Finally, these representations of rape can be understood in relation to the pervasiveness of postfeminism and whiteness in the majority of post-1980 film and television representations of rape that I discuss in chapter 3. Each of these contexts helps illuminate the specificity of the representations I examine in this chapter.

Many African American feminist scholars show how rape has been pervasive in African American women's lives historically, while concomitantly the U.S. legal system, antiracist activism, and most recently (white) feminism downplay or ignore African American women's experiences of rape. Catherine Clinton (1994), for example, argues that "slavery systematically fostered patterns of sexual violence" (206) such that "slaves saw rape as part of a continuum of humiliation, coercion, and abuse" (210). Concomitant with the pervasive threat or experience of sexual violence, as the law was written in most states, women slaves could not technically be raped (e.g., Wriggins 1983; Sommerville 1995). When rape was discussed postslavery, both public discourses and antiracist activism focused primarily on African American men accused of raping white women (Smith 1990).[3] Antilynching activism addressed the irony that false accusations of rape were used to justify the lynching of African American men while, in fact, most lynching was a response to something other than African American men's actual sexuality (such as owning property, voting, or in any other way "crossing the color line" [e.g., Hodes 1993]). Activists also addressed the fact that in the courts, "legal lynching" led to a disproportionate use of the death penalty against African American men convicted of rape (Wriggins).

Despite this focus on African American men in many antiracist discussions of rape, African American women continued to face rape and the threat of rape not only in the context of their family and community lives (as do all women) but also in explicitly racialized contexts by the Klan (e.g., Hodes; Smith, 156) and by their white higher-class employers (particularly in domestic work) (e.g., Wriggins; Hine 1989). As Angela Y. Davis (1985) puts it, "Throughout Afro-American women's economic history in this country . . . sexual abuse has been perceived as an occupational hazard" (8).[4] Darlene Clark Hine (1989) theorizes that this experience led to "the development of a culture of dissemblance among Black women," which she defines as "behavior and attitudes of Black women that created the appearance of openness and disclosure but actually shielded the truth of their inner lives and selves from their oppressors" (912). The impact of these racialized social structures that include rape is borne out by statistics from the second half of the twentieth century that show African American women are more likely to be raped than are white women, but they are less likely to access the criminal justice system. Furthermore, if they do enter the justice system, they are less likely to be considered credible witnesses, leading to a lower conviction rate for the men who raped them (e.g., Clinton, Wriggins, Crenshaw). In addition to racialized social structures that encourage and allow for the rape of African American women, such as slavery and domestic work, scholars argue that these disproportionate statistics are a result of persistent cultural depictions of Black women as, by definition, sexually promiscuous, always already sexually desirous, and therefore unrapable (e.g., Wriggins; Collins 1998; Smith, 159; Crenshaw).

Black women's activism against rape has addressed the specificities I only briefly describe above. For example, Darlene Hine and Kate Wittenstein (1981) discuss the use of refusal, abortion, and even sometimes infanticide by Black women during slavery to resist the use of their bodies for sexual and reproductive purposes. And, at the turn of the twentieth century, the National Association of Colored Women's Clubs (NACW) made one of their primary goals an attack on "negative [and] derogatory" stereotypes (Hine, 917), many of which at least implicitly defined Black women as excessively sexual and therefore unrapable. Additionally, the NACW argued for women's suffrage in part to provide African American women with a means to protect themselves against rape (Hine).

Black feminist antirape activism also includes a critique of the more visible (in popular culture) implicitly white antirape movement. For example, Davis (1985) argues that the existence of the "myth of the Black rapist" makes it difficult for Black women to join a "multiracial antirape movement" that seeks to bring rapists into the justice system, since most men blamed for rape are African American and most rapes discussed are of white women (7).[5] Furthermore, she points out that "the experience of Black women has been that the very same white policeman who would supposedly protect them from rape, will sometimes go so far as to rape Black women in their custody" (10). Additionally, like other women of color who experience rape by men in their own communities, African American women who report rape by African American men (the majority of rapes African American women experience) face the possibility of being "disregarded" or "vilified within the African-American community" (Crenshaw, 1273). In response, Kimberlé Crenshaw (1991) suggests potential changes in rape trials, such as "expanding the scope of voir dire to examine jurors' attitudes toward Black rape victims" or including "expert testimony" about the specificity of African American women's experience of rape analogous to the expert testimony that is now accepted about "battered women's syndrome and the rape trauma syndrome" (1271).[6]

As many scholars point out and as I will develop in more detail in some of my analysis in this chapter, the history of African American women's particular experience of rape and cultural narratives about "black male animalism" (Smith, 161) and Black women as sexually promiscuous and thus unrapable persist (even if in sometimes more veiled forms) in the present. Both Crenshaw and Valerie Smith (1990) refer to the treatment of the 1989 "Central Park jogger" case in the press as evidence of "vestiges" (Crenshaw, 1267) of these cultural narratives.[7] Scholars also point to the racial solidarity that emerged around Mike Tyson— but not around Desiree Washington—during Tyson's trial and conviction for raping Washington (e.g., Crenshaw, 1274). Robyn Wiegman (1993) makes a similar link of the history of lynching as a "disciplinary tool" and as a "narrativizing context that . . . propels the white crowd to action" with George Bush's use of the figure of Willie Horton in a 1988 anti-Dukakis campaign ad.[8] Other scholars link historical representations to the more contemporary cases of Yusuf Hawkins (e.g., Hodes; Crenshaw) and Tawana Brawley (Smith).

Collectively, these examples' primary emphasis on the white female victim illustrates that "certain women's bodies are more valuable than others" (Smith, 162) in contemporary culture and law. They illustrate the "silence" (Smith, Crenshaw, Wallace) and invisibility surrounding African American women's experiences of rape and African American women in popular culture generally, despite relatively high-profile cases like Tyson/Washington and Tawana Brawley.[9] For example, Patricia Hill Collins (1998) argues that, on the one hand, "poor Black women become intensely 'raced'" and thus "become icons for Black women as a collectivity" (36).[10] On the other hand, wealthy and/or successful African American women, such as the fictional Claire Huxtable of *The Cosby Show*, represent the "Black Lady Overachiever" (39) and remain relatively "'unraced' and assimilated" (38). On this end of the spectrum, the representation of an African American woman's blackness serves only to illustrate the possibility of making it, of leaving behind the highly raced experience of poor African American women in order to fit into (white middle-class) society. The existence of this type of representation, then, can effectively neutralize any claim of racial and gender discrimination that a successful African American woman, such as Anita Hill or Bari-Ellen Roberts, might make.[11] Thus, "the success of selected unraced individual middle-class Black women becomes highly visible in blaming intensely raced poor Black women for their own poverty." Both figures "obscure the workings of institutional power" and "the experiences of the majority of actual African-American women, namely, working-class Black women who fall into neither category" (Collins, 42). Collins further argues that "overlaying this new politics of containment is a rhetoric of tolerance, claiming that race and other such categories no longer matter" (35).

Here, Collins offers an idea analogous to my discussion of postfeminist discourses about women when she argues that the particular ways African American people are represented in popular culture disavow any other version of African American experience and insist on the existence of a "colorblind" (Crenshaw) society. In this context, African American women "remain visible yet silenced" (Collins, 38). Wahneema Lubiano (1995), focusing on blackness generally, makes a similar point, arguing that "hypervisibility, the very publicness of black people as a social fact, works to undermine the possibility of actually seeing black specificity" (187). Furthermore, Lubiano points out that the hypervisibility often depends on marks of realism. Thus the poor African American woman and successful African American woman that Collins describes, for example, become even more embedded in popular culture as marks of "reality" or "truth." Overall, Lubiano calls the cultural representations and narratives she describes a "spectacle of race" (187). One might also call this construction of race a cipher.[12] A particular representation of an African American character, then, can simultaneously stand in for all African Americans, for the reality (whether of poverty or success) of all African Americans, *and* for a universal human nature that somehow transcends race. As Lubiano puts it, "Some representations actually empty out race specifics—at the same time they inscribe racialized generalities—leaving narrative vessels that could be anything, could revolve around anyone" (196).

Each of the issues I discuss above—the persistence of the historical representation of African American women as enigmas and the emphasis on the racism African American men experience in relation to rape, as well as the contemporary representation of African American women as highly visible yet simultaneously silenced, of a color-blind assimilated culture in which race no longer matters, and the possibility that race can function as a spectacle and an individual African American character or person as a cipher—helps to explain how infrequently African American women appear in postfeminist narratives. Furthermore, as I argue in chapter 2, even when postfeminist texts do include African American women, they are primarily what Herman Gray (1995) calls assimilationist texts: the African American women have been incorporated into a culture of pervasive whiteness that masquerades as color-blind. More specifically, as I show in chapter 3, postfeminist rape narratives depict rape as a universal experience for women, emphasizing deracialized narratives in which, for example, women generally (but white women implicitly) face the dilemma of acquaintance rape and the court's assumption that they may not have said "no" clearly or loudly enough, confront their responsibility to speak up and use the legal system to protect all women from future rape, or experience post-rape traumas such as the hospital rape kit and an overwhelming need to shower. None of these standard postfeminist representations of rape pays attention to a particular experience of racialized *and* gendered violence.[13]

In the remainder of this chapter, I examine post-1980 film and television representations of Black women's relationship to rape—with the history of African American women's experience of rape and the contemporary field of representations of blackness and postfeminism in mind—in order to further interrogate the boundaries and limitations of postfeminism. I ask, If so many postfeminist rape narratives center whiteness, what happens when gender and race intersect more explicitly in rape narratives? How does the field of representations of blackness and the visible silence of African American women in particular impact these representations? What role, if any, does the history of African American women's specific experience of rape as detailed by African American feminist scholars and activists play in the forms these narratives and representations take? In short, what happens to the representations of Black women, of rape, and of postfeminism when gender and race collide in contemporary rape narratives?

In order to answer these questions, I divide my analysis into three sections. First, I examine texts that displace Black women from narratives explicitly about race and racism, even when they themselves experience the rape on which the narrative depends. In these examples, generally, a Black woman's rape is a highly visible aspect of the text, while attention to her response is conspicuously absent. In some cases, texts write Black women out of the rape scenario altogether, implicitly contributing to cultural definitions of Black women as unrapable and of Black men as those most endangered by rape. While some of these texts intersect with postfeminism, the majority of them separate their emphasis on race from an examination of any kind of feminism.

In the second section of my analysis, I focus on texts that do incorporate postfeminism. Here, I argue that African American women in these narratives either exist next-to-but-just-outside the postfeminist aspects of the narrative or, occasionally, lead to alterations in the standard postfeminist rape narratives. Ironically, unlike in general postfeminist discourses such as those I describe in chapter 2, African American women are *not* generally assimilated into whiteness in postfeminist *rape* narratives. Rather, the texts maintain postfeminism's whiteness by distancing African American women's racialization from the postfeminist aspects of the narratives.

For these first two sections of my analysis, I draw on examples that I consider to be representative of the rape narratives including Black women that have appeared in U.S. film and television since the early 1980s. As in chapter 3, for each example I mention, other possible examples may come to mind that illustrate the same or related modes of representation. My point is not to be exhaustive but to address what I consider to be the major ways representations of Black women intersect with rape in recent popular film and television.

Nevertheless, it is important to point out that the number of texts from which I draw my examples in this chapter is just a tiny fraction of the number from which I draw in chapter 3. Overall, whiteness is by far the dominant racialization of rape in late-twentieth-century fictional films and television shows. Thus, simply by focusing exclusively on Black women in this chapter, I am responding to and resisting the pervasiveness of postfeminism's whiteness. Additionally, by focusing my attention on Black women's experiences of rape in these examples, I hope to draw attention to the possibility that these films and television shows offer a challenge to the historical representation of Black women as unrapable. From this perspective, I ask, What do these texts say about the rapability of Black women?

The final section of the chapter examines the most nuanced representations of African American women's relationship to rape of all the widely distributed films and television shows released in the past twenty years or so. The films are *Rosewood* (1996), *She's Gotta Have It* (1986), and *Daughters of the Dust* (1991).[14] Nevertheless, I argue that, despite the relative complexity of these texts, they continue to depend on many of the modes of representation I describe in the first two sections of the chapter, particularly the centrality of Black *men's* experience of rape.

Overall, then, whether texts focus on issues of race and racism, draw on postfeminism, or strive for analytical nuance in relation to gender, race, rape, and their intersections, they still persistently displace Black women. As my analysis in this chapter shows, collectively these displacements are complex, nuanced, and varied, making them all the more versatile. In response, in the discussion that follows, I focus attention on and center Black women as a mode of critical analysis that resists their persistent displacement.

Race and Racism

The following examples displace Black women and their experiences of rape from the particular stories they tell about race, while often using rapes of Black women to initiate those same stories. These displacements take a variety of forms, defining Black women's experience of rape as a historical problem that is no longer relevant,[15] as a problem that helps reveal white men's villainous racism, or as a problem that affects Black men more seriously than it affects Black women. In each case, the texts neither center nor explore the rapes of the Black women they represent.

Former Rape

An episode of *Dr. Quinn, Medicine Woman* (March 26, 1994) (a television show set in late-nineteenth-century Colorado) provides an example of both historical and metaphorical displacement of African American women from the rape narrative. In this episode, out-of-town members of the Ku Klux Klan attack Grace, an African American woman who owns and runs the only café in town. The assault scene is melodramatic, with crosscutting between Grace working at her café alone and Robert E, her husband, fixing up the house they have just purchased. The Klan has come to town, in fact, in response to this African American couple's purchase of property. Thus, the juxtaposition of Robert E as he works on the house, illustrating his refusal to give up his "right" to own property, with Grace's suffering as a result of his insistence heightens the pathos. While Robert E is unaware of Grace's plight, the editing, melodramatic music, and extreme close-ups naturalize his sudden realization that something is wrong. But, he is too late. By the time he arrives at the café, the Klan has already attacked Grace. Robert E, while trying to function as a protector here, is ineffectual. With both Grace and Robert E powerless in the face of the Klan's racism, the text emphasizes the history of the Klan's violent response to African American property owners, while simultaneously making both Grace and Robert E hypervictims who are completely innocent and entirely unable to defend themselves.

In particular, the fact that the Klan's attack is unambiguous and fully onscreen intensifies the portrayal of Grace's victimization. Admittedly, the Klan men do not literally rape Grace. Instead, the figurative rape consists of hooded Klan men cutting off her long hair with a knife. This violence functions as a metaphorical rape because of the status of Grace's long hair as a mark of her femininity and sexuality. Although she always pins her hair up (in fact until this moment, the series never draws attention to Grace's hair), thus de-emphasizing her femininity and emphasizing her businesslike demeanor, at this moment, her hair comes loose and she is reduced to her feminine body. The sudden appearance of Grace's long hair places her in a very specific relationship to the white feminine sexuality the show generally centers. Dr. Quinn, the central character, has long strawberry blonde hair that she almost always wears down. Characters often comment on her hair's beauty, and her costume and performance draw attention to it as a mark of her sexuality and sexual attraction to her primary suitor and later husband, Sully. On *Dr. Quinn*, then, long hair equals feminine sexuality.[16] The sudden appearance of Grace's long hair thus introduces sexuality into the Klan's attack. In this context, not only does the violence done to her hair highlight her sexual vulnerability, but it also intensifies the episode's condemnation of the history of Klan violence.

Despite this condemnation of a particular aspect of U.S. history, the *metaphorical* nature of the rape also deflects the white out-of-towner men's villainy to a certain extent. While they are clearly evil men, they do not physically hurt Grace; they simply cut off her hair. Additionally, the townsmen, who temporarily join the Klan but do not take part in the attack on Grace, can subsequently reject the organization and thus avoid their own villainization through only temporary association with the Klan. In short, while the text acknowledges a history of white men as rapists of African American women, it does so by constructing a particular history of the Klan, one that distances the problem from the present and diffuses the violence through metaphor. One can even read the metaphorical nature of the rape to *disavow* the violent nature of the Klan. From this perspective, I would point out that the Klan, in fact, does *not* literally rape Grace.

Evil White Men

The evil white men in this episode of *Dr. Quinn* are, in fact, common in texts that deal with interracial rape of Black women. For example, the film *A Time to Kill* (1996) represents purely evil white men, opposing them to a purely innocent African American girl-child. The white men's rape of her not only highlights these opposing depictions, but sets a narrative in motion that offers surficial attention to the spectacle of race while simultaneously addressing in more detail a color-blind morality around men's (actual and imagined) response to the rape of their daughters. The film thus uses and then shifts attention away from African American women, focusing instead on the excessive evilness of (some) white men and on a narrative about deracialized fatherhood and masculinity through which a different white man is redeemed.

The very first moments of the film announce the danger of white racism. Discordant music plays behind the credits and then continues over a shot of an empty field and the additional sound of birds singing. Suddenly, a loud pickup roars by. The two white men in the truck appear in numerous quick, close shots as the truck bounces along. A Confederate flag, a gun on a gun rack, beer, and cigarettes are visible in various frames, as are the men's greasy hair and general unkempt appearance. When the men pass two African American men playing basketball, they call them "boys" and threaten to shoot them as they throw a beer bottle, which breaks against the backboard. These white men are overdetermined as pure, unequivocal racists, perfect villains to conduct the rape that will set the narrative in motion. Setting up a contrast between an idyllic pastoral setting and a violent threat, this opening leads into a rape scene in which stereotypical poor southern white men rape a young African American girl, Tonya.

Crosscutting reveals a well-kept African American girl, hair in neat pigtails, shopping for groceries at a store and speaking politely with the clerk. As the two narrative lines come together, the pickup truck disturbs Tonya, walking along a quiet country road with her groceries, when she hears it approaching her from behind. A well-behaved child, she immediately moves to the side of the road, but the conversation inside the truck reveals that the men will not pass by quietly. Their dialogue contributes to their hypervillainous status, as they discuss whether or not she is "too young." Thus, not only are they racists, not only are they rapists, but they are racist child-rapists. Their evilness and her innocence contrast so as to compound one another: each renders the other more iconic.

During the rape scene, Tonya's body is fragmented or, sometimes, absent altogether when objects and one word stand in for her victimization and innocence. Nevertheless, as in *Dr. Quinn*, the violence is onscreen and explicit. For example, when the men throw a beer bottle at her, beginning the assault, a shot of her groceries falling to the ground stands in for a possible image of her fall. Extreme close-ups, a shaky and blurry camera, and quick cuts show her feet and hands being tied with rope. The rope intensifies the violence of the rape, evoking an image reminiscent of slavery and of the noose of postslavery lynchings. Everything about the men's behavior suggests that they are much more interested in violence toward African Americans than in sex, and their use of the rope underscores this.

In this film a girl initially represents the innocence of African Americans faced with racist white southerners, but after the rape African American women—even girls—no longer matter. Even when Tonya has been found and is with her mother, it is not until her father, Carl Lee Hailey, arrives that Tonya speaks and that the full horror of the event is articulated. When Carl Lee arrives, a close-up reveals his pained face as Tonya's mother cries offscreen and Tonya apologizes for dropping the groceries. The emphasis on men's experience of the rape of "their" women, or more accurately "their" daughters, continues when Carl Lee approaches Jake Brigance, a young white lawyer, and asks, "Jake, if I was in a jam, you'd help me out, wouldn't you?" Carl Lee all but tells Jake, his future lawyer, that he plans to kill the rapists by evoking the image of the vulnerable daughter and asking Jake what he would do if this had happened to his child. While the film makes it clear that racism leads to the rape and undoubtedly will prevent Carl Lee from getting a fair trial in this particular southern town, it is nonracialized masculinity, or more accurately paternity, that is at issue here: Carl Lee is just as interested in what Jake would do as in what he himself is about to do.[17] Furthermore, since the film represents this perspective as an African American man's, it more aggressively claims nonracist color-blindness. Thus, while the film repeatedly draws attention to race and racism and makes race a spectacle, racism is not the central narrative issue. Instead, an abstract concept of morality structures the narrative. For Carl Lee, morality means that because racism will prevent justice, he must kill the rapists. For Jake, morality means that because he would want to do the same if his own daughter were raped (regardless of race), he must defend Carl Lee.

Conveniently, the rape of an overdetermined innocent child whom Jake can consequently deracialize makes it possible for him to win Carl Lee's case. In his closing arguments, Jake asks the jury to close their eyes and imagine the rape scene as he describes it. He says that the rape "shatter[ed] everything innocent and pure" and describes both the scenes depicted in the opening of the film and additional acts of violence to which the spectator had not yet had access.[18] Communicating his own emotional connection to the story, he begins to cry, insisting, "Can you see her? . . . I want you to picture that little girl." Then, after a dramatic pause, he says, "Now imagine she's white." By asking the jurors to imagine a white girl being raped, he renders the rape of an African American girl all the more horrific. With this line, he simultaneously racializes and deracializes Tonya: he reminds the jury (and the audience) that she is African American and that the rape was racist, but he also insists that the violation of a man's child goes beyond race and racism, is a moral crime (against the father as much as against the daughter) that calls for the rapists' death (at the hands of the father). Furthermore, if the jury (or the audience) had been considering finding Carl Lee guilty, Jake's strategy makes it difficult, if not impossible, for them to maintain this position without also seeing their perspective as grounded in racism.

Throughout the film, race is a ploy to articulate a liberal veneer while the real story is about the moral purity of men (regardless of race) protecting their daughters. The overdetermined evilness of the racist rapists, the overdetermined innocence of the African American girl-child, and the explicit onscreen violence of the rape legitimate a story in which an African American man teaches a white man about his right, or rather his moral duty, to protect his daughter and to defend any other man who does so, *regardless of race*. Thus, while the film seems to "scream" "this story is about race!" throughout and while it depends on a gendered and racialized rape as narrative catalyst, in the end the film is most concerned with Jake's imagined role as avenger of the imagined rape of his (white) daughter.[19]

The Tragedy of Rape for Black Men

A third type of representation ignores Black women's experience of rape by placing Black men center stage. One example of this displacement takes place in narratives about false accusations of African American men for the rape of white women; these texts take a masculine perspective on condemning racism and remove African American women from the rape scenario altogether. For instance, *Jungle Fever* (1991) offers a critique of the racist assumption that an African American man is necessarily a rapist.[20] In one scene, two central characters who are having an affair—Angie, an Italian American woman, and Flipper, an African American man—play fight in the street. Flipper pretends to overpower Angie after she hits at him, and she laughs and enjoys the game. Based on the progression of the narrative, Angie and Flipper are clearly both consenting (indeed, their interaction is part of a growing romance); however, an overhead shot emphasizes not what they are experiencing but what an offscreen character assumes is happening: an African American man is raping a white woman. The offscreen character who watches the scene ostensibly makes a standard racist assumption and then calls the police. When the police arrive and put their gun to Flipper's head, Angie protests, saying, "But he's my boyfriend." While they eventually do convince the police that nothing is wrong, Flipper is furious with Angie for saying publicly that they are lovers. From Angie's perspective, as a white woman, her consent is sufficient to guarantee the absence of rape and Flipper's subsequent safety. From Flipper's perspective, however, as an African American man, he knows that her consent may make little difference once he has been accused of rape.

Through their focus on African American men, false accusation narratives leave African American women out of the rape scenario altogether; however, even the rape of a Black woman can lead to narrative attention focused directly on a tragic Black man.[21] For example, during the spring of 1999 several episodes of the television show *ER* included a continuing story line about Mobalage and Kubby Ekabo, a Black couple from Nigeria. In these episodes, Dr. Mark Greene, in particular, interacts with Mobalage, who works as a janitor in the hospital. Almost immediately Mark realizes that something is wrong with Mobalage, and eventually Mobalage admits he is impotent. In the February 4, 1999, episode Mark examines Mobalage, sees massive scars on his back, and assumes (correctly) that he was tortured in Nigeria before coming to the United States. Mark sends Mobalage to a specialist, who prescribes a back surgery that will most likely cure his impotence.

The impending surgery then sets up a multi-episode narrative imperative for Kubby to speak of her prior rape. When Kubby learns that Mobalage will be able to have sexual relations again, she tells nurse Carol Hathaway, "I don't know if I can." Kubby then says that when her husband was arrested in Nigeria for being a student leader, a group of ten soldiers came to their home and each raped her "all night and into the next day." Although Carol says that Kubby should tell Mobalage, Kubby says, "I never told him. . . . It would kill him." Carol immediately discusses the case with Mark, and they agree that the Ekabos need therapy with someone who "specializes in post-traumatic stress disorder in torture victims."

On the one hand, when Kubby tells her about her torture, Carol responds with horror and sympathy; in fact, the editing and cinematography suggest a critique of Mark and Carol's earlier neglect of Kubby's desire to ask questions about the surgery, and Mark and Carol *could* be referring to Kubby's experience of rape as the torture that produced "post-traumatic stress disorder." On the other hand, because no one ever defines the rapes as torture but several characters do repeatedly name Mobalage's experience as such and because Kubby's dialogue shifts attention to Mobalage when she says that speaking of *her* rape would kill *him*, the narrative remains principally concerned with Mobalage. Furthermore, the narrative dispenses with Kubby altogether when later in the episode she arrives at the hospital with stab wounds; Kubby remains in a coma as a result of the wounds for a large portion of the remaining story line. The police officer who brings Kubby in says her husband "freaked out" and jumped out a window. Mark immediately assumes—incorrectly—that Mobalage stabbed Kubby when she told him about the rapes. Because Kubby is in a coma and Mobalage is not speaking, there is no one to correct Mark's assumption. Instead, the episode reveals Mobalage's suffering but emphasizes Mark and Carol's perspective on that suffering.

In the next episode in which the Ekabos appear (March 25, 1999), Mobalage has been brought to the ER from jail because he has refused to eat. Mark and Carol tend to him while Mark talks to him continuously, telling him Kubby has a good chance of coming out of her coma and that he knows Mobalage did not mean to hurt her, that "your response was out of your control." Mobalage does not speak either to confirm or to disconfirm Mark's interpretation of the events. When Kubby wakes from her coma, however, she immediately corrects Mark's false assumption, telling him that she tried to kill *herself*. Unlike early in the February 18, 1999, episode, when the spectator has access to Kubby's experience, from the second half of that episode up until this moment in the subsequent episode the spectator is encouraged to take Mark's perspective. Not only does his use of medical terminology (e.g., post-traumatic stress disorder) suggest this, but Mobalage's statement before he is arrested—"What have I done?"—and his silence in the face of Mark's accusations (no matter how sympathetically made) all encourage the spectator to assume Mobalage did try to kill Kubby. Thus, when she utters the truth almost immediately upon waking from her coma, both Mark and the invited spectator's first response is to worry about *Mobalage*, to feel sympathy for his unjust time spent in jail, heightened by knowledge of his prior experience of incarceration and torture in Nigeria. In short, the particular positioning of Kubby in the narrative depends on the plot elements of her rape and then her attempted suicide to move the narrative forward, but her experience is subsumed by Mobalage's suffering.

In fact, as soon as Mark understands what happened, he realizes that Mobalage ran when the police arrived because of his experiences in Nigeria. When Mark tells Mobalage this, Mobalage begins to speak to him again. He tells Mark that the soldiers "raped her because of me." His discussion and Mark's response support a definition of torture during war as something that happens to men. By extension, the rape of women becomes part of that torture of men. In this series of episodes, then, the rape of a Black woman leads Mark to help a Black man face his past. While the rape is central to the narrative, and while the narration early on seems to criticize Mark and Carol for neglecting Kubby, by the end of the story line the narration suggests that that neglect was a problem only because it prevented Mark from really understanding *Mobalage's* tragic experience.

Many of the examples I describe here lead to particular types of representations that are specific to depictions of Black women and rape and that support the texts' overall displacements of Black women. For example, the emphasis on rape as a problem only for African American girl-children leads to a hypervictimization of the African American girl-child and directs possible attention away from adult African American women's experience of rape. Relatedly, an African American girl's pure innocence can help hypervilify white men as racist rapists. These overdetermined representations use race as a spectacle sometimes to teach a history "lesson" (about the Klan, for example) and sometimes, ironically, to shift attention back to masculinity—either villainous white masculinity, morally advanced color-blind masculinity, or tragic Black masculinity. Additionally, while the hypervictimization of the innocent African American woman or child can be read to replace and critique problematic representations of African American women as hypersexual—by definition—these representations *also* produce a particularly victimized African American female subject. Such stories portray African American women as passive subjects, not as active agents.

While hypervictimization, paradoxically, diverts attention away from African American women's experiences of rape in *Dr. Quinn* and *A Time to Kill*, African American women are perhaps most thoroughly displaced in texts concerned with criticizing the myth of the Black rapist. Although the white man as protector and the African American woman as sexually promiscuous and therefore unrapable are equally important characters in the maintenance of this myth (e.g., Davis 1981a, Smith), the texts examined here, like the antiracist work against lynching discussed above, exclude African American women altogether through their antiracist focus on African American men. Furthermore, although *ER* includes a Black woman in a rape scenario about a tragic Black man, it does so in a way that defines her rape as part of *his* torture.

In addition to the characterization of African American women as hypervictims and the narrative positioning of Black women as irrelevant to the rape scenario, particular representational themes also contribute to these texts' displacements of Black women. For example, the rapes of African American women are often unambiguous, violent, and onscreen. Sometimes the use of rope during the rape evokes both slavery and lynching, heightening the racialized pathos. These explicit representations of violence against African American women emphasize the seriousness of the assaults. Ironically, however, they also naturalize a subsequent narrative neglect of the experience: if the rape is so unquestionable, there is no need to spend time investigating it. Furthermore, the explicit violence contributes to and depends on a cultural definition of African American women's bodies as less valuable and as more available—in this case, available for visualizing representational violence. The onscreen violence also contributes to the hypervictimization that then leads to alternative narrative foci.

In all these examples, Black women may be highly visible and the rapes they face may generate the narratives, but they remain relatively silent—infantilized, hypervictimized, or absent altogether—or they function as spectacles of race that nevertheless advance an ideology of color-blindness. These characterizations, narrative scenarios, and representational themes that contribute to Black women's displacement clearly emerge in these texts that address race and racism, but they are in no way limited to this context. I turn now to an examination of the ways these and other depictions of African American women intersect with postfeminism.

Race and Postfeminism

Despite emphasizing issues of race, some of the previous examples contain postfeminist elements. For example, the *Dr. Quinn* episode addresses the theme of a woman's independence, particularly her right to own and run her own café. However, the historical nature of the narrative combines racial discrimination with gender discrimination without significantly undermining contemporary postfeminism's emphasis on whiteness. While the episode tells a story about the Klan's historical racism, it links the issue of gender discrimination more directly to the present, at least intertextually through the television show's constant attention to (white) women's independence in narratives about fashion, combining work and family, and the difficulty of functioning as a woman in a masculine career, all topics that resonate directly with other present-day postfeminist narratives.[22] Similarly, examples that take place in the present may raise gender issues, but they then conceive of gender as separate from race issues—race issues that are more central to the narrative. For example, *Jungle Fever* represents Angie as an independent woman who stands up to the police and states her right to desire and date whomever she chooses, but Flipper's immediate physical danger diverts attention away from Angie's perspective to a critique of racist definitions of African American men as rapists, as a class. In *ER,* while the text initially offers a critique of the medical institution (represented by Mark and Carol) for neglecting a woman's experience of rape, as soon as Kubby speaks of rape the text concentrates on the racialized experience of an undocumented Nigerian man living in the United States and the weight of his memory of torture. In each case, the specific issue of race is separated from those of gender and feminism.

These examples begin to illustrate how representations of Black women function in the context of narratives about rape and postfeminism. In these examples, Black women are either absent altogether from the rape scenario (as in *Jungle Fever*), or they face rape in a historical context dissociated from the contemporary postfeminist moment (as in *Dr. Quinn*), or they are only momentarily important to a text that is primarily concerned with Black men (as in *ER*). In this second section, I explore narratives about African American women and rape focused more directly on postfeminism. In particular, I address issues of law, women's independence, and attention to women's experience, three important aspects of postfeminist rape narratives, as I describe in Chapter 3. Here I ask, If the previous examples displace Black women from their own stories of racialized rape, what happens when African American women face rape in the context of postfeminist discourses that primarily center white women?

Law

The December 12, 1992, episode of *The Commish* positions an African American woman, as I will argue, "next-to-but-just-outside" a postfeminist representation of the usefulness of rape law. In this case, Stacey Winchester is not quite a pure victim. Not only does she make unsafe decisions, but she responds to being raped through illegal revenge activities. Her revenge activities do evoke some postfeminist rape narratives (see chapter 3); however, the episode depends on a postfeminist use of and response to the law by characters other than Stacey for the narrative development and conclusion. In short, Stacey brushes up against the postfeminist aspects of the episode, but never enters the dominant flow of the postfeminist narrative progression.

The episode begins with a club scene. A clean-cut, attractive white man, Bolchek, picks up a clean-cut, attractive African American woman, Stacey. He tells her in a refined accent about his travels around the world. Playing the perfect gentleman, he says, "I don't wish to appear forward," but offers her a ride anyway. When the valet drives up in Bolchek's red Porsche, Stacey says, "Wow, look at that car," and Bolchek simply walks around the car and gets in without waiting for her answer. Obligingly, she smiles and also gets in the car. This scene establishes typical postfeminist perspectives on rape: wealthy clean-cut white men can be dangerous, and if he seems too good to be true, he is. Given these standard representations of rape, Stacey's willingness to get in the car without a moment's hesitation implies she is particularly thoughtless about her personal safety and has much postfeminist knowledge to learn.

However, her role in a postfeminist narrative as a woman who needs to learn about rape is short-lived. The explicit onscreen violence in the next scene—a post-rape scene—emphasizes the severity of Stacey's victimization, not her naive choices. The scene begins with a low camera shot that tracks forward along the ground until it finds a body and then pulls out and repositions as the body rolls over, revealing that the body is, in fact, Stacey's. Once again, although her race is not explicitly related to the rape, a particularly common racialized depiction of explicit onscreen violence separates the African American woman from the postfeminist aspects of the narrative. Furthermore, in this shot her hands are tied with a thick rope, as are Tonya's in *A Time to Kill*, once again evoking slavery. However, the episode does not develop this fleeting representation of a racially specific history in relation to rape. Instead, it turns out, the rope is important as evidence that this man is a serial rapist who always uses rope, no matter who he rapes. When the Commish, Tony Scali, drives up and asks the police officer who found Stacey if she was raped, the officer responds, "Yes. She was tied with this [holding up the rope]. I thought this guy had gone away." Thus, even the rope's brief visual reference to a historically specific African American experience of slavery and lynching is subsumed under the larger narrative focus on the problem of catching a serial rapist who eludes the police not only because he is wealthy, white, and suave, but also because, as an employee of an embassy, he happens to have the protection of diplomatic immunity.

Furthermore, a white male hero is the legal avenger, thus shifting attention away from Stacey to the *police officers'* experience of the legal system and *men's* relationship to rape. For example, while Cyd Madison, a white female police officer, apologizes to Tony for jumping in during his questioning of Stacey, he contradicts her, saying, "You were clutch back there. You saw how to get to her. A man can't . . . he can be sympathetic, but unless a man can be a victim, he just can't know." While of course a man *can* be a victim, the episode constructs rape as a woman's experience, paradoxically through a white male hero who champions antirape discourse more virulently than anyone else.[23] Thus, the episode has it both ways: insisting on the centrality of a nonracialized woman's perspective but doing so in a way that actually centers a white man's postfeminist perspective on her experience.

As if to prove Tony's claim that a man cannot understand unless he has been a victim, Tony ultimately persuades the ambassador to waive Bolchek's immunity. He does this by manipulating the ambassador's daughter, Anna, into reminding her father of his work during World War II, helping Jews in Romania. Anna says, "My father has forgotten what it's like to be a victim," and so she agrees to pretend to be Bolchek's next victim in order to force her father to empathize with the women's perspectives. While Tony initially resists the idea, saying, "I don't know if I can put another father through that," Cyd persuades him by saying, "The question is, can you let Bolchek put another woman through it, when it is real?" Here, the narrative develops so that a man's understanding of victimization is necessary to prevent further rape.

Tony and Cyd spend their time persuading a white woman (Anna) to help a white man (the ambassador) understand the pain of rape and therefore use the law to the fullest extent possible against a hypervillainized white serial rapist. Stacey, however, spends her time articulating her anger. Thus, the narrative maintains a separation between Stacey's experiences and Tony and Cyd's use of men's empathy to make the legal system work. For example, Bolchek returns to the club and repeats his suave rape-setup behavior with another woman, this time an attractive blonde white woman (contributing to Stacey's deracialization, Bolchek is a color-blind rapist). When the valet pulls up with Bolchek's car and he expects the woman to follow him into it, but she instead gets an odd look on her face. He turns his head, and a cut to a point-of-view shot reveals that someone (i.e., Stacey) has spray painted the word "RAPIST" on the hood of his Porsche.

While Stacey takes part in this kind of illegal revenge behavior throughout the narrative, once Tony manages to draw Bolchek into the U.S. legal system by using Anna to manipulate her father into waiving immunity, Stacey appears to be satisfied. A shot pans from Bolchek in a lineup to Stacey identifying him as the man who raped her. Tony recounts the legal process, telling Stacey that Cyd has some papers for her to sign and that then they will go to trial. Stacey smiles. In the next scene, she gives Cyd a picture of her she has drawn as a gift, and then Stacey violently tears up an angry picture of Bolchek she has also drawn. When Cyd touches her arm, however, Stacey smiles as if to suggest that now she will be "all right." Stacey shifts from expressing her anger to accepting that the legal system (represented by Cyd) is empathetic and able to help her. While her experience of rape *initiates* the narrative, the *development* of the narrative depends entirely on the white characters' use of and response to the legal system. Stacey's acceptance of the legal system at the end simply reinserts her into the dominant postfeminist narrative from which the bulk of the (color-blind, but implicitly white) narrative excludes her.

This episode of *The Commish* illustrates how the rape of an African American woman can function to initiate a narrative about the law and its relationship to postfeminist white men and women who seek to use the law to protect, understand, and/or support women, in general, regardless of race. While this episode does at least offer a parallel narrative about an African American woman's post-rape experience, it also largely excludes her from issues of law and morality with which the main characters are concerned. Overall, the episode primarily represents a color-blind world in which a woman's race is supposedly irrelevant, while simultaneously shifting its focus to white characters who pursue white rapists who rape white and African American women indiscriminately. Stacey is then left on the edge of the postfeminist rape narrative, her race emerging only implicitly through her hypervictimization (even despite her initial unwise behavior). By making questions of law the purview of white postfeminism and locating African American women's more important experiences elsewhere (i.e., revenge), this example draws on and contributes to a long-standing cultural definition of African American women as outside rape law. Thus, even as this example is unusual for post-1980s film and television rape narratives because it acknowledges that African American women do experience rape, it does not go so far as to shift its representation of rape *law* in relation to these women's experiences.

Independent Women

While Stacey can certainly be read as an independent woman, the primary narrative development of the episode concerns a liberal white man's understanding of women's experience of rape and his encouragement of (white) women to take responsibility for making rape law work against rapists. In this section, I examine examples that focus more directly on a woman's right to exist on an independent and equal level with men. I choose two examples at opposite ends of a spectrum: the first views African American women as altogether unrelated to postfeminist questions of women's independence and equality, and the second develops the issue of independence exclusively in relation to an African American woman. In each case, however, the text distances the African American woman's experience from postfeminist questions of independence.

The 1995 made-for-television movie *Inflammable* begins by showing the sexual and racial dynamics on a navy ship. A Hawai'ian theme party on deck reveals primarily white sailors in gender and race drag, dancing. The officers, including one woman whose name—Charlie—is predictably masculine, watch the men with tolerance and humor. Below deck, an African American and/or Latina woman, Santos, continues her work, even when a fellow sailor comes by and urges her to come up to join the party.[24] One more setting reveals Charlie passing through the kitchen, commenting to the cook that the breasts of the woman in his pornography that she happens to see as she passes are fake.

This crosscutting establishes tension around gender: the men, who clearly make up the majority on ship, have the freedom both to play with gender (drag performance) and to objectify women (pornography), while the women—one officer and one enlisted woman—must either tolerate their behavior (Charlie) or compensate for their sexism by working more assiduously than anyone else on the ship (Santos).

As the crosscutting continues, what appears to be the beginning of a rape scene ensues. A shot of just legs and shoes walking toward Santos implies danger. Although Santos recognizes the African American man who approaches her and clearly responds to him as her boyfriend, Raines, sexual danger is implied as she play-struggles away from his embrace, insisting that she has work to do. His response, "You know you want it," evokes rape and, in fact, leads into an actual attempted rape scene when an offscreen voice says, "We all want it." A typical assault scene follows, with a group of masked men running in, close camera work, and non-diegetic music heightening anxiety. Just as the men tear off Santos's outer jumpsuit and imply that her boyfriend has told them about their sexual encounters, the crosscutting culminates when Charlie enters the area, grabs a fire extinguisher as a weapon, and tells them to back off. The scene ends when Charlie helps Santos pull her jumpsuit back on and Santos walks with dignity toward the camera. When Raines reaches out to her, she pushes him away.

Again, the movie explicitly represents a gendered tension when it represents Santos's anger at Raines for bragging to other men about his sexual relationship with her. Furthermore, the representation of sexual danger itself takes place in the context of an attempted rape *and* in the context of the consensual relationship between Santos and Raines. This implies that the presence of actual women in the military context disrupts the illicit, but nonetheless accepted, objectification of women (in pornography) by the sailors. And while the movie emphasizes the gender tensions, it also implies but does not directly address racial tensions, marking an African American man, Raines, as particularly villainous, not only for pressuring Santos to neglect her work in order to be with him and playing with a rape scenario, but more importantly for revealing their private relationship to others, which in turn nearly leads to rape. In short, up until the attempted rape scene, race is a concern of the movie—at least implicitly.

Race, however, drops out as even an implicit issue when the narrative shifts after the attempted rape to the matter of women in the military. Even more tension emerges around gender when a special investigator arrives, Lt. Dollen, a former lover of the white captain, Jack Gutherie, and a traditionally attractive white woman.[25] As Jack watches her arrive, he says, "Behold the legacy of Tailhook," explicitly articulating the tension around women and sexuality in the military with which the movie is concerned. Dollen takes seriously her role as an investigator; for example, she encourages Santos to talk to her, evoking a standard postfeminist definition of women who face rape as responsible for protecting other women from rape by speaking out. Nondiegetic music and close-ups intensify the emotion in their exchange as Santos resists Dollen's pressure, saying, "I have to live with these guys," and Dollen insists on a "zero tolerance" policy and tells Santos that "If we ignore this kind of thing it will happen again, maybe to you, maybe to some other woman." While the scene ends without Santos speaking, a reaction shot of her implies that she is moved by Dollen's argument and may be willing to take on the responsibility Dollen is giving her. She suddenly turns up murdered, however, thus she is unable to act on this postfeminist responsibility.

Here, the attempted rape of an African American woman initiates a narrative concerned with women in the military. The attempted rape precipitates Dollen's arrival, and the bulk of the narrative focuses on her determination to continue her investigation of the attempted rape and now murder, despite being told to back off by both the ship's captain and her own superior. In the end, however, despite her insistence on her right and responsibility to pursue these gendered events, the mystery she ultimately solves has nothing to do with attempted rape or even with inappropriate sexual behavior, such as illegal pornography. While it turns out that the men attempted to frighten Raines by threatening to rape Santos in order to keep Raines from revealing an illegal pornography business in which he, in fact, was involved, this relatively illogical aspect of the mystery has nothing to do with Santos's death. Furthermore, although the movie repeatedly takes Charlie's, Santos's, and Dollen's gendered perspectives (by depicting the majority of the men as at best uneasy with women's presence and at worst assaultive and objectifying of women and by giving the women dialogue that explicitly articulates a vaguely feminist perspective), in the end *Charlie* turns out to be the villain who killed Santos.[26] Charlie had been running not a (by comparison) relatively harmless (gendered) pornography business but a more serious (a-gendered) drug business. When Santos discovers the drugs and naively reports them to Charlie, Charlie kills her. When Charlie's villainy is revealed, she also reveals a disdain for the vaguely feminist principles she had been espousing, laughing at Santos for trusting her just because she "was a woman."

Issues of race are subsumed by those of gender in this movie, resulting in a white woman as hero who insists that "all" women (implicitly, regardless of race) are responsible for upholding the military's "zero tolerance" policy. The movie then further centers whiteness by killing off the one African American woman in the story and providing drug-running as a solution to the mystery that, it turns out, has nothing to do with either rape or the issue of women in the military. That the hero (Dollen) and the villain (Charlie) are both white women underscores the text's emphasis on a deracialized postfeminist question about women's roles and rights in the military. The rape and then murder of Santos are just narrative ploys to set up the primary focus on Dollen and Charlie.

While the African American woman's experience of attempted rape in *Inflammable* helps shift the movie's focus to an exploration of independent (white) women in the military, in the film *What's Love Got to Do with It?* (1993) (a loose biography of Tina Turner) rape is the "final straw" that leads an African American woman to claim her independence. Importantly, however, unlike postfeminist narratives in which white women achieve independence in the *process* of responding to rape and dealing with the legal system, in this film the rape is simply the last event in a long string of events that depict Ike Turner's attempts to control Tina. It is just one example in a continuum of abuse experiences. After the rape, Tina finally leaves Ike, thus taking control of her own music, body, and identity.

This rape is particularly explicit, as are many representations of the rape of African American women. The entire event takes place onscreen; Tina says no and continues to say no; the camera focuses on her face as she struggles against Ike; and the intercourse is clearly violent and painful for Tina. Furthermore, Ike has been abusing Tina emotionally and physically (onscreen) throughout the film and hence already has become an inarguable villain. The literal and unambiguous nature of the rape naturalizes the narrative's subsequent shift in focus: there is no complexity to explore in relation to this rape. Additionally, this shift in focus away from the rape marks a difference between the representation of an African American man and a white man as villain. While the hypervillainized white rapists of African American women in *A Time to Kill* and *The Commish* are all pursued aggressively, in this case an African American man as rapist simply drops into the background of the narrative. His rape of Tina does not mark an excessively racist and sexist character (e.g., *A Time to Kill*) or an abuse of international power (e.g., *The Commish*). Instead, it marks him as ineffectual. Despite/because of his use of rape in an attempt to control Tina, he loses her. He thus becomes more pathetic than villainous. Both he and the rape are beside the point for the remainder of the film.

These series of differences between *What's Love Got to Do with It?* and the other postfeminist examples I discuss highlight further the general implicit whiteness of postfeminism. In other words, in *What's Love Got to Do with It?* a film explicitly about African Americans, many of the typical representations of the rape of Black women coalesce: the rape is onscreen and unambiguous, a Black man is ineffectual in relation to the rape, and law and the process of responding to rape are irrelevant. These modes of representation collectively make rape a given for Tina, and thus a relatively unimportant aspect of the narrative. In the other examples, the rape of an African American woman initiates narratives about white men's relationship to postfeminist law or about white women's equality. In this example, which does not center whiteness, rape may ensure Tina's move toward independence, but the text avoids addressing Tina's experience of rape and its relationship to her pursuit of independence. It is almost as if rape is an African American woman's unremarkable fate.

African American Women's Perspectives

Unlike all the examples I have discussed so far (except *What's Love Got to Do with It?*), *Incognito*, a 1999 made-for-cable (BET) movie, represents a world that centers African American identity and experience.[27] The last example I discuss in this section on postfeminism, *Incognito* offers the most detailed representations of an African American woman's perspective on rape in the context of postfeminist concerns with women's independence and emotional experience. I separate out this example, in particular, because it does include at least some explicit attention to the woman's racialized experiences, unlike *The Commish*, for example, which distances Stacey from the postfeminist narrative about (white) women's responsibility for using the law against rapists but does not address racialized aspects of her experience. *Incognito* is similar to the postfeminist examples I discuss in chapter 3; nevertheless, it *also* draws on many of the specifically racialized aspects of the representations of Black women I discuss in this chapter. Thus, this example explicitly connects African American women to postfeminism more so than do any other examples I have found, and it simultaneously offers more attention to race than do the vast majority of postfeminist texts. Here, rather than standing next-to-but-just-outside a white-focused postfeminism (*The Commish* and

Inflammable), an African American woman is at the center of postfeminism. Paradoxically, then, this example suggests that, of the narratives that include African American women and rape, the more postfeminist they are the more they engage blackness. By explicitly engaging *both* postfeminism *and* blackness, this example offers potential challenges to postfeminism's pervasive whiteness. As I argue, however, the challenges are minor.

Like many rape films, this one begins with a dream/memory sequence. In the dream/memory, a woman witnesses a man murdering another woman and then is kidnapped by him. While this opening sequence does not refer to rape directly, it ends abruptly after the man jumps into the woman's car and forces her to drive where he tells her, making it clear that "something awful" has happened and that something is preventing this woman from leading a happy and "normal" life. In fact, the dream ends when the man (whose names turns out to be Scanlon) jumps in the car, because the woman (whose name turns out to be Erin Cortland) initially can only remember these particular events from that night. Not only did Scanlon assault Erin, but her inability to remember the entire night perpetuates her feelings of victimization. Furthermore, Erin's current life is filled with assaults by men, heightening her role as a vulnerable woman who needs to develop self-confidence and independence. Not only is she living with the blocked memory of Scanlon's rape and now with his stalking in the present, but her father (who is also her boss) insists on controlling her actions, ordering her to use a bodyguard, Hunter, and telling her when she can and cannot come to work. To add intrigue to the plot, her fiancé, Quinn, is not only insensitive to her need to postpone their wedding after the rape, but, it turns out, he is also secretly stalking her.

Erin initially responds to these perpetual masculine assaults by rejecting Hunter, defining his protection as one more assault. She makes this point explicitly when her therapist asks her how having a bodyguard makes her feel. Erin responds, "Like I have no control over anything. Forced, you know. Violated against my will again." Early in the film, then, Erin articulates a postfeminist independence in a way that requires her to reject men entirely. The narrative development, supported by postfeminist therapeutic discourse, then teaches her to combine her independence, produced by her experience of rape and assault, with acceptance of a certain *kind* of heterosexual partner. Specifically, through Hunter, she learns to "trust men again" when—as a good postfeminist man—he listens to her, accepts her right to make her own decisions, protects her from physical harm, and even takes her out of her wealthy but stifling environment into his south central Los Angeles home, where he and his wheelchair-bound sister, Wilhemina, nurture her with food, affection, and attention. In the end, her feelings of violation, produced by her assault, exacerbated by her father's paternalism, and then enacted by Hunter's existence, are replaced by love for and acceptance of an understanding *and* protective man.

In addition to representing Erin as integrating a postfeminist independence in response to rape with a postfeminist acceptance of heterosexual coupling, the movie also explores Erin's perspective in particular scenes that mark her psychological state in relation to the rape. For example, in one scene she takes a bath, rubbing her leg over and over in the same spot, accessing the postfeminist post-rape shower/bath trope. Another typical aspect of post-1980 postfeminist rape films and television shows, the representation of a woman who cannot engage in a loving sexual relationship as a result of a previous rape, also appears. Erin not only puts Quinn off as a result of the rape, but, when she finds herself falling in love with Hunter, initially she is unable to engage with him sexually. When they begin to have sex for the first time, she has a flashback to the rape that, until this moment, she has not been able to remember at all. During the sex scene, Erin sees the cross Hunter wears around his neck, and flashes on the (much larger and more menacing) cross Scanlon wore around his neck while raping her. The editing then intercuts between the rape and Erin with Hunter in the present, depicting a literal substitution of Scanlon for Hunter and Hunter for Scanlon.

When Erin finally undergoes hypnosis and remembers the rape, she becomes an actively resistant survivor, ironically contradicting her sense of herself in the present as a passive victim. In the flashback/memory, either during or after the rape, she is able to hit Scanlon in the face and run. In fact, the last shot of the flashback is of her back as she runs away from Scanlon, escaping from him. In the present, her first words are "I got away." Thus, although her recovered memory does not erase the fact that she was raped, it allows her to reinterpret herself, to remember not only that she tried to defend herself but that she was able to get away, perhaps saving her own life (Scanlon, after all, had just killed another woman). While therapeutic hypnosis allows the detectives to find Scanlon, it simultaneously helps transform Erin from the manipulated woman she explicitly defines herself to be in relation to Quinn, her father, and even Hunter early in the film into a survivor who can take care of herself.[28]

Given that her hypnosis-induced access to her memories helps her re-define her experience of rape so that she is no longer solely a victim, she is now able to inhabit her independent identity without rejecting men entirely.

Erin's racial identity is not relevant to any of these typical aspects of postfeminist rape narratives; her racial identity in this film is not tied to the rape. Nevertheless, I would argue that *Incognito* is what Gray would call a multicultural, rather than assimilationist, movie. It "position[s] viewers, regardless of race, class, or gender locations, to participate in black experiences from multiple subject positions [and it] . . . interro-gat[es] and engag[es] African American cultural traditions, perspectives, and experiences" (90). Erin's entire world, except for a few background characters and the (relatively incompetent white) detective, is populated by African Americans. There are many marks of a specifically African American experience in the film, as well. For example, Erin's mother died of sickle cell anemia when Erin was a child, and Erin's family owns an old and respected insurance company called the Freemen Mutual Corpora-tion, established in 1895. In Hunter and Wilhemina's home, Erin and Wilhemina discuss an African mask on the wall, and African art is also visible throughout Erin's office. In one scene Erin plays the African game Mancala. Thus, unlike in many other post-1980 rape films and television shows, it does not take a resistant critical reading (such as those I offer earlier in this chapter) to center the Black woman's experience in this film. Erin is the center of her world, and her entire world is about African American experience and culture.

While the rape is not linked to the specificity of that experience and culture, as it is, for example, in *Dr. Quinn* and *A Time to Kill*, Erin never-theless is the center of the story. Thus, this film, by offering an entirely African American world and centering an African American woman in that world, offers an unusually sustained look at an African American woman's experience of rape. Furthermore, by drawing on postfeminist themes of women's independence, therapy, and post-rape trauma, *Incog-nito* is a rare example of a rape narrative that brings blackness into post-feminism. Not only does Erin engage in postfeminist post-rape behavior, but *she* is the key to solving the mystery and helping the (relatively inef-fectual) police bring Scanlon to justice. This is not a color-blind postfem-inism that depicts a Black woman as "the same as" white women (thus maintaining whiteness as a standard). Nor is it a displacement that sepa-rates African American women from the postfeminist aspects of the text.

This text places a specifically racialized African American woman in the center both of the text and of the text's postfeminism. Nevertheless, Erin's specific blackness does not transform the structure of the postfeminist *rape* narrative. In other words, *Incognito* offers no analysis of racialized aspects of rape. Thus, while the film may challenge postfeminism's whiteness more than any of the other examples I have examined here so far, it does not challenge postfeminism's deracialized (but white-centered) conception of rape.

Nuanced Depictions

In this last section, I explore three films that offer more nuanced depictions of the relationship between African American women and rape in the context of contemporary representations of *both* blackness and postfeminism. While these examples do draw on some of the strategies of displacement and aspects of postfeminism discussed above, they also go beyond these modes of representation by dealing with rape and its relationship to both race and gender in a more sustained and nuanced manner. In particular, I am interested here in two kinds of examples. First, I look at a film that juxtaposes two different interracial rape scenarios, complicating each in the process. Second, I examine two films that deal in a complex, sustained, and experimental way with women-centered narratives and the place rape plays in those narratives. My goal here is to offer a critical reading of films that can be read to resist standard representations of Black women in all three of the following contexts: blackness, postfeminism, and their intersections with rape. Overall, I argue that the representations of rape in these films offer a much more critical and nuanced understanding of African American women's relationship to rape and sexuality than is typical in post-1980 film and television. Nevertheless, they do so primarily from African American men's perspectives, thus contributing to a cultural silencing of African American women, even in the highly celebrated Black feminist film *Daughters of the Dust*.

Juxtaposing Interracial Rapes

Rosewood, based on a true story, takes place in segregated neighboring towns in 1920s Florida. When Fanny Taylor, a white woman, is beaten by the white man with whom she is having an affair, in order to hide her affair from her husband she claims, "I was beaten, he was so big! He was so Black, that boy!" While nearly everyone except her husband (but including the spectator) knows she is lying about the assailant's racial identity, the town nevertheless takes up her accusation as an excuse for what becomes a white massacre of nearly the entire African American community. Some time after the assault, while Sarah, an African American elder and Fanny's maid, watches from a window in Fanny's house, Fanny steps onto the porch, gathers herself, and begins screaming as if to imply she has just been beaten. The town immediately moves into action, with cuts, close-ups, busy frames, and a mobile camera revealing men gathering their guns and spreading the story. When the white sheriff, Ellis Walker, arrives, he asks, "Who raped you?" introducing rape into the story for the first time. Despite the fact that Fanny clearly states, "I wasn't raped, just beat," the white women gathered around her immediately start saying to each other that she was raped. The scene includes an overhead extreme long shot of Fanny sitting on the ground in the road in front of her house, surrounded by the sheriff and other members of the white community. This shot suggests the inevitability of what will come next: the racist assaults foreshadowed by Sarah's earlier warning to her son, Sylvester, that even winking at a white woman will get an African American man killed.[29] In this case, an actual African American man is not even necessary as the white town takes up a story it knows to be false as an excuse for destroying the people and property of the neighboring African American town of Rosewood.

In contradistinction to the clearly false assumption that Fanny was raped, the sexual relationship between an African American woman and a white man in the film is unclear with regard to coercion and consent. A portion of the opening of the film includes an ambiguous sexual encounter between John Wright, the only white business owner in Rosewood, and Jewel, a young African American woman who works for him. While there are no definitive markers of Jewel's lack of consent, neither are there any definitive markers of her desire. Jewel and John are in the back room of his general store, she lying on a table and he with his back to the camera, standing over and blocking her from the camera's view. She calls his name repeatedly—Mr. Wright—with no clear emotion in her voice. Her relative lack of emotion makes the encounter indistinct, since she could either be calling his name in pleasure or in an attempt to make him stop. However, her use of a title and his last name—Mr.

Wright—makes clear the power relation between them, regardless of co-ercion or consent: not only is she a young African American woman in segregated 1920s Florida, but she depends on this man for her livelihood. Thus, it makes sense to read this scene as a rape in the context of the his-tory of African American women's work experiences, as detailed by Hine, for example. Jewel's lack of emotion, then, could be read not as enigmatic but rather as evidence of a form of the self-protective dissemblance Hine describes as resistance to sexual coercion.

While I consider it important to read this encounter between Jewel and John as rape, I nevertheless am also troubled by this reading, or more accu-rately troubled by the ambiguity the film constructs and then abandons around the scene.[30] To read the scene as rape is to avoid reading Jewel as having sexual agency and desire. In other words, reading the encounter as coercive depends on denying the possibility that Jewel could find pleasure in this relationship. By maintaining at least some ambiguity around the en-counter, the film avoids either a clear-cut condemnation of white men's abuse and expression of racialized and gendered power through rape or a clear articulation of the complexity of African American women's sexuality. It is not that I want to feel free to read Jewel as attracted to John, but that I want the film to address her experience more directly and explicitly. Al-though *Rosewood* avoids the standard representation of unambiguous on-screen sexual violence against African American women that is such a com-mon way of representing African American women as highly visible yet profoundly silent in popular culture, neither does the film ever address Jewel's perspective on the experience.

The problem with the absence of Jewel's perspective is even clearer when comparing this scene with other scenes in the film that articulate white men's sexualized assault of African American women in relation to African American *men's* experience. For example, Sylvester confronts a white man, Mr. Andrews, for whistling at his cousin, Scrappie. While Mr. Andrews is up on a porch, accompanied by another man, and Sylvester is alone, below him on the ground, a low angle shot of Sylvester and his gun emphasizes his size and determination as he tells Mr. Andrews, "I don't like Scrappie feeling scared around nobody." The film represents Syl-vester's perspective on challenging the white man, rather than Scrappie's experience of the assault. Furthermore, the scene is a brief flashback that takes place during a family dinner table conversation in which Sylvester's mother, Sarah, tells him what he did was dangerous: "You can't talk to white people that way and not expect a rope around your neck. . . . They burned a boy last summer for winking at a white woman." This line functions as a history lesson/reminder for the spectator, articulating the historical moment in which the story is being told as one in which lynching was rampant. However, with Sarah's example, the film shifts from addressing an experience that is at least related to an African American woman's experience of white men's sexual assaults (Scrappie and Mr. Andrews), even though it focuses on Sylvester's role in the situation, to a story in which African American women are entirely absent (Sarah tells of an *African American man* killed for winking at a *white woman*), except as matriarchs worried about their sons' lives.

In death, as in life, Jewel represents as much about the men in the film as she does about herself. While other main characters' deaths appear on screen as part of the narrative development (e.g., Sarah), Jewel is killed, and probably raped (again), offscreen. As the massacre proceeds, John repeatedly attempts to stop the escalation and prevent deaths, but he is inevitably unsuccessful. In one of several scenes like it, John and Ellis confer in hushed voices at the edge of the group of white men, trying to decide how to keep the violence to a minimum without actually defending either the law (as Ellis could as sheriff) or their principles (as "halfway decent white men," as Sarah explicitly calls John early in the film). In a vain attempt to keep tempers cool, Ellis convinces John to leave the group. Immediately after this scene, which takes place at night, a daytime shot of the swamp where the remaining African American townsfolk are hiding appears. The next shot shows John at a distance, walking along an empty road. The camera, which is close to the ground, pans to follow him but then picks up and pans across Jewel lying in the grass, dead, with her dress torn. The shot of her face reveals her eyes open and her head turned away from John, toward the camera, staring out at the spectator in death. John, in the background, walks along oblivious to her body lying by the side of the road. This shot communicates several things about John. First, it underlines his obliviousness to the intensity of the violence of which the whites are capable. Second, it foregrounds the futility of his "halfway decent" attitude toward African Americans, emphasizing just how distant he actually is from the African American person to whom he is closest in the film. Third, the implication that Jewel was raped as well as murdered refers back to John's sexual exploitation of her. Thus, while the shot is tragic, the pathos is heightened not in relation to Jewel, whose perspective the film never directly represents, but in relation to the depiction of white masculinity and the profound futility of being "halfway decent" in a fully racist context.

Overall, then, while the film deals with African American women's experience of rape by white men in much more complex ways than many of the other examples I discuss in this chapter, and while it addresses multiple intersections of gender and race with rape through a juxtaposition of two different interracial rape scenarios (Fanny and Jewel), *Rosewood* privileges an African American masculine perspective (and even, in this last example, a white masculine perspective) on African American women's experience of rape. Furthermore, it provides clarity only about a white woman's experience of violent assault (Fanny), a clarity that allows for a much more explicit critique *and* acknowledgment of that woman's experience than of Jewel's racialized experience.

Women-Centered Narratives?

If *Rosewood* privileges a masculine perspective on African American women's experience of rape by excluding African American women or making their voices and perspectives incoherent, the final two films I discuss in this chapter—*She's Gotta Have It* and *Daughters of the Dust*—at least attempt a more sustained representation of African American women's experience of rape in both gendered and racialized ways. Nevertheless, African American male perspectives on the women, sexuality, and rape compete with and generally overpower the women's narration of their own experiences.

In *She's Gotta Have It*, Nola Darling attempts to maintain sexual relationships with three men—Jamie, Mars, and Greer—despite each man's attempt to persuade her to enter a monogamous relationship with him alone. The film begins with an image of Nola (the "she" in the title) looking directly into the camera and consenting to tell her version of "having to have" sex (the "it" in the title). At first it appears that Nola is going to be the narrator of the film. The camera tracks toward her sheet-covered body in her bed until she sits up, adjusts her covers, and looks directly into the camera. As the first character introduced in the film, Nola is the first to "look" at the audience directly and the first to control the narration. By acknowledging the camera, she both consents to being the object of study and draws attention to that process, thus simultaneously asserting some control over narration and making the process of narration explicit. This look is followed by an intertitle introducing her name, and then a close-up during which she continues to look directly into the camera as she begins to speak:

> I want you to know the only reason I'm consenting to this is that I wish to clear my name. . . . I consider myself normal, whatever that means. Some people call me a freak. I hate that word. I don't believe in it. Better yet, I don't believe in labels. But what are you going to do? This was the deal.

The dialogue about the act of narrating and the direct address itself ostensibly put Nola in control of the narration. This implies that Nola will be telling this story from her perspective, resisting the "label" of "freak" and thus challenging the stereotype that women who are interested in sex on their own terms are abnormal.

The film as a whole, however, does not sustain her gendered narration. Although the opening shot ends with her statement, "This was the deal," suggesting that the film will move directly into a flashback from her perspective, the next shot depicts Jamie sitting on a park bench, also looking directly into the camera. Although Nola initially takes the position of narrator, the film immediately provides Jamie with the same narrative position as he looks into the camera and begins to tell the same story to which Nola is referring. While the same topic—Nola's sexuality—is the subject of narration, there is now a tension between the perspectives of two narrators—Nola and Jamie. Not only does the film establish another character as co-narrator, but the cut to Jamie directly following Nola's attempt at initiating the story thwarts the impulse toward the flashback that Nola's dialogue creates. In fact, *Jamie,* not Nola, is the instigator of the flashback when it finally begins immediately after his brief direct narration. Jamie thus interrupts Nola's narrating voice. This move on the level of narration mirrors Jamie's desire for sole sexual and emotional possession of Nola within the diegesis.

In the context of the narrating tension, Jamie's rape of Nola toward the end of the film works both to accept a woman's definition of rape and, paradoxically, to assert Nola's lack of control over her own body, her own sexuality, and the narrating process. By this late point in the narrative, Jamie has tired of Nola's refusal to leave her other lovers and has withdrawn from the relationship. She calls him, says she needs him, and persuades him to come over. When he arrives he is angry to discover that nothing in particular is wrong and that she is not inviting him into the monogamous relationship he desires. His anger culminates in an explicit onscreen rape that both characters acknowledge and name as such in the next scene.[31]

During the rape scene, as in much of the film, Jamie's dialogue shapes the structure of the scene and punishes Nola. For example, while he is raping Nola, he asks her if this is the way she has sex with Greer and Mars. When he says each name, jump cuts replace him with each of them, respectively, giving him—his voice, his imagination—omniscient control over the narration and multiplying her rape by three.[32] Masculinity converges in Jamie here as the text makes explicit his identification with the two men he considers his competitors. As Felly Nkweto Simmonds (1988) argues, Nola "is punished not only because one man, Jamie, rapes her, but because the structure of the scene allows him to punish her for the other men, as he subjects her not only to physical but also to psychological rape" (18). Jamie's question ("Whose pussy is this?") and her response ("Yours") further emphasize his power over both the narration and her speaking/spoken body. As bell hooks (1989b) puts it, while criticizing the film's characterization of Nola,

> She does not assert the primacy of her body rights. She is passive. It is ironic because until this moment we have been seduced by the image of her as a forceful woman, a woman who dares to be sexually assertive, demanding, active. We are seduced and betrayed. When Nola responds to the question, "Whose pussy is this" by saying "yours," it is difficult for anyone who has fallen for the image of her as sexually liberated not to feel let down, disappointed both in her character and in the film. (139)

Jamie and Nola's perspectives are not in *opposition to* each other; their perspectives are in *struggle with* one another for control of the narration and renegotiation of sexualized stereotypes of African American women and men. The rape is the culmination of the gendered struggle for control of Nola's body diegetically and Nola's story narratively, a struggle that is never completely resolved but in which masculinity reasserts control over femininity, at least temporarily.[33] Thus, while *Rosewood* silences African American women altogether, *She's Gotta Have It* gives an African American woman voice only to overpower it through an African American man's narration and rape.

African American women's narrating voices are also central to *Daughters of the Dust*, a film about a Gullah island family, the Peazants, preparing to migrate north in 1902. In fact, Toni Cade Bambara (1992, xiii) argues that the (female) Unborn Child and her mother, Eula, who is pregnant with her throughout the film, co-narrate *Daughters of the Dust*. Unlike in *She's Gotta Have It*, this narrating voice is not in competition with a masculine *narration*. Nevertheless, the film depicts a tension between a focus on Eula's experience of having been raped and Eli's (her husband) response to the rape, arguably emphasizing Eli's need to come to terms with the rape more than it does Eula's.

Daughters of the Dust introduces rape in the Unborn Child's first voiceover, as "my ma and daddy's problem." The images represent that problem as an estrangement, with Eula turning toward Eli in bed and Eli ignoring her. This scene structures the problem between Eula and Eli as one that Eula has to confront but that Eli has to change. Much of the film focuses on Eli's experience of what the director, Julie Dash, in her interview with hooks, calls the "aftereffects" of the rape (1992, 50). For example, early in the film Nana (the oldest living member of the family) confronts Eli about his behavior. Nana articulates a woman-centered logic, suggesting that Eli not worry about whether or not the child Eula is carrying is his "because she get forced." While whether or not Eula was forced is irrelevant to whether or not the child is biologically Eli's, Nana points out that the child is his spiritually because the ancestors have sent it to him. While Eli does not accept Nana's perspective at this early point in the film, she has articulated the two things Eli will learn by the end of the film: the Unborn Child is his daughter and Eli must understand Eula's experience of rape from Eula's (not his own) perspective.

In the process of learning these things, Eli confronts his own spirituality. For example, Eli links the rape to spirituality because it causes him to lose faith. He asks, "Why didn't you protect us Nana?" and he no longer believes that, for example, empty bottles in trees will protect them. In fact, he later destroys the glass bottles in the tree outside his home in anguish and anger. Thus, the rape both causes Eli's (temporary) separation from his culture and—through the Unborn Child's status as both past (ancestors) and future (child)—helps him find his way back to that culture.

Eli's importance in terms of the rape also emerges in relation to his connection to lynching and the antilynching political movement. Not only does Yellow Mary (a family member who has returned to the island after living several years first as a wet nurse and nanny and then as a prostitute) warn Eula not to tell Eli who the rapist is in order to protect Eli from lynching, but twice Eli's decision to remain on the island, rather than to leave with the rest of the family as he originally intended, is linked to lynching. First, the Newlywed Man (Eli's cousin) asks Eli if he will become involved in their antilynching work, whether or not he remains on the island. Second, when the Unborn Child's final voiceover explains that Eula and Eli did decide to remain on the island, she says, "Some say Eli got himself all involved in the antilynching issue. Some say Eula saw too much of herself in Nana Peazant and wanted her children born on this island." Thus, the rape leads both Eula and Eli to remain behind, to reject an idealized attempt at modernization. Only Eli, however, remains for an explicitly politicized reason.

Eula's relationship to the aftermath of rape—which primarily can be understood as Eli's rejection of her—might best be described to be "to wait it out," although the rape links her, too, to culture, spirituality, and politics. Throughout the film, she reaches out to Eli and endures his mistreatment of her, all the while waiting for him to return to her. When he breaks the bottles in the tree, she covers her ears, cowering inside their house. When he enters the house and holds her roughly against the wall, she does not struggle away from him. Nevertheless, she asserts her control over the flow of the narrative by refusing to tell him who raped her. By *not* introducing the identity of the rapist into the story, which would perhaps shift the film to an avenging narrative structured around Eli, she waits for Eli to come to her, Nana's, and the Unborn Child's perspective. She takes the same determined, waiting stance when she, Yellow Mary, and Yellow Mary's friend/lover, Trula, discuss the situation. While Eula gives very few details, she listens to Yellow Mary telling her not to name the rapist because if she did she would have to fear finding her husband hanging from a tree. Yellow Mary also connects Eula's experience to her own, implying that her employer raped her when she served as wet nurse and nanny to his children.[34] This scene not only articulates a reason for Eula's silence, but it also links her experience to a larger historical context in which African American women face rape, often by white men.[35]

Eula drops her waiting stance and finally speaks of the rape only when Eli accepts her back into his life and takes up her perspective on the rape. In a pivotal scene in which Eula confronts the "rifts" (Bambara, xiii) in her family, two separate shots of Eli show him encouraging her to "speak what needs to be spoken." His position here contrasts with his earlier entreaty that she tell him what he wants to know (who did this), thus emphasizing his shift in perspective on the rape. Specifically, Eula articulates her perspective when many of the women in the family reject Yellow Mary and her desire to return home. Eula challenges them, drawing a connection between herself and Yellow Mary as "ruined," as well as between them in the present and all the women of the past. She says,

> If you're so ashamed of Yellow Mary 'cause she got ruined . . . Well, what do you say about me? (gesturing to her pregnant stomach) Am I ruined, too? [. . .] As far as this place is concerned, we never enjoyed our womanhood. . . . Deep inside we believed that they ruined our mothers, and their mothers before them. And we live our lives always expecting the worst because we feel we don't deserve any better. [. . .] If you love yourselves, then love Yellow Mary, because she's a part of you. Just like we're a part of our mothers. [. . .] We carry too many scars from the past. Our past owns us. We wear our scars like armor, . . . for protection. Our mother's scars, our sister's scars, our daughter's scars . . . thick, hard, ugly scars that no one can pass through to ever hurt us again. Let's live our lives without living in the fold of old wounds.[36]

Here, Eula, like Yellow Mary earlier in the film, links her rape and Eli's subsequent rejection of her to a racist culture that defines African American women as "ruined" and gives them scars that separate them from themselves and from others. She asks the family members who would reject Yellow Mary to reconsider their own links to Yellow Mary's circumscribed choices and to Eula's experience of rape. She seeks to persuade the women in her family who reject tradition and desire the northern migration to return to a grounded understanding of the family's relationship to history, culture, and community.

While this speech is powerful and an important articulation of Eula's experience of both the rape and its aftermath, her pregnancy functions oddly in relation to rape here, as it and the Unborn Child do throughout the film. As Dash's 1997 novel that is based on and continues the narrative of the film makes very clear and as the film implies, the Unborn Child is, in fact, Eli's both spiritually *and* biologically.[37] Thus, on the one hand, the Unborn Child represents the aftermath of rape and does the work of resolving both Eula and Eli's trauma after rape; on the other hand, she technically has nothing to do with the rape. This ambiguity, I would argue, undermines the film's privileging of Eula's perspective at the end. By not challenging Eli's and the family's assumption that her pregnancy might be a result of rape or, alternatively, rearticulating Nana's earlier argument that the Unborn Child's biological parentage is irrelevant since the child was sent by the ancestors, Eula (and thus the film) stops just short of challenging what the film itself defines (through Nana) as a masculinist obsession with biological parentage and the possession of women through marriage. Nevertheless, despite this incoherence around rape and pregnancy, of all the films I discuss in this chapter—in fact in the entire book—*Daughters of the Dust* offers the most nuanced, sustained, critical, and feminist representation of African American women's gendered, racialized, and political relationship to rape—even when it emphasizes the effect of rape on African American men by focusing at least as much attention on Eli's relationship to the rape as it does on Eula's.

Conclusion

In this chapter, I have argued that Black women are displaced by contemporary representations of both blackness and postfeminism in numerous ways. These displacements can be historical, defining rape as only a specifically racialized experience for African American women in the past; they can be metaphorical or can infantilize African American women, distancing rape from adult African American women; they can address race by focusing on evil white men or tragic Black men; they can leave African American women out of the rape scenario altogether by addressing false accusations of African American men for raping white women; and they can use race as a spectacle to address a deracialized (white) father's morality. Postfeminist displacements often position African American women next-to-but-just-outside postfeminism, maintaining postfeminism's whiteness by excluding African American women from questions of law, portraying white men as more knowledgeable and more committed to pursuing rapists, and even sometimes holding white women responsible for helping white men in their benevolent endeavors. In almost all these contexts, African American women are highly visible, their rapes are necessary to instigate the narrative, but their voices, perspectives, and experiences are silenced. In each case, a possible specific representation of the intersections of gender, race, and rape is superseded by more simplistic and historically tenacious definitions of the women who matter (to postfeminism) as white, the men who matter (to antiracism) as Black, and the people who *really* matter as white men, because, after all, we (now) have a postfeminist color-blind society in which white men can represent the ideal antiracist, antisexist human as much as (really, more than) anyone else can.

Nevertheless, many of these texts do open up spaces for less hegemonic (and perhaps less sarcastic) readings. For example, the rape's sexualization and then the text's almost immediate desexualization of Grace in *Dr. Quinn* draw attention to her delimited relationship to sexuality and beauty throughout the series. The first half of the first *ER* episode to address Kubby's rape highlights and critiques both the U.S. medical system's and the central characters' willingness to discard her interests and needs in favor of law, citizenship, constructions of Nigerians as torturers, and, most explicitly, a human link between a Black man and a white man (a link which nevertheless is not primarily about race). Stacey, in *The Commish*, offers moments of African American women's activism against rape, including acts of revenge that offer spectatorial pleasure and catharsis. Even though *Incognito* does not address the intersection of rape and race, it does challenge postfeminism's whiteness by representing a nonassimilated African American woman at the very center of a postfeminist text that explores both her emotional response to rape and her role in embracing gendered independence in the process of bringing the rapist to justice.

Furthermore, reading many of these examples through the context of Black women's historically specific experiences of rape reveals moments in which the texts can be read to grapple with Black women's experiences, even if they do so without providing attention to the Black women's perspectives on those experiences and even if it takes purposeful critical attention to draw out these moments. From this critical perspective, *Dr. Quinn* points out that the Klan not only lynched but also raped, *A Time to Kill* insists on a continuing link between racism and sexual violence in the present, *ER* draws attention to the use of rape as a form of torture in war, and *Incognito* suggests the importance of understanding both the nuanced emotional response and the role of law and justice in an African American woman's post-rape experiences.

By addressing the intersection of gender and race with rape, *Rosewood, She's Gotta Have It*, and *Daughters of the Dust* (despite their varying tendencies to emphasize African American masculinity) all can be read to speak back directly to the much more common representations I discuss in this chapter. These films illustrate the possibility of breaking apart both postfeminist and color-blind representations by addressing the intersectionality of gender and race in African American women's experiences of rape. By juxtaposing these more nuanced examples with more typical films and television shows, I hope to have highlighted even further the limits of what postfeminism can address: it cannot address the intersections of gender, race, and rape. And, I hope to have emphasized the fact that postfeminism has its limits: as pervasive as it is, it does not extend to or incorporate *all* contemporary representations of rape in popular culture. Nevertheless, the fact that African American men's perspectives emerge perhaps even more strongly in the more nuanced examples than in the less explicitly critical undermines some of what I read as the resistant potential in these films.

I have also tried to articulate a critical tension in response to some of the specific modes of representation that emerge in relation to Black women and rape. On the one hand, the fact that African American women's rapes are often very explicit, that at least brief references to racism sometimes appear in rape scenes, and that African American women in these narratives more often eschew the law in favor of taking revenge all offer ways out of postfeminism's obsession with whiteness, the ambiguous she said/he said definition of acquaintance rape and (white) women's sexuality, and the usefulness of the law. On the other hand, these modes of representation also illustrate the persistence of a cultural willingness to do/see violence to African American women (in this case, through particularly explicit, onscreen rapes), to let the rape of a Black woman stand in as a marker of a generic racism (which inevitably means racism against Black *men*), and, perhaps most problematically, to define the rape of African American women as outside the law.[38] Similarly, the fact that, unlike more general postfeminist representations, postfeminist rape narratives do *not* tend to assimilate African American women helps highlight postfeminism's whiteness and provides an alternative space for African American women in popular culture. Conversely, the next-to-but-just-outside postfeminist space also ensures that the vast majority of postfeminist rape narratives define rape in a way that contributes to and draws on color-blind (but implicitly white) representations that marginalize African American women.

In short, in this chapter I have tried to illustrate the persistence of Black women's visible silence in popular culture, while simultaneously drawing these examples together and focusing on the parts of the texts (even when they are very brief) that allow for a sustained discussion of the representation of Black women's relationship to rape. This transtextual critical analysis, hopefully, acknowledges but also undermines each example's individual displacement of Black women.

6

Talking Back to Postfeminism?
Rape Prevention and Education Films and Videos

In this final chapter I examine rape prevention and education films and videos (many of which implicitly or explicitly define their projects as feminist) that complicate even further this book's multifaceted examination of representations of rape. These films and videos self-consciously engage and reflect on the process of representation in order to work against rape and other forms of sexual assault and abuse. While the films and television shows I examine in previous chapters have an entertainment emphasis for a (relatively) mass audience, the films and videos I examine in this chapter focus on social change for a classroom, feminist group, or perhaps college dorm audience.[1] These shifts in purpose and intended audience lead me to ask with even more urgency questions about the process of representation, its social meanings, and its capacity to produce social change.

In other words, the stakes are higher in this chapter than in previous chapters because I now confront films and videos that have similar goals to my own in this book: to articulate a complex antirape politics and to be critical and analytical of cultural representations. Given these texts' multilayered (and often feminist-inclined) politicized approaches, I want to examine—with both appreciative respect and critical skepticism—the perspectives on and definitions of rape they collectively represent. How do these perspectives and definitions relate to the more mainstream material I examine in the rest of this book? What alternatives to pervasive postfeminist representations do they offer for feminist antirape activism? What options have not yet been explored in antirape activist films and videos? What other ways of representing rape might one imagine as productive avenues for antirape activism? Collectively, these questions help me to consider the political efficacy of explicitly antirape films and videos.

I collected the films and videos I examine here from several different sources in order to cover the broad range of the prevention and education programs available. I look at many of the videos held by the Violence Prevention Program on my campus, the University of California, Davis. In addition, I examine films and videos carried by an assortment of distribution companies that market their products to university communities.[2] For some of the texts produced in the 1970s that are unavailable to me, I rely on descriptions from Kaye Sullivan's books, *Films for, by and about Women* (1980) and *Films for, by and about Women: Series II* (1985). Collectively, these various sources provide a range of materials that might be available to an educator and/or activist involved in antirape activism; I believe that the thirty-plus films and videos I have seen and the fifty-plus additional descriptions I have read provide sufficient examples for the claims I ultimately make about this genre as a whole.

I divide my analysis of these programs into two sections. First, I examine dominant themes, moving through them roughly as they appear in the programs chronologically. Here, I am concerned with identifying key *repetitive* aspects of these programs and examining how those aspects define rape and women's relationships to rape. In the second section, I focus on two key modes of representation in these texts: the explicit representation of rape and the neglect of any analysis of the relationship between rape and race. Here, I draw on my own feminist critical concerns in order to challenge these films and videos as fully as I do the more mainstream films and television shows I examine in previous chapters.

Overall, through both approaches to critical analysis, I argue that despite an explicitly antirape activist purpose, these films and videos depend on and contribute to postfeminist conceptions of rape more often than they challenge them. Particularly after a mid-1980s shift from a focus on stranger rape and self-defense to a focus on acquaintance rape and therapeutic discourses, antirape prevention and education films and videos participated in a larger postfeminist cultural emphasis on individualized, decontextualized conceptions of rape as an issue of concern primarily for white, middle-class, heterosexual women. In short, while I do find many instances of powerful social critique in the examples I examine in this chapter, collectively they stop short of offering a substantial reconceptualization of rape that would have the potential to challenge significantly the ubiquitous postfeminist representation of rape throughout popular culture.

Rape Prevention and Education Films and Videos, 1970s–Present

While I specifically organize this section around themes, in order to address historical shifts I also follow a roughly chronological order. I begin with themes and arguments more common in 1970s texts and move toward those more common in recent texts, while nevertheless noting later or earlier appearances when they exist. I argue, first, that 1970s and early 1980s texts focus most often either on awareness, prevention, and self-defense or on social and legal change. Second, while overall all these programs tend to emphasize women's perspectives on rape, in the late 1970s and into the mid-1980s some texts spent considerable time exploring the assailant's view of rape. Third, texts that draw on therapeutic discourses or seek to debunk "rape myths" appear throughout the 1970s, 1980s, and 1990s; however, a *primary* and overwhelmingly individualized and interiorized focus on therapeutic responses to rape experiences becomes more prevalent by the 1990s. Concomitantly, a combination of the antimyth that "rape is violence, not sex," with a simultaneous attention to the existence of acquaintance rape in eroticized contexts muddies the examination of rape myths by the 1990s. Unlike Ellen Goodman (1991) and Naomi Wolf (1991a, 1991b), who, as I discuss in chapter 3, (perhaps inadvertently) blame feminism for the muddiness of representations of rape in popular culture, I would suggest that the context of postfeminist culture (not feminist theory or activism) leads to the confused representations in the texts I examine in this chapter. Specifically, I argue that these historical shifts correspond with many of the themes in the postfeminist films and television shows I discuss in chapter 3. This mid-1980s shift toward postfeminist-informed representation is perhaps clearest in the move from representations of activism against stranger rape to representations of individualized therapeutic responses to acquaintance rape. Finally, I discuss programs, primarily from the 1990s, that address cultural contexts for rape, specifically the contexts of war, media culture, and experimental film and video. These few examples thus implicitly resist the move toward postfeminist depictions of rape in the majority of films and videos to appear after the mid-1980s. They are, however, the minority of the antirape films and videos available.

Awareness, Prevention, and Self-Defense

Awareness, prevention, and self-defense are probably the most frequent themes in 1970s rape prevention and education films and videos.[3]

Programs with these themes seek to draw the implicitly female viewer's attention to the potential for rape in her life and to encourage her to develop strategies to avoid "dangerous situations" or to cope with those situations should they occur. The texts provide interviews with police and antirape activist experts, and they define the "dos and don'ts" of how to respond to rape and how to move about in social spaces (e.g., *do* lock your windows, *don't* go out alone at night). These programs also sometimes include representations of women taking part in actual self-defense classes. Many programs stress that rape can happen anywhere to anyone (sometimes showing teen and post-fifty-year-old women to make this point); thus, they suggest that all women must take responsibility for preventing their own potential rapes by being on guard. Some examples also include interviews with actual rapists and women who have been raped to show how actual rapes occur and therefore to suggest strategies for prevention.[4] Overwhelmingly, these programs provide awareness and prevention advice for rapes that are defined as nighttime stranger rapes in which a woman is assaulted in her home or kidnapped off a dark city street by someone she has never seen before. Only two texts that focus on awareness, prevention, or self-defense address the issue of acquaintance rape—*Acquaintance Rape Prevention* (1978) and *Girls Beware* (1980)—and both address a specifically teenage audience.

The most recent film I have seen that focuses primarily on self-defense is *Give It All You've Got* (1984). This film emphasizes confrontational physical self-defense strategies over self-focused awareness and prevention strategies that appear more frequently in the pre-1984 films and videos. By emphasizing response over preparation, the film holds women slightly less responsible for eliminating rape than do the other programs in this category. *Give It All You've Got* combines staged conversations between friends with clips from a self-defense class to illustrate how even just a loud yell can prevent a rape. One sequence, for example, depicts a woman walking down a city street with the film's narrator, telling a story about how she recently was able to use her self-defense skills to prevent an attack. She describes being frightened on the street as a stranger approached her from behind and then says she remembered her self-defense training and turned quickly while letting out a loud yell. Immediately after she demonstrates this to the narrator, a cut to a self-defense class reveals a large group of women practicing the very same move. By providing a success story and, furthermore, intercutting that story with a related self-defense lesson about how to yell to scare off an attacker, this section of the film illustrates nicely its overall argument that self-defense is a powerful and empowering way to prevent sexual assault.

Give It All You've Got is the *only* 1980s program I have found that looks at self-defense in a sustained fashion, and none appear in the 1990s. When these later films and videos do refer to awareness, prevention, and self-defense, they primarily tack these issues on at the end, usually with vague advice such as "trust your instincts." For example, *Summer's Story: The Truth and Trauma of Date Rape* (1992), which is almost entirely made up of one woman's therapeutic post-rape testimony, provides vague self-evident prevention advice such as "establish your limits" and "don't be afraid to make a scene." The video does not explain *how* to define limits or make a scene. One video from the early 1990s, however, does offer potentially empowering images of women who use their bodies and voices to defend themselves. While struggling with how to represent rape in the context of teaching antirape activism in the classroom, Martha McCaughey and Neal King produced *Mean Women*, a collection of clips from contemporary Hollywood films featuring women fighting back against violent men. As they suggest in their essay about the video, McCaughey and King's (1995) goal is to provide an alternative to most contemporary antirape programs that, they argue, frighten women. In *Mean Women* they provide images they hope will empower women and frighten men. While this video is not *about* self-defense per se, it does reintroduce the active and confident depictions of women that appear in *Give It All You've Got* and some of the 1970s films.

Social and Legal Change

Another common element of 1970s programs is the representation of the immediate aftermath of rape, which includes depictions of painful emotions, suspicious police, assaultive court systems, and (usually) unsupportive friends and families. These texts emphasize the need for legal and social reform in response to post-rape experiences, and they call for awareness of and attention to women's experiences of rape, reminding the audience that someone they know may have been raped and may need their understanding and support. Some also explicitly address spectators who have experienced rape (or who may experience rape in the future) when they argue that it is important to report rape in order to help change the court system and society's awareness of rape.[5]

The most recent program that substantially focuses on the need for social and legal reform appeared, like *Give It All You've Got*, in the mid-

1980s. While *Waking Up to Rape* (1985) primarily uses testimony from three women who have experienced rape, which is a technique much more common to late 1980s and 1990s films and videos, it edits their testimony in a way that emphasizes their arguments for social reform and sometimes combines that testimony with documentary footage of the women engaging in the activities they describe. For example, a Latina woman says that learning self-defense helped her cope with her family's silence surrounding her rape. We then see her participating in a self-defense class. In another narrative strand, an African American woman discusses her struggle to work through the emotional and personal aftermath of rape, while also coping with the continuing trauma of her husband's imprisonment for murdering the man who raped her. She explicitly articulates a critique of the legal system as racist and sexist in its dealings with both her and her husband. Furthermore, she says that she is now studying law in order to help her husband get out of prison and to fight the racism of the legal system.

A related group of programs also refers to structural sexism. Rather than emphasizing negative post-rape experiences, they highlight *positive* actions rape crisis and prevention programs, various local police stations, and hospitals take to fight rape and to treat women who experience rape with care, respect, and understanding. While these programs represent community responses to rape with more optimism than do those that detail social and legal barriers to rape law reform, both groups of programs argue for more support of antirape activism and encourage women who have been raped to come forward and speak out.[6] Most shows in this category emerged in the 1970s. The most recent program I have found that primarily emphasizes the success of antirape activism and legal reform is the 1986 *Update Brazil: Women's Police Stations.* This film provides information about Brazil's new police stations for women, in which the police officers are women who fight crimes against women (e.g., rape and domestic violence). The film includes documentary footage of women coming to the police station to report crimes and to get help, as well as of female police officers learning self-defense techniques, arming themselves, and going out into the community to arrest accused men. The narrator as well as a government official argue that these stations have been successful and that more will be built.

The only 1990s video I found that addresses legal and social injustices substantially is a historical dramatization of the life of the artist Artemisia Gentileschi, who lived from 1593 to 1652. This 1994 BBC video, *Women*

Word for Word: A Reputation: The Rape of Artemisia Gentileschi, uses actual court transcripts to construct the dialogue of Gentileschi, her father, the man who raped her, and other key figures in the case.[7] Emphasizing the injustice of the male-dominated art world as well as the church-dominated court system, the video retells this historical event by highlighting Gentileschi's testimony and discrediting the testimony of the other figures in the video, and by providing a scholarly expert to fill in details about the patriarchal structure of the time period. Despite the power of its critique of institutionalized social injustice, this example represents that injustice as a historical problem (as do some of the examples I discuss in chapters 1 and 5), thus moving the problem of rape away from the present era. As a result, this video does not address contemporary social and local injustices, as do the earlier films and videos. Overall, I have not encountered a post-1986 program with a primary focus on contemporary social or legal reform.[8]

The Assailant's View

The two types of programs I have discussed so far—those that focus on awareness, prevention, and self-defense and those that emphasize social and legal change—dominate rape prevention and education films and videos from the 1970s and early 1980s. Late in the 1970s and into the 1980s another type of program became common, one that focused on the rapist's perspective. Set in prisons and mental institutions where men who admit they have raped can be found, these programs reveal the therapeutic treatment of convicted rapists in prison and include interviews with the rapists themselves. Often the men speak from shadows that protect their individual identities (but inadvertently also visually reinscribe their dangerous, threatening character), but some men, especially those who are participants in an Oregon state rehabilitation program, reveal their names and faces. Some of these men, in fact, appear in more than one antirape program.

While these men are all in therapy, most of the programs are at pains to emphasize that the abuse these men are uncovering in their own childhood, and which presumably led to their own abuse of others, should not excuse their behavior. The overarching argument of the programs is that these men's therapy is important for two reasons: to learn more about why men rape and to prevent these men from reoffending when they are paroled. Given that the majority of the men featured are serial rapists and that the psychological and psychiatric experts interviewed in the programs argue that most men who rape do so repeatedly, the programs imply that rehabilitating even just one rapist will go a long way toward preventing future rapes.[9] Some programs also include sensationalistic scenes of the therapeutic process that include group discussions (i.e., confrontations) between convicted rapists and women who have experienced rape, although not by these specific men. These sequences are particularly intense because they depict women voicing their anger and men breaking down emotionally in response. These scenes heighten the programs' overall focus on the men by revealing their emotional acknowledgment of culpability. Concomitantly, the scenes emphasize the men's villainy by including the women's expression of anger.[10]

The only video I have seen from the 1990s that represents the therapeutic treatment of imprisoned rapists and focuses primarily on men who rape is the ABC television 1992 video *Men, Sex, and Rape*, narrated by Peter Jennings.[11] Oddly enough, despite its primary focus on convicted rapists, the initial premise of the video is that the case of William Kennedy Smith (who neither admitted to nor was convicted of rape) has brought more attention to rape as a social problem. Jennings implies that in order to prevent cases such as Smith's in the future, women and men must understand why men rape and men must understand how women experience rape. The fact that Smith was *not* convicted of rape makes Jennings's premise untenable, and this confusion increases when the video turns to the small minority of men who rape—those who are convicted and imprisoned—to offer a general explanation of why Smith (or someone like him) might have raped. The contradictions pile up here: Smith's (legally defined) *non*rape case initiates a program meant to explain why "typical" men (like Smith) *do* rape, and then atypical *convicted* rapists (unlike Smith) serve as sources of information about these supposedly *typical* men.

Other than this one program from the 1990s, films and videos that focus on convicted rapists and that include interviews with them about their views on rape seem to emerge in the late 1970s but then disappear again by the mid-1980s. At that time, films and videos collectively return to a focus on women, their potential actions, and their responsibilities in relation to rape and the threat of rape.

Talk, Testimony, and the Therapeutic

Many programs that focus on women throughout the 1970s, 1980s, and 1990s include interview testimony from women who have experienced rape and represent therapeutic talk (of which testimony is one example) as a way to reclaim one's life and self. Earlier films and videos tend to combine the testimony and therapy with other approaches to representing rape, such as challenging myths and discussing legal reform.[12] More recent films and videos, however, emphasize confessional and individual psychologized modes much more heavily than do these earlier programs. These programs intersect with what Dana L. Cloud (1998) defines as a therapeutic rhetoric, "a set of political and cultural discourses that have adopted psychotherapy's lexicon—the conservative language of healing, coping, adaptation, and restoration of a previously existing order—but in contexts of sociopolitical conflict" (xvi). Here, rape, rape myths, and rape law reform are the sociopolitical contexts in which the therapeutic not only emerges but predominates.

From 1984 on, in fact, all but two of the twenty-three films and videos I viewed include testimony, representation of therapy as imperative to survival and recovery, or both.[13] In fact, four programs from 1985 through 1992 are almost *entirely* made up of women (and one man) describing their experiences of rape and its aftermath during interviews.[14] In many of the films and videos, at some point in the interview, the woman who has been raped explicitly states that the very process of talking through the experience of rape—a process that the audience is watching and listening to—is part of her therapy. The chronological structure of many of the programs supports this claim. For example, *Waking Up to Rape, From Victim to Survivor* (1986), *Summer's Story: The Truth and Trauma of Date Rape, Surviving Rape: A Journey through Fear* (1992), and *Good Things Too: Recovery from Sexual Abuse* (1995) all move from descriptions of a pre-rape naive, innocent, and/or young self; through detailed descriptive discussions of the rape and post-rape despair (during which the person testifying usually begins to cry); to the final segment in which the interviewees describe their feelings of relief and joy at entering therapeutic discussion groups or individualized counseling because in these contexts they learn to speak of their rape and begin the healing process. The final stages of this healing process, are, of course, documented by the program itself. Each of these programs, then, defines individualized therapeutic discourses and practices as the primary appropriate response to rape. This individualized therapeutic management of the inevitable post-rape despair in these late 1980s and 1990s programs completely eclipses both rape prevention and social change, the two most prevalent aspects of antirape programs that appear up until the mid-1980s.

Rape Myths: Rape as Violence, Not Sex

Films and videos that identify and counteract what they define as rape myths, such as "no means yes" or "what women wear can cause rape," are, like the therapeutic texts, prevalent throughout the 1970s, 1980s, and 1990s. Up until the mid-1980s, these films and videos tend to use the term "myth" in the more limited sense of "false," as opposed to in the sense of cultural narrative or mythos.[15] *Rape: An Act of Hate* (1986) even literally prints "myths" on screen as true/false questions for the audience to try to answer. For example, one statement reads, "Rape occurs mostly among strangers," to which the program answers itself: "False." By far, the idea that rape is "just bad sex" is the most common falsity addressed in these programs. These films and videos seek to replace this definition of rape with the idea that rape is "violence, not sex" and the related argument that men rape for "control" and "power" rather than for sexual pleasure. Many films and videos, in fact, address only this one "rape myth."

Despite sustained attention to the argument that rape is violence, not sex, collectively the programs contain many contradictions as they struggle to articulate simplified true/false arguments about rape while simultaneously attempting to acknowledge the complexity of women's (and occasionally men's) experiences of rape, including sexualized experiences. These contradictions are particularly pronounced in films and videos from the 1990s that focus on rape myths in relation to date rape.[16] *Dating Rites: Gang Rape on Campus* (1991), for example, emphasizes that rape is about power by providing interviews with an expert who says that gang rapes tend to be planned and that the most likely victim will be the most vulnerable woman, not the most sexually attractive woman. The program then goes on to dramatize a gang rape that includes a pre-party planning process. However, the dramatization focuses considerable attention on the men's discussions of sex before the party, thus contradicting the expert's earlier argument that rape is entirely about power. Furthermore, the women in the dramatization, during their pre-party preparations, spend the bulk of their time talking about what they are going to wear in order to appear attractive to the men in whom they are interested (and who turn out to be rapists). By including the women's sexualized preparations, the video reintroduces the idea that what a woman wears *is* (somehow) connected to rape.

In one segment of the video, a group discussion among actual male and female college students, who appear to be enlightened (they discuss how to educate men about women's experiences and they discuss their own antirape activism), includes a particularly powerful close-up of one woman lamenting the fact that the existence of rape means not that some men abuse power as the expert claims, for example, but that she has to watch what she wears. This college student's more personal and emotional delivery, as well as her status as similar to the implied college student audience, potentially makes her perspective (that it matters what she wears) more salient than the "talking head" expert's theoretical claim that rape is about planned power, especially since the context in which she speaks, an enlightened group discussion, adds to her ethos. Furthermore, the explicit context of flirting and sexuality that runs throughout the dramatization similarly undermines the expert's authority on the subject.

Overall, then, rape prevention and education programs have addressed rape myths consistently since the 1970s, but with *increasing* levels of contradiction and confusion, particularly around the issue of defining rape as being about power, not sex. No matter what the experts say, women in the programs, whether they have experienced rape and/or are "typical" college students, tend to take responsibility for rape instinctually by focusing on what they wear, where they go, whether or not they drink at parties, and what they say. While their overall goal may be to define rape as violence, not sex, the programs reinscribe a connection between rape and sex by including men who discuss rape in sexualized terms and by including women who take responsibility for preventing rape by reining in their own expression of sexuality. As Monique Plaza (1981) argues,

> In order to combat this naturalist ideology [i.e., it is in men's sexual and biological nature to rape] we have asserted that rape is not ascribable to sexuality. But we must also assert at the same time that rape is sexual, insofar as it refers to social sexing, to the social differentiation between the sexes, and because we must not dissociate heterosexual sexuality from violence. (33)

The films and videos do not, however, take this opportunity to explore or analyze the complex and contradictory relationships among rape, sex, and violence to which they themselves contribute. Marketed to college student audiences, these programs implicitly instruct both men and women on how to behave in eroticized date situations, while simultaneously insisting that rape is not about eroticism or sexuality.

From Stranger Rape to Acquaintance Rape

Perhaps the clearest distinction between programs produced before and those produced after the mid-1980s is a shift in focus from stranger rape to acquaintance rape. Up until the mid-1980s, programs tend to suggest that rape is much like other violent crime that requires preventative measures such as locking one's doors and windows and never traveling alone at night. Even *Give It All You've Got*, which offers a particularly empowering narrative of successful self-defense, reinforces the myth that rape is most often perpetrated by strangers. After the mid-1980s, programs (either directly or indirectly) generally counter this myth by (over)emphasizing acquaintance rape. While a few of the early programs actually do implicitly acknowledge the existence of acquaintance rape because many of the actual rapists and women who have been raped that they interview tell stories about raping or being raped by someone they know, the first program I found to address acquaintance rape directly is the 1978 *Acquaintance Rape Prevention*.[17]

The 1986 *Someone You Know*, while arguing that "you" are more likely to be raped by "someone you know," depends on modes of representation standard to the earlier programs that evoke the stereotypical stranger rapist trope.[18] This program thus functions as a transition from the earlier stranger rape programs to the later acquaintance rape programs. For example, the show begins with a dark night shot of a seemingly empty city street, while a police audiotape of a 911-type call of an in-progress stranger rape plays on the soundtrack.[19] After this tape plays and a transcript of the dialogue between the police officer and the caller appears on the screen, a male correspondent in a typical "journalist's trenchcoat" appears and says that the case we have just heard is *atypical* because it is a stranger rape. Nevertheless, the real police tape has set the stage for the program, and the later interviews with prison rapists (in shadow) reinforce the image of the shadowy, dark rapist who plots to rape any stranger who appears to be vulnerable (as opposed to representing a date culminating in sexual violence).

By the 1990s, films and videos that directly address acquaintance rape replace these frightening dark and shadowy images and sounds of stranger rape with bright images of women and experts talking openly about their experiences of and perspectives on acquaintance rape. *No Means No: Understanding Acquaintance Rape* (1991), for example, dramatizes an acquaintance rape trial as a way to reveal myths about rape (through the voice of the defense attorney and some members of the jury) and to counteract those myths through the dialogue of the prosecutor and the nonscripted discussion of some of the jury. *The Date-Rape Backlash: The Media and the Denial of Rape* (1994) also seeks to clarify, but turns its attention not to acquaintance rape itself but to the *media's representation* of "date rape," arguing that the popular U.S. media acknowledged acquaintance rape as an "epidemic" in the late 1980s but then almost immediately reversed their position. In particular, the media started quoting as fact Katie Roiphe's 1993 book *The Morning After*, in which she argues that date rape accusations are primarily a result of women's regret or bad sex, not rape.[20] Finally, *Summer's Story: The Truth and Trauma of Date Rape* seeks to reveal the "truth and trauma" of date rape entirely through Summer's testimony. Explicitly naming Summer and placing her in a brightly lit setting with soft orange and blonde colors, the video creates a friendly and safe atmosphere in which the truth can be safe and trauma can be healed through therapy. This open and revealing context for telling the story of acquaintance rape can be understood as the opposite of the rapist-in-shadow image from *Someone You Know*.[21]

While, like most late 1980s and 1990s programs, these examples emphasize women's experiences of and perspectives on rape, many also address men's perspectives as *potential* rapists in order to elucidate how it is possible for a formerly trusted acquaintance to rape. Using group discussions among college students, these films and videos seek to reveal the stereotypes and myths that some men hold about women, dating, and rape. Rather than including interviews with convicted rapists, many of whom knowingly hide their identities in shadows, these programs depict men who *unknowingly* reveal what the programs depict as their problematic attitudes toward women and thus who are not even aware that it might be in their best interest to be depicted in identity-hiding shadows. For example, *No Means No: Understanding Acquaintance Rape* depicts groups of same-sex students in two separate collective discussions about rape, intercutting the discussions with each other. The women express fairly mainstream rape reform ideas about rape; for example, they state what the overall video claims—that acquaintance rape is real rape. The men are a different story. While they do not discuss actual rapes in which they have participated, their conversation reveals attitudes (such as "no means yes") that suggest they might "inadvertently" rape (or have raped) a woman. These attitudes directly contradict the overall video that, for example, provides talking head experts who offer more accurate "facts" about rape, such as the actual title for the video: "no means no." In this context, the men, who appear to be typical college students, become threatening when they themselves articulate as "truths" the "myths" about rape that the video challenges. Overall, the acquaintance rape programs seek to reveal the existence, "truth, and trauma" of acquaintance rape, while often simultaneously depicting men as unknowingly contributing to the problem through their attitudes and ostensibly the behaviors that might follow from those attitudes.

Rape in Cultural Contexts: War, Media Culture, and Experimental Film and Video

Other than the 1970s and early 1980s programs that address social and legal change, the majority of antirape programs do not address cultural aspects of rape. Even the acquaintance rape videos that reveal young men's unwitting beliefs in rape myths tend to represent the problem in individual and psychological terms. Similarly, the programs that set out to debunk rape myths do so by separating those myths from the cultural and institutional contexts that produce and maintain them, using true/false statements for effect instead. There are, however, three additional important types of antirape films and videos that appear occasionally, all of which place rape in a larger cultural context and appear mainly in the 1990s.

The earlier *Women's Political Dance* (n.d.) and the more recent *Calling the Ghosts* (1996), *In Harm's Way* (1996), and *In the Name of the Emperor* (1994 or 1995) all put rape in the context of war. *Women's Political Dance* represents Vietnamese dances as responses to U.S. bombings, one of which is an "antirape dance [that] demonstrates a deep sensitivity to the needs of women and the earth" (Sullivan 1980). *Calling the Ghosts* depicts Muslim civilian women whom Serbian soldiers imprisoned and repeatedly raped during the Bosnia-Herzegovina war. Drawing on these women's testimony, journalist-collected footage of male prisoners from war camps, interviews with family members and various journalists, depictions of these women's post-imprisonment activism, and the war tribunal, the documentary defines rape as one aspect of war that can function as both torture and genocide, and it calls for international activism. *In the Name of the Emperor* is similar, although it focuses on the historical example of rape in the context of World War II. Using interviews with professors, journalists, and Japanese officials; excerpts from diaries of Western missionaries who chose to stay in

China during the war; found footage from newsreels and from private films taken by one of these missionaries; and testimony from soldiers, missionaries, children of those missionaries, and civilian survivors of the war, the documentary details the metaphorical rape of Nanjing and the literal rape of the women of Nanjing by Japanese soldiers. Placing these rapes in the context of global war, the documentary traces a link between the invasion of Nanjing, the international response to the brutality, and the subsequent policy of the Japanese military of providing "comfort women," primarily from Korea, as replacements for the civilian rapes they had previously implicitly encouraged. The documentary does not equate rape with forced prostitution; rather, it places both forms of sexual violence in the context of international relations and draws attention to the ease with which these forms of sexual violence replace one another.

Finally, *In Harm's Way* places rape in the context of the cold war. The first half of the film details the complex and sometimes ironic ways fear of the cold war was instilled in the narrator/filmmaker: images from educational films, television, and newsreels teach "duck and cover" techniques and the supposed "danger" of reading comic books or looking at pornography. The second half of the film is markedly different, shifting to a detailed description of a stranger rape the narrator/filmmaker neither expected nor had been taught to fear. Throughout each section, the film repeatedly intersperses an image of a young girl skipping in a playful manner, presumably happily, away from the camera. This image serves as a link between the two sections of the film, highlighting the incongruity between what young women are taught to fear and the complexities of their actual experiences, in this case a rape experience.

In Harm's Way fits into another category as well: texts that understand rape in the context of a larger media culture. While *In Harm's Way* addresses the inadequacies and inappropriateness of culturally produced fears when it comes to avoiding rape, other programs look directly at what they often term "rape culture," examining how media images, advertising, bar scenes, and social expectations about exchanging money (from men to marketers for products to give as gifts to women) for sex (from women to men) on a date collectively produce a culture that accepts, if not encourages, rape.[22] Perhaps the most interesting example here, *After the Montreal Massacre* (1990), addresses links between the murder of female engineering students and social attitudes about women, feminism, and violence. The video weaves together testimony from a woman who survived the massacre, comments from people on the street attending memorial services for the murdered women, interviews with journalists who covered the massacre, self-defense lectures, group discussions with college students, and public presentations on the global context in which the continuum of violence against women exists. Not specifically about rape per se, the video still draws attention to a specific cultural context in which rape, fear of rape, and other forms of sexual violence both respond to and seek to contain changes in women's social existence.

Finally, some of these films and videos about rape are experimental. More recent experimental texts about rape include *In Harm's Way, Philomela Speaks* (1996), and *Rape Stories* (1989).[23] As does *In Harm's Way, Philomela Speaks* draws attention to Hollywood images and sounds, such as those from the television show *Bewitched* and the film *The Wizard of Oz* (1939), that encourage women to be generally fearful and to remain vulnerable. It then opposes those images to home movie footage and narration that documents the stealing of women's voices. Drawing on the myth of Philomela, whose brother-in-law cut out her tongue to prevent her from revealing that he raped her (but who resistantly wove a tapestry in order to tell her sister of the rape), this video "speaks" the story of rape on multiple narrational levels. And *Rape Stories* takes one rape event, which happened to the filmmaker years before she finished the film, and tells the story several times, from several different perspectives. Addressing post-rape experiences in more complexity than do any of the other programs I have seen, *Rape Stories* represents fantasies of killing the rapist, fears of elevators, ironic images of the futility of running/exercise, and an intuition the filmmaker had that she would be raped. Filmed in part two weeks after the rape and in part ten years later, the film repeatedly intercuts between these two very different stories about the rape in ways that avoid the typical chronological progression from pre-rape naïveté to post-rape recovery that most films and videos that depend on testimony reproduce. Furthermore, the film does not take up the pedagogical or argumentative voice that many of these rape prevention and education programs use. Instead, *Rape Stories* invites the spectator to reflect on the contradictions, pain, anger, long-lasting effects, and even humor that often follow rape.

Overall, while not all programs fit within a strict chronological order, and while certain themes (such as therapeutic discourses and dispelling rape myths) appear throughout the 1970s, 1980s, and 1990s, in general, as the above analysis reveals, a definite shift occurs in these antirape programs' focus in the mid-1980s. Specifically, the majority of the films and videos from the 1970s and early 1980s emphasize stranger rape and the need for awareness and self-defense. While focusing on these topics, the programs incite fear by emphasizing convicted serial rapists' perspectives and the painful experience of being disbelieved by friends and the courts after a rape, but they then often suggest that women can overcome that fear by learning self-defense techniques and taking advantage of new rape crisis centers and legal reforms. Almost always, the programs present an argument for reporting rape and engaging in antirape activism, an argument that (like the emphasis on self-defense) primarily holds women responsible for preventing and responding to rape. Furthermore, they seek to redefine rape as "violence, not sex." While contradictions emerge when later videos make such a claim while simultaneously defining rape as a potential part of an eroticized date or party context, the logic in these earlier videos is primarily consistent. They depict rape as taking place between strangers, and the rapists who speak from prison articulate a desire to have power and control over another person as their reason for raping. Additionally, both the rapists and the women who have been raped tend to describe extremely violent rapes that almost always include a weapon such as a knife or gun.

By the late 1980s, rape prevention and education programs shift their attention from stranger rape and self-defense to acquaintance rape and therapeutic responses to rape. Rather than encouraging women to report their rapes and friends and family to believe and support someone who has been raped, as do the 1970s and early 1980s programs, these films and videos encourage women (and now sometimes men) to seek therapy after being raped and remind friends and family members to play an active role in the therapeutic process. This stronger emphasis on therapy over social and legal reform in the more recent programs still tends to hold women (rather than society, for example) responsible for dealing with rape, in this case through personal, therapeutic transformation.

Similarly, while the modes for inciting fear shift, the programs continue to draw on fear as a means of persuasion. The earlier programs often insist that rape can happen to anyone, anywhere, but they tend to represent both rape and even journalistic reporting about rape as taking place late at night, and they frequently depict convicted serial rapists, often protected by identity-hiding shadows. Hence, while the earlier films and videos do use scare tactics to encourage the audience to "pay attention" to rape, by representing limited locations and depending only on convicted serial rapists, they do not really suggest that *anyone* in the audience could actually be raped or could commit a rape. The more recent films and videos, however, spread anxiety about rape further by representing rape as taking place not in dark and so-called dangerous neighborhoods but on sunny college campuses. The shift here from areas one could presumably avoid (by being aware) to areas the implied college student audience could not possibly avoid does suggest that "anyone" could be raped or could commit a rape.[24] Furthermore, the shift to a focus on acquaintance rape evokes ambivalence and confusion about rape by emphasizing poor communication and conflicting interpretations as reasons for rape, although many of the films and videos do juxtapose the women's personal testimony with reenactments that emphasize their experiences and thus implicitly shore up their perspectives.

In short, while the majority of these texts incite fear and hold women responsible for preventing and/or responding to rape, they do so through themes and modes of representation that shift in the mid-1980s. This shift ironically *intensifies* the incitement of fear and the level of personal responsibility women are to claim in the more recent programs, as rape appears everywhere and women must now individually move into their own psyches—rather than take activist steps collectively to challenge the legal system, for example—in order to deal with rape. Furthermore, over time what rape is becomes *less* clear in these programs as they introduce eroticized dates as contexts for rape without giving up the now clichéd "fact" that rape is violence, not sex, and without developing an analysis of how violence, power, and control relate to the institution of heterosexual dating and coupling in ways that can lead to rape.

These shifts in the strategies and themes of antirape films and videos, shifts that move *away* from feminist activism and arguably place women in a worse relationship to rape than do earlier programs, clearly intersect with the emergence of postfeminism in the larger popular culture. By the mid-1980s, feminist activism for rape law reform already had experienced some success.[25] Furthermore, as I illustrate in chapter 3, mainstream postfeminist representations of rape had begun to absorb some rape law reform arguments, making them widely accessible to a general audience.[26] As a result, it would be redundant for rape prevention and education programs released after the mid-1980s to seek to prove that rape exists, that it is horrific, and that one must speak out in order to change social and legal injustices. These were givens of both law reform and postfeminist popular culture by the mid-1980s. Additionally, by this time postfeminist cultural representations had begun to redefine not only rape but also what feminism and feminist activism might mean. Since post-1980 postfeminist discourses in popular culture implied that feminism had already been successful and was hence no longer needed, if antirape films and videos were to argue for continued social activism against rape, they would need to argue simultaneously *against* this larger cultural assumption that feminist activism was no longer necessary.

While a few 1990s programs, such as *The Date-Rape Backlash*, do challenge postfeminism's complacency, films and videos produced after the mid-1980s primarily sidestep issues of activism, reform, and transformation in favor of an emphasis on individualized therapeutic talk. As I argue in chapter 3, the therapeutic is an aspect of postfeminist representations of rape that helps to depoliticize feminism. From this perspective, despite their antirape challenges, the late 1980s and 1990s rape prevention and education films and videos function as *part of* postfeminist media culture much more than they provide an activist challenge to that culture. In other words, they participate in popular culture's general emphasis on the individual and de-emphasis of social analysis and activism. Furthermore, they target women themselves as in need of individualized and psychologized personal transformation, drawing on and reiterating the kinds of discourses found in television, film, magazines, and the rest of popular culture on a daily basis.

Only the few more recent texts that examine rape's role in war, address a link between rape and the organization of media culture, or use filmic experimentation to explore the complexity of rape move toward a more nuanced understanding of rape that does not reinscribe an individualized postfeminist subject as victim, survivor, or self-aware avoider of rape. Instead, these texts suggest that rape is an embedded aspect of an international militaristic, media, and voyeuristic culture. Unfortunately, these films and videos are the clear minority of those available to educators and antirape activists.

Representational Strategies

While I describe a large number of antirape films and videos in broad thematic and historical terms in the previous section, I turn now to more specific elements of these texts that raise questions about the process of representing rape as an antirape strategy. The topics I address in this section—rape scenes and constructions of race—are two that emerged for me repeatedly as problematic aspects of these programs' representations of rape, and thus seem to call for careful critical analysis. These topics in particular are disturbing because they illustrate ways I think these texts ultimately work at cross-purposes with their own goals, drawing on particular representational strategies in order to achieve antirape, antisexism, and antiracism goals but often reinscribing rape, sexism, and/or racism in the process. My goal here is not to discount these individual programs altogether, especially since I share many of their goals in relation to rape. Rather, my hope is to identify sometimes insidious representational practices that appear in numerous programs and that can inadvertently undermine those very perspectives and goals.

The Presence of Rape, Eroticism, and Violence

Many of these programs represent the act of rape itself in ways that can increase spectatorial anxiety and intensify the spectator's experience of rape. Whether through dramatizations, reenactments, descriptive detail in testimony both from convicted rapists and from women or men who have been raped, or the sound of a police tape of an actual rape as it is taking place, these depictions are horrific in their violence and detail. I acknowledge that these representations occur in an antirape context, one that uses explicit representations in order to convince an audience that rape exists, that it is horrific, and that "something must be done." These representations are not "gratuitous" violence or "excess" in the sense of moments in the texts that are irrelevant to the flow of the narrative or the structure of the plot.[27] This filmic violence has a specific antiviolent political purpose. Nevertheless, the specificity and detail in these representations do reproduce and extend the violence in the acts being described.[28]

In almost all the films and videos, both women who have been raped and rapists provide detailed, descriptive information when telling their stories. Many programs add reenactments or dramatizations of rape scenarios to these descriptions, intensifying the representation. For example, *Rape: An Act of Hate* includes a dramatization of a man jumping through the open window of a woman's house as she prepares for bed. Before the man enters her house, the camera shows the woman walking past the window from the rapist's point of view, repositioning slightly as though the rapist is moving to get a better look. Next, a low angle shot shows him jumping through the window with a bandanna covering his face, and several quick shots (edited in rhythm with the nondiegetic music on the soundtrack) show him grabbing her and pulling her toward himself. The sequence ends as it begins, with a shot from the rapist's point of view as the woman screams. This sequence not only provides explicit details, but it also aligns the spectator's vision with the rapist/attacker's. It is shot and edited to heighten spectatorial anxiety and discomfort and to illustrate the danger of leaving one's window open and unlocked. As Carol J. Clover (1992) argues in relation to horror films, texts that provide the spectator with an attacker's point of view do not necessarily *equate* the spectator with the villain. Rather, the representation of the attacker's visual point of view provides the spectator with more knowledge than the vulnerable woman in the text, using suspense to increase anxiety for and identification with her. To put it somewhat reductively, these scenes encourage the spectator to yell "Watch out!" rather than "Here I come." In this antirape context, providing this point of emotional identification with the woman under attack through a rapist's visual point of view of her insists that rape is violent and horrific but does so by transmitting some of that horror to the spectator.

In opposition to rapists' visual point-of-view sequences, some more recent films and videos emphasize the point of view of the woman who is raped. This shift corresponds loosely with the mid-1980s shift from films and videos that depict stranger rape and interviews with admitted rapists to programs that emphasize acquaintance rapes and therapeutic testimony from the women who have been raped. Despite the shift, however, the programs continue to show characters' point of view to increase spectators' sense of vulnerability. For example, the last shot of the dramatization in *Dating Rites: Gang Rape on Campus* shows a group of men in a darkened room from a low angle as they approach a bed on which a woman (and in this shot the camera/spectator) is lying. Thus, the spectator literally sees what the woman sees. *Women Word for Word: A Reputation* takes the emotional, although not visual, point of view of Gentileschi. When the video arrives at the point in the narrative when the villain first rapes her, it cuts back and forth between her testimony (which is a dramatization itself) and a dramatization of the rape. For example, on the one hand, when she says she scratched his face, the video cuts to a close-up of his face with bloody scratches, doubling her perspective. On the other hand, when he testifies in court that he never had "carnal intercourse" with her, the video cuts back to the dramatized rape scene, showing him to be lying. Thus, the structure of the narration emphasizes and supports the perspective Gentileschi articulates in her courtroom testimony, despite several other characters who testify that the rape never took place. While these examples provide the woman's point of view before and during the rape, *Rape: An Act of Hate* provides one sequence of the woman's literal point of view during a medical exam following rape. The video does not identify the woman as either a real person or a specific character in a dramatization; hence, she can more fully stand in for the spectator. The handheld camera moves into an examining room, moving from the face of the (male) doctor to the (female) nurse, and then subsequent shots show a woman's hands in the foreground moving nervously, her knees in the middle of the frame, and the doctor toward the back of the frame patiently explaining what will take place as he examines her. Her missing head and face (replaced by the camera) further invite the (implied female) spectator to place herself in the vulnerable position of the woman who has been raped and now faces a post-rape exam.

Overall, then, programs primarily from the 1970s and early 1980s use the horror film convention of a rapist's point of view sequence to highlight the vulnerability of women and construct fear for the spectator. While spectators see in parallel with the rapist, that *physical* positioning only strengthens their *emotional* positioning with the vulnerable and victimized woman who faces rape. In the context of antirape programs, this use of rapist point of view shots in the process of representing rape scenes asks the spectator to be aware of the extreme violence and criminality of rape. Nevertheless, this representational strategy also encourages the spectator to arrive at that awareness by *increasing* an experience of fear either for one's self as a woman or for women generally. After the mid-1980s, the programs tend to replace the fear of an impending attack revealed through the stranger rapist's point of view with the attack itself, experienced from the visual and/or emotional point of view of the woman who faces rape. While this shift in representational strategy and emotional positioning of the spectator offers a more complex understanding of an experience of rape than do the earlier films and videos, it nevertheless does so by potentially heightening the fear of rape for the spectator even more. To put it somewhat reductively again, these later representations encourage the spectator to yell, "Oh no, here he comes!" rather than the more protective self-defense response evoked by the earlier programs that represent the rapists' point of view: "Watch out!" In short, I am arguing that the visual and emotional point-of-view shots/sequences in all these films and videos expand, heighten, and perpetuate the experience of rape, as well as its (representational) existence. These shots/sequences work, at least in part, at counterpurposes with the programs' overall antirape goals of decreasing the existence of rape. Instead, these sequences augment the violence and power of the rapist and intensify the victimization of the woman he assaults.

While it is theoretically possible for a viewer to resist the fear encouraged by the film or video and/or even to derive erotic pleasure from these rape scenes, the structure of the programs I discuss above tends to define the rape scenes as "violence, not sex," and they do so in part by inviting the spectator into an experience of violence devoid of any explicit sexuality. A few examples, however, do draw on more erotic images of women's bodies to argue against sexualized violence. For example, both *Men, Sex, and Rape* and a series of Los Angeles Commission on Assaults against Women public service announcements (1996) show women wearing revealing clothes in order to argue that no matter how erotic these images appear to be (e.g., giving away a phone number, kissing, wearing sexy clothing), "This is not an invitation to rape me." (The public service announcements explicitly print this phrase in red lettering that appears over the black and white imagery at the end of each spot.) Sut Jhally's *Dreamworlds* (1994) also uses sexualized images of scantily clad women, intercutting clips of women from MTV videos with the rape scene from the film *The Accused* (1988) to suggest that "images of this kind [the easy sexual availability of women in the media, particularly MTV] might cultivate attitudes that could legitimize rape" (represented by the fictionalized rape scene from *The Accused*) (Jhally 1994, 153).

Both the Los Angeles public service announcements and *Dreamworlds* are powerful critiques of rape; by using aspects of media culture (such as fashion photography and music videos) against themselves, they argue that media can lead men to *think* (erroneously) that the way a woman dresses may be a sexual invitation. They identify a source of a particular rape myth without reducing that myth to a true and false dichotomy. Unlike the films and videos that depict frightening and *de*contextualized (although horrific) rape scenes, these examples emphasize the relationship between rape and the larger masculinist media culture in order to make a theoretical point about the media's symbiotic relationship to cultural attitudes about women's sexual availability, while still insisting that rape is horrific.

Nevertheless, while the red lettering that appears on the screen at the end of the public service announcements insists the images are not an invitation to rape, they do not go so far as to suggest, for example, that they are not an invitation to have sex, or not an invitation to attract the heterosexual male gaze. In fact, they themselves explicitly *address* the heterosexual male spectator: The red lettering says, "This is not an invitation to rape *me*" (emphasis added), drawing a distinction between the spectator and the women the ad depicts and acknowledging that someone (i.e., a heterosexual man[29]) is looking at something (i.e., an objectified woman) that is not to be read as an invitation. In short, while these images may not invite rape, they *do* invite a heterosexual male gaze.[30]

Relatedly, in *Dreamworlds*, while the juxtaposition of the MTV images with *The Accused* invites the spectator to see MTV in a new and critical way, unfortunately, this re-representation of sexually violent images actually can perpetuate representations of rape through repetition. McCaughey and King, for example, argue that because *Dreamworlds'* goal is to shock its audience by rendering television as defamiliarized "entertainment," the video may provide—even encourage—the same kind of pleasures for men and fears for women that MTV videos do and that *Dreamworlds* attempts to criticize.[31]

In response to their dissatisfaction with *Dreamworlds* as a pedagogical tool, McCaughey and King created an alternative video for use in rape prevention and education contexts: *Mean Women*. In their essay on rape education videos, they describe their strategy of constructing a teaching video out of a collection of film clips of what they call "mean women" to use in place of videos such as *Dreamworlds*, which emphasize "dangerous men." They argue,

> Images of "mean women" in film are uncommon. Thus the experience of seeing these images collected reminds many viewers of their rarity, and has the same effect as traditional consciousness raising about the aggression faced by women. . . . The promise of the "mean women" fantasy, then, is not that women may be driven to oppressive violence but rather that men may gain a different sense of women's responses to assault. (385–86)

Here McCaughey and King explicitly state that their goal in producing *Mean Women* is to shift responsibility for changing rape culture from women to men, in part by imagining alternative responses to men's sexualized violence. They edit together various clips from Hollywood films of women fighting back against assault, without the derogatory scenes of sexual violence against women that precede and/or follow the vengeful acts. By showing moments in which "bitches from hell" (to evoke

Thelma and Louise, two prominent figures in this video) protect themselves, McCaughey and King hope to engage in rape prevention education that reverses what they argue is *Dreamworlds'* paradigm of women's fear and men's pleasure. Furthermore, they hope that Hollywood images of men's violence against women will become more strange, less naturalized, for the viewers as a result of this recontextualization of gendered violence.

Although *Mean Women's* thirty minutes of sustained women's power can and does provide pleasure and empowerment for some women viewers, I would argue that this critical strategy of "reversal" will work only when the spectator is able to maintain an unusually high level of suspension of disbelief.[32] Some of *Mean Women's* images of women fighting back are so well known that even if a viewer has not seen the original film s/he may remember the violent attack that precedes (e.g., Harlan's rape of Thelma in *Thelma and Louise* [1991]) or follows (e.g., the alien's attack on Ripley in the *Alien* series) the woman's powerful resistance. The *Total Recall* (1990) clip clearly illustrates how excerpts of women's revenge in the video exist outside the context of the overall violence against women in the original film: *Mean Women* shows Sharon Stone fighting back against Arnold Schwarzenegger, but, immediately following the clip included in *Mean Women*, in the actual film he pulls out a gun and shoots her, declaring in an oft-quoted line: "Consider that a divorce." As in this example, *Mean Women* decontextualizes the images and thus disavows the original films' association of women's power with men's increased violence against women. Furthermore, at least in the *Total Recall* example, the video might even suggest to viewers who recontextualize the clip of Sharon Stone within the entire film (in which she is quickly murdered in response to her aggression) that *not* fighting back is safer than using self-defense. Finally, because popular culture texts in which men attack women sexually far outnumber the relatively few clips re-represented in this short video and because the video may remind the viewer of this fact, *Mean Women*—like *Dreamworlds*—inevitably draws attention to the problem of representations of sexual violence against women in a way that may contribute to it (through implicit reference) rather than provide a significant challenge to it, as McCaughey and King intend.

Overall, then, these rape prevention and education programs *heighten* the representation of rape and sexualized violence when they include descriptive detail, duplication of details on image- and soundtracks and through testimony combined with reenactments of that testimony, visual point-of-view shots for both the rapist and the woman being raped, emotional point-of-view sequences of women who have been or are being raped, eroticized images of women, and occasionally the physical self-defense of either actual or fictional women who experience sexualized violence. Importantly, this heightened representation takes place in the context of films and videos that are primarily produced, marketed, and exhibited as antirape activism. From this perspective, explicit onscreen/ onsoundtrack violence is *de*sensationalized and arguably *under*stated in relation to the general social problem of rape to which these programs respond. These aspects of the programs seek to approximate the experience of rape in order to evoke the horror of the act of rape. This argumentative narration addresses the spectator both emotionally and intellectually as an agent of social change and as a political actor who can use fear and anger to work toward awareness, self-defense, legal reform, and therapeutic transformation in both social and personal ways.

Nevertheless, these representations also "give" rape to the spectator, in the sense that their argumentative narration is *based on* "transferring" an aspect of the experience of rape to the spectator in order to increase understanding and to fulfill an educational goal of informing the general public about rape. The underlying argument of such programs seems to be, "If people understand what rape is like, maybe they will do something to stop it." Paradoxically, however, this aspect of the texts also ultimately increases the existence of rape in the larger culture. I want to emphasize that I am *not* arguing here for a metaphorical understanding of rape in which one might say the films and videos "rape" the audience. This perspective would only add one more layer to the proliferation of rape by *using* rape (as a metaphor) to respond to rapes (as film and video representations) that are already responses to rape (as a physical act). Rather, I am arguing that paying careful attention to the *effectivity of representation in antirape films and videos* is, itself, an antirape strategy. As some of these programs suggest themselves, rape is embedded in media culture and exists not only in people's lives but also in a larger representational field that in turn shapes the understandings and experiences of rape that people often encounter. These programs are also part of this relationship between media representation and the existence and social understanding of rape, and thus they necessarily contribute to an ever expanding set of rape representations.

I am also *not* arguing that the best way to decrease rape would be to cease producing and showing antirape films and videos. A structured absence of attention to rape is only another way of representing rape; indeed, as I discuss in the book's introduction, it is a particularly problematic long-standing way of representing rape (Higgins and Silver 1991). Rather, I am arguing here that the *particular* ways these programs tend to represent the act and experience of rape are troubling because they distill (in the sense of bringing together and intensifying within a text) and personalize (in the sense of making emotional and visceral for the spectator). The conundrum is that to do the opposite—to dilute (and therefore disempower) and defamiliarize (and therefore excise) rape—is virtually if not literally impossible in the cultural context (detailed throughout this book) in which rape is pervasive, not only in our everyday lives but also in our representational worlds. Antirape films and videos cannot will rape away. Nevertheless, the many programs that depend on explicit representations of rape, eroticized sexual violence, and/or decontextualized media images contribute to (even as they challenge) the representational existence of rape.

The Absence of Race

A second troubling aspect of many of these antirape films and videos is the way they curtail attention to the cultural relationship between rape and race. This is troubling, not only because of the lack of attention to antiracism work, but also because it corresponds so directly to the whiteness of postfeminist representations. Like the presence of therapeutic discourses, the absence of race in these programs draws on and supports relatively acritical postfeminist representations of rape. In these films and videos, experts, rapists, and those who have experienced rape are overwhelmingly white, and when they are Asian American, African American, or Latina/o, for example, the texts rarely address any specific way racialized identity might play a role in their experience of rape. On the one hand, much like in postfeminist representations of rape in mainstream film and television, the lack of men of color as rapists in these programs can be understood as an implicit rejection of the long-standing "myth of the Black rapist" (Davis 1981a), which depends on a cultural stereotype of African Americans as overly sexual, presumably leading African American men to rape and African American women to be "unrapable."[33] Concomitantly, a cultural stereotype of white men as in control of their sexuality and white women as simultaneously sexually desirable and passively asexual makes the white man the idealized protector of the white woman, the idealized victim. The representation in almost all these programs of all rapists as white implicitly challenges the part of this cultural narrative that is about men.[34] In these films and videos, men of color cease to exist as rapists (but also as people altogether), while white men become villains and thus lose their privileged status as protectors by definition. Women in this narrative, on the other hand, remain firmly in their racialized roles, with African American and other women of color seemingly unrapable (through their absence) and white women the idealized, standard victim.[35] White women become the primary object of sympathy and care—the ones who deserve spectatorial attention.

Despite this overwhelmingly dominant, although unarticulated, representation of rape as an event that takes place almost entirely among white people, a few of the films and videos do address race more directly. For example, during the dramatization of the planning stage of a gang rape in *Dating Rites: Gang Rape on Campus,* the only man who objects to the plan and refuses to attend the party is African American. All other characters in the dramatization are white. While this video is similar to the films and videos that include one or two token people of color without addressing the issue of race, it does more directly counter the myth of interracial rape of white women by men of color by casting an African American man as a detractor. He is a passive detractor, however; he simply disappears from the dramatization, taking with him the momentary and oblique attention to the cultural racialization of rape and leaving the white men behind to carry out the rape.

Good Things Too: Recovery from Sexual Abuse (1995) also addresses race, but without dialogue or narration to counter the racism embedded in many social understandings of rape. Because race is nevertheless central to the organization of the video, I offer a somewhat extended analysis of this example. Rather than casting a man of color as the (momentary) hero as does *Dating Rites,* this video makes the unusual move (for the 1990s) of casting an Asian American man as the ultimate villain. Furthermore, it represents an Asian American teen, this man's daughter, as the least idealized post–sexual abuse subject in the video.

This video is a dramatization of a fictional teen therapy group, complete with a sympathetic counselor and two male teens and three female teens who have experienced abuse. The counselor's primary role in the video is to assure the teens that their feelings of guilt, responsibility, self-hate, and loneliness are "typical" but unnecessary, since the abuse is not their fault, they are good people, and they now can depend on each other in a therapeutic context. Taking place across several months, the video's segments show the passage of time during the healing process, representing a different character telling her or his story to the group at each session. As they tell their stories, animated flashbacks represent their memories while quick intercuts to brief shots in the present show them talking and their groupmates listening sympathetically.

Given this obvious repetitive structure, it is clear very early in the video that each of the five teens will tell their stories. However, Melissa, an Asian American teen, seems reluctant to do so. Furthermore, while everyone else looks at each other during their reaction shots and smiles, cries, or nods sympathetically, Melissa never looks up during her reaction shots, performing a stereotypical passive Asian American popular culture identity. Given that the entire video's therapeutic structure suggests that it is important to speak about one's experience of sexual abuse in order to achieve "good things too" through "recovery," Melissa's silence makes her the least ideal example of a therapeutic subject because she refuses to engage in a "talking cure." Furthermore, the video's implicit promise that each story will be told constructs a spectatorial desire to hear and see the story of Melissa's abuse. In this way, it not only represents Melissa as the least ideal member of the group, but it also demands that she leave her (stereotypical) racial and cultural specificity behind and conform to the majority model. Inevitably, she does.

When she tells her story, two aspects of how the video represents what she says are particularly troubling in relation to race. First, her response to her abuse is not self-destructive; rather, she throws herself into her schoolwork. While this presumably is a "real" response that some people have to the experience of sexual abuse (and while lack of self-destructive behavior is generally a good thing), by dramatizing Melissa as the only character who responds in this way, the video draws on and reinforces the myth of the Asian American model minority.[36] For example, the fact that she works hard might imply that she will be okay, and thus she does not need the kind of support and care that the other teens do.

Additionally, the representation of Melissa's father, the man who assaulted her, is troubling. While the assailants in the other stories sometimes appear, often as shadowy figures, the emphasis in the other characters' flashbacks is on the person having the memory and her/his family's response to the assault. For example, during the blonde woman's flashback we never see her abuse or the man who abused her (her brother). Instead, we see her alone in her room, looking frightened, and we see her consume an entire pan of brownies as an example of her bulimia. We also see her mother catch her eating the brownies and respond in a sympathetic way that leads to her ultimate entry into therapy and hence recovery. In Melissa's flashback, however, not only do we see her father, but we see him in a particularly menacing way. Shot from below to appear huge, he hovers over her, placing his hand on her shoulder. Then we see him again, speaking to her in a threatening way as he insists that she sit on his lap. While touching her shoulder and asking her to sit on his lap could be relatively innocuous actions between a father and a daughter, his threatening voice and the low camera angle together construct Melissa's father as the most frightening of all the characters who sexually abuse in this video. He is also the only assailant of color to appear in the video.

One of the Los Angeles Commission on Assaults against Women's public service announcements similarly reinscribes racialized cultural identities. The press release materials as well as several articles in mainstream and alternative Los Angeles papers all claim that these spots, as well as coordinated posters, are powerful critiques because they represent "almost every possible target and situation of rape" (Nichani 1997, 10).[37] Yet, the kinds of rape that appear break down along racial lines. The fashion model images of women who wear sexy clothing that is not an invitation of rape all feature white women. They are beautiful, but aloof; the most they do (not to invite rape) is give their phone number or smile. The one image that expresses eroticism and sexuality through action rather than fashion and clothing, however, features an African American heterosexual couple kissing passionately. Thus, at least in relation to the other announcements, this spot reinforces a cultural stereotype that African Americans are more sexually expressive than are whites, while white women are more erotically appealing, more to-be-looked-at, than are African American women.

Overwhelmingly, rape education films and videos from the early 1970s through to the present simply ignore race by portraying the social world as primarily if not entirely made up of white people. When people of color do appear or the programs do directly address race, as in the few examples I discuss here, the moment is either brief or tends to reinscribe, rather than challenge, racist ideology. Through tokenization, many of these images suggest that a few individuals can represent whole groups of people. Overall, the best the films and videos do is *ignore* the historical links between racism and narratives about rape, leaving those links to continue to operate at an insidious, unspoken level and thus to reinforce an overall cultural tendency to see whiteness as simultaneously invisible and pervasive.

Conclusion: Alternatives?

Several years ago, as part of my ongoing research on and activism against rape, but before studying rape prevention and education programs as closely and critically as I do here, I decided to become a rape crisis line counselor. I did have some trepidation about this decision because I feared that the kinds of narratives I encountered in popular culture and that I discuss throughout this book might resurface in this antirape training context, despite its explicitly feminist goals. Unfortunately, while I did learn many useful skills during the training, one day late in the four-week course some of my original fears about the representational power of rape narratives were confirmed. After discussing the "facts" of rape repeatedly over the four weeks (e.g., rapists are most likely to know their victims and to be of the same race as their victims), the instructor decided to show an episode of *20/20* (or perhaps it was *60 Minutes* or *Primetime Live*). This episode directly contradicted the "facts" the instructor had been articulating. Specifically, the episode told a story about an African American man who had been convicted of committing a series of rapes and was now up for parole. The correspondent's deep and serious voice, the backdrop of the dusty, wind-blown, empty prison yard, and the entire episode's trajectory toward the *unresolved* narrative climax of whether or not the man would be granted parole all encouraged spectatorial anxiety about the violence of the dark-skinned serial stranger rapist who was likely to jump out from behind the nearest bush or car during the night to attack an (implicitly white) innocent victim. Furthermore, the episode's structure and focus on a relatively unusual case of a "convicted serial rapist" reinscribed racist and anti–civil rights discourse about locking away those "animals" for good.

The conversation after the video did not turn to how the ideas in the video might or might not be useful to us when we got our first crisis line call; instead, we discussed with fear and anger the then recent case of a man a grand jury had initially refused to hold over for trial because the woman he had allegedly raped (who was a stranger to him) had asked him to wear a condom (thus presumably implying consent). This conversation was no more helpful than the video; in fact, it only intensified the anxiety about and attention to the type of case we were least likely to get on the crisis line and encouraged racist and simplistic thinking about rape. Despite the four weeks of training, the conversation reproduced U.S. cultural stereotypes that feminist and antiracist activists have been arguing for years inhibit rape prevention, fair court practices, and successful counseling for people who have been raped.[38]

At the time, I wondered why the instructor had not chosen a feminist rape prevention and education program, one that would resist standard postfeminist narrative forms for rape and focus on a variety of skills for fighting and responding to both representations and acts of rape. But, as my discussion in this chapter hopefully illustrates, the "perfect" feminist antirape film or video that I wished for during my own training does not exist. While some of the programs do seek to shift the social definition of rape—away from men of color as rapists or toward a critique of rape culture, for example—they also often heighten anxiety, reproduce a masculine gaze at women's sexualized bodies, recenter whiteness, and individualize rape by providing women with strategies for awareness, prevention, and therapy rather than social action. Furthermore, they leave the institutions of heterosexuality and the male gaze intact and uncriticized. In short, while antirape films and videos have explicit goals different from those of mainstream postfeminist texts (educational and activist goals rather than entertainment-focused and market-driven goals), the antirape programs draw on and contribute to postfeminist culture more than they challenge its circumscribed depiction of rape. In particular, their mid-1980s shift away from stranger rape and self-defense and toward acquaintance rape and therapeutic discourses corresponds to a postfeminist absorption of feminist antirape activism into depoliticized representations of rape. Thus, while these programs' acknowledgment of acquaintance rape illustrates an important shift in feminist arguments, it also undermines that acknowledgment by disconnecting it from the more activist inflection of the earlier videos. Focusing on acquaintance rape goes only so far when the problem is defined as one that affects only middle-class college-educated white women and that can be solved by a turn to individualized therapeutic practices.

Even empowering self-defense models, such as *Give It All You've Got* and the more recent *Mean Women*, tend to individualize rape, thus separating it from its cultural contexts. Shannon Jackson (1993) argues that some self-defense courses teach focused and ritualized narratives about and performances of self-defense and that these narratives and performances leave students unprepared for a variety of experiences that exist outside the scripted encounters, during which instructors at times intentionally leave openings so that students can "successfully" defend themselves. Furthermore, she points out that at least the self-defense classes she studied leave the implicit model of the stranger rapist uncriticized. Certainly, her critique of the self-defense classes she studied can be applied to *Give It All You've Got*.

Yet self-defense culture is much more complex than it appears to be in the films and videos I study here or the model mugging classes Jackson studies. As Martha McCaughey (1997) argues, women's self-defense is becoming more and more popular, not only through more traditional classes like model mugging, but also through women's use of guns, courses that fuse aerobic and self-defense (such as "Cardio Combat"), and I would add television characters like Buffy the Vampire Slayer and television episodes about self-defense (e.g., episodes of *Designing Women*, *Ellen*, and *Sister, Sister*, to name a few). I would argue that this popularity of women's self-defense links it to postfeminist representations of women who can have it all: both physical power and feminine sexuality. From another perspective, however, McCaughey urges feminist theory and criticism to take self-defense culture seriously by considering how it can help locate theories of self and gender viscerally in the body, can help give them materiality and corporeality. McCaughey offers a powerful argument for a task I am willing to take on in relation to my own examination of antirape films and videos, but only with a concomitant historical awareness of the gaps in what these programs offer and an imagination for what else they might offer.

For example, I have argued that the mid-1980s shift from stranger rape and physical self-defense to acquaintance rape and therapeutic recovery in these programs can be understood in relation to the emergence of postfeminist culture in the 1980s. In this way, antirape films and videos, like McCaughey's self-defense culture, are embedded in popular media culture, and thus are a part of the very thing against which they at least initially and implicitly struggle. What would a video that combined attention to acquaintance rape and self-defense look like, for example? If a program combined attention to sexual violence in the everyday contexts of institutions like family, education (high school, college), waged work, and dating with attention to the possibility of self-defense, the definition of both dating and self-defense would have to change. Rather than reifying an image of heterosexual dating as the norm and seeking to help women and men participate more happily in this institution, as do most contemporary antirape films and videos, the video I imagine here might offer ways to defend oneself against the institution of heterosexual dating. Indeed, what if a video addressed sexual violence in lesbian, gay, bisexual, and transgendered relationships? Could it do so without stigmatizing lesbian, gay, bisexual, and transgender people as somehow prone to violent sexuality and without dissociating that violence from violence in heterosexual relationships; celebrated violence against women, lesbians, gays, bisexuals, and transgendered people in popular culture; and the absence of nuanced cultural representations of lesbians, gays, bisexuals, and transgendered people? Or, what if a video not only analyzed how the media contribute to a popular culture that disbelieves women who report rape, as does *The Date-Rape Backlash*, but also acknowledged that the women who get to speak about rape publicly so that they can then be disbelieved in the media are almost always white and thus that the "date rape backlash" is both antiwoman and pro-whiteness, both sexist *and* racist?

Since I have not found these videos yet, on a very practical pedagogical level, as someone who teaches both film studies and women and gender studies, I would choose to show my students some of the videos I discuss here that address rape in various social contexts and encourage their audiences to think beyond the boundaries of both the crazed stranger seeking control over women (not sex with women) and the heterosexual, middle-class, white college acquaintance rapist. *After the Montreal Massacre*, in particular, places rape and sexual violence in both the very local everyday contexts of the home and the street and links those forms of violence to global contexts in which rape is used as a tool of war. Furthermore, by linking the murder of the Montreal women engineering students to rape and other forms of sexual violence, the video is able to make a historically specific argument about how sexual violence is related to antifeminism, which in turn is linked to misogyny. This video is thus simultaneously about rape, feminism, activism, and the structure of media culture itself.

Nevertheless, given that even this complex video separates rape from cultural narratives about race and sidesteps a careful examination of everyday violence within the formerly all-male institutions (such as engineering) into which the video itself points out women are now entering, I would argue that an even more productive approach to using, teaching, and producing rape prevention and education films and videos would be not only to seek out projects like *After the Montreal Massacre* but also to combine two or more of these kinds of programs or approaches in an attempt to invite viewers and students to understand rape in multiple ways *simultaneously*. Monica Chau (1993) makes a similar argument in relation to a 1993 Whitney Museum of American Art exhibition on "the subject of rape" that she helped curate. She chose videos that "bespeak the need for a new cultural literacy that acknowledges different voices, contesting the silence, myths, and fallacies that surround representations of rape" (80). Collectively, she argues, the videos she curated "represent multiple vantage points on the part of the women and men who are both the speaking subject(s) [and] object(s)" (84). In short, I argue here that in order for an antirape program to make good on its promise to challenge rape, it must struggle not only against rape, but also against the pervasive and persuasive power of the cultural narratives about rape and the cultural imperatives to represent it in particular ways. Finally, when teaching film (so much of which includes rape and attempted rape), studying rape in women and gender studies, and participating in antirape activism, I would ask, How else might we represent rape, how else might we use the power and politics of representation against itself?

Conclusion

Despite examining hundreds of films and television shows that represent rape, attempted rape, or the threat of rape in some way, in this book I have really only touched the surface of the plethora of representations of rape in twentieth-century U.S. popular culture. I have even covered only a fragment of the many representations that saturate the last twenty years or so of film and television. Representations of sexual violence pervade our social lives, occupying both public (e.g., movie theaters) and intimate (e.g., living rooms) spaces and defining gendered and racialized social relations. Whether this ubiquity naturalizes depictions of rape for us so that we hardly notice them, draws our attention to them so that we feel overwhelmed by their presence, or places us somewhere in between along this continuum of awareness, it is impossible to avoid encountering representations of rape *often* in our daily lives.

Given this ubiquity (coupled with the general lack of attention to rape in media scholarship generally), feminist media scholarship needs to respond to, make sense of, challenge, and work against the insidiousness of rape representations. One way to do this is to explore their complexity in specific contexts. As I suggest in the book's introduction, rape narratives in various historical and social contexts define and organize social relations in a variety of ways. In this book, I focus on rape narratives in the particular context of post-1980 U.S. postfeminist discourses and film, television, and video texts. I argue that, since about 1980, rape narratives and postfeminist discourses have existed in a co-constitutive relationship, depending on and supporting each other. Postfeminist discourses rely on rape as an easily recognizable and hence salient feminist issue; rape narratives rely on postfeminist assumptions about women's desires, goals, and experiences. In the process, they work together to define feminism in particularly limited ways in terms of gender, race, class, and sexuality. The totality of late-twentieth-century feminist theory and activism certainly is more complex than the feminism postfeminist rape narratives discursively produce, but in popular culture feminism in general includes only white, middle-class women who want (and have) individualized choice and equality in relation to work, family, and (hetero)sexuality, and the few women of color and men who share these visions.

I am not arguing that white, middle-class, heterosexual women should not have access to choice and equality. (Although I would argue that they might want to ask, What forms of disadvantage are produced by supposed access to choice and equality? What other choices are untenable because of access only to the particular forms of equality available?) Rather, I am suggesting that when a pervasive set of discourses defines feminism in these (or any other) limited ways, other options are closed down, other experiences are unaccessed, other possibilities are denaturalized, and other forms of activism are discouraged. On the one hand, I would argue that the larger popular cultural process of incorporating social movements, such as feminism, is basic to mainstream U.S. popular culture. Media function to identify, absorb, transform, and therefore at least partially to disempower movements for social change, even as they give those movements voice within popular culture. It is no surprise that this has happened to feminism so systematically. On the other hand, it is nevertheless important to identify the particular ways theories and practices of social change, such as feminism, are transformed in popular culture. By focusing on one important area of feminist research, activism, and concern—rape—I have tried to identify some of the implications of the particular limits postfeminist discourses place on feminism. Specifically, I argue that postfeminism's version of feminism assumes that antirape activism is no longer necessary, ultimately holds women responsible for responding to rape, often recenters white men in the name of feminist antirape activism, and perpetuates a long-standing tradition of excluding women of color, particularly Black women, from rape scenarios in ways that negate rape's complexity and frequency in their lives.

Throughout this book, I also look at the relationship between postfeminism's version of feminism and rape from the opposite direction—from rape to feminism. On the one hand, films such as *The Accused* (1988) and *Thelma and Louise* (1991) do raise awareness; challenge rape myths and patriarchy; produce public discussions of rape and antirape activism; perhaps influence judges, lawyers, and juries to think through a rape case from a woman's (if not a feminist) perspective; and even, ideally, influence some men to give up or never engage in sexually coercive behavior. Many other films and television shows also include important components of feminist antirape logics, such as an acknowledgment that rape often occurs in such masculine contexts as the military, sports, and fraternities; programs also demonstrate an understanding of some of some women's post-rape experiences, such as feeling a constant need to bathe, being uncomfortable with physical touch, and desiring or engaging in revenge. On the other hand, I also argue that rape films and television shows contribute to the production of the limited versions of feminism that postfeminist discourses propagate. Counterintuitively, these films and television shows, collectively, define rape as *necessary* to feminism. Even while acknowledging some feminist antirape logic, they often simultaneously offer narratives in which a woman's experience of rape releases a supposedly already available latent feminist consciousness with which she pursues abstract equality in the name of family. In these texts, rape empowers feminism. Other rape films and television shows might define feminism as responsible for the existence of rape, for example when independent behavior or the pursuit of equality with men leads to rape or when feminist perspectives make it *more* difficult to tell the difference between coercion and consent. *When rape narratives produce and maintain feminism or suggest that feminism leads to rape, then feminism is used against (other potential versions of) itself.* Furthermore, these texts overwhelmingly subsume rape under a depoliticized version of feminism that is interested only in an unacknowledged whiteness. *When rape narratives perpetuate a social separation of gender and race in the name of a universalized (and therefore implicitly white) feminism, then, again, feminism is used against (other potential versions of) itself.*

In this book, I respond to these co-constitutive relationships between representations of rape and postfeminist discourses about feminism in two general ways. First, in chapters 1, 2, and 3 I describe the relationships I see among rape, feminism, and postfeminism in film and television. Here, my goals are to identify typical representational forms for rape and to identify the most common ways that discourses about rape and postfeminism support each other in their construction of feminism. In pursuit of these goals, I emphasize multiple examples, arguing that no one film or television show matters in and of itself. For example, the relationship between women and independence that runs throughout the history of rape films is available in the 1980s to help postfeminist texts link particular kinds of independence (those related to heteronormativity, corporate capitalism, and the family) to women's social identities. And, the role of rape as narrative instigator, as the fulcrum of narrative causality, again, has long been central to fictional rape films (among other forms of representation) and thus naturalizes post-1980 texts that depend on rape to tell stories about postfeminism's version of feminism. Together, these two aspects of the history of rape in film normalize more recent films and television shows that represent rape as the cause of a woman's actions, actions that lead her directly to make postfeminist choices and to seek postfeminist equality.

In chapters 4, 5, and 6, however, I explore the "limits" of postfeminist discourses, developing three types of case studies and using my critical practice to resist and work against postfeminism as a social concept. In the chapter on *Thelma and Louise,* I look for aspects of a single film that move beyond postfeminist definitions of rape and of feminism. This case study illustrates that one single film, even a mass-mediated film such as *Thelma and Louise,* offers possibilities for escaping the bounds of its critical reception, and will always allow for more meanings and critical readings than any one reception context (such as the popular press) acknowledges. On the one hand, as I also emphasize through my readings of *Duel in the Sun* (1946), *Shanghai Express* (1932), and *Sadie Thompson* (1928) in chapter 1, this means that theoretically any rape film has the potential to be read in ways that are feminist and resistant. Hence, spectators can empower themselves through their responses to texts that bring (representations of) rape into their lives. On the other hand, I would also argue that when feminist media critics (including myself) provide these alternative readings, as so many have with *Thelma and Louise,* we should do so with consciousness of how representations of rape may facilitate our readings. Unfortunately, very few scholars who have written about *Thelma and Louise* address the role of rape in the film, revealing a relative blind spot about rape in feminist media studies.

In chapter 5, I challenge postfeminism from another perspective. Rather than examining and partially reclaiming a highly mediated film that has been used by the popular press in decidedly postfeminist ways, in this chapter I seek out representations that are generally excluded from postfeminist discourses: those that represent Black women. Here, I resist postfeminist discourse that ignores Black women by selecting less common examples for analysis. Then, through my critical reading practices, I resist how those very texts often decenter Black women from the stories that nevertheless depend on their experiences of rape. In other words, I turn my critical attention both to postfeminist discourses and to where many of these films and television shows that include Black women suggest it does not belong: on Black women themselves. Furthermore, in anticipation of the final chapter, which moves away from mainstream examples altogether, in chapter 5 I spend a significant amount of time exploring the representation of African American women in relation to rape in some films that exist on the margins of mainstream cinema; these films are produced by African American film-makers (John Singleton, Spike Lee, and Julie Dash) who define themselves as antiracist activists and consider their filmmaking part of that activism. This critical move both challenges postfeminist discourses by moving away from the mainstream context in which they thrive and challenges the films for the ways they, to varying degrees, collude with postfeminist discourses' displacement of African American women.

In the final chapter, I look to antirape activist films and videos in the hopes of finding alternative forms of representation for rape, forms that might undermine postfeminism's definitions of rape, feminism, and their intersections. Unfortunately, these antirape activist programs illustrate more how pervasive postfeminist ideas are than how antirape activism has been able to resist and undermine those ideas. This particular approach to studying the representation of rape—exploring texts that one would expect to be both feminist and critical of more mainstream representations—is especially important in a project such as mine that seeks both to understand and to challenge how far-reaching postfeminist discourses are.

Overall, I speak back to postfeminism in the second half of the book, and the critical approaches I take to the texts (reading a media spectacle rape film from multiple perspectives, focusing critical attention where it is discouraged, and examining nonmainstream activist films and videos) do illustrate some spaces into which postfeminist discourses do not go and do help broaden those spaces through critical practice. Nevertheless, collectively chapters 4, 5, and 6 also illustrate just how pervasive postfeminism is and how tenacious particular forms of representations of rape are. For example, the absent presence of rape in myriad texts, codified in the self-regulating Hollywood Production Code, reemerges in some feminist media criticism that grapples with important questions of feminist possibility in more recent popular culture texts, such as *Thelma and Louise*. And, the myopic focus on Black men and white women in (some) antiracist and feminist antirape activism, respectively, emerges in the relatively few films and television shows that do represent a relationship between Black women and rape, even a highly praised feminist film such as *Daughters of the Dust*. Furthermore, postfeminist and rape discourses do not only support each other in their discursive constructions of feminism in mainstream post-1980 fictional films and television shows, but they also function co-constitutively in activist films and videos designed for an educational context in which one might hope critical perspectives on mainstream culture, on popular definitions of feminism, and on rape would emerge.

What does the tenaciousness of postfeminist logics and particular (limited and limiting) types of rape representations mean for feminist media criticism and for antirape activism? It means a need to be vigilant, as I have tried to be throughout this book, about identifying and challenging representations of rape for their contributions to discursive definitions of gender, race, class, sexuality, nationality, and feminism. It means a need to be open, again as I have tried to be throughout this book, to the complexity of narrative and of representation, to the possibility that the overwhelming presence of rape in our representational world does not function only to debilitate, frighten, and confine. In other words, I hope this book provides strategies for confronting the inevitable representations of rape and sexual violence that pervade contemporary U.S. media culture, strategies that open up spaces for alternative definitions of rape, feminism, antirape activism, and media generally.

One of the reasons I consider a critique of both postfeminist discourses and rape narratives to be imperative is because of the ways they function pedagogically. In defining pedagogy, Henry A. Giroux (1994) writes, "There is no absolute sign under which pedagogy can be defined. Instead, pedagogy refers to the production of and complex relationships among knowledge, texts, desire, and identity" (29–30). Given this definition, he includes popular culture as a "pedagogical apparatus" (43) generally. More specifically, not only the educational antirape films and videos I discuss in chapter 6, which explicitly depend on pedagogical discourses, but also many of the mainstream postfeminist texts I discuss throughout the book draw on sound bites of feminist antirape logics to "teach" the audience how to understand rape, feminism, and women's experience.

This teaching function of texts such as *The Accused* and *Rosewood* (1996), for example, is troubling, because the particular versions of feminist antirape activism they teach are limited and even sometimes internally contradictory. In other words, when *The Accused* instructs its audience, through the character of Ken, that it is imperative to speak out when one sees a rape, to bear witness, it evades the question of why Ken did not try to stop the rape itself. When *Rosewood* draws on a "real" historical example to teach its audience that racist white lynchings and massacres of African American men and communities were often supported by cultural myths about rape produced and sustained by (not individual white women but) entire white communities and actively supported by powerful white institutions such as the police, it leaves another lesson as only an implicit and muted aspect of the film: that African American women simultaneously face repeated and unavoidable sexual coercion in multiple areas of their work and daily life. This is not an argument that the media should (or could) represent rape in a way that is complex enough to address the nuances of the theoretical and activist feminist perspective I draw on and articulate throughout this book: I am not arguing for "better" representations here. Rather, I am arguing for critical thought and pedagogy that draw attention to the ways even well-meaning profeminist and antiracist texts and discourses in popular culture can simultaneously reinscribe sexism and racism.

Despite the downright exhausting ubiquity of representations of rape in the entire history of film and more recently in postfeminist discourses of late-twentieth-century fictional U.S. films and television shows, I hope this book suggests strategies for responding to, researching, and teaching about these texts. In other words, this book offers methods for drawing attention to the role of rape in the history of film (and thus by implication in film studies), for addressing the pervasiveness of representations of rape, and for challenging the ubiquity of postfeminism.

Notes

1. After two separate hung jury trials, during which five women testified against him, University of California, Davis, student Robert Lugo pled no contest to four of the original "21 rape-related charges" in order to avoid a pending third trial (Keene 1999).

2. Relatedly, during a class presentation when one of my students asked her classmates how old they were when they first found out about rape, *every one* of the students who responded reported first encountering rape through the mass media. Their examples included the film *The Accused* (1988), the television show *Little House on the Prairie*, and *Parents* magazine.

3. Parent and Wallace base this claim on interviews with ex-slaves. In no way am I suggesting either that this strategy was altogether effective or that slaves did not often fiercely resist these sometimes subtle attempts at indoctrination. My point is that slave holders intended to use rape as a means for social control.

4. On racial specificity in antebellum law, see, for example, Bardaglio and Sommerville. Overall, African American men faced much harsher and more frequent punishments for rape than did white men. Jennifer Wriggins (1983) makes this point and connects it to continued racism in early 1980s court practices. See Kimberlé Crenshaw (1991) for a discussion of continuing racism in U.S. rape convictions and sentencing in the 1990s.

5. For example, see Ida B. Wells-Barnett (1909), Angela Y. Davis (1981a), Bardaglio, Sommerville, Martha Hodes (1993), and Robyn Wiegman (1993).

6. Davis criticizes the following feminist analyses of rape: Susan Brownmiller, *Against Our Will: Men, Women, and Rape* (1975); Shulamith Firestone, *The Dialectic of Sex: The Case for Feminist Revolution* (1971); Jean MacKellar, *Rape: The Bait and the Trap* (1975); and Diana E. H. Russell, *The Politics of Rape: The Victim's Perspective* (1975). Other scholars who challenge racism in Brownmiller's highly influential *Against Our Will* include Wriggins (128 n.155), Valerie Smith (1990, 158), and Catherine Clinton (1994, 206).

7. Davis's discussion is a reminder of Wells-Barnett's discussion of this myth. Also see Hazel V. Carby (1985; 1987).

8. By moving from the beginning of the twentieth century (in this section) to the last few decades of the twentieth century (in the next section), I do not mean to imply either that rape narratives did not continue to function in various ways in between these two periods, or that feminist activism did not begin to discuss rape until the 1970s. Rather, I choose to focus on the 1970s because this was the first time feminism and rape were both highly visible in popular culture, often appearing in concert with each other. For discussions of rape in the intervening years, see, for example, Mary E. Odem (1995) on the increase in age of consent laws through the 1920s as a means of both controlling young women and addressing their experiences of abuse; Patricia A. Turner (1993) on rumors about interracial rape contributing to a June 1943 riot in Belle Isle, Detroit (51); Elaine Tyler May (1988) on cold war era "hysteria" over an "alleged wave of sex crimes" (96); and Ruth Rosen (2000) on Betty Millard's 1947 suggestion that "it might be interesting to consider the question of rape as a form of violence practiced against women" (quoted in Rosen, 31) rather than as a form of "aggressive sex" (Rosen, 31). This "rape reform concept" of rape as violence, not sex, did not become a commonly accepted feminist truth until the 1970s.

9. See Davis (1975) for a discussion of the Joanne Little case.

10. For more detailed discussions of the history of rape law reform, see Nancy A. Matthews (1994), Cassia Spohn and Julie Horney (1992), and Carole Goldberg-Ambrose (1992).

11. See Crenshaw for a more recent discussion of these continuing racist structures in rape law and in some feminist antirape work.

12. See Jeanne March, Alison Geist, and Nathan Caplan (1982); Susan Estrich (1987); and Gregory M. Matoesian (1993).

13. For a cogent and varied discussion of rape culture, see the anthology *Transforming a Rape Culture*, edited by Emilie Buchwald, Pamela R. Fletcher, and Martha Roth (1993).

14. Susan Jeffords (1988) offers an excellent discussion of rape in war and the military from a media/cultural studies perspective. On rape in the context of masculine sports, see Jeffrey R. Benedict (1998).

15. While Laura Mulvey (1975) does not discuss rape per se, I borrow her concept of women as objects-to-be-looked-at, developed in her feminist psychoanalytic analysis of classical Hollywood cinema.

16. See Liz Kelly (1988) on sexual violence as a continuum. For a cogent analysis of sexual harassment on the street as one example of the "everydayness" of sexual violence, see Carol Brooks Gardner (1995).

17. See Tami Spry (1995) for a thoughtful discussion of the limiting nature of *both* "victim" and "survivor" as terms to describe women who have been raped. In order to avoid the passivity of "victim" and the implicit reference to trauma in the term "survivor," throughout this book I have chosen to use the admittedly more unwieldy phrase "women who have been raped." I make an effort to avoid

even saying "her rape" or "her rapist" in order to resist defining rape as something that "belongs" to women or is somehow their responsibility.

18. See Martha McCaughey (1997) for a brief discussion of the history of feminist self-defense classes and for an analysis of the more recent movement of self-defense into popular culture generally. See Shannon Jackson (1993) for a race- and class-based critique of some self-defense classes and for a discussion of their overreliance on a stranger-rape model. I discuss self-defense more fully in chapter 6.

19. I draw the information in this paragraph from my own experience during training and as a volunteer at a rape crisis center and from the following two essays: Amy Fried (1994) and Rebecca Campbell, Charlene K. Baker, and Terri L. Mazurek (1998).

20. For more on a critique of traditional rape crisis and domestic violence centers and on the specificity of centers geared toward the needs of women of color, see Anannya Bhattacharjee (1997), Crenshaw, Sandyha Shukla (1997), and United States Commission on Civil Rights (1992, 174–80). In particular, I develop a discussion of African American women's relationship to rape more fully in chapter 5.

21. I do not conceive of my activism and my scholarship as separate; nevertheless, they do sometimes lead me to ask the different kinds of questions and to make the different kinds of arguments I discuss in this paragraph.

22. Girls, boys, and men, while not the primary focus of this book, also face rape.

23. Also see Cuklanz (2000) for a discussion of this process during this time period, particularly in relation to television.

24. Jeffords (1991) argues that the roles of victim, protector, and villain in the long-standing tradition of the captivity narrative helped to facilitate and possibly bring about the fighting of the Persian Gulf War (208). She argues that this narrative had "the overall purpose of requalifying the United States as international and national protector . . . [and served] the very construction of citizenship in the new world order" (210). Furthermore, she points out that in this context rape functioned primarily as a metaphor to justify U.S. protectionism; the popular press rarely mentioned actual rapes of Kuwaiti women during the war and never mentioned actual rapes of Iraqi, Saudi, and U.S. women. Public discourse about the rape of Bosnian women by Serbian forces, however, figured prominently in constructing the United States as primary protector and thus central citizen of the "new world order" (e.g., see the following cover stories: "A Pattern of Rape: War Crimes in Bosnia," in *Newsweek* [Post et al. 1993] and "Exclusive! New Testimony from the Rape/Death Camps Reveals *Sexual Atrocities Being Used as Pornography*" in *Ms.* [MacKinnon 1993]). During the more recent Kosovo situation, as during the Gulf War, rape functioned only metaphorically until late in the U.S. news coverage. However, in April 1999 the *New York*

Times reported mass rapes in one short paragraph (Perlez 1999). By June, rape became a featured topic in a front-page *New York Times* article, entitled "Deny Rape or Be Hated: Kosovo Victims' Choice" (Bumiller 1999). On rape as genocide in Rwanda, see the *New York Times* editorial "When Rape Becomes Genocide" (1998).

25. See Esther Madriz (1997) for an ethnographic study of the way fear of crime, including rape, constrains women's lives in ways that are not only inconsistent with, but also directly contradictory to, statistics on the prevalence of rape and other violent crime.

26. See Kyra Pearson (1995), Rosalind Pollack Petchesky (1981), Katha Pollitt (1990), and Sheila Scraton (1994), respectively, for analyses of the intersections of these topics with postfeminism.

27. On Davis's discussion of pre-1980s women of color feminism, see Rosa Linda Fregoso (1999). Fregoso also cites Lisa Lowe (1997) on this point.

28. For a fuller discussion of how strategic whiteness has functioned historically to elide issues of race, see Sarah Projansky and Kent A. Ono (1999).

29. For analyses of print journalism depictions of actual cases, see Helen Benedict (1992) and Marian Meyers (1997). For analyses of rape on television, see Cuklanz (1996; 2000) and Sujata Moorti (1995). For analyses of rape narratives in a non-U.S. context, see Jenny Sharpe (1993). Some important work has been done on rape in U.S. film (e.g., Jeffords [1988], Julia Lesage [1981], Gina Marchetti [1993], and Shohat [1991a]), and I rely on this scholarship throughout this book. Nevertheless, to my knowledge no book-length study of rape in film has been published before now.

30. See Kathleen Rowe (1995b) for a discussion of her approach to a similar cross-media project focused on "a 'topos' . . . of the unruly woman" (54).

31. For books on these media spectacles, see Cynthia Baughman (1995), David Lavery (1995), Robert Gooding-Williams (1993), Toni Morrison (1992), Susan Jeffords and Lauren Rabinovitz (1994), and Taylor Harrison, Sarah Projansky, Kent A. Ono, and Elyce Rae Helford (1996), respectively.

32. For example, see Henry Jenkins (1992) and Jacqueline Bobo (1995).

33. For an analysis that does address audience response to representational violence, see Philip R. Schlesinger et al. (1992).

34. See Lynn A. Higgins and Brenda R. Silver (1991) for a discussion of the long-standing absent presence of rape in narrative.

35. Chapter 5 primarily examines representations of African American women, but it does include one example of a Black woman from Nigeria living in the United States. Hence, I shift back and forth between the terms "Black" and "African American," as appropriate. While narratives about the rape of all women of color offer potential challenges to postfeminism's whiteness, I choose to focus on Black women in particular in this chapter because they are the second most common racialized group to appear in rape narratives, after white women. See

chapter 5 for a fuller discussion of the logic behind and admitted limitations of my choice.

NOTES TO CHAPTER 1

1. This leaves the study of the specificities of the representation of rape in independent, alternative, avant-garde, and activist film and video for a separate project. I examine some of these texts in chapter 6.

2. I begin with 1903 because, although I assume there must be earlier examples, this is the first year in which I have found a representation of rape in film. I end with 1979 because the remainder of this book addresses rape films in the context of post-1980 postfeminist culture.

3. For example, see Lynn A. Higgins and Brenda R. Silver (1991) and Ella Shohat (1991a).

4. Vasey draws on Lea Jacobs (1991) to make this point.

5. A look through *Reader's Guide to Periodical Literature* from the late 1800s to the present supports this linear argument about popular culture texts' increasing attention to rape. The entries under "rape" and related categories held fairly steady at a few citations per decade until the 1970s, but since then they have grown exponentially. I do not mean to imply that the *actual* numbers of rapes have increased; rather, I would suggest that the *explicit* public discussion of rape has increased. Additionally, the explicitness of article titles shifts, for example, from "Night of Terror, a Lifetime of Anguish" (Bernstein 1956) to "Women against Rape" (1973).

6. Molly Haskell implicitly makes the same point with the title of her 1973 book, *From Reverence to Rape*, one of the first book-length studies of women and film. While her discussion of rape in the book is cursory, her title implies that female characters in film were protected during the Production Code era; whereas, by the early 1970s they more often faced assault. Scholars such as Vivian C. Sobchack (1977), Susan L. Brinson (1989), and Carol J. Clover (1992) make similar arguments. For example, Clover writes that although "rape—real, threatened, or implied—has been a staple of American cinema more or less from the beginning," it was "typically a side theme . . . until the early 1970s" (137).

7. "Internet Movie Database," http://us.imdb.com/search.html, and "Motion Picture: Database," http://www.tvguide.com/MovieDb/MovieSearch.asp. Additionally, I used the keyword search function available with the CD-ROM "Cinemania 97."

8. For example, I draw on Julia Lesage's (1981) and Gina Marchetti's (1993) work on *Broken Blossoms* (1919).

9. I also have relied heavily on suggestions from friends and colleagues who are aware of my research. I cannot overstate how valuable these chance references have been.

10. For example, without providing examples of the other "rape fantasies" to which she refers, in an otherwise excellent analysis Marchetti writes, "*As in many rape fantasies, [The Cheat* (1915)] offers a peculiar invitation to women to identify with the attacker, to see themselves as pitted against the same authority that he opposes in trying to possess her" (23, emphasis added). Similarly, Joel Shrock (1997) overgeneralizes when he writes, "Popular films reflected and capitalized upon these sexual, ethnic, racial, and cultural tensions by depicting evil rapists as African Americans and immigrants of the criminal classes. The rapist in these early films *always* represents cultures that were considered uncivilized and underdeveloped by native-born Americans of the middle and upper classes" (73, emphasis added). Even more problematically, Haskell virtually ignores rape in *From Reverence to Rape*, even though the title seems to promise a substantial analysis of the topic.

11. For example, see *The Jungle* (1914), *The American Beauty* (1916), *The Fool's Revenge* (1916) (drugged); *Body and Soul* (1915) (amnesia); and *Infidelity* (1917) (hypnotism). One film, *The Girl o' Dreams* (1916), uses a childlike state, produced by the shock of a shipwreck, as a mark of hypervictimization.

12. For example, see *La Vie de Boheme* (1916) and *Faith of the Strong* (1919).

13. For example, see *The Innocence of Ruth* (1916) and *The Devil's Circus* (1926).

14. For example, see *The Human Orchid* (1916), *The Ragged Princess* (1916), and *A Man's Law* (1917).

15. Both Halliwell (1988) and Wayne Wilson (1988) claim *Johnny Belinda* is the first post–World War II film to represent rape directly.

16. *Peyton Place* (1957) also represents a rape that transforms a woman into a silent figure.

17. For example, see *Pull Down the Curtains, Suzie* (1904).

18. For example, see *What Happened in the Tunnel* (1903).

19. For example, see *The Miller's Daughter* (1905).

20. Many other films include employer attacks. For example, see *The Hand of Destiny* (1914), *Help Wanted* (1915), *Pearls of Temptation* (1915), *The End of the Rainbow* (1916), *The Shop Girl* (1916), *The Love That Lives* (1917), *The Devil's Playground* (a serial that ran from May 1917 to June 1918), and *The Grain of Dust* (1918). Not only working-class jobs are dangerous for women. See *When a Woman Sins* (1918) and *The Call of the Soul* (1919) (nurses), *Something New* (1920) (writer), and *The Arab* (1915) and *Auction of Souls* (1919) (missionaries). Also see my discussion below of rape in the context of the art, singing, dance, and theater worlds. This link between work and rape is particularly common in the 1910s, but later films include it as well. For example, see *$20 a Week* (1935), *The House by the River* (1950), and *Killer's Kiss* (1955). In the 1970s, anxiety about women in public spaces emerged in relation to women in prison in rape films such as *Terminal Island* (1973) and *Caged Heat* (1974).

21. For example, see *The Unbroken Road* (1915), *Mr. Goode, the Samaritan* (1916), and *The Sunset Princess* (1918).

22. For example, see *The Great Divide* (1915), *June Friday* (1915), and *The Sunset Princess* (1918). *The Unbroken Road* (1915) combines both an elopement and a false marriage.

23. For example, see *Maiden and Men* (1912), *Betty and the Buccaneers* (1917), *The Little American* (1917), *The Painted Lie* (1917), *Beach of Dreams* (1921), *The Sheik* (1921), *The Thief of Bagdad* (1924), *My Official Wife* (1926), and *Son of the Sheik* (1926).

24. Also see, for example, *The Almighty Dollar* (1916), *Barbary Sheep* (1917), *The Devil's Assistant* (1917), *Easy Money* (1917), *A Woman Alone* (1917), *A Desert Wooing* (1918), *Her Husband's Honor* (1918), and *A Modern Salome* (1920). In some films, the flirtatious woman does not face rape but is replaced in her husband's or lover's life by a vulnerable woman whom he rescues from rape. In this context, a vulnerable woman who is nearly raped enters marriage while an independent woman now faces undesired solitude. For example, see *Tangled Lives* (1918) and *Two Women* (1919).

25. For example, see *Woman Hungry* (1931), *Call Her Savage* (1932), *The Painted Woman* (1932), *Panama Flo* (1932), *Riding for Justice* (1932), *Stowaway* (1932), *Tess of the Storm Country* (1932), *Three Wise Girls* (1932), *Man of the Forest* (1933), *She Had to Say Yes* (1933), and *The Ship of Wanted Men* (1933).

26. On sexual tension in screwball comedies, see, for example, Stanley Cavell (1981), Kathleen Rowe (1995a), and David R. Shumway (1991).

27. *Breakfast for Two* (1937).

28. *Next Time I Marry* (1938).

29. Like many screwball comedies, this film also includes violence directed at the man by the woman; in fact, it includes *sexual* violence from the woman to the man. For example, in addition to Doris slapping Stephen, a later scene reverses this exchange when he slaps her in frustration and she kisses him in response. Nevertheless, the violence is primarily directed against the woman. As in *His Girl Friday* (1940) and many other screwball comedies, in *We're Not Dressing* the constant shifting between the man and the woman having the upper hand ends with his control both over the culmination of the narrative and over her.

30. For example, see *The Round Up* (1941), *Frenchman's Creek* (1944), and *Jubal* (1956). Also see *Strange Illusion* (1945), in which a widow recklessly dates a villain who attempts to rape her daughter.

31. For example, see *I Was a Shoplifter* (1950).

32. For example, see *The Accused* (1949).

33. For example, see *Anatomy of a Murder* (1959).

34. For example, see *A Streetcar Named Desire* (1951).

35. For example, in *Seven Brides for Seven Brothers* (1956), based on "The Rape of the Sabine Women," the narrative itself functions as a coercive agent that requires the "brides" to fall in love with the "brothers."

36. For example, see *Miss Sadie Thompson* (1953).

37. See *Kitty Foyle* (1940), in which Mark coerces Kitty into a date by threatening to reveal the fact that she is faking a feminine faint if she does not comply.

38. Also see *The Chapman Report* (1962), *Of Love and Desire* (1963), *Candy* (1968), *Puzzle of a Downfall Child* (1970), and *A Walk in the Spring Rain* (1970).

39. This tension is based on nationality as well as class. The film takes place in England, Amy's home, but David is from the United States.

40. Films that celebrate the possibility of cross-class romance, depending on rape as a plot device, include *Highway of Hope* (1917) and *The Little Runaway* (1918). A few films, such as *La Vie de Boheme* (1916), depict romantic relationships between people of different classes as doomed.

41. See Marchetti (27–32) and Staiger (1995) for a development of this argument.

42. For example, see *Hand of Destiny* (1914), *Samson* (1915), *The Road Called Straight* (1919), and *The Road of Ambition* (1920). More tempered films that depict wealthy men as villainous include an additional character from the same class (and usually from the same family) who saves the woman from rape. For example, see *Help Wanted* (1915), *A Woman's Honor* (1916), *Beloved Jim* (1917), and *The Shuttle* (1918).

43. For example, see *The Mischief Maker* (1916), *The Cabaret Girl* (1918), *A Desert Wooing* (1918), and *The Mask* (1918).

44. For example, see *The Cheat* (1915), *Diamonds and Pearls* (1917), *The Mask* (1918), and *A Modern Salome* (1920).

45. For example, see *The Littlest Rebel* (1914), *Into the Primitive* (1916), *Hell Morgan's Girl* (1917), and *A Rich Man's Plaything* (1917).

46. Lesage writes, "It seems clear beyond the need for any more elaboration here that Burrows' breaking into the closet with an ax and dragging the cowering Lucy out between the broken boards visually symbolizes rape" (52). Lesage's claim that this scene clearly symbolizes rape "beyond the need for any more elaboration" is perhaps unpersuasive. Part of the goal of feminist criticism that analyzes connotative rape, as I argue throughout this book, is to provide the elaboration Lesage claims is unnecessary. Interestingly, despite her claim, she does provide specific examples to support her point. In addition to discussing the examples I include here, she discusses the "role of the bed in the visual composition and mise-en-scène" (52).

47. Both Lesage and Marchetti argue that an intertitle that assures the spectator that Cheng's interest in Lucy is not sexual functions to introduce and reinforce the idea that it is, in fact, sexual. Furthermore, Marchetti argues that Burrows "reacts to the theft of Lucy as a rape" (36).

48. For example, see *The Jungle* (1914), *The House of a Thousand Scandals* (1915), *Unprotected* (1916), *A Rich Man's Plaything* (1917), *Cheating the Public* (1918), and *The Belle of the Season* (1919).

49. Nevertheless, in the 1935 film *Crime and Punishment* a woman loses her job because she resists her employer's husband's attempt to rape her, throwing her family further into poverty. A villainous wealthy man appears again in the 1940 film *Secrets of a Model*.

50. Films that depict the entertainment world as dangerous to women through the theme of rape or attempted rape include *The Butterfly Girl* (1917), *Man and Woman* (1920) (circus); *The Cabaret Girl* (1918) (cabaret); *Bobbie of the Ballet* (1916), *The Quest for Life* (1916), *The Stolen Kiss* (1920) (dance); *The American Beauty* (1916), *The Mischief Maker* (1916), *Not My Sister* (1916), *The Soul of Kura-San* (1916), *The Painted Lie* (1917), *It Happened in Paris* (1919) (art world); *The On-the-Square-Girl* (1917), *Runaway Girls* (1928) (clothes modeling); *Bend in the Bone* (1915), *The Luring Lights* (1915), *Bread* (1918) (acting setting); *The Bravest Way* (1918) (singing); and *Modern Love* (1918) (acting and art world). Some films depict male artists as saviors but do not place the rape narratives in the context of an art world: for example, *The Twin Triangle* (1916), *Unprotected* (1916), and *The Auction of Virtue* (1917). Other films depict male artists as rapists, but again do not place the rape narratives in the context of the art world: for example, *The Saintly Sinner* (1917) and *The Black Gate* (1919).

51. For example, see *The Sins of Nora Moran* (1933).

52. For example, see *Panama Flo* (1932).

53. For example, see *Cheating Blondes* (1933) and *Killer's Kiss* (1955).

54. For example, see *Law of the Sea* (1931), *Stowaway* (1932), *Tess of the Storm Country* (1932), and *Moontide* (1942).

55. Also see, for example, *Riot in Juvenile Prison* (1959) and *Riot on Sunset Strip* (1967). For additional examples of "violent youth" films, see *Mad Dog Coll* (1961), *Lady in a Cage* (1964), *Change of Habit* (1969), and *Gas-s-s-s* (1970). *The Violent Years* (1956) represents a violent *female* youth who rapes an innocent young man. Films also link rape to other social class groups, including motorcycle gangs: for example, *Devil's Angels* (1967), *The Glory Stompers* (1967), *The Savage Seven* (1968), *The Cycle Savages* (1969), *Satan's Sadists* (1969), *C.C. and Company* (1970), *The Peace Killers* (1971), *The Young Graduates* (1971), and *Sharks* (1974); alcohol users (especially in the 1910s during the debate over prohibition): for example, *The Luring Lights* (1915), *The Silent Battle* (1916), *Susan Rocks the Boat* (1916), *The Fringe Society* (1917), *Hell Morgan's Girl* (1917), *The Highway of Hope* (1917), *Coals of Fire* (1918), *The Family Skeleton* (1918), and *The Sign Invisible* (1918); and drug users: for example, *Black Fear* (1915), *June Friday* (1915), *The Devil's Needle* (1916), *The Devil's Assistant* (1917), *The Border Raiders* (1918), *A Romance of the Underworld* (1918), *Riot on Sunset Strip* (1967), *The Hooked Generation* (1968), and *The Cycle Savages* (1969).

56. See Herman Gray (1995) for a discussion of a similar process in late-twentieth-century assimilationist television texts. I discuss his argument in more depth in chapter 2.

57. For a related argument about the reification of racial categories in a recent video about mixed race people (*Doubles: Japan and America's Intercultural Children* [1995]), see Kent A. Ono (1998).

58. Of course, Cheng is too late actually to rescue Lucy, which is another bend in the standard narrative.

59. I should point out that (the examples I discuss in this section notwithstanding) the overwhelming majority of rape films sublimate race by depicting rape as something that happens between white women and white men who are not aware of themselves as racialized.

60. For example, see Angela Y. Davis (1981a), Hazel V. Carby (1985), and Patricia A. Turner (1993).

61. For example, Asian American men (Ono 1997).

62. Also see, for example, *Forgiven; Or, The Jack of Diamonds* (1914) and *The Great Divide* (1915).

63. It is important to point out that Gus never actually attempts to rape Little Sister in *Birth of a Nation*; he simply chases her until in fear she jumps to her death. Nevertheless, characters in the film, contemporary spectators (see Staiger 1992), and many scholars interpret his actions as attempted rape. Scholars address the diverse roles rape plays in this film, for example, to signify white men as saviors of civilization (Shrock), to produce a new representational mode (Ferguson 1987), to produce both racist and resisting spectators (Diawara 1988), and to explain public protest (Staiger 1992).

64. *Red River* (1948).

65. *The Searchers* (1956).

66. *The Searchers.*

67. *Stagecoach* (1939).

68. *Stagecoach* and *Union Pacific* (1939). See J. P. Telotte (1998) for a discussion of differences between the two scenes of (almost) murder as protection from rape in *Stagecoach* and *Union Pacific*. Telotte also discusses a similar scene in *Birth of a Nation*.

69. See Peter Lehman (1990) for a fuller discussion of the many ways rape functions in *The Searchers*. About *The Searchers* Clover writes,

> Outright rape is rare in the western, but it could be argued that the possibility of sexual violation inheres in the abduction situation. It certainly hovers about the abduction of Lucy in *The Searchers*. "They'll raise her as one of their own, until she's of age to . . ." an experienced frontiersman predicts, his voice discreetly trailing off. When her body is found, her brokenhearted fiancé asks, "Did they . . . Was she . . . ?" "Don't ask!" comes the brusk answer. (136–37)

70. For example, see *Comanche Station* (1960), *Duel at Diablo* (1966), *Cannon for Cordoba* (1970), and *Ulzana's Raid* (1972).

71. In *Blazing Saddles* (1974), another self-defined antiracist comedic western, a one-line joke—"people stampeded and cattle raped"—turns on a reversal of two standard western tropes.

72. For example, see *A Continental Girl* (1915), *The Sign Invisible* (1918), and *Just Squaw* (1919).

73. Also see, for example, *The Promise* (1917). In chapter 5 I develop a fuller analysis of the historical displacement of Black women's experience of rape.

74. For example, *Baree, Son of Kazan* (1918) also deals with a white man's attempted rape of a Native American woman. *A Fallen Idol* (1919) offers a similar narrative about a Hawai'ian princess.

75. This ending is significantly different from the films in which white women in the United States face rape by men of color: those "couples" are rarely, if ever, reconciled.

76. The same narrative structure appears in *The Savage Seven* (1968), although it takes place in contemporary times and depicts a battle between Native Americans and a white motorcycle gang.

77. Micheaux's *Body and Soul* (1925) also confronts stereotypes of African American men as rapists, although perhaps in a less challenging way. By representing an African American man as a rapist, and then "taking it back" by making that rape only part of an anxious mother's dream, the film emphasizes the power of the stereotype but simultaneously reproduces that stereotype. The dream does not alter the stereotype, as does the complex crosscutting sequence of the (separate) rape and lynching in *Within Our Gates*; instead, the film simply defines the stereotype as false.

78. *Massacre* (1934) and *Naked in the Sun* (1957), for example, have very similar narrative trajectories.

79. Also see, for example, *The Lawless* (1950), *Sergeant Rutledge* (1960), and *The Intruder* (1961). Some 1970s films continue to distance racism as a historical problem. For example, in *Soldier Blue* (1970), a western, soldiers rape and massacre a group of Native Americans who are coming to make peace with them. Rape is also distanced through comedy, as in *Hi, Mom!* (1970) when African American actors put blackface on the liberal white audience that has come to see their performance and then beat, rob, and rape them to show them what it is like to be African American. A white police officer (who is one of the performers), of course, does not believe the white audience's stories.

80. *Lady Sings the Blues* is relatively unusual (although not surprising, given a general villainization of African American men) among the films I examine here because it depicts a man of color raping a woman of color in a contemporary U.S. context. As Ella Shohat and Robert Stam (1994) and Shrock argue, films rarely depict women of color as sympathetic rape victims, if they depict them as victims at all. Shohat and Stam and Davis (1981a) point out that this invisibility helps mask the history of sexual violence as a form of gender and racial

oppression of women of color, as Davis puts it, rendering African American women "unrapable." Much of Shohat and Stam's work on this topic is based on Shohat's 1991 article "Gender and Culture of Empire: Toward a Feminist Ethnography of the Cinema."

81. See Susan Jeffords (1988) for a development of the enemy/friend argument in relation to a more recent film, *Opposing Force* (1986).

82. Films from the 1910s that address immigration in contexts other than white slavery include *The Lure of New York* (1913), *The Jungle* (1914), and *The Yellow Passport* (1916).

83. Like some of the films discussed above, this shift also links fears of abduction to fears about women in public spaces of the city.

84. Also see Shelley Stamp (2000) on white slavery films. Stamp also discusses public anxiety over sexual dangers for women in the space of the movie theater itself.

85. Furthermore, the white rapist is sometimes reformed, or at least martyred, in the process of protecting other whites from the attack by indigenous people. Titles here include *The Last Egyptian* (1914), *The Next in Command* (1914) (Arab world), and *The Explorer* (1915) (Africa).

86. Also see, for example, *Beware* (1919), *Fires of Faith* (1919), and *Something New* (1920).

87. See Nadine Naber (2000) for a discussion of a "media-type [that] portrays generic Arab–Middle Eastern–Muslim men as irrationally violent, particularly towards women" (44). She argues that this media-type continues into the present.

88. Richard Koszarski (1990) lists both *The Thief of Bagdad* and *Son of the Sheik* as the top third and fourth popular films during their years of release, respectively (33). Shrock lists both *The Sheik* and *The Thief of Bagdad* as two of the five top grossing films during their years of release (87).

89. Studlar identifies a similar conversion through planned and thwarted rape in a later Fairbanks film, *The Gaucho* (1928).

90. Films that include a sea setting function similarly to desert locale narratives. While the villain is most often white in these films, he is most often also coded as "outside" society as a result of his life at sea. Furthermore, the woman's sexual vulnerability defines the peril of being lost at sea. For example, see *The Sea Wolf* (1913), *The Girl o' Dreams* (1916), *Into the Primitive* (1916), *The Ship of Doom* (1917), *When a Man Sees Red* (1917), *The Call of the Soul* (1919), *Beach of Dreams* (1921), and *The Black Pirate* (1926).

91. Also see, for example, *East of Borneo* (1931), *The Savage Girl* (1932) (Africa), *The Flaming Signal* (1933) (Hawai'i), *Picture Brides* (1933) (South America), and *Island Captives* (1937).

92. In addition to films that take place in colonial settings, a few films depict the "foreign" man's "invasion" of the United States. For example, see *Infidelity* (1917) and *Love Letters* (1917).

93. Also see, for example, *The Captive* (1915) and *The Outlaw's Revenge* (1915).

94. For example, see *The War of Wars; Or, The Franco-German Invasion* (1914), *Three of Many* (1916), *The Little American* (1917), *A Daughter of France* (1918), and *Beware* (1919).

95. See especially *The Little American* (1917) and *The Child Thou Gavest Me* (1921).

96. Titles here include *The Birth of a Race* (1918), *The Kaiser, the Beast of Berlin* (1918), *To Hell with the Kaiser* (1918), *Behind the Door* (1919), *The Great Victory, Wilson or the Kaiser? The Fall of the Hohenzollerns* (1919), *The Heart of Humanity* (1919), and *The Unpardonable Sin* (1919). By the early 1920s World War I films with rapes were less common, although the reformation narrative reappears, for example, in *The Child Thou Gavest Me* (1921). It also appears in a modified version in *The Devil's Circus* (1926), in which a German American rapist becomes an object of pity because he is blinded while fighting for Germany during the war. Other late 1910s, 1920s, and early 1930s films deal with the Russian Revolution rather than World War I generally, using rape as a defining element of a "foreign" character's villainy. Titles include *At the Mercy of Men* (1918), *Her Story* (unknown date, 1920, 1921, or 1922), *My Official Wife* (1926), *The Red Sword* (1929), *Resurrection* (1931), *The Yellow Ticket* (1931), and *Rasputin and the Empress* (1933).

97. Also see, for example, *First Yank in Tokyo* (1945) and *Women in the Night* (1948) for films that use rape to depict Japanese men's villainy. See Michael Renov (1989) for a discussion of similar World War II depictions in nonfilm U.S. propaganda.

98. Also see, for example, *Dragon Seed* (1944).

99. Additional films that depict the villainy of Nazis through rape include *Assignment in Brittany* (1943), *The Strange Death of Adolf Hitler* (1943), *Enemy of Women* (1944), *The Hitler Gang* (1944), and *The Unwritten Code* (1944).

100. Also see, for example, *Cry of Battle* (1963), *In Harm's Way* (1965), *A Time for Killing* (1967), *The Desperados* (1969), and *Hornet's Nest* (1970). Relatedly, some westerns depict tensions between white outlaws and white heroes that are heightened by rape as a way to tell a story of nation formation. For example, see *The Arizona Gunfighter* (1937), *Day of the Outlaw* (1959), *The Deadly Companions* (1961), *Posse from Hell* (1961), *Hud* (1963), *Welcome to Hard Times* (1967), *Hang 'em High* (1968), *The Stranger Returns* (1968), *Two Mules for Sister Sara* (1970), and *The Magnificent Seven Ride!* (1972).

101. For example, see *My Old Man's Place* (1972), *The Visitors* (1972), and *Welcome Home, Soldier Boys* (1972).

102. While there were films that dealt with suffrage (see Stamp Lindsey 1995), none of the *rape* films I found directly referenced women's suffrage.

103. See Nancy F. Cott (1987) and Davis (1981b) on early-twentieth-century feminism, and see Kathy Peiss (1986), Staiger (1995), and Lauren Rabinovitz (1998) on links between that feminism and entertainment culture.

104. On 1960s and 1970s feminism, see, for example, Davis (1981b), Barbara Ryan (1992), and Ruth Rosen (2000). On the representation of feminism in 1960s and 1970s popular culture, see, for example, Susan J. Douglas (1994) and Bonnie J. Dow (1996b).

105. See Staiger (1995) for an analysis of the representation of consumer culture in *The Cheat*. She argues that the film grapples with both the dangers and the necessities of consumerism. The problem for the text is to find just the right amount of and context for women's capitalist consumption.

106. Also see, for example, *A Continental Girl* (1915), *The Ragged Princess* (1916), *Treason* (1933), and *Daughter of Shanghai* (1938).

107. A prerelease screening of this film was held for the Brooklyn Women's Bar Association. At this time, women served on juries in only six states; New York was not among them. It was not until 1975 (with *Taylor v. Louisiana*, 95 S. Ct. 692) that the Supreme Court struck down all state laws restricting women's service on juries (Otten 1993, 86).

108. *Bobbie of the Ballet* (1916) also represents a threatened family and even challenges family law in the process. This film deals with the legal right of a single woman to raise her own brother and sister.

109. Several films, including *The New Moon*, were made about a nonexistent Soviet law that outlawed marriage, making women "public property" (Brownlow, 448). *The New Moon* "made inventive use of the American Expeditionary Force to Russia; troops arrive in the nick of time to rescue the women from a fate worse than death" (Brownlow, 449).

110. Emma Goldman, in particular, advocated free love from a feminist perspective. See Candace Falk (1990) and Emma Goldman (1910).

111. Also see, for example, *The Island of Regeneration* (1915), *The Mischief Maker* (1916), and *Empty Arms* (1920).

112. See the introduction for a brief overview of 1960s and 1970s feminist antirape activism.

113. Also see, for example, the earlier film *The Sinister Urge* (1961).

114. For example, in *Against Our Will* Susan Brownmiller (1975) writes, "Any female may become a victim of rape. Factors such as extreme youth, advanced age, physical homeliness, and virginal life-style do not provide a foolproof deterrent or render a woman impervious to sexual assault" (388).

115. Even feminist scholars who are generally understood to be arguing that pornography causes rape place the causal link between pornography and rape in a social context. Furthermore, they *reject* the concept that only "crazy" men, such as "mad bombers," are susceptible to pornography's influence. For example, see Catharine A. MacKinnon and Andrea Dworkin (1997) and Dworkin and MacKinnon (1988). For an analysis of pornography as one of many "sex debates" within feminism and an argument for moving beyond either rejecting or em-

bracing pornography from a feminist perspective, see Lynn S. Chancer (1998). For feminist analyses of pornography from film, media, and cultural studies perspectives, see Linda Williams (1989) and Jane Juffer (1998).

116. Also see, for example, *Sunshine Molly* (1915), *The Family Skeleton* (1918), *Love's Battle* (1920), and *Beach of Dreams* (1921).

117. See the debate structured around *Stella Dallas* in *Cinema Journal* for a useful illustration of various feminist perspectives on the representation of oppression, spectatorial positioning, and feminism in melodrama (Gallagher 1986; Gledhill 1986; Kaplan 1985a, 1985b, 1986; Petro and Flinn 1985; Williams 1984, 1986).

118. *Sadie Thompson* was remade as *Rain* in 1932 and as *Miss Sadie Thompson* in 1953.

119. Title cards explicitly say that "Pago Pago" is in the "sultry south seas," where (implicitly white) U.S. marines are in exile from both "white men" and "white women."

120. This footage has been lost and thus is reconstructed with publicity stills and intertitles in the surviving print. The representation of rape available to modern audiences, then, is only suggested by stills of Alfred looming behind Sadie, reaching toward her with claw-like hands. The surviving moving images begin again the next day, after the rape.

121. In other sections of the film, the cinematography and editing often allow the spectator to share Lewt's perspective, including, for example, point of view shots of Pearl that show her hips swinging as she walks away from the camera and her bare shoulders as she swims alone.

122. Also see, for example, *Outrage* (1950).

123. Mayne writes, "In this space of heterosexual coupling, in other words, the women exercise far more control than they did in the roadhouse. The confines of the college offer the women control over the rituals of heterosexual courtship, a control not available to them once they leave the safe space of the college for the roadhouse" (136).

124. Paradoxically, this scene contributes to the film's implication that another woman who does *not* defend herself is at least partially at fault for her own subsequent rape.

125. For example, see *The Hunting Party* (1971), *Last House on the Left* (1972), *Enter the Dragon* (1973), *Buster and Billie* (1974), *Death Wish* (1974), *Massacre at Central High* (1976), and *Another Man, Another Change* (1977). *Deliverance* (1972) displaces women altogether, making a man the victim and men the avengers of rape.

126. Also see Barbara Creed (1993). Both Clover and Creed complicate their discussions of these films as potentially feminist by theorizing how it is that male viewers gain pleasure from rape-revenge films. Also see Lehman (1993) on this question. Here, however, I am more interested in women's (whether characters or

spectators) potential pleasure in a revenge made necessary because of the failure of men, culture, and law to address the feminist understandings of rape these films articulate.

127. Additional 1970s rape-revenge films include *The Animals* (1970), *Death Weekend* (1977), and *Messidor* (1978). As Clover, Creed, and Lehman (1993) discuss, the genre continues in the 1980s as well.

128. I return to a discussion of this issue in chapter 6.

129. See note 10 for a critique of this tendency in some scholarship.

130. For important film studies work on rape, see, for example, Shohat (1991a), Shohat and Stam, Marchetti, and Lesage.

NOTES TO CHAPTER 2

1. *Time* magazine, in particular, has been particularly invested in depicting postfeminism. Amelia Jones (1992) makes this point and mentions five issues of *Time* over a three-year period that feature postfeminism: December 4, 1989, Fall 1990, January 20, 1992, March 9, 1992, and May 4, 1992.

2. For a discussion of nineteenth-century feminism's roots in the abolition movement, see Barbara Ryan (1992, 14–16) and Angela Y. Davis (1981b, 30–45).

3. For example, in Anthony's "Constitutional Argument" speech, delivered throughout 1872 and 1873, she said,

> An oligarchy of wealth, where the rich govern the poor; an oligarchy of learning, where the educated govern the ignorant; or even an oligarchy of race, where the Saxon rules the African, might be endured; but this oligarchy of sex which makes father, brothers, husband, sons, the oligarchs over the mother and sisters, the wife and daughters of every household; which ordains all men sovereigns, all women subjects—carries discord and rebellion into every home of the nation. (473)

Also see Davis (1981b, 110–26) for an analysis of racism in some nineteenth-century and early-twentieth-century feminism.

4. On the history of "first-wave" feminism, see, for example, Nancy F. Cott (1987), Davis (1981b), and Ryan.

5. Not to mention that there is a long and rich history of women's activism that preceded the "naming" of a U.S. woman's movement in the mid-1800s. See, for example, the anthology *Women Imagine Change: A Global Anthology of Women's Resistance from 600 B.C.E. to Present* (Delamotte, Meeker, and O'Barr 1997).

6. See the March 9, 1992, cover of, yet again, *Time* magazine, featuring Steinem with Susan Faludi as representative 1990s feminists.

7. Patrice McDermott (1995) details this trend in the early 1990s, citing cover stories and articles from *Mother Jones* and the *Atlantic*. Additionally, see "Is the Left Sick of Feminism?" (Hochschild 1983); "The Awful Truth about Women's

Lib" (Jong 1986); "When Feminism Failed" (Dolan 1988); "Is Feminism Dead?" (1989); "Onward, Women!" (Wallis 1989), a *Time* story advertised on the cover with the question "Is there a future for feminism?"; and "Why the Women Are Fading Away" (Collins 1998). Although some of these articles are written by at least fairly well-known self-defined feminists who hope to save some version of feminism (such as Arlie Hochschild and Erica Jong), their titles alone nevertheless invite an anxious look at feminism and suggest that feminism may well be dead or dying, no matter what the author's stated perspective is on that death.

8. The "strident and lesbian" feminists reference that Jones criticizes comes directly from Claudia Wallis's 1989 *Time* article.

9. For an analysis of *The Blackman's Guide to Understanding the Blackwoman* as an example of antifeminist backlash, see Kimberlé Crenshaw (1991, 1253).

10. McDermott discusses some of these authors in the context of the early 1990s, focusing the most attention on Sommers. But a decade earlier, Hochschild pointed out in *Mother Jones* that "leftist" scholars were participating in a backlash against feminism, particularly Jean Bethke Elshtain (1981) with her book *Public Man, Private Woman*.

11. I hesitate to include Wolf in this list because she is the only one of these authors who is likely to appear on women's studies syllabi as an example of a pro-feminist feminist and because her first book, *The Beauty Myth* (1992), has been so influential for feminism and includes important insights about and critiques of a beauty culture. Nevertheless, *Fire with Fire*, in particular, shares with the other books I list here a characterization of all feminisms other than its own as victim feminism, thus implying that women who do not "choose" to take "control" and access their "power" are at fault for their own oppression. In that sense, I would argue that Wolf's *Fire with Fire* champions antifeminist feminist postfeminism.

12. Also see, for example, Wallis.

13. For a critical analysis of popular press representations of African American women as inadequate single mothers, see June Jordan (1993) and Wahneema Lubiano (1992).

14. Dow is quoting Phyllis Japp (1991) here.

15. Later in her discussion, Dow does address the subsequent seasons in which Murphy has a child but argues that, because the series represents Murphy as responding to a "biological imperative" (151) and because "almost everyone around Murphy (all men, interestingly enough) is better at motherhood than she is" (155), the pregnancy and birth are "consistent with [the show's] original premise that Murphy approaches life much like a man would" (158).

16. Faludi also cites Bolotin as the first to use the term "postfeminism."

17. While making class distinctions, Ehrenreich cites a spring 1986 Gallup poll that shows working-class and "'non-white'" women to be more favorably disposed to feminism than are middle-class women (216).

18. Ginia Bellafante (1998) makes a similar argument in *Time*: feminism is "dead because it has won. Some wags have coined a phrase for this: Duh Feminism" (58).

19. Ehrenreich does point out that the media probably overemphasize the existence of this young woman, but she still claims that she exists on college campuses.

20. In the context of abortion, Probyn (1993) points out that "we have to recognize that the choice in prochoice opens up a semiotic space now occupied by antiabortionists. Thus the discourse of choice is redirected and comes to mean that fetuses have the right to choose" (279).

21. Scholarly critics writing about postfeminism (e.g., Dow 1996b; Walters 1995) often point to the lack of structural analysis in even the more feminist-friendly postfeminist representations. While I share this critique and am making it here, I would not want to forward a structural analysis as the only potential feminist response to postfeminist discourses in popular culture. For one thing, many articles about postfeminism in the popular press *do* include at least some structural analysis, pointing out that women hit a "glass ceiling" and that they face sexual harassment as a class, rather than as individuals, for example (e.g., Wallis, Bellafante). Additionally, I would argue that an analysis of social structure is not sufficient because it implies a division between "representation" (individualistic postfeminism) and "materiality" (analysis of social structure) that avoids the materiality of representation.

22. He bases this claim on the publication of fiction that defines itself as "chick lit." For example, see Cris Mazza and Jeffrey DeShell's (1995) anthology *Chick-Lit: Postfeminist Fiction*. While this fiction does represent a type of postfeminism, I do not discuss it in this chapter because it does not generally appear in the mainstream press. Also see *Making for the Open: The Chatto Book of Post-Feminist Poetry, 1964–1984* (Rumens 1985). Similar to the postfeminist fiction, some artists define themselves or are defined by art critics as "postfeminist" (e.g., see Carson et al. 1987; Gagnon 1990; and Plagens). Again, because this art does not generally circulate in mass-mediated culture, I do not discuss it here. This literature and art, both of which *embrace* the term "postfeminism," have some similarities to the small amount of scholarly theory that embraces the label "postfeminism" (e.g., Mann 1994; Brooks 1997).

23. Ruth Shalit (1998) claims that the phrase "do-me feminists" was coined by *Esquire* magazine. Regardless, it appears fairly frequently in popular press postfeminist representations (e.g., see Friend 1994 and the related concept of "rock-me feminism" [France 1996]).

24. See Jones (1991) for a discussion of masquerade film theory in relation to the "bad news" film *Presumed Innocent*.

25. The now defunct site was www.pfplayground.com.

26. While I focus on her discussion of popular film here, Modleski also weaves this analysis together with a critique of "men in feminism" as a form of postfeminist theory in the academy.

27. Dow's (1996b) analysis of the mid-1980s sitcom *Designing Women* breaks with this linear history slightly because she argues that it is more feminist than postfeminist, primarily because it presents a form of consciousness-raising through women's bonding. Nevertheless, she points out that much of the *explicit* feminist rhetoric that appeared in *The Mary Tyler Moore Show* and *One Day at a Time* is no longer present in *Designing Women*.

28. For a discussion of postfeminism in the 1920s, see Susan Bordo (1990, 152) and Cott (282).

29. See Virginia Valian (1999) for a discussion of some of these continued forms of gender discrimination.

NOTES TO CHAPTER 3

1. On the virgin/vamp dichotomy, see Benedict's title and Meyers's chapter 4.

2. For a brief discussion of some of the major arguments of feminist antirape activism, see the introduction.

3. For an analysis of the gray spot or "blue blob" that covered Patricia Bowman's face during the trial, as well as a feminist discussion of the complexities of naming and of the representation of rape, see Jann Matlock (1993).

4. *Glamour*'s "Are You a Bad Girl?" (Wolf 1991b) is a reprint of the *Washington Post* article "We're All 'Bad Girls' Now" (Wolf 1991a). I cite from the *Glamour* version here.

5. See the antirape video *The Date-Rape Backlash* (1994) (which I discuss in chapter 6) for a discussion of the complex links between Roiphe and Gilbert. See Sharon Johnson (1992) for a critique of Gilbert's work as a (poorly researched) "conservative backlash." Gilbert's two primary articles on this topic are the earlier "The Phantom Epidemic of Sexual Assault" (1991), which Roiphe does not cite, and "Realities and Mythologies of Rape" (1992), which she does cite.

6. The press comments on this trend from time to time. For example, see Caryl Rivers (1974), Daniel Goleman (1984), Dorothy Rabinowitz (1991), Claudia Dreifus (1992), and Michael Logan (1994).

7. For example, see the films *Superman II* (1980), *Pretty Woman* (1990), *Braveheart* (1995), *Strange Days* (1995), and *The Messenger: The Story of Joan of Arc* (1999) and the television shows *Equalizer* and *Law and Order*.

8. *The Accused* has received a great deal of both scholarly and popular attention and is the film that people—from my family, to friends, to colleagues, to feminist activists, to students, to hairdressers, to video store clerks—most often mentioned when I told them the topic of this book, throughout the writing process.

9. For additional examples of arguably progressive texts that nevertheless include particularly assaultive rape scenes, see the films *Sophie's Choice* (1982), *Casualties of War* (1989), *Handmaid's Tale* (1990), *Dead Man Walking* (1995), and *Higher Learning* (1995) and the made-for-cable movie *Bastard Out of Carolina* (1996).

10. On explicit battle scenes in antiwar films, see, for example, Jeanine Basinger (1986, 98), Andrew Kelly (1993, 220), and Claudia Springer (1988). There is an important difference between antiwar films and antirape films, however. Some people would argue that war is necessary, despite its violence, while no one (or at least very few people) would argue that rape is "necessary." In other words, it is socially acceptable to believe that some wars are necessary, but it is not socially permissible to argue that some rape is necessary. Thus it is possible to argue that explicit war scenes are more "necessary" than explicit rape scenes in order to prove that war is "horrific."

11. Also see my discussion of explicit rape scenes in antirape films and videos in chapter 6.

12. For an analysis of audiences that found *The Accused* "disturbing" in much the same way I discuss it here, see Philip Schlesinger et al. (1992, 166).

13. Many horror/thriller films use rape or the threat of rape as a fulcrum for a narrative about the transformation of a meek woman into a powerful independent woman who protects herself and sometimes her friends and family. In addition to *Trial by Jury*, see the films *The Hand That Rocks the Cradle* (1992), *The Juror* (1996), *Scream* (1996), and *Kiss the Girls* (1997).

14. While Killearn does not immediately die from Mary's stab wound, both the wound and her decision to keep the rape secret from Robert contribute to his later death.

15. For example, also see the made-for-television movie *Settle the Score* (1989) and the films *Clan of the Cave Bear* (1986), *Sleeping with the Enemy* (1991), and *Moll Flanders* (1996).

16. White defines this narrative trajectory, but without directly addressing rape.

17. Also see, for example, the films *Robin Hood: Prince of Thieves* (1991), *Alien 3* (1992), *Bad Girls* (1994), and *Nell* (1994) and the made-for-television movie *Without Her Consent* (1990).

18. For a discussion of how masculinity functions in an additional military film, see Nancy Armstrong (1998) on *G.I. Jane* (1997).

19. On the racialization of the enemy rapist, see, for example, chapter 1, Jeffords (1991), Kent A. Ono (1997), Michael Renov (1989), and Ella Shohat (1991b).

20. See Elizabeth Gleick (1996) for an example of public discussions of rape in the military in relation to Tailhook.

21. On rape in the military, see Jeffords (1988); on rape and sports, see Jeffrey R. Benedict (1998); and on rape and fraternities, see Peggy Reeves Sanday (1990). Also see my discussion of this feminist antirape argument in the introduction to this book.

22. For example, see Craig Donegan (1996) and Alycee J. Lane (1994). As Lane argues, it is important not to conflate the arguments against and experiences of African Americans with those of lesbians and gays in the military. Instead, she offers an *intersectional* analysis of gender, race, and sexuality in her essay. Nevertheless, the examples she includes of arguments against African Americans (e.g., "black bodies as filthy" [1076]) and against lesbians and gays (e.g., "lifting the ban would threaten the 'safety' of all Americans because it would result in the creation of a 'second class' military" [1080]) illustrate a general logic that the inclusion of "others" in the military causes a problem.

23. I would argue, for example, that Bobby Trippe, who is raped in the earlier film *Deliverance* (1972), plays this more straightforward emasculated role. The lead character, Lewis Medlock (played by Burt Reynolds), not Bobby, takes over the narrative after the rape.

24. For additional examples of men who face rape or attempted rape and thus come to understand women's experiences more fully, see, for example, the film *Switch* (1991) and the October 9, 1998, episode of *Sabrina the Teenage Witch*.

25. Cuklanz (2000) argues in her later book, in fact, that "sympathy for and legitimation of victim experiences of rape were the most common rape reform ideas to find acceptance in the mainstream mass media examined [1980s prime-time television episodes]" (156).

26. I would not want to push this optimistic reading of *Beverly Hills 90210* too far, however. Laura's reinterpretation of the encounter, her subsequent unstable mental health (see the May 4, 1994, episode), and Steve's status as a regular sympathetic character all point toward a reading of this example as part of a larger antifeminist backlash suggesting that women who claim rape cannot be trusted.

27. For additional bathing scenes, see, for example, the made-for-television movies *Without Her Consent* (1990) and *The Rape of Dr. Willis* (1991) and the films *The Jagged Edge* (1985) and *Thousand Pieces of Gold* (1991).

28. For examples of hospital scenes, see various episodes of *ER, Law and Order, In the Heat of the Night,* and *Cagney and Lacey*. Also see *The Rape of Richard Beck* and *The Accused*. Cuklanz discusses numerous hospital scenes throughout her book *Rape on Prime Time*. Also see Deborah D. Rogers (1991), who discusses an examination scene in the soap opera *Santa Barbara*.

29. For a related argument to the one I present in this section, see Cuklanz (2000), especially chapter 3.

30. For discussions of Sarah's lack of a flashback see, for example, Carol J. Clover (1992, 150) and Cuklanz (1996).

31. This made-for-television movie is a remake of the 1948 film of the same title that I discuss in chapter 1.

32. For example, see the episode of *L.A. Law* discussed below and the made-for-television movies *The Advocate's Devil* (1997) and *Our Guys: Outrage in Glen Ridge* (1999).

33. For example, see the films *Higher Learning* (1995) and *School Daze* (1988) and the *Beverly Hills 90210* episode discussed above.

34. For example, see *Leaving Las Vegas* and *The Accused*.

35. For example, see *The Accused, Our Guys: Outrage in Glen Ridge, Leaving Las Vegas*, and *The General's Daughter*.

36. *School Daze* (1988), which takes place on a historically Black college campus, is an important exception.

37. See chapter 5 for an analysis of the much less frequent representation of Black women's relationship to rape.

38. For a related analysis of this episode of *L.A. Law*, see Michael Awkward (1995).

39. In 1992 my local affiliate was KWWL, Cedar Rapids, Iowa.

40. And, as the Tyson example illustrates, this racialized figure does emerge, especially in the news. See my discussion in the introduction of this chapter of Cuklanz's (1996) analysis of fiction as more progressive than the news and Benedict's (1992) and Meyers's critique of racism in news reporting on rape. Also see Moorti's discussion of the Mike Tyson and the Central Park jogger cases in relation to the William Kennedy Smith case.

41. While I also would critique some feminist antirape activism for privileging whiteness (see chapter 6), I would point out that some feminist literature on rape does address the specificity of race (e.g., Bhattacharjee 1997; Crenshaw 1991; Davis 1981a; Shukla 1997; and Smith 1990). See chapter 5 for a fuller discussion of this point.

42. On the concept of "rape culture," see the anthology *Transforming a Rape Culture* (Buchwald, Fletcher, and Roth 1993). On the male gaze as sexually assaultive in this context, see Sarah Ciriello's chapter of this book.

43. For example, see the films *My Bodyguard* (1980), *Superman II* (1980), *Diner* (1982), *Back to the Future III* (1990), *Cape Fear* (1991), *Joy Luck Club* (1993), *Mary Shelley's Frankenstein* (1994), *Circle of Friends* (1995), *Just Cause* (1995), *Eraser* (1996), *The Real Blonde* (1997), and *Gladiator* (2000).

44. For example, see the film *Matewan* (1987).

45. For example, see the made-for-television movie *Blood and Orchids* (1986) and the films *Passage to India* (1984) and *Rosewood* (1996).

46. For example, see the films *Heaven's Gate* (1980), *Untamed Heart* (1993), *Braveheart* (1995), *Con Air* (1997), and *Out of Sight* (1998).

NOTES TO CHAPTER 4

1. For examples of relatively recent discussions of *Thelma and Louise*, see Terry Diggs (1998) and Jay Maeder (1997).

2. "Should We Go Along for the Ride: A Critical Symposium on *Thelma and Louise*," edited by Toni Kamins and Cynthia Lucia for *Cineaste* in 1991, and "The

Many Faces of *Thelma and Louise*," edited by Ann Martin for *Film Quarterly* in 1991–92.

3. Janet Abrams (1991), Manohla Dargis (1991), and Amy Taubin (1991).

4. Essays and book chapters include Ann Althouse (1992), Jane Arthurs (1995), Michael Atkinson (1994), Marleen Barr (1991, 1993), Jack Boozer (1995), Mia Carter (1993), Peter N. Chumo II (1991–92, 1994), Dana L. Cloud (1998), Jane Collings (1996), Brenda Cooper (1999), Linda Frost (1998), Cindy L. Griffin (1995), Cathy Griggers (1993), Lynda Hart (1994), Jim Healey (1995), Susan N. Herman (1992), Karen Hollinger (1998), Barbara Johnson (1993), Louise J. Kaplan (1993), Pat MacEnulty (1992), Glenn Man (1993), Cara J. MariAnna (1993), James F. Maxfield (1996), David Metzger (1991), Joyce Miller (1996), Susan Morrison (1992), Ann Putnam (1993), Janice Hocker Rushing (1992), Elizabeth V. Spelman and Martha Minow (1992), Shirley A. Wiegand (1997), and Sharon Willis (1993, 1997).

5. For example, I have inadvertently come across discussions of *Thelma and Louise* in the following sources: Carol J. Clover (1992), Teresa de Lauretis (1994), Judith Grant (1993), Philip Green (1998), Camilla Griggers (1997), Douglas Kellner (1995), Kirsten Marthe Lentz (1993), Patricia S. Mann (1994), Martha McCaughey (1997), Patricia Mellencamp (1995), Shari Roberts (1997), Yvonne Tasker (1993, 1998), and Suzanna Danuta Walters (1995). Essays in anthologies that address *Thelma and Louise* but do not focus their entire analysis on the film include Christine Holmlund (1993), Peter Lehman (1993), and Mann (1996a, 1996b).

6. *The Accused* (1988) is probably a close second. However, most of the discussion surrounding that film does not address women's pleasure nor has the film or its characters been taken up as feminist icons for women generally, as I argue is the case for *Thelma and Louise*. Furthermore, the public discussion surrounding *Thelma and Louise* has continued far longer than did that surrounding *The Accused*.

7. Furthermore, much of the scholarly criticism defines the rape in the film as an "attempted rape" or "would be" rape, as does the popular press, thus taking Harlan's perspective over Thelma and Louise's perspectives. I discuss this point further below. For example, see Arthurs, Leo Braudy (1991–92), Griffin, Griggers (1993), Susan Morrison, and Walters (1995).

8. See Griggers (1993) on "packing [as] Thelma and Louise's first excess" (136).

9. Although the dialogue and mise-en-scène, which depicts dusk, imply that some time has passed, the editing takes Thelma and Louise almost directly from leaving town to deciding to stop.

10. Theoretically, one could interpret what happened to Louise in Texas as a rape from the moment she first mentions Texas in this scene, or one could *never* interpret what happened to Louise in Texas as rape. Louise neither confirms nor denies Thelma's assumption that Louise hates Texas because she was raped there;

and although Hal finds out "what happened" in Texas, he never says it aloud. While I choose to interpret Texas as a site of rape for my reading of the representation of rape in the film in this chapter, in another context I would resist the film's pressure to understand this unspoken offscreen event that propels the narrative as rape, imagining a different past for Louise, and thus implicitly respecting the fact that Louise never says she was raped.

11. Several scholars offer an analysis of *Thelma and Louise* in relation to the lower-budget rape-revenge films I discuss in chapter 1. For example, see Clover and Lehman (1993).

12. Similarly, when a police officer stops them for speeding, they take or destroy all his symbols of power: his gun (law), his sunglasses (gaze), and his radio (language).

13. While Thelma could be understood to be referring only to Harlan's death and thus to be blaming Louise here, I understand Thelma to be referring to both the death and the rape and thus to be holding *Harlan* responsible.

14. Or Harlan believes himself to be attractive. Thelma, at least, is attracted to him initially.

15. Technically, it is not even date rape, since Thelma only agrees to dance with Harlan in a public bar. Does Louise also have a "date" with the man with whom she dances? Thelma's encounter with Harlan becomes a "date" only in retrospect, after the rape. Their interaction hardly even qualifies as acquaintance rape. However, I believe Holmlund is referring to the fact that the rape follows eroticized heterosexuality rather than being a violent assault by a man Thelma has never seen before the moment at which he physically assaults her—what would generally be called stranger rape.

16. A few scholarly articles call the biker "Rastafarian," presumably because of his locks and because he is smoking pot. He never self-identifies as Rastafari, however. See Dargis (16). Holmlund quotes Dargis and calls him a "Rasta biker," but she also uses the character's absence from all but Dargis's review to challenge the overwhelming whiteness of the film and its critical response. She writes, "Deadly doll films, which overtly acknowledge that white American men are weaklings and/or nincompoops while at the same time insisting that heterosexual passion is still possible, will not—cannot—simultaneously acknowledge cross-racial alliances and relationships. . . . No wonder even the black male Rasta biker of *Thelma and Louise* disappeared from the critics' view" (151).

17. Every time I have taught this film, many of my students first laugh not when he blows the smoke into the trunk of the car (for me, the point of the joke) but *when he appears on screen*. The same thing happened when I saw the film in theatrical release in an Iowa City, Iowa, public theater with a primarily white audience.

18. Griggers (1993) argues that this is "the only non-negative image of a man" (138) in the film, but, as I suggest here, the depiction of him as an excessive spectacle for comedic effect corresponds with long-standing "negative" stereo-

types of Blacks in popular culture. On these stereotypes, see, for example, Jannette L. Dates and William Barlow (1993, 283–304) and Herman Gray (1995, 75).

19. While most of the men in the film (Darryl is an important exception) at least mimic a southern gentleman, Thelma specifically calls J.D. "gentlemanly."

20. When talking to Louise about her night with J.D., Thelma says, "I finally understand what all the fuss is about now."

21. See Mary Cantwell (1991).

22. See "Cartoon" (1991).

23. For example, see *Boys on the Side* (1995).

24. See Griggers (1993, 132) for both this claim about the popular press and a reading of lesbianism in the film. For additional readings of lesbianism in the film, see Holmlund (140) and Tasker (1993, 29). Johnson (1993) tries out, but is relatively unconvinced by, a lesbian reading of the film.

25. I first made this argument about the critical response to *Thelma and Louise* in my doctoral dissertation (1995). See Arthurs, Frost, and Walters (1995) for related arguments about the discussion of feminism in the press. None of these authors, however, address the ways the postfeminist subjectivities ascribed to Thelma and Louise are then offered up to (ostensibly) all women (but, practically, white middle-class–identified women) as invited spectators/readers.

26. Frost writes, "*Time*'s article on *Thelma and Louise* [Schickel 1991] enacts its own dismissal of this topic [rape]; the article features pictures of four of the movie's male characters in its 'Rogues' Gallery.' One face, however, is conspicuously absent—that of Harlan, the rapist and catalyst for the film's central action" (159).

27. See Holmlund on the need to justify women's violence in "deadly doll" films.

28. A few reviews argue that the film is not feminist enough. These articles, however, appear in magazines and newspapers with relatively small circulations and are never quoted in the popular press's characterization of the debate surrounding *Thelma and Louise*. See the reviews of the film in *Off Our Backs* ("*Thelma and Louise*" 1991) and *SpareRib* (Bader 1991).

29. See Lauren Rabinovitz (1989) for a related study of star discourse that contains the independence of the characters those stars portray. Rabinovitz draws on Serafina Bathrick's (1984) work on Mary Tyler Moore and *The Mary Tyler Moore Show*.

30. I base this characterization of the advertising on the entertainment sections of the Friday and Sunday *New York Times* from May through August 1991. "Lay off Thelma and Louise" comes from an article by Janet Maslin (1991) in which she argues that the violence is mild in comparison to *Total Recall* (1990) and *Another 48 Hours* (1990). Her article is an example of the popular press's move to an easy acceptance of women's nonviolent and nonresistant independence. See John M. Sloop (1994) for a similar argument in relation to public discourse about the musical group Public Enemy.

31. I am not arguing against the pleasurable and resistant potential of fantasy here. As I discuss below, many scholars (e.g., Barr 1991, 1993; Willis 1993) focus on the film's fantasy in opposition to much of the popular press's preoccupation with realism. However, I am arguing that a story about four women on the streets of Chicago with imaginary pistols responding to a truck driver's obscenity does deflect Thelma and Louise's more radical and confrontational responses to the *persistence* of sexual assault in their lives, in particular their killing of Harlan and the truck driver's truck.

32. While I implicitly criticize this scholar's comment here, I also want to acknowledge that her comment—as well as her published scholarship on *Thelma and Louise*—have helped me to develop my own work on the film.

33. See chapter 2 for a discussion of Dow's definition of postfeminism.

34. This resistant critical reading position is analogous to the one I take in chapter 1 in order to find feminist resistance to sexual assault in a film like *Duel in the Sun* (1946).

35. A number of critics point out that the popular press that found the film wanting, either for being too feminist or for not being feminist enough (e.g., "female chauvinist" [Novak] or "Thelma, as she is written, is almost pathologically bimbo. The day after she is brutally assaulted and nearly raped, she invites a stranger into her motel room" [Cross 1991]), often responded to the film in terms of reality, thus missing "the complexity of terms like fantasy" and "operat[ing] to silence the other stories to which [popular films] attempt to give a voice" (Tasker 1993, 8). Also see Arthurs (98) and Tasker (1993, 153–54, 156).

36. Griggers (1993) writes,

> Thelma and Louise, as prototypes of the mainstreaming of the new butch-femme, don't become butch because they're lesbians; they become lesbian because they've already become butch to survive. And surviving in this context means staying alive while escaping the traps of the dependent housewife, the bad marriage, the innocent victim, and the single-working woman who's going it alone and not getting enough. Lesbian identity is represented in this film as a social condition rather than an "innate" sexual orientation. (140)

37. MariAnna writes, "The last words spoken by these great sisters were 'let's keep going.' So they took the leap, a leap into freedom, into a new time and space, and they invited us to follow. This mythic cycle is about creation, birth and beginnings" (95).

38. Later in the book Mellencamp argues that the film "begins after 'happily ever after' has gone sour. While the women's revolt against sexism is doomed by their narrative—their progress impeded by their bungling—their rage is real and logical. They kill a rapist, rob a store, capture a cop, and blow up a gasoline truck. They leave femininity, rely on friendship, and achieve fearlessness" (117).

39. My own, less literal, reading in the first section of this chapter does find "self-defense" and "justifiable violence" in the film from a perspective that links Harlan's "actual" rape to the pervasiveness of physical, verbal, and visual sexual assault of women in everyday life.

40. Also see Ann Brooks (1997), whose embrace of the term "postfeminisms" is similar to Mann's embrace of the term "postfeminism." Frost offers a partial review of literature that addresses postfeminism as a theoretical position in the academy. Also see *Introducing Postfeminism* (Phoca and Wright 1999).

41. See Braudy, Chumo (1991–92), Dargis, Harvey R. Greenberg (1991–92), Kamins and Lucia, Kinder, Mellencamp, and Linda Williams (1991–92). Scholars have also used *Thelma and Louise* to address issues of rhetorical criticism (Griffin, Rushing) and concepts of film authorship (Arthurs), for example.

42. Also see Dargis, who writes, "While *Thelma and Louise* doesn't pretend to remedy a heritage of oppression, it does make tracks as a feminist road movie" (17). Pat Dowell's (1991) "The Impotence of Women" is one of the few scholarly articles that resists reading the film as feminist. Interestingly, Dowell argues that it is the representation of "raped women as somehow damaged goods" in *Thelma and Louise* that is "uncomfortably" problematic (30). Nevertheless, like many other articles that praise the film as feminist, Dowell argues that the film is "bracing" because it "puts sisterhood back on Hollywood's agenda" (30). Similarly, Rapping writes, "I certainly don't think it's a feminist movie," but then goes on to say that "while it certainly veers far from making any clear political statements, it is intelligent and serious enough in its attention to details of genre convention and contemporary gender issues to have made a lot of people committed to the sexual and cultural status quo very uneasy" (30). See Alice Cross (1991) for a more consistent read of the film as not feminist. Holmlund criticizes the film for representing "fear of lesbianism" and "a deeper, more immobilizing terror of racial difference" (149), offering a challenge to the film that goes beyond the dichotomous question, "Is it or is it not feminist?"

43. Certainly, one can read lesbian desire between Thelma and Louise even before the rape (e.g., see Griggers 1993), but here I am arguing that it is the rape that motivates the subsequent narrative development in which they more fully confront and embrace that desire.

44. Obviously, no one essay can address all issues in a text. Thus, even as I suggest that some of the feminist scholarship on *Thelma and Louise* depends on the film's representation of rape without acknowledging that it does so, I leave myself open to similar critiques. For example, by not spending more time on the representation of homoeroticism and race in the film, I contribute to the dominance of heterosexuality and whiteness in both this film and popular culture generally. And, there are of course other issues I have not even imagined that my analysis nevertheless represses and perpetuates. However, simply pointing out

that one can never address all aspects of a film does not diminish a critique of some of the particular ways an argument is circumscribed.

45. Some other scholarly critics do acknowledge the representation of rape in the film, but they do not build their argument around that representation. See, for example, Tasker (1993) and Mellencamp.

NOTES TO CHAPTER 5

1. While all but one of the examples I use in this chapter depict African American women, one does depict a Nigerian woman living in the United States. Hence I move back and forth between the more inclusive term "Black" and the more specific term "African American," as appropriate.

2. Representations of Native American women and Asian (particularly Vietnamese) women, for example, also appear, but with much less frequency. See my discussion of representations of Native American women in westerns in chapter 1 and a Vietnamese woman in *Casualties of War* (1989) in chapter 3. Nevertheless, fuller analysis of the specificity of the relationship between rape and these or other racialized social groups in cultural representations is necessary. For example, see Erin Addison (1993) and Ella Shohat (1991b) on Arab American women, Inés Hernandez-Avila (1993) and Cherríe Moraga (1983) on Chicanas, and Veronica C. Wang (1990) on Chinese American women.

3. On postslavery public discourses about rape, see Ida B. Wells-Barnett (1909), Robyn Wiegman (1993), and Jennifer Wriggins (1983).

4. Also see Patricia Hill Collins (1998, 24).

5. Also see Davis (1981a) and Wriggins.

6. For a discussion of African American women's antirape activism in relation to a particular case—Mike Tyson's—see Aaronette White (1999).

7. Also see Wahneema Lubiano (1995), who argues that in most Hollywood film "race representation . . . [is a] re-presentation, is a rewrite, or a newer picture, of older narratives about race, about masculinity, and about patriarchy" (187).

8. For a transcript of the television ad, see John Fiske (1996, 144). Horton was a convicted murderer who was issued a weekend pass during which he stabbed a man and raped a woman. Smith also mentions this case.

9. Even Smith, who offers a particularly nuanced discussion of the impact the cultural narrative about African American men as rapists of white women has on African American *women*, emphasizes only interracial rapes between African American men and white women in her discussion. Although Smith makes a point of introducing both African American men's rape of white women and white men's rape of African American women as examples of interracial rape, the examples she emphasizes—the Central Park jogger case and Alice Walker's (1981) story "Advancing Luna—and Ida B. Wells"—are about African American men's rape of white women.

An interesting comparison pairing might be an analysis of the relationship between the coverage of the Tawana Brawley case and, for example, Octavia E. Butler's 1979 novel *Kindred*. See Wriggins on most scholars' tendency to use the term "interracial rape" to mean only African American men's rape of white women, thus contributing to the neglect of African American women's experiences of rape.

10. Collins draws on Lubiano's (1992) discussion of Clarence Thomas and Anita Hill here.

11. Bari-Ellen Roberts was the highest-ranking African American woman executive at Texaco in 1994. She filed a racial discrimination suit when she was continually passed over for promotion.

12. For a theoretical and critical development of the concept of a cipher to describe a figure in popular culture as able to stand in for a series of shifting meanings while being simultaneously emptied of any racial and cultural specificity, see Kent A. Ono and Derek Buescher (2001). Specifically, they discuss the figure of Pocahontas in relation to the Disney film *Pocahontas* (1995), its marketing, and its popular press reception.

13. See Charlotte Pierce-Baker (1998) for an ethnographic and autobiographical analysis of African American women's experiences of rape that incorporates some standard postfeminist themes (such as the feeling of never being clean) but also addresses a racialized experience of rape (for example, shame over experiencing fear of African American men after being raped by African American men).

14. I have chosen to leave out an analysis of one additional important film, *Sankofa* (1993), because it has not enjoyed as wide a distribution as have the three films I examine here. Nevertheless, I acknowledge that this decision is somewhat arbitrary, since all the films I discuss here exist in a tension between mainstream Hollywood and independent film production. *Daughters of the Dust*, in particular, had little support from the Hollywood industry in terms of either production or distribution. Nevertheless, it is often discussed as "the first" feature-length film by an African American woman to have a theatrical release (Dash 1992a, 26), and it is accompanied by a "making of" book (Dash, Bambara, and hooks 1992) and, more recently, by a novel (Dash 1997) based on and continuing some of the characters in the film.

15. This historical displacement has precedents, as some of the examples I discuss in chapter 1 illustrate.

16. For a fuller development of this argument, see my essay on *Dr. Quinn* (1997).

17. Emphasizing the town's racism, Carl Lee reminds Jake of another case in which "four white boys . . . got off" for raping an African American woman, thus suggesting that if he does not do something these men will also go free.

18. Here, he functions as a "witness" analogous to Ken in *The Accused* (1988).

19. The film *A Family Thing* (1996) also uses the rape of an African American woman to define a white man as villainous and, also like *A Time To Kill*, focuses on masculinity in response to interracial rape.

20. Also see a two-episode arc in which Jonathan Rollins, a central *L.A. Law* character, is arrested on false suspicion of rape (Feb. 14 and Feb. 21, 1991), an episode from the fourth season of *The Real World* (1994–1995), and the film *The Color Purple* (1985). On *The Real World* example, see Mark P. Orbe (1998).

21. *Dr. Quinn*, for example, puts emphasis on Robert E as an ineffectual savior, although Grace does ultimately remain the central focus of the narrative. In *A Time to Kill* Carl Lee takes over from Tonya as the primary figure affected by the rape, although ultimately he too is displaced—in this case by the central white male hero, Jake.

22. For a development of this argument, see my essay on *Dr. Quinn* (1997), as well as Bonnie J. Dow (1996a).

23. See chapter 3 for a discussion of postfeminist films and television shows about men who are raped.

24. Santos appears to be African American, with relatively dark skin and frizzy hair, but she also has a Latina-coded name and hence can be read as both African American and Latina.

25. The first image of Lt. Dollen includes high heels and stocking-clad legs below a skirt that inadvertently reveals most of her thighs as she gets out of a helicopter.

26. The women's vaguely feminist perspectives are illustrated when Charlie calls God "she," Dollen declares "zero tolerance," and Santos resists Raines's objectification of her, for example.

27. *Incognito* was directed by independent African American filmmaker Julie Dash. Dash also directed *Daughters of the Dust*, which I discuss later in this chapter. Without moving too far into an insupportable "auteurist" argument, I would suggest that some of the complexity and nuance in *Incognito* can be associated with Dash's experience working as an antiracist, feminist independent filmmaker.

28. Through hypnosis Erin remembers that Scanlon took her somewhere that smelled overwhelmingly of flowers and thus the detective and Hunter deduce (correctly) that Scanlon must be living near the flower market.

29. Here, the film offers a "history" lesson by gesturing forward to the 1953 lynching of Emmett Till for whistling at a white woman. See Davis (1981a).

30. I want to thank my friend and colleague Ella Maria Ray for pointing out to me some of the complexities in this scene and for insisting on the importance of reading it as a rape scene.

31. Nola calls it a "near rape," and Jamie responds by saying, "I never did anything like that before in my life."

32. Mark A. Reid (1993) calls this "montage sequence . . . [a] group rape" (95).

33. For a fuller discussion of the process of narration in *She's Gotta Have It* and for a discussion of the popular press's response to the film, see my doctoral dissertation (1995).

34. The script, in a scene that was cut, makes this more explicit, describing the employer's hand caressing one of Yellow Mary's breasts from behind while a child suckles at her other breast (Dash 1992b, 126).

35. Hooks interprets the rape as interracial (hooks and Dash, 50); however, hooks acknowledges that the film, like Eula, never reveals *any* information about the rapist.

36. This dialogue is taken from the script (Dash 1992b, 155–57).

37. While the film remains ambiguous on this point, and thus emphasizes spirituality over biology, the novel spends a good deal of time emphasizing how much the Unborn Child, now born and named Elizabeth, looks like the Peazants, and like her father (Dash 1997, e.g., 8).

38. On the rape of Black women as a marker of generic racism, see Crenshaw: "To the extent rape of Black women is thought to dramatize racism, it is usually cast as an assault on Black manhood, demonstrating his inability to protect Black women" (1273).

NOTES TO CHAPTER 6

1. Given my analysis throughout the book of the social implications of popular entertainment, I hope it is obvious that I do not mean to suggest that Hollywood entertainment films cannot produce social change or that activist films and videos cannot be entertaining. Rather, I mean to draw attention here to differences in production, marketing, and distribution practices, differences that at least seem to promise more support for feminist antirape activism in the prevention and education texts.

2. I would like to thank the following universities and distributors for providing me with access to many of the films and videos I discuss in this chapter: the University of California, Los Angeles, Film and Television Archives; the University of California, Davis, Campus Violence Prevention Program; Filmakers' Library; Films for the Humanities and Sciences; Insight Media; and Women Make Movies.

3. Titles from the 1970s and early 1980s that primarily focus on awareness, prevention, and self-defense include *Nobody's Victim* (1972), *Fear* (1973), *How to Say No to a Rapist and Survive* (1974), *Rape: A Preventive Inquiry* (1974), *Rape Alert* (1975), *Rape: The Right to Resist* (1975), *Rape Prevention: No Pat Answers* (1976), *Beware the Rapist* (1977), *No Exceptions* (1977), *Common Sense Self-Defense* (1978), *Nobody's Victim II* (1978), *Rape: Victim or Victor* (1979), *Fighting Back* (n.d.), *Rape: Escape without Violence* (n.d.), *Rape: The Savage Crime* (n.d.), *Women against Rape* (n.d.), and *Women's Self-Defense* (n.d.).

4. When rapists appear, the interviewers invariably ask them what advice they have for women who want to protect themselves; the men most often suggest locking windows and doors. It seems particularly paradoxical to turn to rapists for advice on how to prevent rape, not only because their advice is so limited and often would not have prevented the actual rapes they describe committing anyway, but also because turning to this source for advice requires women to pay even more attention to men who rape, men whom the programs themselves define as anything but trustworthy in every other way.

5. Examples in this category include *No Tears for Rachel* (1974), *On the Question of Justice* (1975), *The People v. Inez Garcia* (1975), *Sex and Violence* (1975), *The Trouble with Rape* (1975), *Rape: A New Perspective* (1976), *Rape, Incest and Abortion* (1979), *Trial for Rape* (1979, Italy), *The Rape Tape* (n.d.), *Women against Rape* (n.d.), and *Women and the Law: Rape* (n.d.).

6. Titles here include *Rape* (1975), *Sex and Violence* (1975), public service announcements out of Seattle and the San Francisco Bay area (1975, 1976), *A Community Fights Rape* (1978–79), *Working against Rape* (1979), *Who's There for the Victim* (1981), and *If It Happens to You: Rape* (n.d.).

7. This video was released in the United States in 1997.

8. *Calling the Ghosts* (1996) does call for reform of international law in relation to rape as a war crime, but I would argue that its primary focus is on documenting (rather than changing) the fact that rape is a tool of war.

9. For example, in *Rapists: Can They Be Stopped* (1986 or 1988) the head of the treatment center explicitly states that the five men featured in the program have collectively committed more than 150 rapes.

10. Films and videos in this category include *Rape and the Rapist* (1978), *Sexual Assault: The Assailant's View* (1979), *Why Men Rape* (1980), *Rape* (1984), *Rape: An Act of Hate* (1986), and *Someone You Know* (1986).

11. Although this video is an ABC news special, it is now distributed as an educational antirape video by Insight Media. Thus, I include it in this chapter.

12. Titles here include *No Tears for Rachel* (1974), *Sex and Violence* (1975), *The Trouble with Rape* (1975), *Rape: The Hidden Crime* (1977), *Common Sense Self-Defense* (1978), *Shattered* (1978), *Rape* (1979), *Rape, Incest and Abortion* (1979), *Working against Rape* (1979), *The Rape Tape* (n.d.), and *Women against Rape* (n.d.).

13. *Mean Women*, which is not professionally distributed and therefore is not widely available, and a series of 1996 public service announcements produced by the Los Angeles Commission on Assaults against Women do not represent women giving personal testimony in interviews about their experiences of rape, nor do they represent a therapeutic solution to rape or post-rape trauma.

14. See *Waking Up to Rape* (1985), *From Victim to Survivor* (1986), *Rape Stories* (1989), and *Summer's Story: The Truth and Trauma of Date Rape* (1992).

15. Titles up until 1986 include *The Trouble with Rape* (1975), *Rape: The Hidden Crime* (1977), *Shattered* (1978), *This Film Is about Rape* (1978), *Sexual Assault: The Assailant's View* (1979), *The Date* (1980), *National Crime and Violence Test: The Rape* (1982), *Rape* (1984), *Waking Up to Rape* (1985), *Rapists: Can They Be Stopped* (1986 or 1988), *Someone You Know* (1986), *Women against Rape* (n.d.), and *Women and the Law: Rape* (n.d.).

16. Titles include *No Means No: Understanding Acquaintance Rape* (1991), *Men, Sex, and Rape* (1992), *Summer's Story: The Truth and Trauma of Date Rape* (1992), and *The Date-Rape Backlash: The Media and the Denial of Rape* (1994). One other text from the 1990s also addresses rape myths: the Los Angeles Commission on Assaults against Women's public service announcements. The theme of these announcements is that no matter what a woman looks like or does—wearing a revealing shirt, kissing a man, marrying a man—she is not inviting rape. Thus, they counteract the myth that a woman can "invite" or "want" rape. Unlike the other examples I discuss here, these public service announcements do not provide a "desire for power and control" as an alternative explanation for rape's existence. Their focus is on challenging rape rather than understanding it.

17. Other early programs with acquaintance rape as their primary subject include *The Date* (1980), *Girls Beware* (1980), and *Not Only Strangers* (1980).

18. Also see *Rape: An Act of Hate*.

19. This very same audiotape also plays in *Rapists: Can They Be Stopped*. It is particularly chilling because not only is it an explicit representation of a rape taking place, but it is a sound recording of an *actual* rape taking place, as opposed to the fictional dramatizations of rape scenes that are common in many of these films and videos. I will return to the issue of the explicit representation of rape in a later section.

20. See chapter 3 for a discussion of *The Morning After*'s relationship to post-feminism.

21. Other 1990s acquaintance rape titles include *When a Kiss Is Not Just a Kiss* (1994), *He Raped Me: Date Rape: From the Victim's Perspective* (1996), *Date Violence: A Young Woman's Guide* (1997), and *The Rape Drug: A New Menace* (1997 or 1998).

22. For examples from the 1970s and 1980s, see *Rape Culture* (1975), *Rape, Parts I and II* (1975), *Rape* (1979), and *Someone You Know* (1986). Films and videos from the 1990s include *Men, Sex, and Rape* (1992), *The Date-Rape Backlash: The Media and the Denial of Rape* (1994), the Los Angeles Commission on Assaults against Women public service announcements (1996), *Philomela Speaks* (1996), and *Mean Women* (n.d.).

23. Earlier experimental rape films include Yoko Ono's *Rape* (1969) and *No Lies* (1973). For a discussion of *Rape*, see Joan Hawkins (2000); for a discussion of *No Lies*, see Vivian C. Sobchack (1977).

24. I say "presumably" because the programs do not address the issue of socioeconomic class in relation to what areas one might be able to avoid. This is not to say that more rapes actually take place in poor city neighborhoods late at night; however, the earlier programs tend to represent these areas as the most dangerous.

25. For example, see Cassia Spohn and Julie Horney (1992) and Lisa M. Cuklanz (1996, 2000).

26. Also see Cuklanz (1996).

27. See Kristin Thompson (1986) for a formalist discussion of this definition of excess. Other scholars shift the focus away from narrative structure and argue that excess is meaningful on multiple registers, particularly in relation to melodrama (e.g., Byars 1991; Haralovich 1990; Joyrich 1988). Regardless, I am not suggesting that these prevention and education programs' depictions of rape are excessive in either sense.

28. As I discuss in chapter 3, this conundrum appears in *The Accused* (1988), and in nonrape contexts as well. For example, antiwar films must grapple with the problem of representing the violence of war in order to argue against war.

29. Technically, that someone could be a lesbian spectator, but the scenarios all depict men and women interacting in some way, making this reading difficult to sustain.

30. While helping me to copyedit this manuscript, my research assistant supported my claim here when she wrote the following in the margin of the text: "This guy from my dorm sophomore year had one of these ads up in his room because he thought the woman was 'hot.'"

31. Sut Jhally (1994) does acknowledge that "some men might find the tape arousing[,] . . . but I saw this more as an opportunity than a threat. . . . I could get their attention. Could that attention then be directed against the images that were the focus of the watching?" (158). In his analysis of some audience responses to *Dreamworlds*, he uses written responses to the video to argue that he *was* successful, although he does not address the probability that at least some men might not redirect their focus. Similarly, he avoids the criticism that the tape reproduces women's victimization by arguing that many female viewers wrote that they appreciated being alerted to this victimization (160). By taking this perspective, he avoids considering nonvictimizing ways a video might inform spectators about victimization.

32. I feel compelled to say that sometimes when I view this video I am able to suspend my disbelief—rather easily, in fact—and do feel empowered, as McCaughey and King say they intend. However, this is not always the case for me. In the several contexts in which I have viewed this video or similar clip tapes with public groups, a portion of the discussion always turns to the primarily female audience members' feelings of fear and discomfort in response to watching women being violent in the same ways men are so often violent in films. Primar-

ily, the audience members sidestep the issue of *gendered* violence when they express a discomfort with violence generally.

33. While Davis describes this myth in relation to the history of the enslavement of African Americans in the United States, a version of this narrative also functions culturally in relation to men of color generally. For discussions of historically specific examples of this cultural narrative in relation to other racialized groups, see Antonia I. Castañeda's (1993) discussion of military depictions of Native Americans during the colonization of the United States and Kent A. Ono's (1997) discussion of depictions of Japanese, Japanese Americans, and Native Americans in relation to the particular case of a proposed purchase of the Seattle Mariners professional baseball team.

34. When these programs include interviews with rapists, every man who speaks appears to be white. In one or two of the programs that represent a prison group therapy session, one or two African American men are present, but remain in the background. In a few texts, men of color appear in a more nuanced fashion as rapists; I discuss these texts later in this chapter.

35. While the overwhelming majority of these films and videos represent all women who have experienced rape as white, a few offer testimony from women of color, primarily African American women. *Someone You Know*, for example, provides testimony from three women, two of whom are white and one of whom is African American. As is typical in all but one of the programs I viewed (*Waking Up to Rape*), none of these women address their own racial identity or that of the man who attacked them. Furthermore, people on the street or groups of college students interviewed in the programs about their attitudes toward rape are also overwhelmingly white. *After the Montreal Massacre* is one notable exception: in a group discussion among college students, an African American man and an African American woman not only appear but spend a significant amount of time articulating their perspectives. Nevertheless, neither they nor anyone else in the video—people on the street, women who have been assaulted, or experts—acknowledge or articulate an argument about a relationship between race and sexual violence.

36. On the model minority myth, see Keith Osajima (1988).

37. One of the posters even appeared in the September 28, 1997, issue of *TV Guide*.

38. I should point out that this was my own experience with one rape crisis center. I have also had more encouraging experiences with the Violence Prevention Program on my current university campus, for example, where I have often accepted invitations to speak about the representational nature of rape. Some available research implies that this approach also exists more widely. For example, a recent study of feminist rape education programs argues explicitly that "the erotic and . . . dominance themes that characterize our culture's *representations* of rape need to be openly addressed" (Fonow et al. 1992, 119, emphasis added).

Amy Fried's (1994) work on rape crisis centers as organizations emphasizes the variety of types of organizations in existence and points to the ways fluidity and conflict in feminist organizations can lead to alliances that contribute to the transformation of "gendered social structures" (581). Nevertheless, none of this work addresses race.

Works Cited

Abrams, Janet. July 1991. "*Thelma and Louise.*" *Sight and Sound*: 55–56.

Addison, Erin. 1993. "Saving Other Women from Other Men: Disney's *Aladdin.*" *Camera Obscura* 31: 5–25.

Ali, Shahrazad. 1989. *The Blackman's Guide to Understanding the Blackwoman.* Philadelphia: Civilized Publications.

Alleva, Richard. 13 Sept. 1991. "Over the Edge? *Thelma and Louise.*" *Commonweal*: 513–15.

Allis, Sam. Fall 1990. "What Do Men Really Want?" *Time*: 80–82.

Althouse, Ann. 1992. "*Thelma and Louise* and the Law: Do Rape Shield Rules Matter?" *Loyola of Los Angeles Law Review* 25.3: 757.

Amiel, Barbara. 11 July 1994. "The Tyranny of Modern-Day Feminism." *MacLean's*: 13.

Angeli, Michael. Dec. 1993. "Women We Love: Teri Hatcher, Woman of Steel." *Esquire*: 98–99.

Anthony, Susan B. 1872–73. "Constitutional Argument." *Issues in Feminism: An Introduction to Women's Studies.* Ed. Sheila Ruth. Mountain View, CA: Mayfield, 1990. 471–75.

Armstrong, Nancy. 1998. "Captivity and Cultural Capital in the English Novel." *Novel* 31.3: 373–98.

Arthurs, Jane. 1995. "*Thelma and Louise*: On the Road to Feminism?" *Feminist Subjects, Multi-Media: Cultural Methodologies.* Ed. Penny Florence and Dee Reynolds. Manchester: Manchester University Press. 89–105.

Atkinson, Michael. 1994. "Crossing the Frontiers." *Sight and Sound* 4.1: 14–17.

Awkward, Michael. 1995. "Representing Rape: On Spike, Iron Mike, and the 'Desire Dynamic.'" *Negotiating Difference: Race, Gender, and the Politics of Positionality.* Chicago: University of Chicago Press. 95–135.

Bader, Eleanor J. July 1991. "*Thelma and Louise.*" *SpareRib*: 19–20.

Bambara, Toni Cade. 1992. "Preface." *Daughters of the Dust: The Making of an African Woman's Film.* Julie Dash, with Toni Cade Bambara and bell hooks. New York: New Press. xi–xvi.

Bardaglio, Peter W. 1994. "Rape and the Law in the Old South: 'Calculated to Excite Indignation in Every Heart.'" *Journal of Southern History* 60.4: 749–72.

Barr, Marleen. 1991. "*Thelma and Louise*: Driving toward Feminist SF; Or, Yes, Women Do Dream of Not Being Electric Sheep." *Foundation* 53: 80–86.

———. 1993. "*Thelma and Louise*: Driving toward Feminist Science Fiction." *Lost in Space: Probing Feminist Science Fiction and Beyond*. Chapel Hill: University of North Carolina Press. 21–29.

Basinger, Jeanine. 1986. *The World War II Combat Film: Anatomy of a Genre*. New York: Columbia University Press.

Bathrick, Serafina. 1984. "*The Mary Tyler Moore Show*: Women at Home and at Work." *MTM: Quality Television*. Ed. Jane Feuer, Paul Kerr, and Tise Vahimagi. London: BFI. 99–131.

Baughman, Cynthia, ed. 1995. *Women on Ice: Feminist Essays on the Tonya Harding/Nancy Kerrigan Spectacle*. New York: Routledge.

Bellafante, Ginia. 29 June 1998. "Feminism: It's All about Me!" *Time*: 54–60.

Benedict, Helen. 1992. *Virgin or Vamp: How the Press Covers Sex Crimes*. New York: Oxford University Press.

Benedict, Jeffrey R. 1998. *Athletes and Acquaintance Rape*. Thousand Oaks, CA: Sage.

Bernstein, C. June 1956. "Night of Terror, a Lifetime of Anguish." *Coronet*: 107–12.

Bhattacharjee, Anannya. 1997. "A Slippery Path: Organizing Resistance to Violence against Women." *Dragon Ladies: Asian American Feminists Breathe Fire*. Ed. Sonia Shah. Boston: South End. 29–45.

Bizjak, Tony. 26 July 1995. "Jurors in Rape Cases Often Struggle to Decide What's True." *Sacramento Bee*: A1, A4–A5.

Bobo, Jacqueline. 1995. *Black Women as Cultural Readers*. New York: Columbia University Press.

Bolotin, Susan. 17 Oct. 1982. "Voices from the Post-Feminist Generation." *New York Times Magazine*: 28–31, 103, 106–7, 114, 116–17.

Boozer, Jack. 1995. "Seduction and Betrayal in the Heartland: *Thelma and Louise*." *Literature/Film Quarterly* 23.3: 188–96.

Bordo, Susan. 1990. "Feminism, Postmodernism, and Gender-Skepticism." *Feminism/Postmodernism*. Ed. Linda J. Nicholson. New York: Routledge. 133–56.

Braudy, Leo. 1991–92. "Satire into Myth." *Film Quarterly* 45.2: 28–29.

Brinson, Susan L. 1989. "TV Rape: Communication of Cultural Attitudes toward Rape." *Women's Studies in Communication* 12.2: 23–36.

Brooks, Ann. 1997. *Postfeminisms: Feminism, Cultural Theory, and Cultural Forms*. New York: Routledge.

Brownlow, Kevin. 1990. *Behind the Mask of Innocence: Sex, Violence, Prejudice, Crime: Films of Social Conscience in the Silent Era*. Berkeley: University of California Press.

Brownmiller, Susan. 1975. *Against Our Will: Men, Women, and Rape*. New York: Bantam Books.

Buchwald, Emilie, Pamela R. Fletcher, and Martha Roth, eds. 1993. *Transforming a Rape Culture*. Minneapolis: Milkweed Editions.

Bumiller, Elisabeth. 22 June 1999. "Deny Rape or Be Hated: Kosovo Victims' Choice." *New York Times*: A1, A13.

Butler, Octavia E. 1979. *Kindred*. Garden City, NY: Doubleday.

Byars, Jackie. 1991. *All That Hollywood Allows: Re-Reading Gender in 1950s Melodrama*. Chapel Hill: University of North Carolina Press.

Campbell, Rebecca, Charlene K. Baker, and Terri L. Mazurek. 1998. "Remaining Radical? Organizational Predictors of Rape Crisis Centers' Social Change Initiatives." *American Journal of Community Psychology* 26.3: 457–83.

Cantwell, Mary. 13 June 1991. "What Were the Women 'Asking' For?" *New York Times*: A28.

Carby, Hazel V. 1985. "'On the Threshold of Woman's Era': Lynching, Empire, and Sexuality in Black Feminist Theory." *Critical Inquiry* 12.1. Rpt. in *"Race," Writing, and Difference*. Ed. Henry Louis Gates, Jr. Chicago: University of Chicago Press, 1986. 301–16.

———. 1987. *Reconstructing Womanhood: The Emergence of the Afro-American Woman Novelist*. New York: Oxford University Press.

Carlson, Margaret. 24 June 1991. "Is This What Feminism Is All About?" *Time*: 57.

Carson, Juli, Howard McCalebb, Michael Shodahl, and Michael Syrquin. 1987. *Blue Angel: The Decline of Sexual Stereotypes in Post-Feminist Sculpture*. New York: Bronx Council on the Arts.

Carter, Mia. 1993. "The Strange Case of Callie Khouri: Public and Private Responses to *Thelma and Louise*." *Texas Journal of Women and the Law* 2.1: 125.

"Cartoon." 8 July 1991. *New Yorker*: 28.

Castañeda, Antonia I. 1993. "Sexual Violence in the Politics and Policies of Conquest: Amerindian Women and the Spanish Conquest of Alta California." *Building with Our Hands: New Directions in Chicana Studies*. Ed. Adela de la Torre and Beatríz M. Pesquera. Berkeley: University of California Press. 15–33.

Castro, Peter. 10 June 1991. "Chatter: Buddying Up." *People*: 122.

Cavell, Stanley. 1981. *Pursuits of Happiness: The Hollywood Comedy of Remarriage*. Cambridge: Harvard University Press.

Chancer, Lynn S. 1998. "Feminist Offensives: Beyond Defending Pornography." *Reconcilable Differences: Confronting Beauty, Pornography, and the Limits of Feminism*. Berkeley: University of California Press. 61–81.

Chau, Monica. 1993. "Tall Tales or True Stores: The Subject of Rape in Recent Video Art." *The Subject of Rape*. Hannah J. L. Feldman, Hannah Kruse, Jennifer Kabat, and Monica Chau. New York: Whitney Museum of American Art. 79–85.

"Cheers 'n' Jeers." 2 Feb. 1985. *TV Guide*: 22.

Chumo, Peter N., II. 1991–92. "*Thelma and Louise* as Screwball Comedy." *Film Quarterly* 45.2: 23–24.

Chumo, Peter N., II. 1994. "At the Generic Crossroads with *Thelma and Louise*." *Post Script* 13.2: 3–13.

Ciriello, Sarah. 1993. "Commodification of Women: Morning, Noon, and Night." *Transforming a Rape Culture*. Ed. Emilie Buchwald, Pamela R. Fletcher, and Martha Roth. Minneapolis: Milkweed Editions. 265–81.

Clinton, Catherine. 1994. "'With a Whip in His Hand': Rape, Memory, and African-American Women." *History and Memory in African-American Culture*. Ed. Geneviève Fabre and Robert O'Meally. New York: Oxford University Press. 205–18.

Cloud, Dana L. 1998. *Control and Consolation in American Culture and Politics: Rhetoric of Therapy*. Thousand Oaks, CA: Sage.

Clover, Carol J. 1992. *Men, Women, and Chain Saws: Gender in the Modern Horror Film*. Princeton: Princeton University Press.

Collings, Jane. 1996. "The Hollywood Waitress: A Hard-Boiled Egg and the Salt of the Earth." *The Hidden Foundation: Cinema and the Question of Class*. Ed. David E. James and Rick Berg. Minneapolis: University of Minnesota Press. 264–83.

Collins, Gail. 25 Oct. 1998. "Why the Women Are Fading Away." *New York Times Magazine*: 54–55.

Collins, Patricia Hill. 1998. "The More Things Change, the More They Stay the Same: African-American Women and the New Politics of Containment." *Fighting Words: Black Women and the Search for Justice*. Minneapolis: University of Minnesota Press. 11–43.

Cooper, Brenda. 1999. "The Relevancy of Gender Identity in Spectators' Interpretations of *Thelma and Louise*." *Critical Studies in Mass Communication* 16: 20–41.

Cott, Nancy F. 1987. *The Grounding of Modern Feminism*. New Haven: Yale University Press.

Creed, Barbara. 1993. *The Monstrous-Feminine: Film, Feminism, Psychoanalysis*. New York: Routledge.

Crenshaw, Kimberlé. 1991. "Mapping the Margins: Intersectionality, Identity Politics, and Violence against Women of Color." *Stanford Law Review* 43: 1241–99.

Cross, Alice. 1991. "The Bimbo and the Mystery Woman." *Cineaste* 18.4: 32–34.

Cuklanz, Lisa M. 1996. *Rape on Trial: How the Mass Media Construct Legal Reform and Social Change*. Philadelphia: University of Pennsylvania Press.

———. 2000. *Rape on Prime Time: Television, Masculinity, and Sexual Violence*. Philadelphia: University of Pennsylvania Press.

Dargis, Manohla. July 1991. "Roads to Freedom." *Sight and Sound*: 15–18.

Dash, Julie. 1992a. "Making *Daughters of the Dust*." *Daughters of the Dust: The Making of an African Woman's Film*. Julie Dash, with Toni Cade Bambara and bell hooks. New York: New Press. 1–26.

———. 1992b. "The Script: *Daughters of the Dust*." *Daughters of the Dust: The Making of an African Woman's Film*. Julie Dash, with Toni Cade Bambara and bell hooks. New York: New Press. 73–164.

————. 1997. *Daughters of the Dust: A Novel*. New York: Dutton.

Dash, Julie, with Toni Cade Bambara and bell hooks. 1992. *Daughters of the Dust: The Making of an African Woman's Film*. New York: New Press.

Dates, Jannette L., and William Barlow. 1993. *Split Image: African Americans in the Mass Media*. 2d ed. Washington, DC: Howard University Press.

Davis, Angela Y. June 1975. "Joanne Little: The Dialectics of Rape." *Ms.*: 74–77, 106–8.

————. 1981a. "Rape, Racism and the Myth of the Black Rapist." *Women, Race and Class*. New York: Vintage Books, 1983. 172–201.

————. 1981b. *Women, Race and Class*. New York: Vintage Books, 1983.

————. 1985. "Violence against Women and the Ongoing Challenge to Racism." Latham, NY: Kitchen Table: Women of Color Press.

de Lauretis, Teresa. 1994. *The Practice of Love: Lesbian Sexuality and Perverse Desire*. Bloomington: Indiana University Press.

Delamotte, Eugenia C., Natania Meeker, and Jean F. O'Barr, eds. 1997. *Women Imagine Change: A Global Anthology of Women's Resistance from 600 B.C.E. to Present*. New York: Routledge.

Diawara, Manthia. 1988. "Black Spectatorship: Problems of Identification and Resistance." *Screen* 29.4: 66–76. Rpt. in *Black American Cinema*. Ed. Manthia Diawara. New York: Routledge. 211–20.

Diggs, Terry. 13 Apr. 1998. "The Real Reason Why Working Women Have Snubbed Paula Jones." *Legal Times*: 23.

Doane, Mary Ann. 1982. "Film and the Masquerade: Theorizing the Female Spectator." *Screen* 23.3–4: 74–87.

"Documents on the Genesis of the Production Code." 1995. Compiled by Richard Maltby. *Quarterly Review of Film and Video* 15.4: 33–63.

Dolan, Mary Anne. 26 June 1988. "When Feminism Failed." *New York Times Magazine*: 20–23, 66.

Donegan, Craig. 26 Apr. 1996. "New Military Culture: Do Women, Blacks and Homosexuals Get Fair Treatment?" *CQ Researcher* 6.16: 361–84.

Douglas, Susan J. 1994. *Where the Girls Are: Growing Up Female with the Mass Media*. New York: Random House.

Dow, Bonnie J. 1996a. "The Other Side of Postfeminism: Maternal Feminism in *Dr. Quinn, Medicine Woman*." *Prime-Time Feminism: Television, Media Culture, and the Women's Movement since 1970*. Philadelphia: University of Pennsylvania Press. 164–202.

————. 1996b. *Prime-Time Feminism: Television, Media Culture, and the Women's Movement since 1970*. Philadelphia: University of Pennsylvania Press.

Dowell, Pat. 1991. "The Impotence of Women." *Cineaste* 18.4: 28–30.

Dreifus, Claudia. 14 Mar. 1992. "Women in 'Jep.'" *TV Guide*: 22–25.

Dworkin, Andrea, and Catharine A. MacKinnon. 1988. *Pornography and Civil Rights: A New Day for Women's Equality*. Minneapolis: Organizing Against Pornography.

Dyer, Richard. 1988. "White." *Screen* 29.4: 44–64.

Edmonds, Patricia. 23–25 Oct. 1998. "'Now the Word Is Balance.'" *USA Weekend*: 4–6.

Ehrenreich, Barbara. July–Aug. 1987. "The Next Wave." *Ms.*: 166–68, 216–18.

Elshtain, Jean Bethke. 1981. *Public Man, Private Woman: Women in Social and Political Thought.* Princeton: Princeton University Press.

English, Deirdre. Nov.–Dec. 1992. "Through the Glass Ceiling." *Mother Jones*: 49–52, 73.

Epps, Garrett. 28 June 1987. "It's De-Witching Hour: After Two Decades as New Men, We Say the Devil with It." *Washington Post*: C5.

Estrich, Susan. 1987. *Real Rape: How the Legal System Victimizes Women Who Say No.* Cambridge: Harvard University Press.

Falk, Candace. 1990. *Love, Anarchy, and Emma Goldman.* New Brunswick: Rutgers University Press.

Faludi, Susan. 1991. *Backlash: The Undeclared War against American Women.* New York: Crown.

Ferguson, Frances. 1987. "Rape and the Rise of the Novel." *Representations* 20: 88–112.

Firestone, Shulamith. 1971. *The Dialectic of Sex: The Case for Feminist Revolution.* New York: Bantam Books.

Fiske, John. 1996. *Media Matters: Race and Gender in U.S. Politics.* Rev. ed. Minneapolis: University of Minnesota Press.

Fonow, Mary Margaret, Laurel Richardson, and Virginia A. Wemmerus. 1992. "Feminist Rape Education: Does It Work?" *Gender and Society* 6.1: 108–21.

France, Kim. 3 June 1996. "Rock-Me Feminism." *New York*: 36–41.

Fregoso, Rosa Linda. 1999. "On the Road with Angela Davis." *Cultural Studies* 13.2: 211–22.

Fried, Amy. 1994. "'It's Hard to Change What We Want to Change': Rape Crisis Centers as Organizations." *Gender and Society* 8.4: 562–83.

Friedan, Betty. 1963. *The Feminine Mystique.* New York: Norton.

Friedman, Susan S. 1995. "Beyond White and Other: Relationality and Narratives of Race in Feminist Discourse." *Signs* 21.1: 1–49.

Friend, Tad. Feb. 1994. "The Rise of 'Do Me' Feminism." *Esquire*: 48–56.

Frost, Linda. 1998. "The Decentered Subject of Feminism: Postfeminism and *Thelma and Louise.*" *Rhetoric in an Antifoundational World: Language, Culture, and Pedagogy.* Ed. Michael Bernard-Donals and Richard R. Glejzer. New Haven: Yale University Press. 147–69.

Gagnon, Monika. 1990. "Beyond Post-Feminism: The Work of Laura Mulvey and Griselda Pollock." *Canadian Women's Studies* 11.1: 81–83.

Gaines, Jane. 1993. "Fire and Desire: Race, Melodrama, and Oscar Micheaux." *Black American Cinema.* Ed. Manthia Diawara. New York: Routledge. 49–70.

Gallagher, Tag. 1986. "Dialogue: Tag Gallagher Responds to Tania Modleski's 'Time and Desire in the Woman's Film.'" *Cinema Journal* 25.2: 65–67.

Garber, Marjorie, Jann Matlock, and Rebecca L. Walkowitz, eds. 1993. *Media Spectacles*. New York: Routledge.

Gardner, Carol Brooks. 1995. *Passing By: Gender and Public Harassment*. Berkeley: University of California Press.

Gevinson, Alan, ed. 1997. *American Film Institute Catalog: Within Our Gates: Ethnicity in American Feature Films, 1911–1960*. Berkeley: University of California Press.

Gibbs, Nancy. 9 Mar. 1992. "The War against Feminism." *Time*: 50–55.

Gilbert, Neil. 1991. "The Phantom Epidemic of Sexual Assault." *Public Interest* 103: 54–65.

———. 1992. "Realities and Mythologies of Rape." *Society* 29.4: 4–10.

Giroux, Henry A. 1994. "Politics and Innocence in the Wonderful World of Disney." *Disturbing Pleasures: Learning Popular Culture*. New York: Routledge. 25–45.

Gledhill, Christine. 1986. "Dialogue: Christine Gledhill on *Stella Dallas* and Feminist Film Theory." *Cinema Journal* 25.4: 44–53.

Gleick, Elizabeth. 25 Nov. 1996. "Scandal in the Military." *Time*: 28–31.

Goldberg-Ambrose, Carole. 1992. "Unfinished Business in Rape Law Reform." *Journal of Social Issues* 48.1: 173–85.

Goldman, Emma. 1910. "Marriage and Love." *Anarchism and Other Essays*. New York: Mother Earth Publishing. Rpt. in *Red Emma Speaks: An Emma Goldman Reader*. Ed. Alix Kates Shulman. Atlantic Highlands, NJ: Humanities Press, 1996. 204–13.

Goldman, Robert, Deborah Heath, and Sharon L. Smith. 1991. "Commodity Feminism." *Critical Studies in Mass Communication* 8: 333–51.

Goleman, Daniel. 28 Aug. 1984. "Violence against Women in Films." *New York Times*: C1, C5.

Gooding-Williams, Robert, ed. 1993. *Reading Rodney King/Reading Urban Uprising*. New York: Routledge.

Goodman, Ellen. 10 Jan. 1989. "The Post-Feminist Message of *Working Girl*." *Washington Post*: A23.

———. 9 Dec. 1991. "Postfeminist Images Begin to Blur." *Los Angeles Times*: B5.

Grant, Judith. 1993. *Fundamental Feminism: Contesting the Core Concepts of Feminist Theory*. New York: Routledge.

Gray, Herman. 1995. *Watching Race: Television and the Struggle for "Blackness."* Minneapolis: University of Minnesota Press.

Green, Philip. 1998. *Cracks in the Pedestal: Ideology and Gender in Hollywood*. Amherst: University of Massachusetts Press.

Greenberg, Harvey R. 1991–92. "*Thelma and Louise*'s Exuberant Polysemy." *Film Quarterly* 45.2: 20–21.

Grieveson, Lee. 1997. "Policing the Cinema: *Traffic in Souls* at Ellis Island, 1913." *Screen* 38.2: 149–71.

Griffin, Cindy L. 1995. "Teaching Rhetorical Criticism with *Thelma and Louise*." 44.2: 165–76.

Griggers, Camilla. 1997. *Becoming-Woman*. Minneapolis: University of Minnesota Press.

Griggers, Cathy. 1993. "*Thelma and Louise* and the Cultural Generation of the New Butch-Femme." *Film Theory Goes to the Movies*. Ed. Jim Collins, Hilary Radner, and Ava Preacher Collins. New York: Routledge. 129–41.

Halliwell, Leslie. 1988. *Halliwell's Filmgoer's Companion*. 9th ed. New York: Scribner's.

Handelman, David. Mar. 1996. "Postfeminist Mystique." *Vogue*: 286, 295.

Hanson, Patricia King, executive ed., and Alan Gevinson, assistant ed. 1988. *The American Film Institute Catalog of Motion Pictures Produced in the United States: Feature Films, 1911–1920*. Berkeley: University of California Press.

———. 1993. *The American Film Institute Catalog of Motion Pictures Produced in the United States: Feature Films, 1931–1940*. Berkeley: University of California Press.

Hanson, Patricia King, executive ed., and Amy Dunkleberger, assistant ed. 1999. *American Film Institute Catalog of Motion Pictures Produced in the United States: Feature Films, 1941–1950*. Berkeley: University of California Press.

Haralovich, Mary Beth. 1990. "*All That Heaven Allows*: Color, Narrative Space, and Melodrama." *Close Viewings: An Anthology of New Film Criticism*. Ed. Peter Lehman. Tallahassee: Florida State University Press. 57–72.

Harmetz, Aljean. 30 Sept. 1973. "Rape—an Ugly Movie Trend." *New York Times*: sec. 2, 1, 11.

Harrison, Taylor, Sarah Projansky, Kent A. Ono, and Elyce Rae Helford, eds. 1996. *Enterprise Zones: Critical Positions on Star Trek*. Boulder: Westview.

Hart, Lynda. 1994. "'Til Death Do Us Part: Impossible Spaces in *Thelma and Louise*." *Journal of the History of Sexuality* 4.3: 430–46.

Haskell, Molly. 1973. *From Reverence to Rape: The Treatment of Women in the Movies*. New York: Penguin Books.

Hawkins, Joan. 2000. "Exploitation Meets Direct Cinema: Yoko Ono's *Rape* and the Trash Cinema of Michael and Roberta Findlay." *Cutting Edge: Art-Horror and the Horrific Avant-Garde*. Minneapolis: University of Minnesota Press. 117–39.

Healey, Jim. 1995. "'All This for Us': The Songs in *Thelma and Louise*." *Journal of Popular Culture* 29.3: 103–19.

Heinzerling, Lisa. Oct. 1990. "A New Way of Looking at Violence against Women." *Glamour*: 112.

Helford, Elyce Rae. 2000. "Postfeminism and the Female Action-Adventure Hero: Positioning *Tank Girl*." *Future Females, the Next Generation: New Voices and*

Velocities in Feminist Science Fiction Criticism. Ed. Marleen S. Barr. Lanham, MD: Rowman and Littlefield. 291–308.

Herman, Susan N. 1992. "Thelma and Louise and Bonnie and Jean: Images of Women as Criminals." *Southern California Review of Law and Women's Studies* 2.1: 53.

Hernandez-Avila, Inés. 1993. "In Praise of Subordination, Or, What Makes a Good Woman Go Bad?" *Transforming a Rape Culture.* Ed. Emilie Buchwald, Pamela R. Fletcher, and Martha Roth. Minneapolis: Milkweed Editions. 375–92.

Hewlett, Sylvia Ann. 1986. *A Lesser Life: The Myth of Women's Liberation in America.* New York: Morrow.

———. 1987. *A Lesser Life: The Myth of Women's Liberation in America.* Warner Books ed. New York: Warner Books.

Heywood, Leslie. 4 Sept. 1998. "Hitting a Cultural Nerve: Another Season of *Ally McBeal.*" *Chronicle of Higher Education*: B9.

Higgins, Lynn A., and Brenda R. Silver, eds. 1991. *Rape and Representation.* New York: Columbia University Press.

Hine, Darlene Clark. 1989. "Rape and the Inner Lives of Black Women in the Middle West: Preliminary Thoughts on the Culture of Dissemblance." *Signs* 14.4: 912–20.

Hine, Darlene, and Kate Wittenstein. 1981. "Female Slave Resistance: The Economics of Sex." *The Black Woman Cross-Culturally.* Ed. Filomina Chioma Steady. Cambridge, MA: Schenkman Books. Rpt. in *Feminist Frontiers III.* Ed. Laurel Richardson and Verta Taylor. New York: McGraw-Hill, 1993. 431–36.

Hochschild, Arlie. June 1983. "Is the Left Sick of Feminism?" *Mother Jones*: 56–58.

Hodes, Martha. 1993. "The Sexualization of Reconstruction Politics: White Women and Black Men in the South after the Civil War." *Journal of the History of Sexuality* 3.3. Rpt. in *American Sexual Politics: Sex, Gender, and Race since the Civil War.* Chicago: University of Chicago Press, 1993. 59–74.

Hollinger, Karen. 1998. "The Political Female Friendship Film: *Nine to Five, Outrageous Fortune, Thelma and Louise, Mortal Thoughts, Leaving Normal.*" *In the Company of Women: Contemporary Female Friendship Films.* Minneapolis: University of Minnesota Press. 106–38.

Holmlund, Christine. 1993. "A Decade of Deadly Dolls: Hollywood and the Woman Killer." *Moving Targets: Women, Murder and Representation.* Ed. Helen Birch. Berkeley: University of California Press. 127–51.

hooks, bell. 1981. *Ain't I a Woman: Black Women and Feminism.* Boston: South End.

———. 1989a. *Ain't I a Woman*: Looking Back." *Talking Back: Thinking Feminist, Thinking Black.* Boston: South End. 148–54.

———. 1989b. "'Whose Pussy Is This?': A Feminist Comment." *Talking Back: Thinking Feminist, Thinking Black.* Boston: South End. 134–41.

hooks, bell. 1994. "Dissident Heat: Fire with Fire." *Outlaw Culture: Resisting Representations.* New York: Routledge. 91–100.

hooks, bell, and Julie Dash. 1992. "Dialogue between bell hooks and Julie Dash." *Daughters of the Dust: The Making of an African Woman's Film.* Julie Dash, with Toni Cade Bambara and bell hooks. New York: New Press. 27–67.

Hume, Ellen. 3 Sept. 1986. "Race of Two Women for Nebraska Governorship Is Viewed as Start of Post-Feminist Political Era." *Wall Street Journal:* 58.

"Is Feminism Dead?" Feb. 1989. *Los Angeles:* 114–18.

Jackson, Shannon. 1993. "Representing Rape: Model Mugging's Discursive and Embodied Performances." *Drama Review* 37.3: 110–41.

Jacobs, Lea. 1991. *The Wages of Sin: Censorship and the Fallen Woman Film, 1928–1942.* Madison: University of Wisconsin Press.

Japp, Phyllis. 1991. "Gender and Work in the 1980s: Television's Working Women as Displaced Persons." *Women's Studies in Communication* 14: 49–74.

Jeffords, Susan. 1988. "Performative Masculinities, Or, 'After a Few Times You Won't Be Afraid of Rape at All.'" *Discourse* 13.2: 102–18.

———. 1991. "Rape and the New World Order." *Cultural Critique* 19: 203–15.

———. 1994. *Hard Bodies: Hollywood Masculinity in the Reagan Era.* New Brunswick: Rutgers University Press.

Jeffords, Susan, and Lauren Rabinovitz, eds. 1994. *Seeing through the Media: The Persian Gulf War.* New Brunswick: Rutgers University Press.

Jenkins, Henry. 1992. *Textual Poachers: Television Fans and Participatory Culture.* New York: Routledge.

Jhally, Sut. 1994. "Intersections of Discourse: MTV, Sexual Politics, and *Dreamworlds.*" *Viewing, Reading, Listening: Audiences and Cultural Reception.* Ed. Jon Cruz and Justin Lewis. Boulder: Westview. 151–68.

Johnson, Barbara. 1993. "Lesbian Spectacles: Reading *Sula, Passing, Thelma and Louise,* and *The Accused.*" *Media Spectacles.* Ed. Marjorie Garber, Jann Matlock, and Rebecca L. Walkowitz. New York: Routledge. 160–66.

Johnson, Sharon. Mar.–Apr. 1992. "Rape: The Conservative Backlash." *Ms.:* 88–89.

Jones, Amelia. 1991. "'She Was Bad News': Male Paranoia and the Contemporary New Woman." *Camera Obscura* 25–26: 297–320.

———. 1992. "Feminism, Incorporated: Reading 'Postfeminism' in an Anti-Feminist Age." *Afterimage* 20.5: 10–15.

———. 1994. "Postfeminism, Feminist Pleasures, and Embodied Theories of Art." *New Feminist Criticism: Art, Identity, Action.* Ed. Joanna Frueh, Cassandra L. Langer, and Arlene Raven. New York: HarperCollins. 16–41.

Jong, Erica. Apr. 1986. "The Awful Truth about Women's Lib." *Vanity Fair:* 92–93, 118–19.

Jordan, June. 1993. "Don't You Talk about My Momma!" *Technical Difficulties: Selected Political Essays.* London: Virago. 65–80.

Joyrich, Lynne. 1988. "All That Television Allows: TV Melodrama, Postmodernism and Consumer Culture." *Camera Obscura* 16: 129–53. Rpt. in *Private Screenings: Television and the Female Consumer.* Ed. Lynn Spigel and Denise Mann. Minneapolis: University of Minnesota Press, 1992. 227–51.

Juffer, Jane. 1998. *At Home with Pornography: Women, Sex, and Everyday Life.* New York: New York University Press.

Kaminer, Wendy. 1990. *A Fearful Freedom: Women's Flight from Equality.* Reading, MA: Addison-Wesley.

Kamins, Toni, and Cynthia Lucia, eds. 1991. "Should We Go Along for the Ride? A Critical Symposium on *Thelma and Louise.*" *Cineaste* 18.4: 28–36.

Kaplan, E. Ann. 1985a. "Dialogue: Ann Kaplan Replies to Linda Williams's 'Something Else Besides a Mother: *Stella Dallas* and the Maternal Melodrama.'" *Cinema Journal* 24.2: 40–43.

———. 1985b. "E. Ann Kaplan Replies." *Cinema Journal* 25.1: 52–54.

———. 1986. "E. Ann Kaplan Replies." *Cinema Journal* 25.4: 49–53.

Kaplan, Louise J. 1993. "Fits and Misfits: The Body of a Woman." *American Imago* 50.4: 457–80.

Keene, Lauren. 17 Aug. 1999. "Plea Deal Ends Lengthy UCD Rape Case." *Davis Enterprise:* A1, A4.

Kellner, Douglas. 1995. *Media Culture: Cultural Studies, Identity and Politics between the Modern and the Postmodern.* New York: Routledge.

Kelly, Andrew. 1993. "The Brutality of Military Incompetence: *Paths of Glory* (1957)." *Historical Journal of Film, Radio and Television* 13.2: 215–27.

Kelly, Liz. 1988. *Surviving Sexual Violence.* Minneapolis: University of Minnesota Press.

Kinder, Marsha. 1991–92. "*Thelma and Louise* and *Messidor* as Feminist Road Movies." *Film Quarterly* 45.2: 30–31.

Klawans, Stuart. 24 June 1991. "*Thelma and Louise.*" *Nation:* 862–63.

Koszarski, Richard. 1990. *An Evening's Entertainment: The Age of the Silent Feature Picture, 1915–1928.* Berkeley: University of California Press.

Krafsur, Richard P., ed. 1976. *The American Film Institute Catalog of Motion Pictures: Feature Films, 1961–1970.* New York: Bowker.

Krupp, Charla. Aug. 1991. "Why *Thelma and Louise* Scares the Devil out of Some Men—and Women." *Glamour:* 142.

Lane, Alycee J. 1994. "Black Bodies/Gay Bodies: The Politics of Race in the Gay/Military Battle." *Callaloo* 17.4: 1074–88.

Lavery, David, ed. 1995. *Full of Secrets: Critical Approaches to Twin Peaks.* Detroit: Wayne State University Press.

Lehman, Peter. 1990. "Texas 1868/America 1956: *The Searchers.*" *Close Viewings: An Anthology of New Film Criticism.* Ed. Peter Lehman. Tallahassee: Florida State University Press. 387–415.

Lehman, Peter. 1993. "'Don't Blame This on a Girl': Female Rape-Revenge Films." *Screening the Male: Exploring Masculinities in Hollywood Cinema*. Ed. Steven Cohan and Ina Rae Hark. New York: Routledge. 103–17.

Lentz, Kirsten Marthe. 1993. "The Popular Pleasures of Female Revenge (or Rage Bursting in a Blaze of Gunfire)." *Cultural Studies* 7.3: 374–405.

Leo, John. 10 June 1991. "Toxic Feminism on the Big Screen." *U.S. News and World Report*: 20.

Lesage, Julia. 1981. "*Broken Blossoms*: Artful Racism, Artful Rape." *Jump Cut* 26: 51–55.

Lewis, James R. 1992. "Images of Captive Rape in the Nineteenth Century." *Journal of American Culture* 15.2: 69–77.

Logan, Michael. 18 June 1994. "Rapists: Unlikely Heartthrobs." *TV Guide*: 42.

Lowe, Lisa. 1997. "Interview with Angela Davis: Reflections on Race, Class, and Gender in the USA." *The Politics of Culture in the Shadow of Capital*. Ed. Lisa Lowe and David Lloyd. Durham: Duke University Press.

Lubiano, Wahneema. 1992. "Black Ladies, Welfare Queens, and State Minstrels: Ideological War by Narrative Means." *Race-ing Justice, En-gendering Power: Essays on Anita Hill, Clarence Thomas, and the Construction of Social Reality*. Ed. Toni Morrison. New York: Pantheon. 323–63.

———. 1995. "Don't Talk with Your Eyes Closed: Caught in the Hollywood Gun Sights." *Borders, Boundaries, and Frames: Essays in Cultural Criticism and Cultural Studies*. Ed. Mae G. Henderson. New York: Routledge. 185–201.

MacEnulty, Pat. 1992. "*Thelma and Louise*: A Feminist Fable." *Mid-Atlantic Review* 13.2: 102–7.

MacKellar, Jean. 1975. *Rape: The Bait and the Trap*. New York: Crown.

MacKinnon, Catharine A. 1993. "Turning Rape into Pornography: Postmodern Genocide." *Ms.* 4.1: 24–30.

MacKinnon, Catharine A., and Andrea Dworkin, eds. 1997. *In Harm's Way: The Pornography Civil Rights Hearings*. Cambridge: Harvard University Press.

Madriz, Esther. 1997. *Nothing Bad Happens to Good Girls: Fear of Crime in Women's Lives*. Berkeley: University of California Press.

Maeder, Jay. 8 Sept. 1997. "Crime and Punishment." *U.S. News and World Report*: 12.

Maltby, Richard. 1995. "The Genesis of the Production Code." *Quarterly Review of Film and Video* 15.4: 5–32.

Man, Glenn. 1993. "Gender, Genre, and Myth in *Thelma and Louise*." *Film Criticism* 18.1: 36–53.

Mann, Patricia S. 1994. *Micro-Politics: Agency in a Postfeminist Era*. Minneapolis: University of Minnesota Press.

———. 1996a. "On the Postfeminist Frontier." *Socialist Review* 24.1–2: 223–41.

———. 1996b. "The Postfeminist Frontier Is Global." *Frontiers* 17.3: 24–26.

Mansfield, Harvey. 17 July 1998. "The Partial Eclipse of Manliness: What Room Is There for Courage in a Post-Feminist World?" *Times Literary Supplement*: 14–16.

March, Jeanne, Alison Geist, and Nathan Caplan. 1982. *Rape and the Limits of Law Reform*. Boston: Auburn House.

Marchetti, Gina. 1993. *Romance and the "Yellow Peril": Race, Sex, and Discursive Strategies in Hollywood Fiction*. Berkeley: University of California Press.

MariAnna, Cara J. 1993. "The Seven Mythic Cycles of *Thelma and Louise*." *Trivia* 21: 82–99.

Martin, Ann, ed. 1991–92. "The Many Faces of *Thelma and Louise*." *Film Quarterly* 45.2: 20–31.

Maslin, Janet. 16 June 1991. "Lay Off *Thelma and Louise*." *New York Times*: sec. 2, 11, 16.

Matlock, Jann. 1993. "Scandals of Naming: The Blue Blob, Identity, and Gender in the William Kennedy Smith Case." *Media Spectacles*. Ed. Marjorie Garber, Jann Matlock, and Rebecca L. Walkowitz. New York: Routledge. 137–59.

Matoesian, Gregory M. 1993. *Reproducing Rape: Domination through Talk in the Courtroom*. Chicago: University of Chicago Press.

Matthews, Nancy A. 1994. *Confronting Rape: The Feminist Anti-Rape Movement and the State*. New York: Routledge.

May, Elaine Tyler. 1988. *Homeward Bound: American Families in the Cold War Era*. New York: Basic Books.

Mayne, Judith. 1994. *Directed by Dorothy Arzner*. Bloomington: Indiana University Press.

Maxfield, James F. 1996. "'We Don't Live in That Kind of World, Thelma': Triumph and Tragedy in *Thelma and Louise*." *The Fatal Woman: Sources of Male Anxiety in American Film Noir, 1941–1991*." London: Associated University Presses. 168–80.

Mazza, Cris, and Jeffrey DeShell, eds. 1995. *Chick-Lit: Postfeminist Fiction*. Normal, IL: Unit for Contemporary Literature, Illinois State University.

McCaughey, Martha. 1997. *Real Knockouts: The Physical Feminism of Women's Self-Defense*. New York: New York University Press.

McCaughey, Martha, and Neal King. 1995. "Rape Education Videos: Presenting Mean Women Instead of Dangerous Men." *Teaching Sociology* 23.4: 374–88.

McDermott, Patrice. 1995. "On Cultural Authority: Women's Studies, Feminist Politics, and the Popular Press." *Signs* 20.3: 668–84.

Mellencamp, Patricia. 1995. *A Fine Romance: Five Ages of Film Feminism*. Philadelphia: Temple University Press.

Metzger, David. 1991. "Rhetoric and Death in *Thelma and Louise*: Notes toward a Logic of the Fantastic." *Journal of the Fantastic in the Arts* 4.4: 9–18.

Meyers, Marian. 1997. *News Coverage of Violence against Women: Engendering Blame*. Thousands Oaks, CA: Sage.

Miller, Joyce. 1996. "From *Bonnie and Clyde* to *Thelma and Louise*: The Struggle for Justice in the Cinematic South." *Studies in Popular Culture* 19.2: 277–86.

Modleski, Tania. 1991. *Feminism without Women: Culture and Criticism in a "Postfeminist" Age*. New York: Routledge.

Moorti, Sujata. 1995. "Screening Sexuality: Democratic Sphere and Television Representations of Rape." Ph. D diss. University of Maryland, College Park.

Moraga, Cherríe. 1983. "A Long Line of Vendidas: Chicanas and Feminism." *Loving in the War Years: Lo que nunca pasó por sus labios.* Boston: South End. 90–144.

Moraga, Cherríe, and Gloria Anzaldúa, eds. 1981. *This Bridge Called My Back: Writings by Radical Women of Color.* 2d ed. New York: Women of Color: Kitchen Table Press, l983.

Morrison, Susan. 1992. "Pearl, Hilda, Thelma, and Louise: The 'Woman's Film' Revisited." *Cineaction* 30: 48–53.

Morrison, Toni, ed. 1992. *Race-ing Justice, En-gendering Power: Essays on Anita Hill, Clarence Thomas, and the Construction of Social Reality.* New York: Pantheon.

Mulvey, Laura. 1975. "Visual Pleasure and Narrative Cinema." *Screen* 16.3. Rpt. in *Feminism and Film Theory.* Ed. Constance Penley. New York: Routledge, 1988. 57–68.

Munden, Kenneth W., ed. 1971. *The American Film Institute Catalog of Motion Pictures Produced in the United States: Feature Films, 1921–1930.* New York: Bowker.

Naber, Nadine. 2000. "Ambiguous Insiders: An Investigation of Arab American Invisibility." *Ethnic and Racial Studies* 23.1: 37–61.

Nichani, Kiran. Feb. 1997. "Charles Hall: Inviting Change." *FEM: L.A.'s Feminist Newsmagazine*: 10–11.

Novak, Ralph. 10 June 1991. "Picks and Pans: *Thelma and Louise.*" *People*: 19.

Odem, Mary E. 1995. *Delinquent Daughters: Protecting and Policing Adolescent Female Sexuality in the United States, 1885–1920.* Chapel Hill: University of North Carolina Press.

Ono, Kent A. 1997. "'America's' Apple Pie: Baseball, Japan-Bashing, and the Sexual Threat of Economic Miscegenation." *Out of Bounds: Sports, Media, and the Politics of Identity.* Ed. Aaron Baker and Todd Boyd. Bloomington: Indiana University Press. 81–101.

———. 1998. "Communicating Prejudice in the Media: Upending Racial Categories in *Doubles.*" *Communicating Prejudice.* Ed. Michael L. Hecht. Thousand Oaks, CA: Sage Publications. 206–20.

Ono, Kent A. and Derek Buescher. 2001. "*Deciphering Pocahontas*: Unpackaging the Commodification of a Native American Woman." *Critical Studies in Media Communication* 18.1: 23–43.

Orbe, Mark P. 1998. "Constructions of Reality on MTV's *The Real World*: An Analysis of the Restrictive Coding of Black Masculinity." *Southern Communication Journal* 64.1: 32–47.

Osajima, Keith. 1988. "Asian Americans as the Model Minority: An Analysis of the Popular Press Image in the 1960s and 1980s." *Reflections on Shattered Windows: Promises and Prospects for Asian American Studies.* Ed. Gary Y. Okihiro, Shirley Hune, Arthur A. Hansen, and John M. Liu. Pullman: Washington State University Press. 165–74.

Otten, Laura A. 1993. *Women's Rights and the Law*. Westport, CT: Praeger.

Overholser, Geneva. 19 Sept. 1986. "What 'Post-Feminism' Really Means." *New York Times*: A34.

Parent, Anthony S., Jr., and Susan Brown Wallace. 1993. "Childhood and Sexual Identity under Slavery." *Journal of the History of Sexuality* 3.3. Rpt. in *American Sexual Politics: Sex, Gender, and Race since the Civil War*. Chicago: University of Chicago Press, 1993. 19–57.

Patai, Daphne, and Noretta Koertge. 1994. *Professing Feminism: Cautionary Tales from the Strange World of Women's Studies*. New York: Basic Books.

Pearson, Kyra. 1995. "A Rhetorical Analysis of the Cultural Narrative of Battered Women Who Kill: 1975–1995." Undergraduate thesis. University of California, Davis.

Peiss, Kathy. 1986. *Cheap Amusements: Working Women and Leisure in Turn-of-the-Century New York*. Philadelphia: Temple University Press.

Perea, Juan. 1997. "The Black/White Binary Paradigm of Race: the 'Normal Science' of American Racial Thought." *California Law Review* 85.5: 1213–58.

Perlez, Jane. 10 Apr. 1999. "Serbs Seal Off 700,000 Refugees Who Face Starvation, U.S. Says." *New York Times*: A1, A6.

Petchesky, Rosalind Pollack. 1981. "Antiabortion, Antifeminism, and the Rise of the New Right." *Feminist Studies* 7.2: 206–46.

Petro, Patrice, and Carol Flinn. 1985. "Dialogue: Patrice Petro and Carol Flinn on Feminist Film Theory." *Cinema Journal* 25.1: 50–54.

Phoca, Sohpia, and Rebecca Wright. 1999. *Introducing Postfeminism*. New York: Totem Books.

Pierce-Baker, Charlotte. 1998. *Surviving the Silence: Black Women's Stories of Rape*. New York: Norton.

Pistono, Stephen P. 1988. "Susan Brownmiller and the History of Rape." *Women's Studies* 14: 265–76.

Plagens, Peter. 30 Sept. 1996. "Lady Painters? Smile When You Say That. Surrealism's the Name, Postfeminism Is the Game." *Newsweek*: 82–83.

Plaza, Monique. 1981. "Our Damages and Their Compensation: Rape: The Will Not to Know of Michel Foucault." *Feminist Issues* 1.3: 25–35.

Pollitt, Katha. 26 Mar. 1990. "'Fetal Rights': A New Assault on Feminism." *Nation*. Rpt. in *The Politics of Women's Bodies: Sexuality, Appearance, and Behavior*. Ed. Rose Weitz. New York: Oxford University Press, 1998. 278–87.

Post, Tom, with Alexandra Stiglmayer, Charles Lane, Joel Brand, Margaret Garrard Warner, and Robin Sparkman. 4 Jan. 1993. "A Pattern of Rape: War Crimes in Bosnia." *Newsweek*: 32–36.

Probyn, Elspeth. 1990. "New Traditionalism and Post-Feminism: TV Does the Home." *Screen* 31.2: 147–59.

———. 1993. "Choosing Choice: Images of Sexuality and 'Choiceoisie' in Popular Culture." *Negotiating at the Margins: The Gendered Discourses of Power and*

Resistance. Ed. Sue Fisher and Kathy Davis. New Brunswick: Rutgers University Press. 278–94.

Projansky, Sarah. 1995. "Working on Feminism: Film and Television Rape Narratives and Postfeminist Culture." Ph. D. diss. University of Iowa.

———. 1997. "Shifting Bodies, Changing Texts: Representing Teenage Womanhood on *Dr. Quinn, Medicine Woman.*" *Critical Approaches to Television.* Ed. Leah R. Vande Berg, Lawrence A. Wenner, and Bruce E. Gronbeck. Boston: Houghton Mifflin. 315–35.

Projansky, Sarah, and Kent A. Ono. 1999. "Whiteness as Strategic Nothingness in Contemporary Hollywood Cinema." *Whiteness: The Communication of Social Identity.* Ed. Thomas K. Nakayama and Judith Martin. Newbury Park, CA: Sage. 149–74.

Putnam, Ann. 1993. "The Bearer of the Gaze in Ridley Scott's *Thelma and Louise.*" *Western American Literature* 27.4: 291–302.

Rabinovitz, Lauren. 1989. "Sitcoms and Single Moms: Representations of Feminism on American TV." *Cinema Journal* 29.1: 3–19.

———. 1998. *For the Love of Pleasure: Women, Movies, and Culture in Turn-of-the-Century Chicago.* New Brunswick: Rutgers University Press.

———. 1999. "Ms.-Representation: The Politics of Feminist Sitcoms." *Television, History, and American Culture.* Ed. Mary Beth Haralovich and Lauren Rabinovitz. Durham, NC: Duke University Press. 144–67.

Rabinowitz, Dorothy. 20 May 1991. "Television: Sweeps-Month Obsessions." *Wall Street Journal*: A16.

Rafferty, Terrence. 3 June 1991. "Outlaw Princesses." *New Yorker*: 86–87.

Rapping, Elayne. 1991. "Feminism Gets the Hollywood Treatment." *Cineaste* 18.4: 30–32.

Reid, Mark A. 1993. *Redefining Black Film.* Berkeley: University of California Press.

Renov, Michael. 1989. "Advertising/Photojournalism/Cinema: The Shifting Rhetoric of Forties Female Representation." *Quarterly Review of Film and Video* 11.1: 1–21.

Rhodes, Joe. May 1991. "Straight Shooter." *Harper's Bazaar*: 140, 141 (pic.), 175.

Rivers, Caryl. 6 Oct. 1974. "TV Has Fun with Robbery, Arson and Rape." *New York Times*. Rpt. in *More Joy Than Rage: Crossing Generations with the New Feminism.* Hanover: University Press of New England, 1991. 107–9.

Roberts, Shari. 1997. "Western Meets Eastwood: Genre and Gender on the Road." *The Road Movie Book.* Ed. Steven Cohen and Ina Rae Hark. New York: Routledge. 45–69.

Rogers, Deborah D. 1991. "Daze of Our Lives: The Soap Opera as Feminine Text." *Journal of American Culture* 14.4: 29–41.

Rohter, Larry. 5 June 1991. "The Third Woman of *Thelma and Louise.*" *New York Times*: C21, 24.

Roiphe, Katie. 1993. *The Morning After: Sex, Fear, and Feminism.* Boston: Little, Brown.

———. 1994. *The Morning After: Sex, Fear, and Feminism.* 1st paperback ed. Boston: Little, Brown.

Rosen, Ruth. 2000. *The World Split Open: How the Modern Women's Movement Changed America.* New York: Viking.

Rowe, Kathleen. 1995a. "Romantic Comedy and the Unruly Virgin in Classical Hollywood Cinema." *The Unruly Woman: Gender and the Genres of Laughter.* Austin: University of Texas Press. 116–44.

———. 1995b. "Studying *Roseanne.*" *Feminist Cultural Theory: Process and Production.* Ed. Beverley Skeggs. Manchester: Manchester University Press. 46–61.

Rumens, Carol, ed. 1985. *Making for the Open: The Chatto Book of Post-Feminist Poetry, 1964–1984.* London: Chatto and Windus, Hogarth Press.

Rushing, Janice Hocker. 1992. "Introduction to 'Feminist Criticism.'" *Southern Communication Journal* 57.2: 83–85.

Russell, Diana E. H. 1975. *The Politics of Rape: The Victim's Perspective.* New York: Stein and Day.

———. 1982. *Rape in Marriage.* New York: Macmillan.

Ryan, Barbara. 1992. *Feminism and the Women's Movement: Dynamics of Change in Social Movement Ideology and Activism.* New York: Routledge.

Sanday, Peggy Reeves. 1990. *Fraternity Gang Rape: Sex, Brotherhood, and Privilege on Campus.* New York: New York University Press.

Schickel, Richard. 24 June 1991. "Gender Bender: A White-Hot Debate Rages over Whether *Thelma and Louise* Celebrates Liberated Females, Male Bashers, or Outlaws." *Time*: 52–56.

Schlesinger, Philip, R. Emerson Dobash, Russell P. Dobash, and C. Kay Weaver. 1992. *Women Viewing Violence.* London: BFI.

Scraton, Sheila. 1994. "The Changing World of Women and Leisure: Feminism, 'Postfeminism' and Leisure." *Leisure Studies* 13.4: 249–61.

Searles, Patricia, and Ronald J. Berger, eds. 1995. *Rape and Society: Readings on the Problem of Sexual Assault.* Boulder: Westview.

Shalit, Ruth. 6 Apr. 1998. "Canny and Lacy: Ally, Dharma, Ronnie, and the Betrayal of Postfeminism." *New Republic*: 27–33.

Shapiro, Laura. 17 June 1991. "Women Who Kill Too Much." *Newsweek*: 63.

Sharpe, Jenny. 1993. *Allegories of Empire: The Figure of Woman in the Colonial Text.* Minneapolis: University of Minnesota Press.

Shohat, Ella. 1991a. "Gender and Culture of Empire: Toward a Feminist Ethnography of the Cinema." *Quarterly Review of Film and Video* 13.1–3: 45–84.

———. 1991b. "The Media's War." *Social Text* 28. Rpt. in *Seeing through the Media: The Persian Gulf War.* Ed. Susan Jeffords and Lauren Rabinovitz. New Brunswick: Rutgers University Press, 1994. 147–54.

Shohat, Ella. 1998. "Introduction." *Talking Visions: Multicultural Feminism in a Transnational Age.* Ed. Ella Shohat. Cambridge, MA: MIT Press. 1–63.

Shohat, Ella, and Robert Stam. 1994. *Unthinking Eurocentrism: Multiculturalism and the Media.* New York: Routledge.

Shrock, Joel. 1997. "Desperate Deeds, Desperate Men: Gender, Race, and Rape in Silent Feature Films, 1915–1927." *Journal of Men's Studies* 6.1: 69–89.

Shukla, Sandyha. 1997. "Feminisms of the Diaspora Both Local and Global: The Politics of South Asian Women against Domestic Violence." *Women Transforming Politics: An Alternative Reader.* Ed. Cathy J. Cohen, Kathleen B. Jones, and Joan C. Tronto. New York: New York University Press. 269–83.

Shumway, David R. 1991. "Screwball Comedies: Constructing Romance, Mystifying Marriage." *Cinema Journal* 30.4: 7–23.

Simmonds, Felly Nkweto. 1988. "*She's Gotta Have It*: The Representation of Black Female Sexuality on Film." *Feminist Review* 29: 10–22.

Sloop, John M. 1994. "'Apology Made to Whoever Pleases': Cultural Discipline and the Grounds of Interpretation." *Communication Quarterly* 42.4: 345–62.

Smith, Valerie. 1990. "Split Affinities: The Case of Interracial Rape." *Conflicts in Feminism.* Ed. Marianne Hirsch and Evelyn Fox Keller. New York: Routledge. 271–87. Rpt. in *Theorizing Feminism: Parallel Trends in the Humanities and Social Sciences.* Ed. Anne C. Herrmann and Abigail J. Stewart. Boulder: Westview, 1994. 155–70.

Snead, James. 1994. *White Screens, Black Images: Hollywood from the Dark Side.* Ed. Colin MacCabe and Cornel West. New York: Routledge.

Snowden, Lynn. Mar. 1992. "Thelma and Louise, Part II." *Working Woman*: 99–100, 102, 109.

Sobchack, Vivian C. 1977. "*No Lies*: Direct Cinema as Rape." *Journal of the University Film Association* 29.4: 13–18.

Sommers, Christina Hoff. 1994. *Who Stole Feminism? How Women Have Betrayed Women.* New York: Simon and Schuster.

Sommerville, Diane Miller. 1995. "The Rape Myth in the Old South Reconsidered." *Journal of Southern History* 61.3: 481–518.

Sontag, Susan. 1990. *Illness as Metaphor; and, AIDS and Its Metaphors.* New York: Doubleday, 1990.

Spelman, Elizabeth V., and Martha Minow. 1992. "Outlaw Women: An Essay on *Thelma and Louise*." *New England Law Review* 26: 1281–96.

Spohn, Cassia, and Julie Horney. 1992. *Rape Law Reform: A Grassroots Revolution and Its Impact.* New York: Plenum.

Springer, Claudia. 1988. "Antiwar Film as Spectacle: Contradictions of the Combat Sequence." *Genre* 21: 479–86.

Spry, Tami. 1995. "In the Absence of Word and Body: Hegemonic Implications of 'Victim' and 'Survivor' in Women's Narratives of Sexual Violence." *Women and Language* 18.2: 27–32.

Stacey, Judith. 1987. "Sexism by a Subtler Name? Postindustrial Conditions and Postfeminist Consciousness in the Silicon Valley." *Socialist Review* 17: 7–28.

Staiger, Janet. 1992. *Interpreting Films: Studies in the Historical Reception of American Cinema.* Princeton: Princeton University Press.

———. 1995. *Bad Women: Regulating Sexuality in Early American Cinema.* Minneapolis: University of Minnesota Press.

Stam, Robert, Robert Burgoyne, and Sandy Flitterman-Lewis, eds. 1992. *New Vocabularies in Film Semiotics: Structuralism, Post-Structuralism, and Beyond.* New York: Routledge.

Stamp, Shelley. 2000. *Movie-Struck Girls: Women and Motion Picture Culture after the Nickelodeon.* Princeton: Princeton University Press.

Stamp Lindsey, Shelley. 1995. "'Eighty Million Women Want—?': Women's Suffrage, Female Viewers and the Body Politic." *Quarterly Review of Film and Video* 16.1: 1–22.

Studlar, Gaylyn. 1996. *This Mad Masquerade: Stardom and Masculinity in the Jazz Age.* New York: Columbia University Press.

Sullivan, Kaye. 1980. *Films for, by and about Women.* Metuchen, NJ: Scarecrow Press.

———. 1985. *Films for, by and about Women: Series II.* Metuchen, NJ: Scarecrow Press.

Suplee, Curt. 3 May 1987. "The Myth of the New Man." *Washington Post*: B1, B4.

Sykes, Plum. May 1998. "Internal Affairs." *Vogue*: 142, 144.

Tasker, Yvonne. 1993. *Spectacular Bodies: Gender, Genre and the Action Cinema.* New York: Routledge.

———. 1998. *Working Girls: Gender and Sexuality in Popular Cinema.* New York: Routledge.

Taubin, Amy. July 1991. "Ridley Scott's Road Work." *Sight and Sound*: 18–19.

Telotte, J. P. 1998. "A Fate Worse Than Death: Racism, Transgression, and Westerns." *Journal of Popular Film and Television* 26.3: 120–27.

"Thelma and Louise." 1991. *Off Our Backs* 21.8: 19–20.

Thompson, Kristin. 1986. "The Concept of Cinematic Excess." *Narrative, Apparatus, Ideology: A Film Theory Reader.* Ed. Philip Rosen. New York: Columbia University Press. 130–42.

Turner, Patricia A. 1993. *I Heard It through the Grapevine: Rumor in African-American Culture.* Berkeley: University of California Press.

United States Commission on Civil Rights. 1992. *Civil Rights Issues Facing Asian Americans in the 1990s.* Washington, DC: United States Commission on Civil Rights.

United States Department of Justice. July 1993. *Violent Crime in the United States.* FBI Annual Report. Washington, DC.

Valian, Virginia. 1999. *Why So Slow? The Advancement of Women.* Cambridge: MIT Press.

Vande Berg, Leah R. 1993. "*China Beach*, Prime Time War in the Postfeminist Age: An Example of Patriarchy in a Different Voice." *Western Journal of Communication* 57: 349–66.

Vasey, Ruth. 1995. "Beyond Sex and Violence: 'Industry Policy' and the Regulation of Hollywood Movies, 1922–1939." *Quarterly Review of Film and Video* 15.4: 65–85.

Walker, Alice. 1981. "Advancing Luna—and Ida B. Wells." *You Can't Keep a Good Woman Down*. New York: Harcourt Brace Jovanovich. 85–104.

Wallace, Michele. 1990. "Introduction: Negative/Positive Images." *Invisibility Blues: From Pop to Theory*. New York: Verso. 1–10.

Wallis, Claudia. 4 Dec. 1989. "Onward, Women." *Time*: 80–82, 85–86, 89.

Walters, Suzanna Danuta. 1991. "Premature Postmortems: 'Postfeminism' and Popular Culture." *New Politics* 3.2: 103–12.

———. 1995. *Material Girls: Making Sense of Feminist Cultural Theory*. Berkeley: University of California Press.

Wang, Veronica C. 1990. "Rape, Madness, and Silence: Breakdown and Recovery in Maxine Hong Kingston's *Woman Warrier*." *South Dakota Review* 28.3: 137–44.

Warshaw, Robin. 1988. *I Never Called It Rape: The Ms. Report on Recognizing, Fighting, and Surviving Date and Acquaintance Rape*. New York: Harper and Row.

Wells-Barnett, Ida B. 1909. "Lynching, Our National Crime." Rpt. in *The Rhetoric of Struggle: Public Address by African American Women*. Ed. Robbie Jean Walker. New York: Garland, 1992. 95–102.

"When Rape Becomes Genocide." 5 Sept. 1998. *New York Times*: A23.

White, Aaronette. 1999. "Talking Feminist, Talking Black: Micromobilization Processes in a Collective Protest against Rape." *Gender and Society* 13.1: 77–100.

White, Mimi. 1989. "Representing Romance: Reading/Writing/Fantasy and the 'Liberated' Heroine of Recent Hollywood Films." *Cinema Journal* 28.3: 41–56.

———. 1992. *Tele-advising: Therapeutic Discourse in American Television*. Chapel Hill: University of North Carolina Press.

Wiegand, Shirley A. 1997. "Deception and Artifice: Thelma, Louise, and the Legal Hermeneutic." *Oklahoma City University Law Review* 22: 25–49.

Wiegman, Robyn. 1993. "The Anatomy of Lynching." *Journal of the History of Sexuality* 3.3. Rpt. in *American Sexual Politics: Sex, Gender, and Race since the Civil War*. Chicago: University of Chicago Press, 1993. 223–45.

Williams, Linda. 1984. "'Something Else Besides a Mother': *Stella Dallas* and the Maternal Melodrama." *Cinema Journal* 24.1: 2–27.

———. 1986. "Linda William Replies." *Cinema Journal* 25.2: 66–67.

———. 1989. *Hard Core: Power, Pleasure, and the Frenzy of the Visible*. Berkeley: University of California Press.

———. 1991–92. "What Makes a Woman Wander." *Film Quarterly* 45.2: 27–28.

Williams, Raymond. 1977. *Marxism and Literature*. Oxford: Oxford University Press.

Willis, Sharon. 1993. "Hardware and Hardbodies, What Do Women Want? A Reading of *Thelma and Louise*." *Film Theory Goes to the Movies*. Ed. Jim Collins, Hilary Radner, and Ava Preacher Collins. New York: Routledge. 120–28.

———. 1997. *High Contrast: Race and Gender in Contemporary Hollywood Film*. Durham: Duke University Press.

Wilson, Wayne. 1988. "Rape as Entertainment." *Psychological Reports* 63: 607–10.

Wolcott, James. 20 May 1996. "Hear Me Purr: Maureen Dowd and the Rise of Postfeminist Chick Lit." *New Yorker*: 54–59.

Wolf, Naomi. 4 Aug. 1991a. "We're All 'Bad Girls' Now: Our Lives Are Just as 'Lurid' as Those of Alleged Rape Victims." *Washington Post*: C1–C2.

———. Nov. 1991b. "Are You a Bad Girl?" *Glamour*: 212, 274–75.

———. 1992. *The Beauty Myth*. New York: Anchor, 1991.

———. 1993. *Fire with Fire: The New Female Power and How It Will Change the Twenty-first Century*. New York: Random House.

———. 1994. *Fire with Fire: The New Female Power and How to Use It*. New York: Fawcett Columbine.

"Women against Rape." 23 Apr. 1973. *Time*: 104B.

Wriggins, Jennifer. 1983. "Rape, Racism, and the Law." *Harvard Women's Law Journal* 6: 103–41.

Index of Film and Television Titles

General Index

About the Author

Sarah Projansky is an assistant professor of women and gender studies at the University of California, Davis, where she also teaches film studies and is a member of the cultural studies M.A./Ph.D. program. She received her Ph.D. in film studies from the University of Iowa in 1995. As an undergraduate student she studied film with Jeanine Basinger at Wesleyan University.

She is a coeditor of *Enterprise Zones: Critical Positions on Star Trek* (Westview 1996) and has published in *Signs, Cinema Journal, Quarterly Journal of Speech, Women's Studies International Forum*, and various anthologies. Her next project, currently titled *Spectacular Girls: Crises of Body, Sexuality, and Nation in Contemporary U.S. Media*, explores moments in which girls and their bodies disrupt media stories about them.

AEC-6155

WITHDRAWN

Gramley Library
Salem Academy and College
Winston-Salem, N.C. 27108